THE PAGEANT OF
MIDDLE AMERICAN HISTORY

GULf
of
MEXico
PACIFIC OCEAN
N
S
W
E

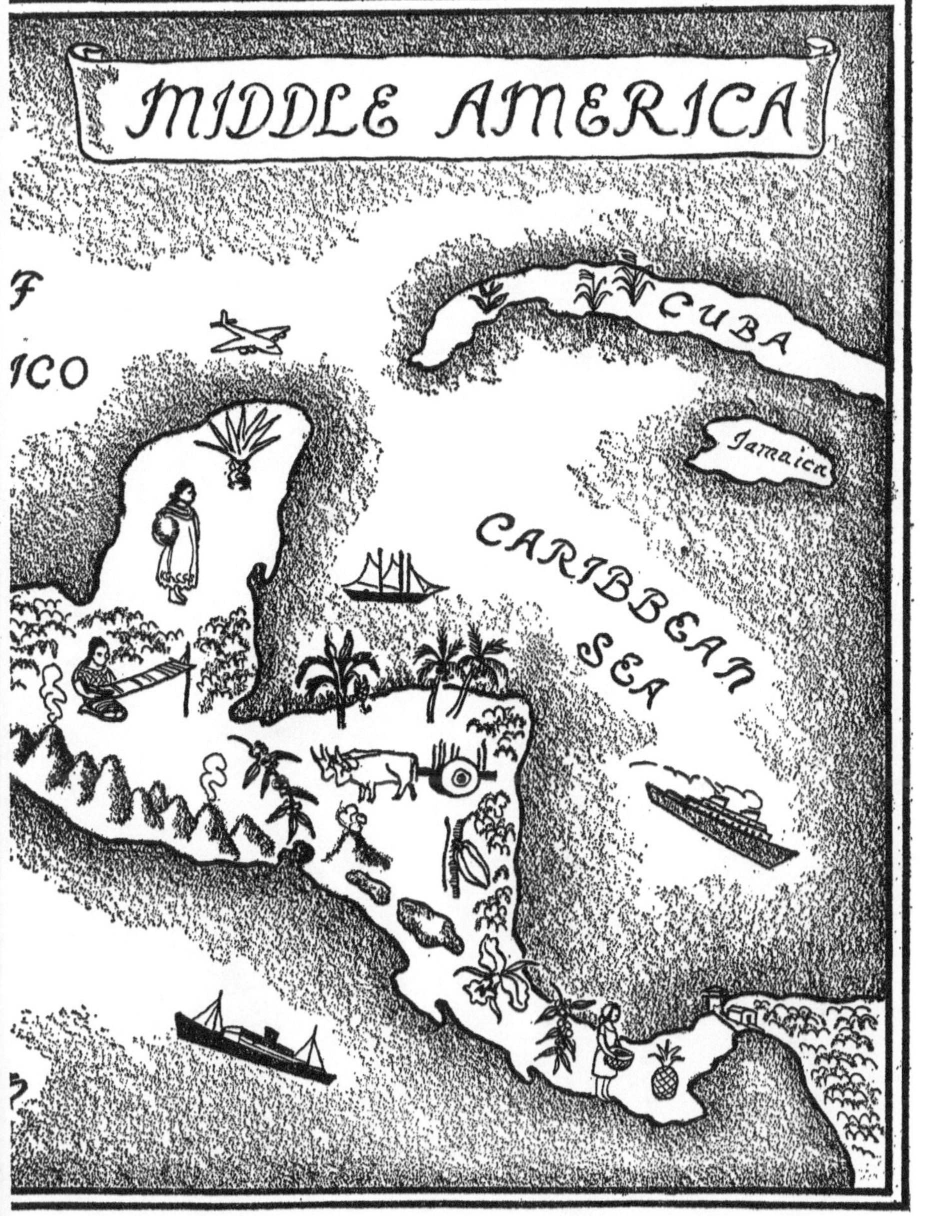

MIDDLE AMERICA
CUBA
Jamaica
CARIBBEAN SEA
F
ICO

THE PAGEANT OF MIDDLE AMERICAN HISTORY

Anne Merriman Peck

Simon Publications

2001

Library of Congress Card Number: 47002138

ISBN: 1-931313-59-8

Distributed by Ingram Book Company

Printed by Lightning Source Inc., La Vergne, TN

Published by Simon Publications, Safety Harbor, FL

MANY individuals and many books have helped in the compiling of material for this story of Middle American lands. There is a goodly company of men and women in Mexico and Central America—writers, educators, journalists, librarians—who gave freely of their interest and time to aid me in understanding their people and to whom I am grateful.

Among them are Angela Acuña de Chacón, Aida Golcher, Don J. García Monge and Don Roberto Brenes Mesén of Costa Rica; Dr. David Vela, Dr. Antonio Goubaud, C. and Lilly de Jongh Osborne of Guatemala; Argentina Diaz Lozano, Ing. Arturo Lopez Rodezno and Lic. Jorge Fidel Duron of Honduras; and Josefa T. de Aguerri of Nicaragua.

Others, chance acquaintances met in train and bus travel or in small towns, helped by their friendliness and interest in my inquiries. There were also some North Americans, doing good service for inter-american understanding, whose counsel was valuable.

My thanks go to friends, both North American and Latin American, who gave me letters to their friends, and to Mrs. Concha Romero James of the Pan American Union whose introductions opened many doors. Officials of the United Fruit Company received this inquiring traveler with hospitality, arranged trips, and made it possible for me to visit banana plantations and other projects of the Company.

Months of intensive research preceded and followed travel.

My appreciation goes to the librarians of the University of Arizona in Tucson, and more especially to the wise and helpful librarians of Room 300 of the New York Public Library where most of the study was done. I am deeply indebted to the late Dr. George C. Vaillant for his criticism of the chapters on Indian cultures, and to Dr. William Bridgewater of the Columbia University Press for his stimulating comments and criticism on the whole manuscript. It is my hope that this book, condensed though it is, will help North Americans to become better acquainted with the good friends in the beautiful lands grouped here as Middle America.

ANNE MERRIMAN PECK

CONTENTS

MAPS

THE PAGEANT OF
MIDDLE AMERICAN HISTORY

CHAPTER I

THE MIDDLE LANDS

A COMMON PAST links the countries between the United States and South America. Long before Europeans discovered the Western Hemisphere there were kingdoms of beautiful sculptured stone cities in these middle lands, created through slow centuries by aboriginal Americans who were artistic peoples.

Then came the indomitable Spaniards to conquer a new world for King, Church and their own glory. From Mexico to Panama they explored the wilderness, trampled on the Indian cultures, and built a new civilization blended of the two races, Indian and Spanish.

Only when the men of Spanish blood, but bred in the New World, broke away from the mother country did this region of common history become separated into national states. Despite their distinct nationhood and national spirit these states are closely related by their past and by their present interests.

These middle lands, lying between two oceans, narrow down from Mexico to the slim link with South America, Panama. Indians and Spaniards went back and forth, fought and built, over an area that nature had provided with a geographical environment alike throughout. From mid-Mexico to Panama the lands lie in the tropic zone. Heat and rainfall give them fringes of dense vegetation and jungle forests. Prehistoric convulsions raised up the land mass in crumpled mountain ranges and towering volcanoes, with fertile plateaus between, and rivers rushing through deep gorges to the sea.

The lands are still uneasy with the grumblings and hidden fires of volcanic forces that break out in eruptions and destructive earthquakes. From the snow-clad giants of Mexico to the spectacular procession of volcanic peaks marching down the western side of Central America, volcanoes have played a part in human history. In these lands hurricanes, floods, earth upheavals have been the lot of the inhabitants, and the violence of nature has been reflected in the stormy, dramatic history of the peoples.

Central America should be a title to cover all this territory, the middle of the Americas; but it has come to denote the five small republics—Guatemala, El Salvador, Honduras, Nicaragua, Costa Rica—that were once the United Provinces of Central America. Mexico stands apart, and tiny Panama was historically more related to South America than to the countries of the wider isthmus of Central America.

Archeologists have given the title Middle America to these lands of many Indian peoples where Maya, Toltec and Aztec created aboriginal civilizations of art and priestly learning. Other writers have followed suit, sometimes including the islands of the Caribbean Sea in the comprehensive title, Middle America.

The theme of this book is the interlocking history and present relationships of the peoples of Middle America. It is the bold attempt to tell the story as a whole, in broad sweeps, picking out the highlights, following the threads that link them together. Details must be neglected, history telescoped into a small space, but this is the story of peoples rather than academic history.

The tale must begin with the peoples whose homeland this was before white men from Europe discovered it. Scholars are generally agreed that the aboriginal inhabitants of the American continents, who became the countless tribes over thousands of years, came originally from Asia, probably by way of Bering Strait between Siberia and North America. The Asiatic type of head, the color ranging from yellow-brown to red, of the American Indian seem to bear out this conclusion.

Did the racial groups that evolved sculpture and architecture, social and religious systems, develop that culture in the primeval New World? On that question scholars differ so much that one can only state the theories and take one's choice. Some argue that, having come from the cradle of ancient Asiatic civilizations, tribes brought with them the germs of art and religious ideas which, over the course of centuries, developed into American Indian cultures. Others believe that the peoples who advanced farthest in civilization were influenced by "culture bearers" from India, China or Egypt who somehow reached the shores of America.

Still other scholars maintain that the aboriginal inhabitants of the Americas created their own arts and religious beliefs without contact with the Old World. The story is unfolding bit by bit as archeologists and ethnologists delve deeper into America's past. New discoveries from year to year cause some theories to be discarded and others to take their place.

White inhabitants of the Americas, immigrants all in one age or another, may take pride in the knowledge that the culture of native races goes back into the dim past in the so-called New World; that the most advanced peoples had well-ordered social, artistic and ceremonial life long before Europeans knew that there were continents across the unexplored ocean.

The peoples of Middle America were descendants of tribes who had lived for thousands of years in the Western Hemisphere. Faced with the mysteries of the awesome world of nature they invented gods to worship, personifying the powerful forces of nature, the sun, moon and stars, creatures of forest and stream important to their lives. With imagination and the skill of their hands they built and carved and molded pottery, evolving art forms and symbolic designs truly their own.

The study of their lives and works is essential to the story of civilization in this region, for the native people survived the cruelties of the Spanish conquest to mingle their blood with that of the conquerors and to become an integral part of Spanish colonial life. Indian character and customs color civilization to this day in most of the countries. The arts and architecture of their distant ancestors are cherished with pride as a national heritage.

Middle America is really the heartland of the Americas, for it was not only the home of the most advanced peoples, with the exception of some in Peru and the Colombian highlands, but the place where wandering tribes first learned to farm and thus have a settled existence.

Somewhere in the sunny uplands of Guatemala or Mexico certain tribes, more ingenious than their fellows, learned to domesticate a wild grass plant and develop its seed into ears of corn. This was maize, native to the New World, the foundation of civilized life in ancient America.

Generations of men sowed and harvested the maize, developing its fruitfulness as time went on, learning to irrigate the fields where rainfall was insufficient. As the people advanced in agricultural skill beans and other native plants were added to the crops that fed the tribes.

This epochal change in human life in America began thousands of years ago. Some scholars date it as far back as 4000 B.C. From the farming people of the Central American highlands it is generally believed that the knowledge of maize cultivation spread northward and southward, until it became the staff of life for most tribes who then advanced from a wandering existence to one of settled culture.

Tribes with a secure food supply could take time to invent tools and implements for daily use, to weave fibers into baskets or garments, to shape clay into cooking pots and jars. The prehistoric farming folk had leisure to add to their tribal customs and ceremonies. They expressed their ideas of nature deities in little images modeled in clay. Deep down in the soil of Middle America archeologists find the possessions and images belonging to tribes in this stage of culture.

Succeeding these people many tribes, differing in characteristics and language, lived out their span and were superseded by yet others in Mexico and Central America. Their handiwork, surviving the centuries, is the chief source of information about their lives and ideas. We know that the semi-civilized men of Middle America were marvelously skilled in hewing and carving stone, although they had only stone tools to work with. Human labor was plentiful but it took engineering ability as well to transport huge blocks of stone from the places where they were quarried to religious sites, and to arrange them in ceremonial patterns. Some blocks were sculptured into the forms of primitive gods, others were carved in relief to serve as altars.

These people also built, by the labor of hundreds of men, the great platforms of stone and rubble on which temples were set. One by one the centers of worship of vanished peoples are being unearthed from the mass of vegetation, brush and trees which have covered them for centuries.

The ancient stone-workers also carved hard volcanic rock into seats and metates, or grinding stones. Smoothed to a concave surface these grinding stones are beautifully finished and are often set on the backs of carved animals. Metates are found everywhere, of the same shape as those used by Indian women of today. Evidently the corn-eaters of Middle America passed on from one generation to another an identical method for grinding soaked kernels of corn to make meal.

Many semi-civilized tribes were artists in pottery making. In the ruins and graves of temple sites are found bowls, jugs and plates, expertly shaped and decorated. Craftsmen of individual tribes followed traditional motifs, but geometrical design pleased them all because of their feeling for pattern. Revered creatures—birds, animals, serpents—were evolved into stylized forms for pottery decoration. To archeologists these beautiful pieces are precious records in their study of artistic ideas and the relationship between peoples.

The inhabitants of Panama and lower Costa Rica worked skillfully in gold, obtained from stream beds or rude mines in the mountains. In technique and design their ornaments are similar to those of tribes in Colombia, so it seems likely that there was communication between widely separated populations by way of rivers or jungle trails.

Often the sites of settlements and temples were abandoned by their builders because of some disaster or war with other tribes. Then the structures were gradually worn down by weather and the fierce encroachment of tropical vegetation. Sometimes new people occupied the sites and built their structures upon the ruins of the old. The possessions of successive tribes, the treasures laid away in the graves of priests and rulers, were buried under the soil, under temples or were smothered in the forests. They remained hidden until modern explorers began their excavations.

The invading Spaniards, with a craving for gold, seized all they could lay hands on of the finely wrought ornaments of Indian goldsmiths. Although they sometimes paused to admire the delicate workmanship their main object was to melt the Indian treasures into gold bricks for the King and themselves. They took all they could wring from the living by hunt or torture, but they missed hundreds of graves where cherished possessions were buried with dignitaries of the tribes. Exquisite objects of wrought gold and silver have come to light as burial places are excavated by explorers in search of lost cultures instead of loot. These examples of Indian art have come to rest in museums or private collections.

Only the archeologists can interpret the treasures found in the graves of priests or rulers, or deduce something about the lives of vanished peoples from their implements and tools, their design and building. Theirs is fascinating work, piecing together bits of information, relating one group of people to another, as they clear vegetation from fallen temples and find layers of human products buried deep down in the earth.

Archeologists are coming to the conclusion that tribes of unknown antiquity, in the Caribbean coastal area of Mexico, originated cultural ideas and artistic skills which passed from them to other peoples. Perhaps this fecund land in the present states of Vera Cruz and Tabasco provided a good environment for advancement in civilized living.

The region is hot and moist, with fertile soil and abundance of tropical plants and fruits. Food could be obtained without much effort so craftsmen had time to work with increasing skill, with their primitive tools, in the carving of stone and jade for the service of the gods. The priests, served by the people, were free to evolve religious concepts and ceremonies.

It may be that the priests of the Maya people began their astronomical calculations and development of their calendar in this rich coastal region. A small statuette found at San Andrés Tuxtla, Vera Cruz, bears the oldest Mayan date yet known. It is equivalent to 98 B.C. in Dr. Herbert Spinden's reckoning of Mayan time counts. At Cerro de las Mesas a record stone was found with a date earlier than those found in the cities of the Guatemalan jungles.

Artists of some peoples in this region succeeded in carving the hardest rock with great technical skill and feeling for design. Animal forms are extremely stylized, representations of deities are somber or terrifying. Sometimes, however, the artists looked at the people around them and modeled clay into most expressive human figures. Heads of jolly, laughing fellows, others with subtle smiling expressions, are variations from the usual solemn, symbolic art forms of the pre-Columbians.

The great builders of some semi-civilized peoples erected the massive carved stones and pyramidal temple platforms of the religious centers in coastal Mexico and in the highlands. One site with an immense arrangement of sculptured stones and altars was found in Panama.

Skilled tribes from the lowlands began the building of temples on the hill called Monte Alban near the city of Oaxaca in southern Mexico. Later, on their foundations an accomplished people, the Zapotecs, made of Monte Alban a great center of ceremonial civilization, with lofty temples, palaces and great courts, built into the contours of the hills.

They were joined by another civilized people, the Mixtecs, whose palace center at Mitla is a rare example of pre-

Columbian American architecture. The walls of the buildings are banded with a mosaic of cut stone in geometric designs suggestive of textile patterns. Once the mosaic was painted white against a red background, and these beautiful walls, above the red-painted floors of the great courts, must have been a vivid setting for ceremonials.

It is believed that the artistic and religious ideas of civilized people in this region of southern Mexico spread northward to influence less advanced tribes in the Valley of Mexico.

The Mayas had their stone cities, magnificent in architecture and sculpture, in the jungles of southern Mexico, Honduras and Guatemala. Fallen into ruin, buried in the forests, they now have been explored and studied by archeologists and scholars of Europe, the United States and Mexico.

Scholars have amassed a store of knowledge through study of architecture, sculpture and pottery; through study of Mayan hieroglyphs carved on record stones or painted in books. The picture writing of the Mexicans, tribal legends and chronicles, have aided in the understanding of these ancient peoples' beliefs and history.

To scholars this search for knowledge of ancient peoples has the absorption of a mystery story. Eagerly they follow clues, link one discovery with another, as they add to the picture of life in Indian America. The picture is incomplete in details, but rich in the color and symbolism evolved by people who lived very close to the natural world.

CHAPTER 2

THE MAYA, ARTISTS AND SCIENTISTS

HIDDEN in the depths of tropical forests in southern Mexico, Honduras and Guatemala, the cities of the Maya rested for ages in oblivion. Great trees grew on temple terraces, their roots undermined walls and façades, reducing them to heaps of stone. Exuberant vegetation took possession of the pyramids, smothering them in vine and bush. In the green twilight of the forest, exotic beings, sculptured on towering monoliths called stelae, brooded over the ruins, their faces framed in sweeping plumes.

Life had vanished from these cities long before the Spaniards made their conquering marches through the country. Only a few were ever seen by Spaniards. The later civilization of the Maya in Yucatán had degenerated into conflicts between competing clans when the conquerors first met the natives.

Spanish priests gleaned some knowledge of Mayan history and customs from chiefs of the conquered people, and from a Mayan chronicle, written after the conquest, called the *Books of Chilam Balam*. The priesthood had a store of books containing the accumulated learning of the race, and perhaps their history. They were painted in hieroglyphic symbols on sheets of deerskin and paper made from the fiber of the wild fig tree, amate. Most of them were destroyed during wars with the Toltecs and by the fanatical Spanish bishop, Diego de Landa. Only a few survived and are preserved in museums of Europe, a valuable source of study for scholars. Tribes of Mayan stock in the highlands of Guatemala also had a chronicle, the *Popul Vuh,* which has been useful to scholars.

Those ruined cities in the jungle lowlands, when discovered by modern archeologists and scholars, provided new clues to Mayan civilization. Tall shafts of stone, the stelae, were erected to mark intervals of time. Worked into the flamboyant pattern of sculptured ornament were rows of glyphs, recording the dates when the stones were erected, and perhaps historical events as well. Scholars have learned to decipher dates on the stelae, but whatever else the tantalizing symbols may tell of the Mayan story remains a mystery.

No race of ancient America has captured more fully the imagination and curiosity of modern minds than the Maya, the most creative and learned, the most highly civilized of all aboriginal Americans. After years of intensive study scholars have learned a great deal about the religious symbolism which was the source of their complex and sophisticated art. The remarkable scientific achievements of the ancient astronomer-priests are known.

Scholars have found a way to correlate dates in the Mayan system of reckoning time with those of the Gregorian calendar used by the modern world. They do not, however, agree in the results of their study. There is a difference of about two hundred and sixty years in the dates as figured by Doctor Herbert Spinden and the system followed by Doctors Thompson, Goodman and others. When the records of a race are in the form of hieroglyphs, archeological discoveries provide the best clues to their history.

However much they may differ in specific dates, scholars agree that, during the early centuries after the birth of Christ, those cities in the jungles were busy centers of religion and government for large populations. The men who built the first cities were not primitive people. They were already advanced in architectural and sculptural skill and had their calendar fully developed. Where did these people come from, and how long had they been living in the lowlands before they began recording dates on stone? There is no answer to that question, but scholars reckon that the history of the Maya, from their beginnings to the end of their empire in Yucatán, spanned nearly two thousand years. Probably the first dates and sculpture were done on wood and so perished in the damp climate.

It is believed that the Maya reached the forested lowlands after a series of migrations from their place of origin. That place is a matter of speculation, but there is reason to believe that they must have lived for some time in the Caribbean coastal area of Mexico. Discovery of typical Mayan hieroglyphs in this region was mentioned in the last chapter.

Eventually they migrated to the peninsula of Yucatán where some of the wanderers remained to build the oldest of the beautiful cities found in ruins in the bush. Others went on to found the empire which grew up in the jungle lowlands of Guatemala, Honduras and the Mexican state of Chiapas.

Tribal legends of the Yucatecan Mayas describe a priestly leader, Itzamná, who gave his people the calendar and system of time counting, who taught them arts and agriculture. According to legend Itzamná commanded the people to build a city dedicated to the Rain God at the place of two great wells, Chichén. So it seems that famed Chichén Itzá was a holy site from the earliest times. The oldest ruins, half buried in bush, are supposed to be those of the first city. Some scholars believe that this city was built during the eighth century. The site was abandoned and built upon again two and a half centuries later.

Yucatán was called by its people the Land of the Pheasant and the Deer; also El Mayab, the Place of the Few.

The people in Yucatán and those who settled in the lowland forests were of the same race, with the same artistic and religious ideas. Yucatecan Mayas were trading, farming and building at the same period when the cities in Guatemala and Honduras were expanding. Doubtless there was communication by way of the traders between the two groups of Mayan people. The civilization in the jungles is called the Old Empire because it was the first flowering of the Mayan genius.

The people of the Old Empire lived in a tropical country of steamy heat, where a long rainy season made vegetation grow with overwhelming luxuriance. Great trees and lush underbrush had to be cleared away for the maize fields on which life depended. After the felled bush was dried in the sun it was burned and maize was planted in holes made with a planting stick. When they were not busy in the fields the humble folk and skilled builders, who labored for their rulers, were occupied year in and year out in the construction of the proud cities, which were religious and civic centers. The working population lived in villages of thatched huts among the surrounding fields.

The Mayan workmen were exceedingly skilled in the cutting and handling of stone, quarrying their blocks from the most convenient hills of limestone, andesite or sandstone. Thousands of workers must have labored like the ancient Egyptians to transport the huge blocks to city sites. Masons and sculptors made expert use of limestone mortar, plaster and stucco in building and decoration.

Sometimes a natural hill was used as base for the terraces above which temples were erected, but most of the pyramids and smaller mounds were man-made. They were solid masses of earth and rubble faced with mortar or cut stone. Every building of consequence was raised on a mound above the level of the courts. Long low buildings on the smaller mounds are believed to have been dwellings for the priesthood and nobility. Temples and palaces were ranged in imposing patterns around great plazas and sunken courts where religious pageants and ceremonial games took place.

In their towering pyramids crowned with temples the Mayas reached for the sky, perhaps to make the buildings dedicated to the gods impressive against the crowding forest. The pyramidal bases were built in terraces of diminishing size, each set back from the one below. The lift of the terraces, and the ascending line of steep stone stairways mounting from one terrace to the next, led the eyes and spirits of worshippers to the temple built on the flat top.

Mayan architects did not know the principle of the keystone arch. Their rooms were built with walls of solid stone above which overlapping courses of stone were laid until the opening could be closed with a flat slab. The walls were then covered with smooth stucco. This made a long narrow room with a pointed vault for ceiling. The outer room of a temple was like a portico with the roof supported on pillared blocks covered with sculptured ornament. A doorway led into the windowless sanctuary, its walls covered with brilliant frescoed designs or sculptured panels. If a second story was built it was set back over a solid core of stone to support the weight. This gave the architecture, particularly of palaces, its interesting set-back character. Often temples were heightened by crowning the flat roof with a tall sculptured screen called a roof comb. Aspiration was the keynote of this temple architecture, an expression in art of the religious spirit of the race.

In the great plazas were placed the record stones, the stelae. They were immense shafts from fifteen to thirty feet high, carved on all four sides with symbolic ornament and groups of hieroglyphs. On the face of the stones, carved in deep relief, were figures richly costumed, the plumes of their flamboyant headdresses sweeping up to complete the design of the whole shaft. In some cities a stela was set up every twenty years, in others at intervals of five or ten years. The dates, in symbolic glyphs, marked the historical progress of the city.

In the lowlands of northeastern Guatemala, called El Petén, the earliest cities grew to splendor; Uaxactún, with the oldest stelae, Tikal, of tremendously lofty temples, Yaxchilan, Piedras Negras. This region is traversed by rivers, three of which join to form the broad tropical stream of the Usumacinta, a highway for travel in canoes from one center to another, and to the sea. The cities were surrounded by large populations and cultivated fields until El Petén, now mostly a forested wilderness, was astir with civilized life.

Other centers of religion and learning were added to the Maya Empire; cities such as Copán in Honduras, Quiriguá in Guatemala, Palenque in Chiapas. In Palenque art and architecture reached their climax of style and elaborate beauty; temples were less thick-walled and lofty, palaces were as important as temples. There was a marvelous grace and elegance in the sculptural reliefs done in molded stucco.

In the Maya Empire the plantations, where industrious folk worked the earth, framed the groups of temples in living green. From their villages the people came to the great plazas to take part in the gorgeous ceremonials that marked their year of worship. With vivid pageantry processions of priests mounted the stone stairways to the temples to make sacrifices to the gods in a mist of copal incense. Copal, a resinous gum, was used for incense by all Middle American people.

It is considered likely that these temple and palace centers were city-states, each with its nobility and the priestly hierarchy, chief rulers of an intensely religious race. There was commerce between the city-states, trade in the products of the soil and work of skilled craftsmen. The Mayan people were great traders, sending their merchants far and wide by river or trail through the forests. Probably it was through these travelers that the influence of Mayan art and religion spread to less civilized people, their contemporaries.

The craftsmen of individual cities specialized in arts. From one place came exquisite carved jade plaques and ornaments, from another fine pottery. The workshops of other cities produced fine woven cottons. None survived in the hot, damp climate, but evidence of their skill is found in the patterned costumes on frescoed and sculptured figures. These beautiful things were distributed by the traders in exchange for goods needed in the cities.

The aristocratic rulers of this empire were not interested in war and conquest. Indeed, it may be deduced from the absence of battle scenes and warrior figures in their reliefs that the Maya of the Old Empire were a most peaceful people. Farming, building and masonry, or craftwork, occupied the lower ranks. The sculptors were absorbed in the carving of stelae and reliefs in stone and stucco. The labor of multitudes set free the priestly aristocracy for endless speculation and study.

Their minds were steeped in abstract calculations, fascinated by concepts of time and the study of the stars in their courses.

Earliest of their achievements was the evolution of a calendar which was fundamentally a farmers' almanac, to inform the people of the seasons and the time to begin agricultural operations. There was also a great deal of astrological calculation connected with the study of months and days. Observations of the sun, moon and planets were checks for the agricultural year.

The Maya evolved a year of eighteen months, each of twenty days, making 360 days. The five additional days needed to make up the sun year of 365 days were considered very unlucky. People tried to avoid disaster by staying home and doing as little as possible. Each month had its pictured sign and name. The Mayan sun calendar was as accurate as that by which we live. The priests also evolved a ceremonial calendar connected with feasts, fasts and prayers.

Generations of priests must have made their calculations in developing the elaborate system of time counts. The day was the unit and the Maya counted in twenties and employed the symbol zero long before it was known to Europeans. All dates in Mayan chronology were reckoned from a mythical event in the past corresponding, according to Doctor Spinden, to 3373 B.C.

In addition to these studies the priests evolved the symbolism of religion, with the round of ceremonies and sacrifices necessary to keep the gods in favorable mood toward the people. In time, the personification of natural forces worshipped by a primitive people grew into a pantheon of gods with many attributes. Their pictured forms, grotesque and loaded with symbols, appear in hieroglyphs and design.

Everywhere in sculptured decoration stylized serpent forms wind in and out. This creature was universally worshipped by ancient Americans as the symbol of life-giving water. In the

Mayan religion the serpent became a powerful and mystic divinity, god of water, wind and sky, associated with the planet Venus. The undulating body of Kulkulcan, the Feathered Serpent, represented his control over water, while the bird feathers in which he was clothed indicated his control of the air. The serpent god was sometimes given human attributes as well as those of beast divinities.

Priestly scholars also devised and passed on the system of writing. Their hieroglyphs were somewhat like Chinese characters in that they composed a sacred writing without an alphabet. Each pictograph or glyph stood for a word or idea.

These astronomer-priests were aloof from the material aspects of life, far above the people they ruled. It is possible that the impressive figures on the stelae were actual portraits, or at least the idealized type of the class. The subtle faces with heavy-lidded eyes, prominent noses and strongly modeled lips are those of beings who might well have inspired awe in humble folk.

Only the priests could manipulate the complex calendars, interpret the wishes of the gods and the meaning of the heavens. Only they and the educated nobility could read the hieroglyphs. The people took part in ceremonies and prayers decreed by the priests and made their own offerings of flowers, fruit and copal incense to the small intimate deities of earth and fertility who would give them abundant crops.

Mayan sculptors, working within the framework of tradition and symbolism imposed by the priests, created a distinctive art, masterly in form and design. As it developed, the artists attained a grace and freedom in treatment of human figures surpassing the art of the Egyptians. The later temples and stairways leading to them were enriched with carved reliefs, masks and figures. Color, in frescoes and exterior ornament, glorified the buildings. The sculptors showed their plastic talent in the molding of stucco relief, of which the most beautiful was found at Palenque. The few wooden beams and door lintels not destroyed by the climate are carved with exquisite skill.

It is evident from all their works of art that the Maya were mature, sophisticated people, their minds so steeped in the symbolic meanings of their world of thought that the expression in art is almost unintelligible to us.

Mayan design is very intricate, rich and, in the later period, flamboyant. If we cannot understand it, we may at least enjoy the beauty and rhythm of its patterns. We cannot appreciate most of their strange representations of gods, but the sculptured busts of the Maize God are most appealing. This deity, so important to a people dependent on corn, is represented as a beautiful exotic youth, his almond-shaped eyes downcast, his lips half open as though addressing the people. His head is crowned with curly corn leaves.

The ordered life of the Old Empire, so rich in ceremonial and art, existed for centuries and had a wide influence on other peoples. Then, quite suddenly, it came to an end. One by one the thriving cities were deserted. Whole populations abandoned the temples of their gods, their homes and fields, to trek through the wilderness in search of a new dwelling place. Gradually the centers of once-busy life were taken over by lush jungle growth and the birds and animals of the forest. This wholesale migration is believed to have taken place sometime between the seventh and ninth centuries.

No one knows the reasons for such a migration. There may have been destructive pestilence, failure of water supply, attacks by barbaric tribes or warfare between city-states. Some scholars think that it was no longer possible to grow enough maize for the increasing population. The farmers were in the habit of letting the fields lie fallow between plantings so they must have had to go farther and farther from the centers to clear new land. Successive burnings and plantings destroyed the fertility of the soil. It may be, too, that the priests, for reasons of their own, decreed the migration.

After centuries of sleep in the smothering jungle some of those wonderful cities of ancient America have been cleared of bush and trees by archeological expeditions; their sculptures revealed, fallen stones of temples and stairways set back in place. People who fly in planes over El Petén see the white tops of Tikal's ruined temples in the sea of forest. Work-a-day planes, taking out chicle, land beside the ruins of Uaxactún, deep in the bush.

Some of the migrants from the city-states may have gone into the highlands of Guatemala; most of them made their way to the peninsula of Yucatán where they settled among people of their own race. They merged with those of Yucatán and in the course of a few centuries new glories of Mayan art were created in a renaissance of culture, called the New Empire.

The migrants settled in a very different environment from that of their old homes. Yucatán is a flat land with a thin layer of soil over limestone rock, no surface rivers and much scrubby forest. The people were dependent for water on deep natural wells in the porous limestone called cenotes, and subterranean pools in caverns, both fed from underground rivers. They also managed to store some water during the rainy season.

The farmers, however, adapted themselves to new conditions, raising maize, beans, squash, tomatoes, chili peppers. The people had an abundance of tropical fruits as well as wild turkeys and deer to vary the vegetable diet. Cacao, or chocolate, was valued by the Mayas as it was by other Middle American people. The rich oily beans taken from the seed pods of the native cacao tree were an article of trade between tribes and often used for money. The Mayas, like the Mexicans, made a thick beverage by mixing ground and heated chocolate with maize gruel and chili.

Few record stones have been found in Yucatán, so it is believed that the priests then recorded dates and historical events in their books which were destroyed. The later chronicle of *Chilam Balam* gives a legendary account of the rivalries of three ruling clans—the Xius, Cocoms and Itzás. There were wars between them, during which the control of cities frequently changed hands. Uxmal became the capital of the lordly Xius while the Itzás occupied Chichén.

Uxmal was one of the most beautiful of the cities. Soaring above the surrounding country on terraced platforms and pyramids, its temples and palaces of white limestone, touched with color, must have been brilliant in the sunlight. The outer walls of the buildings were banded with the most exquisite sculptured reliefs and patterns. Partly restored by archeologists, Uxmal today is a beautiful example of Mayan art of the renaissance in Yucatán.

Chichén Itzá, the name meaning Wells of the Itzás, was always a holy city. One of the deep cenotes, or wells, was the source of the town's water supply. Steps were cut in the rock wall to reach the unfailing water far below. In the days of Chichén's glory there must have been a constant procession of slaves with their water jars going to and from the pool.

The other cenote was the Sacred Well, abode of Yum Chac, the Rain God. It was a huge pit a hundred and sixty feet wide with perpendicular sides, the green water about seventy feet

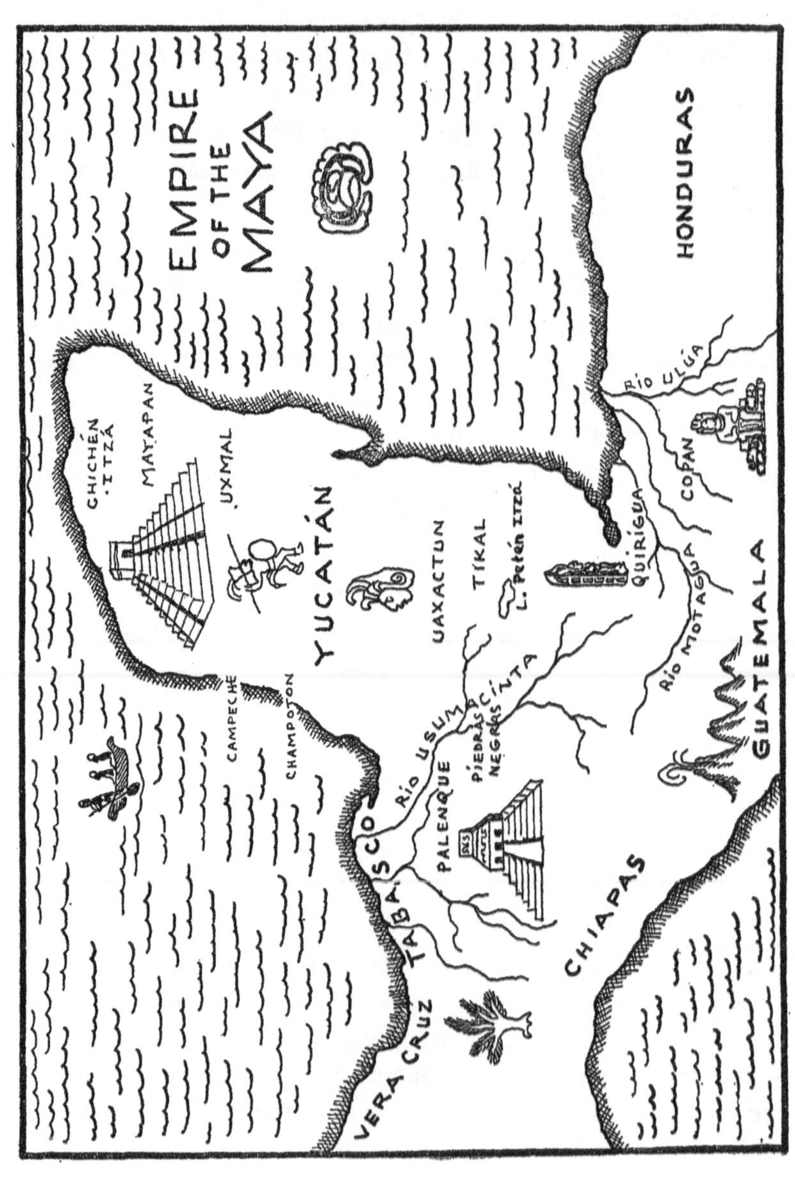

EMPIRE OF THE MAYA
HONDURAS
RIO ULÚA
COPAN
CHICHÉN ITZÁ
MAYAPAN
UXMAL
YUCATÁN
UAXACTUN
TIKAL
L. Petén Itzá
QUIRIGUA
Rio Motagua
GUATEMALA
CAMPECHE
CHAMPOTON
Rio Usumacinta
PIEDRAS NEGRAS
PALENQUE
TABASCO
CHIAPAS
VERA CRUZ

below the surface. From the earliest times sacrifices were made there to the Rain God, a much honored deity in that land of drought.

A new element came into the life of Yucatán about the beginning of the eleventh century, according to more or less legendary accounts. It was a stimulus from outside which was to bring about great changes in art, religion and social life. This new influence centers about the most fascinating figure of the ancient American story—Quetzalcoatl. If he was a real person, he was leader of the Toltecs, the most civilized people of the Valley of Mexico. Their story will be told in the next chapter.

Some scholars believe there was a human Quetzalcoatl, some do not. In legend he is described as a wise leader, later deified as the hero-god of the Toltecs. This god had many of the attributes of Kulkulcan of the Maya—he was the Feathered Serpent. If there was a human leader of this name he may have been a priest of the god and so took the sacred name.

In Yucatán Quetzalcoatl is a mysterious, legendary figure. One story has it that, as a young prince, he was captured in battle and sacrificed to Yum Chac, the Rain God, in the Sacred Well. It was the practice to throw victims into the pool at daybreak, and if they survived until noon it was taken as a sign that the god wished them to live. They were then hauled out and acquired divine rank, having taken on some of the god's spirit through sacrifice. According to this story Quetzalcoatl survived the ordeal and was thenceforth regarded as a god on earth. Another legendary account tells of the conquest of the Yucatecans by Quetzalcoatl and his warriors, after which he became their ruler. These stories of Quetzalcoatl in Yucatán, the leader who came from outside the country, coincide with the invasion by powerful Toltecs from the Valley of Mexico.

Quetzalcoatl organized life in Yucatán with the civilized

ideas always associated with him. He united the rival clans—Xius, Cocoms, Itzás—in the League of Mayapán of which he was supreme lord. The large walled city of Mayapán was built for the governing center of the League. There the tribal chieftains lived, ruling their cities through subordinate chiefs. Chichén Itzá remained the religious center and the shrine of the Feathered Serpent God—Quetzalcoatl to the Toltec, Kulkulcan to the Maya.

The new leader and his followers brought with them the worship of the Toltec Feathered Serpent and they found adoration of the same deity in Yucatán. The two were blended in devotion to Kulkulcan who was raised to the position of supreme god at Chichén Itzá.

Before the coming of the Toltecs, Chichén of the Itzás was a city of purely Mayan architecture. There were richly carved and painted temples set on terraced pyramids, dwellings of priests and nobles adorned with sculpture. Great masks of the Rain God with upward curling snouts, were set in the friezes and jutted out from cornices of temples.

Under Toltec influence the city was rebuilt to be a place of grandeur in honor of Kulkulcan. Toltec ideas of the Feathered Serpent were used in sculpture and ornament. Huge serpent heads with gaping jaws and feathered collars adorned the balustrades of stairways and thrust out from cornices. Serpent bodies formed the pillars of temple porticos, their heads on the floor and their tails supporting the roof.

In this rebuilding some of the older temples were buried within larger and more imposing structures. The beautiful Temple of the Warriors, nucleus of an immense pattern of pillared courts and plazas, preserved in its heart a smaller shrine with walls frescoed in designs of warriors in full battle array. Another shrine was buried in building the temple of

Kulkulcan, the most lofty and impressive of them all. It was called El Castillo by the Spaniards and retains the name to this day.

When the Carnegie Institution Expedition, with the collaboration of the Mexican government, was working at Chichén Itzá, they discovered the buried temples in the course of their diggings. In the heart of El Castillo they found, standing in the sanctuary of the older shrine, the famous jaguar throne. It was carved from stone and painted red, with turquoise spots and eyes of shining jade. Who knows what lordly priests of the Itzás may have sat upon that throne!

In many beautiful cities the Toltec influence was responsible for changes in architecture and design. Under the League of Mayapán there was peace, so that the empire prospered through far-flung commerce. Explorers are now tracing out some of the water routes of the Mayan traders along the coasts of Yucatán. They became navigators, sailing among the islands of the Caribbean Sea in their great canoes. Mayan textiles—patterned cotton goods and feather mantles—were one of the chief exports to other peoples.

Overland trade brought in materials for the skilled artisans; jade and obsidian from Mexico, turquoise from Oaxaca. Wrought gold ornaments came from Costa Rica, perhaps even from South America, and the iridescent plumes of the sacred quetzal bird for headdresses were brought from the highlands of Guatemala.

Broad causeways of white limestone were built above the level of the land to connect important cities. Highway of pilgrimage was the road from Chichén Itzá to Cobá and thence to the coast opposite the island of Cozumel, a place of revered shrines. The great roads knew only the feet of men—there were no beasts of burden, no vehicles. Slaves and carriers trotted over them laden with produce, groups of traders made their journeys with their bundles of goods carried on human backs, bands of barbarically decked warriors marched from city to city. At times of religious festivals pilgrimages filled the roads, with feather banners floating and musicians beating on drums and blowing conch-shell trumpets.

When drought threatened the crops pilgrims came from far and near for the sacrifices to the Rain God at Chichén Itzá. There was a causeway leading from the great temple of Kulkulcan to the Sacred Well, over which a procession of priests and musicians led the victims to be sacrificed. They were children, maidens, or young men captured in battle. After prayers and the burning of copal incense, the victims were flung out over the brink to fall into the green water far below. Yum Chac was appeased by human sacrifices and by offerings of jade, gold, mosaic and other treasures thrown in by the pilgrims.

Some Mexican archeologists believe that the pillared courts and plaza below the Temple of the Warriors were for the use of the throngs of pilgrims who came to make offerings. One can imagine the swarm of people camped among the columns, chattering softly in their Mayan tongue, cooking over little fires in the Indian fashion.

The nobility in this Maya-Toltec empire was a luxurious class, served by many slaves in their city palaces. They were clothed in girdles and mantles of fine cotton and feather fabrics, adorning themselves with great earplugs of gold or jade, necklaces, and headdresses of quetzal plumes. The heads, sloping to a point above big noses and lips, are unpleasing to modern eyes, but that was beauty to the Maya. The admired sugar-loaf shape of head was artificial, obtained by binding their babies' soft skulls between boards.

Young men of the nobility were trained in religion and astrology, history and the calendar. Children of workers learned at an early age the occupations of their parents; boys to hunt, fish and till the fields, girls to weave and to grind maize, chili and cacao beans for food.

Pageants and games drew crowds in the cities. At Chichén Itzá the ceremonial ball game of the ancient Americans was played in a great walled court, with carved stone rings for goals set high against opposite walls. The teams played with a hard rubber ball, hitting it with the hand, hip or other parts of the body. To win, by driving the ball through one of the stone rings, required great skill and agility. Spectators followed the play with all the passion of bullfight *aficionados* in Spanish life. Although the game was connected with religion it was the occasion for lively betting.

Innumerable festivals for the great gods brought the workers from their shops, looms and fields to take part in worship before the temples. Then there was dancing on plazas strewn with green leaves and flowers, weird music, and heavy drinking of the ceremonial beverage, *balche*. It was made of honey brewed with plant juices and the bark of a certain tree.

Life was bound up with religion and, as always, based on agriculture. Each villager had a piece of land for crops of maize and vegetables. The farmers worked together to till their fields and raise food for their aristocracy and priesthood, as well as cotton for the weaving industry. Before the brush was cleared and burned and the fields planted the farmers spent a night of feasting and prayer. Each process of agriculture was accompanied by prayers and the burning of copal to the gods of the earth.

Every trade had its patron deity and special feast—the hunters and fishermen, the farmers, beekeepers, traders and craftsmen. Beekeepers were numerous because honey was used for food as well as to make the ceremonial balche.

After two hundred years of peace the rivalry of warlike chiefs brought the League of Mayapán to an end. Gradually the Cocoms made themselves overlords in Mayapán and extended their tyranny over the country, causing wars with the Xius and Itzás. Mexican soldiers brought in by the Cocoms added to the confusion and disunity.

Finally the Cocoms became so overbearing that the clans rose against them in force. The strong city of Mayapán was besieged and conquered in A.D. 1451. The Cocoms were slaughtered and the city left in ruins. That was the end of peace and prosperity, and of the League of Mayapán. It was split up into many clan groups ruled by their chiefs in individual cities. The Itzás left their beautiful Chichén to migrate through the wilderness to Lake Petén in Guatemala. There they built an island city and lived in security long after the Spaniards had conquered Yucatán.

Within less than a century from the fall of Mayapán white men from across the sea would reach Yucatán. Mayan priests, looking into the future, foretold the doom of their race. In the *Books of Chilam Balam* the warning chant of the Tiger Priest is written:

> Eat, eat, thou hast bread;
> Drink, drink, thou hast water;
> On that day dust possesses the earth;
> On that day a cloud arises,
> On that day a mountain rises,
> On that day, a strong man seizes the land,
> On that day, things fall to ruin,
> On that day, the tender leaf is destroyed,

On that day, the dying eyes are closed,
On that day, three signs are on the tree,
On that day, three generations hang there,
On that day, the battle flag is raised,
And they are scattered abroad in the forest.

The prophecy was fulfilled as disasters added to the disintegration of civilization in Yucatán. One year a terrific hurricane devastated the land, uprooting forest trees, destroying villages and ruining the crops. Drought brought the people near to starvation in other years, or widespread pestilence decimated the population. Although the Yucatecans fought white-skinned invaders fiercely in tribal groups, native civilization met its doom when the Spaniards landed on the coast of Yucatán.

CHAPTER 3

IN ANÁHUAC, THE VALLEY OF MEXICO

THOUSANDS of years ago primitive men first chose the Valley of Mexico for their homes. High above the hot, humid coasts, the highlands enfolded by mountains were an inviting place to live. Great shallow lakes, reflecting the luminous sky, attracted wandering tribes to settle on their shores. Wild birds, haunting the reed beds of the lakes, and deer from the mountain slopes, augmented the diet of the early farming folk. Men looked up from their work to the immense volcanoes, Popocatépetl and Ixtaccíhuatl, glistening white against the sky, and worshipped them with fear and awe.

Peaceful farming tribes lived for ages near the lakes. They inhabited villages of thatched huts, cultivated maize and other crops, ground their corn on stone metates, and had various tools and clay vessels for daily use.

About the third or fourth century of the Christian era, new people entered the Valley from more civilized regions to the south and east. They brought more skilled techniques in handiwork and the idea of building platforms of earth and stone to hold their temples.

Eventually another tribe entered the lake region, probably from the north; people who were to attain a position of great prestige in the myths of ancient Mexico. They were a Nahua tribe and, as succeeding waves of migrants belonged to the same language group, Nahuatl became the principal language of central Mexico. It is not even known whether Toltec was the real name of these accomplished people, or whether it was a name applied by later migrants to the civilized tribes they found in the Valley of Mexico. So entangled with myth and tribal annals is the story of the Toltecs that they are seen through a veil of mystery.

However it may be, the people called Toltecs, the Master Builders, developed an influential center of civilization at Teotihuacán during the early centuries of their life in the Valley of Mexico. There they became good farmers, expert craftsmen and builders, while through their superior arts, learning and powerful religion, they dominated other tribes of the Valley. This period of Toltec life is called that of the Classical Toltecs.

Teotihuacán lies northeast of the great salt Lake Texcoco, not far from modern Mexico City. Even now the place is tremendously impressive with the huge truncated pyramids of the Sun and Moon looming above the plain. It must have been majestic indeed when temples and priests' dwellings stood on the pyramids and other platform bases, linked by a long ceremonial roadway. According to tradition the temples on the two massive pyramids were dedicated to a Sun God and Moon Goddess. Across a little river the temple of Quetzalcoatl stood on a lofty platform, its sides faced with carved stone. A great stairway, on one face of the platform, led up to the shrine. Huge serpent heads, brightly painted, with eyes of obsidian, thrust out from terraces and balustrades, and undulating serpent bodies decorated the base. The serpent heads are like those on temples at Chichén Itzá, supposed to have been inspired by Toltec ideas.

The people had many gods but the divine being most closely associated with the Toltecs was Quetzalcoatl, the Feathered Serpent, god of learning and civilization. In their mythological history of the universe, divided into four "Suns," Quetzalcoatl ruled the world during the Wind Sun. He taught human beings farming and the arts and then disappeared in the East, promising to return. Some legends say that he sailed over the sea to the place of the sun's rising on his magic serpent raft.

Priests serving this god took his name. Some myths credit Quetzalcoatl with giving the people the knowledge of astronomy, their calendar and picture writing. This may indicate the time when priests evolved such useful knowledge.

All the advanced peoples of central Mexico had a system of time counting, a calendar, and hieroglyphic symbols. Whether each group evolved the knowledge separately, or whether the creative Mayas were the original source, we cannot know. Among the Toltecs years were counted in fifty-two year cycles and their calendar, like that of other peoples, had three hundred and sixty days.

The Toltecs are credited with introducing the ceremonial ball game to the Valley of Mexico and with the invention of *pulque,* the liquor made from the fermented sap of the maguey plant.

At Teotihuacán the common folk, busy with their crops and crafts, lived in large communal dwellings of adobe brick outside the ceremonial center of temples. The costumes worn by the upper ranks became the mode in the Valley of Mexico, as they were adopted by tribes who succeeded the Toltecs. Men wore breechclout and mantle, women a square sleeveless blouse called a *huipil* with a strip of cotton wrapped about the waist and legs for a skirt. Priests were distinguished by miter-shaped headdresses and long black robes. Chiefs also wore long robes and decked themselves with necklaces and ornamental ear-plugs. Warriors had suits of quilted cotton and fought with spears, shields and wooden clubs edged with sharp blades of obsidian.

The custom of earlier people of making tiny images for votive offerings was perfected by the Toltecs. Thousands of little heads and figurines, modeled in clay or carved in stone and obsidian, have been unearthed at Teotihuacán. Deposits of this black volcanic glass, obsidian, were near by. The hard substance could be chipped into flakes for knife blades, used for eyes of images, and its clear black surface appealed to the sculptors.

These Classical Toltecs were the creators of the most beautiful masks ever found in Mexico. Carved out of jade, obsidian or milky stone, they are the work of master sculptors, superb in style and finish. Skill in carving large pieces of stone is shown in the serpent heads of Quetzalcoatl's temple and the monumental statue of the Water Goddess, a terrifying creature. The craftsmen were also skilled in the art of pottery. Rarely beautiful pieces were made for ceremonial purposes and passed by way of the traders to other peoples. Through these travelers, who brought in materials for the craftsmen, Toltec culture was spread both north and south.

Within a few centuries the rulers of Teotihuacán extended their dominion over towns in the Valley of Mexico and other regions. They took over the site of an earlier tribe at Cholula in the Puebla region, building a great maze of temples. Quetzalcoatl was the reigning god at Cholula. In later generations all the courts and temple bases were filled in to make the enormous pyramid for which Cholula is famous.

At Teotihuacán the followers of Quetzalcoatl, tribal hero and most honored god, had the greatest power. Their control was challenged in a later period by worshippers of new deities. In the religious conflicts which ensued prosperous life was disrupted; the followers of new gods prevailed and the temples were rebuilt, using the old structures as cores for the new. Archeological excavations revealed this fact. The bulk of the pyramids was increased and the gorgeous stairway of Quetzalcoatl's temple was buried under earth and stone in building a larger pyramidal base. This pyramid was surrounded by a great walled enclosure. Hidden thus, the stairway with the Feathered Serpent heads was unknown until modern excavations brought it to light.

Tradition has it that during the tenth and eleventh centuries Teotihuacán was gradually abandoned due to religious wars, although the people continued to live in the region. It was late in this period, also according to tradition, that Toltecs and their leader, arriving in Yucatán, began to impose their influence on Mayan civilization.

After the dispersion of people from Teotihuacán the Valley of Mexico, or Anáhuac, was overrun by a succession of warlike hunting tribes from the north. The name Chichimecs, wearers of skins, was given in a general way to all these uncivilized tribes. One after another these bands entered the region of cultivated fields and thriving towns, each group bearing the image of its tribal god. Superior prowess in war enabled them to conquer the sedentary people, but they in turn were conquered by the civilization they found.

They learned skill in agriculture and handiwork, adopted

the social customs and gods of the subdued people. Toltec prestige was still great, so that barbaric chieftains founded dynasties by marrying into noble families of the civilized people, and called themselves Toltec lords. Each tribe with its ruling class occupied its city-state, and the most powerful chiefs dominated other towns, exacting tribute from them. During this period of competition between clans which lasted well into the fourteenth century, fine cities of stone houses and temples grew up around the shores of Lake Texcoco.

The city which was to become the most advanced in arts and learning, Texcoco, was founded by one of the barbaric tribes, who built up a proud lineage of chieftains through intermarriage with the conquered. Later, accomplished Mixteca people from the region of Oaxaca brought their cultural gifts to the city-state. They introduced the worship of the Sky God Tezcatlipoca, and taught the people picture writing. The lords of Texcoco conquered other cities, adding to their wealth from tribute, so that Texcoco became a dominating power in the Valley. Other tribes, the Xochimilcos and Chalcas, had their towns on the sweet-water lagoons below huge Lake Texcoco.

Into this cultivated highland region came a late band of Nahua-speaking wanderers. Their beginnings were humble, but they were destined by superior intelligence and aggressive character to become the rulers of Indian Mexico. They became known as the Aztecs, but they were originally a nomadic tribe called the Tenochcas. When they had become proud and powerful the story of their origin was preserved, and the record of their wanderings set down in picture manuscripts.

According to one legend the tribe came into the world from a mythical place of Seven Caves, a common origin myth in America. Another version is that the people first lived on islands in a lake of western Mexico. There they found in a cave an image of the god Huitzilopochtli, who became their tribal deity. Following a prophecy, probably announced by their priest, the Tenochcas set forth in search of a place where they would find an eagle perched on a cactus plant with a serpent in its mouth. There they were to found their kingdom.

This prophetic sign is supposed to have been found on the island where the Tenochcas or Aztecs built their marvelous city. The nation of Mexico, creation of Indian and Spaniard, has taken for its emblem the Aztec eagle perched on a cactus.

The Aztecs, according to their own story, began their wanderings in the twelfth century. It was a slow progress and they did not reach Lake Texcoco until about the middle of the thirteenth century. Too weak as yet to wrest good land from powerful chieftains, they made their settlement on the hill of Chapultepec near the lake shore, where they lived for some time. These interlopers made themselves thoroughly disliked in the neighborhood by their rough, aggressive ways. When they made a marauding expedition to steal wives from a lake town, the other tribes rose against them and drove them from Chapultepec. Some of the Aztecs took refuge on the islands in the lake while others lived in servitude.

Gradually the tribe increased in numbers and strength, gaining a reputation for prowess in battle. In their island town called Tenochtitlán thatched huts were replaced by houses of adobe and stone. Tenochtitlán began its career as the Aztec city-state when the tribal council elected their first ruler, Acamapichtli, about A.D. 1376.

The Aztec chiefs took every opportunity to make alliances with the strong cities around the lake. They helped the young exiled lord of Texcoco, Nezahualcoyotl, to regain his rule over the city. Thenceforth the alliance between the city-states of

Texcoco and Tenochtitlán enabled them to dominate the other tribes in the Valley of Mexico.

The remarkable success of the newcomers in winning power over their more civilized neighbors was due to their intelligence and genius for organization as well as to their skill in war. Like the Romans of the Old World they were clever in assimilating the ideas and arts of people they conquered, and were adaptors rather than creators.

Social customs, learning and gods were taken over by the Aztecs from their neighbors. Their craftsmen and artists outdistanced the people from whom they learned, their government and society were organized more efficiently than in other tribes. On the basis of what they found the Aztecs developed the interesting civilization known by their name, which was in full flower when the Spaniards arrived to destroy it. The span of the Aztec Empire was only a hundred and fifty years, a much shorter period than those of the civilizations preceding it.

During the fifteenth century these vigorous people built up their kingdom by wars of conquest and strategic alliances, until their last ill-fated chief, Montezuma II, ruled a realm extending from sea to sea and from Anáhuac to the Isthmus of Tehuantepec. For all their prowess, the Aztec armies never subdued the Tarascans who had their towns around Lake Patzcuaro in the Michoacán region, or the independent Tlascalans whose kingdom lay between the Valley of Mexico and Vera Cruz. Tribute was taken from the Zapotec kingdom to the south and a road was opened through their territory to obtain tropical products from Tehuantepec.

The Spaniards called this realm an empire, but it was not that in the European sense. Conquered tribes were obliged to

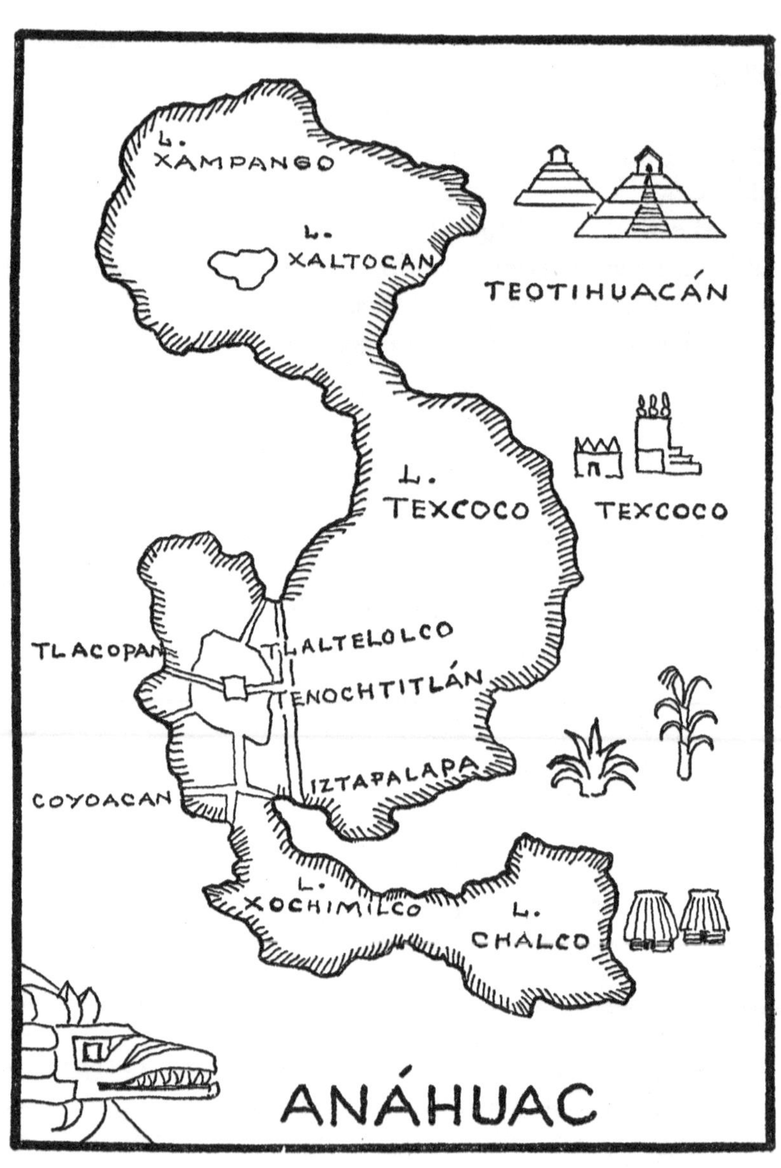

L. XAMPANGO
L. XALTOCÁN
TEOTIHUACÁN
L. TEXCOCO
TEXCOCO
TLACOPAN
TLALTELOLCO
TENOCHTITLÁN
COYOACAN
IZTAPALAPA
L. XOCHIMILCO
L. CHALCO
ANÁHUAC

pay tribute of their produce, raw materials and craftwork to the lordly Aztecs. They were vassals, expected to provide armies for warfare, but their chiefs continued to rule in their own cities. The whole realm was well organized for the gathering of tribute and assembling of armies but the Aztec lords were obeyed out of fear, and there was little real unity in the empire. It was greatly to the advantage of the Spaniards that most of the subject peoples hated the rulers of Tenochtitlán. Only the Incas of Peru, among pre-Columbian people, had the ability to blend many regions and their people into one well-knit empire.

Each chief of the Aztec dynasty added to the splendor of their island capital, Tenochtitlán. It was connected by three broad stone causeways to towns on the lake shores. Pure water from the springs of Chapultepec was led to the city through a stone aqueduct. Dikes were built for protection from floods in the rainy season. The people showed great ingenuity in utilizing their situation—island, water and marsh—for their needs. To provide land for crops they invented the famous *chinampas,* erroneously called "floating gardens." Mud from the lake bottom was scraped up to fill frames of reed and stakes, forming nests of wet, fertile earth in which to raise maize and vegetables. As trees and bushes took root the little islands increased in size and became solid. Clear water between the chinampas formed canals over which the amphibious farmers paddled in dugout canoes. Thatched huts for farmers' families nestled on the larger islands. By this ingenious scheme marshes were transformed into bowery islands of enchanting beauty, covered with flowers, trees and vegetable gardens.

The Xochimilcos and Chalcos, lake-dwellers on the lagoons, also grew their crops on chinampas. Although their lakes are almost gone, Indians of today still live among canals and islands in that region, growing fruit, vegetables and flowers for Mexico City. They speak the Aztec language and live in the same kind of thatched huts as those of their ancestors.

The verdant chinampas with their farmers' huts fringed the stately capital. In canoes people traversed the city by a network of canals, bordered by footpaths and crossed at convenient intervals by wooden bridges. Houses with walls of adobe or stone were built on stone bases, surrounding courts and gardens.

Over all the delightful city of waterways, gardens and dwellings towered the *teocalli,* the temples. The center of civic and religious life was an enormous plaza called the Tecpán. There, on an imposing pyramid, stood the temples of Huitzilopochtli, the War God, and Tlaloc, the God of Rain. The Sun God, Tonatiuh, also had his temple in the Tecpán. Schools, priests' dwellings and palaces of the ruling family were gathered around the courts. People assembled in the Tecpán to take part in festivals and dances for the gods, or to watch games in the great ball court. There were temples to Huitzilopochtli and Quetzalcoatl in the neighboring island town, Tlaltelolco, which was joined to Tenochtitlán by bridges. In the great plaza of Tlaltelolco trade in all the produce and crafts of Mexico took place on market days.

Small wonder that the island capital of the Aztecs was regarded by all the people with pride and admiration. It was indeed unique among cities, riding on the lake waters in its frame of gardens like something out of legend. It was a place of order and beauty, prepared for happy living.

Texcoco also became a very beautiful city under the wise rule of Nezahualcoyotl, one of the most interesting personalities to emerge from the dim Indian past of Mexico. He was a statesman and philosopher, learned in astronomy, renowned as a poet and orator. Nezahualcoyotl made of Texcoco a city unsurpassed in the Valley for art and civilized living. When this great prince died in 1472 the alliance between Tenochtitlán and Texcoco was weakened. The arrogant lords of Tenochtitlán dominated the other city and extended their political control over the peoples of central Mexico.

Aztec government began as a simple tribal organization composed of clans, or related families. The chiefs of clans administered the affairs of the members. Distinguished leaders of clans were chosen to join the tribal council which elected the "chief of men," the ruler. This system became more complex in the highly organized empire and the leadership of the Aztecs became hereditary. When a ruler died some man of his lineage —son, brother or uncle—was chosen to succeed him.

Land belonged to the state and was allotted to the different groups for use. Warriors and chiefs received lands obtained in conquest in return for their service to the state, which were worked for them by tenants and serfs. Other lands were cultivated communally for the support of the priesthood, the ruler and noble families. Each chief divided the portion of land allotted to his clan among heads of families, so that everyone had fields to cultivate for subsistence.

In the austere Aztec state an individual gained prestige by the value of his service, for everyone was expected to contribute to the community by his labor, his special skill, or ability in warfare. In this respect the Aztec system was democratic, as a man attained rank and privilege through his achievements rather than from inherited social position.

Young men trained for the priesthood could advance through their learning in astronomy and ritual, their disciplined lives and devotion to religious practices, even though of humble family. The same was true of the young men who served the state as warriors. Those who showed great skill in battle and unflinching bravery might join one of the military orders, the Knights of the Eagle, or Knights of the Ocelot, and wear the brilliant trappings and great masks of the order. In a state built on conquest, warriors were naturally an honored class. The Aztec aristocracy, as the empire grew in wealth, had many privileges and lived luxuriously.

The last phase of Indian civilization in Mexico was at its height when the Spaniards disrupted it with the devastating force of an alien race and culture. Spanish chroniclers described native customs, scholarly priests studied the native language, learning from educated Aztecs the meanings of their ceremonial world of myth and religion before it was overlaid by Christianity.

Indian character, thought and customs are woven into the very fabric of modern Mexico. Art works of the pre-Columbian races are part of the nation's cultural heritage and Indians of the present produce the fascinating folk arts of Mexico. Native plants cultivated by the Indians are basic in Mexican agriculture. Aztec words in the language of today, Aztec foods, some festivals and the social customs of villagers are a direct inheritance from the past. Since that past is not dead in Mexico the Indian manner of life in its full flower deserves a chapter to itself.

CHAPTER 4

LIFE IN THE AZTEC REALM

AT THE CLOSE of the fifteenth century the inhabitants
of Anáhuac had behind them generations of settled, productive life. There was no reason to suppose that it would ever
change, so long as the dread supernatural powers were propitiated with prayers and sacrifices, for no enemy would dare to
invade the Aztec realm. The farmers followed the agricultural
round of sowing, cultivation and harvest. They looked up from
their peaceful work to see, passing on the roads, bands of warriors vivid with feather banners, headdresses and weapons.
They were marching on raids of conquest, a warfare with twin
objectives—to capture prisoners alive for sacrifice to the gods,
and to add the wealth of other tribes to the empire.

Beauty surrounded the inhabitants of towns and villages;
the eternal majesty of mountains against the sky, cultivated
fields, shimmering lakes fringed with gardens and white-
walled towns. The people were responsive to the loveliness of
their land, content with the orderly succession of work, festival
and worship decreed by law and long-established custom.

Each individual had his place in the pattern of communal
life. Some served the state as warriors or craftsmen. As there

43

were no beasts of burden some sections of the population spent their lives carrying loads on their backs for their lords. Other laborers worked on roads, canals and bridges, or quarried stone and made adobe bricks. Farming families passed on to their children the work of cultivating the earth to feed the population. Although laborers and farmers were poor in this world's goods, few were hungry or without shelter.

Every family had a thatched hut and a garden patch for the raising of maize, beans and chili peppers. These were the Mexican staples in Aztec times as they are today. Women spent hours grinding corn on the metates with stone rollers, to make meal for the daily corn cakes, tortillas. The pat-pat of tortilla-makers' hands shaping the flat cakes was as universal and homely a sound in Aztec villages as in those of modern Mexico.

Maize, and the maguey plant, raising its urnlike clusters of blueish green leaves to the sky, were the two plants of fundamental importance in ancient Mexico. The thick solid leaves of the maguey made good roofs for huts. Fiber from the leaves was woven into cloth for garments of humble folk or made into carrying bags. From the heart of the maguey came the sweet sap, fermented to make the ceremonial liquor called *octli* by the Aztecs, the pulque of modern times. Drinking of pulque enhanced the religious ecstasy of festivals, and on those occasions it was permissible to get drunk.

The Aztec family of workers was self-sufficient, making everything needed for labor and household by hand. Those who were especially industrious or skillful might surpass their neighbors in the workmanship of clay dishes, reed mats or tools.

Other people of the lower ranks won distinction as merchants or craftsmen. Feather-workers, jewelers, potters, sculptors and builders had their guilds and were respected for their achievements. Certain artists were skilled in painting picture manuscripts. Aztec books were long strips of amate-fiber paper coated with white size to take color, folded like an accordion when finished. These manuscripts were more objective and pictorial than the Mayan books with their complex hieroglyphs and abstruse designs of gods.

Aztec drawing was flat and angular, but the little pictures were quite expressive. Historic events, conquests or ceremonies, were recorded in a combination of picture and symbol. War was indicated by a shield and bundle of lances surrounded by footsteps. The symbol of a town's name with a lance thrust through it, or a temple on fire, described a conquest. Footsteps leading from one picture to another indicated sequence of events. Enchanting picture maps were drawn for the rulers, describing visually the trees, roads, towns and products of a region. A palm tree represented the tropics and a maguey plant the highlands. The little pictures in many colors were accented by black outlines.

Trade was vital to communities and the empire, so merchants were a privileged class. They had their own god to whom they made sacrifices before starting on journeys. Astrologers were consulted to learn the lucky days for beginning expeditions, and on the safe return from journeys incense was burned and festivals made, to give thanks to the god of merchants. With their trains of carriers loaded with goods, the traders traveled in groups over Mexico and beyond, hundreds of miles on foot through difficult country.

These men knew where to find the most precious materials for the workshops of artisans and artists; pebbles of jade, lumps of turquoise, tortoise shell, skins, feathers, sea shells, gold. In the hot country they exchanged such articles as cotton cloth, fiber rope and obsidian for tropical products. Many things were obtained by barter, but cacao beans were universally used for currency, and sometimes little quills of gold dust. Cacao beans were always in demand for the favored frothy drink of the nobility, chocolatl. On their journeys among people of distant regions the merchants acted as spies for their rulers. They learned local dialects and cleverly picked up information as to the strength of towns or wealth of products to report to the chiefs at Tenochtitlán for purposes of conquest.

The products of home fields and workshops, goods and raw materials brought from other regions, were bartered in the market places of towns. The age-old custom of market day meant as much to the Aztec people as to their descendants in modern Mexican villages.

Undoubtedly the causeways leading to Tenochtitlán were crowded with men and women trotting along with loads on their backs to reach the renowned market of Tlaltelolco. Produce was brought across the lake to the basin by the market place in fleets of canoes. The Spaniards' eyes popped at the wonders of that market when first they saw it. Let Bernal Diaz del Castillo, one of Cortés' captains, describe what they saw:

"Let us begin with the dealers in gold, silver and precious stones, feather mantles and embroidered goods. Then there were other wares consisting of Indian slaves, both men and women, tied to long poles with collars round their necks so they could not escape. Next there were other traders who sold great pieces of cloth and cotton and articles of twisted thread and those who sold cacao. In this way one could see every kind of merchandise that is to be found in New Spain. There were those who sold cloths of henequen and ropes, and sandals with which they are shod made from the same plant, and sweet cooked roots and other tubers which they get from this plant, all were kept in one part of the market in the place assigned to them. In another part were skins of tigers and lions, of otters and jaguars, deer and other animals, some tanned and some untanned. Let us go on and speak of those who sold beans and sage and other vegetables and herbs in another part, and those who sold fowls, cocks with wattles, rabbits, hares, deer, mallards, young dogs, and let us also mention the fruiterers and the women who sold cooked food, dough and tripe in their own part of the market; then every sort of pottery made in a thousand forms from great water jars to little jugs, these also had a place to themselves; then those who sold honey and other dainties like nut paste, and those who sold lumber, boards, blocks and benches, and vendors of ocote firewood. Paper, which in that country is called amate, and reeds scented with liquid ambar and full of tobacco, and yellow ointments and things of that sort, and much cochineal is sold under the arcades which are in that great market place, and there are many vendors of herbs and other sorts of trades. There are also those who sold stone knives, and fisherwomen, and others who sold cakes, and axes of copper and tin, and gourds and gaily painted jars made of wood."

Bartering went on quietly, with courtesy and the soft murmur of Aztec speech, as it does in village markets today. Then as now, the market was not only a place to buy and sell, but a social center, a place to exchange news and talk to friends.

The privileged ranks of society were well provided with fruits and foods of both hot country and highlands, obtained from vassal states. Beautiful materials and handwrought articles were theirs, distributed from the stores collected as tribute from subject tribes.

The tribute collectors traveled to distant cities in great state and were received with the best the people had to offer. Elegantly dressed and haughty in manner, these emissaries sniffed at bouquets of flowers as they checked over the goods demanded from the inhabitants. In Tenochtitlán the warehouses were filled with the foodstuffs and treasures of the empire. Officers in charge of the stores kept records for the ruler, painted on amate-fiber paper. In pictures and number symbols were set down the amount and kind of tribute received; such as raw materials, produce, textiles, costumes, gold, silver, precious stones, etc.

Aztec law and custom made life disciplined and rather austere. Those who were rebellious or unsocial were severely punished. Children were strictly brought up, trained at an early age to take their part in life by some useful work.

There were two schools for boys at Tenochtitlán, the Tepuchcalli for civil and military service to the state, and the Calmecac where youths of noble family were taught the learning and history of their race, and were trained to serve the gods as priests. Parents brought their little boys to the teachers humbly and with tears, offering them "like a jewel or a precious plume." Thenceforth the boys lived in the common house of the school, disciplined by hard labor such as cleaning the temples, cutting firewood in the forest, digging canals and making adobes. Boys who were to be warriors were hardened by carrying the shields and weapons of fighting men as they accompanied them on raids. After days spent in manual work the boys must worship the gods with chants and beating drums at night. To obtain blood to offer to the deities they pricked themselves with sharp maguey thorns.

The training of girls was not so severe, but they, too, were brought up away from home in schools like nunneries. Their duties were to tend the temple fires, prepare food for the priests and make costumes for the idols.

Marriages were arranged by parents and matchmakers. After

the bride had been carried into her husband's house her mantle and that of the young man were tied together, symbolizing the union. Not until the young pair had listened to moral lectures from their elders and had fasted and prayed, were they free to settle down to their new life.

The well-ordered, productive life of the Aztecs was overshadowed by superstition. They lived in fear of many supernatural powers bent on doing harm to human beings unless they were propitiated. The gods of other tribes were added to the Aztec pantheon, so that the worship of such a host required constant prayers, penances and sacrifices, swamping daily life with observances.

Tezcatlipoca was feared and worshipped as the God of Darkness, the all-powerful, who saw everything that was done on earth in his smoking mirror and dealt out reward or punishment accordingly.

Tlaloc, the Rain God, ranked with Tezcatlipoca, for without his favor the crops in that semi-arid land would fail. The Aztecs believed that Tlaloc had four assistants, the Tlaloque, and that in the courtyard of his palace stood four great jars containing rain from the four world directions—east, west, north and south. Thunder roared when the Tlaloque struck the jars with rods, letting loose the rain. Hundreds of little slaves, the raindrops, assisted in its distribution.

Like other pre-Columbian people, the Aztecs made much of the symbolism of the four world directions, each having its god and sacred color. This probably developed from the need of primitive tribes to orient themselves in their wanderings. The Mayas, as well as the Aztecs, represented the world directions as four trees growing from the body of Mother Earth in a cruciform design. They called this symbolic design the tree of life, but when Spanish priests saw it on temple walls they jumped to the conclusion that one of the twelve apostles had done missionary work in America and introduced the Cross.

Among the great gods ferocious Huitzilopochtli was supreme in Tenochtitlán. He was the War God and the Aztecs' tribal protector. Their success was attributed to his favor, and the people believed Huitzilopochtli demanded the blood and hearts of human victims in return for his guidance of their affairs. Human sacrifice had been practiced by other Mexican tribes, but as the Aztecs imposed their religious ceremonials it became a fearful cult, the nucleus of their worship. Every important deity must be appeased and nourished with blood. The shedding of blood had its mystic meaning as well, symbolizing the fertilization of the earth. Wars were undertaken as much to obtain victims for sacrifice as to gain wealth and expand power.

In the peculiar psychology of the Mexicans there was no terror in this wholesale offering of human beings to the gods. Warriors considered it the most honorable death, sometimes offering themselves voluntarily. Victims for the altars were believed to represent the deities to whom they were sacrificed and were much honored.

For the great festival to Tezcatlipoca a youth was chosen as the people's offering. He was surrounded for months with every luxury and pleasure, then went to his death decked with jewels and flowers, playing on a flute as he ascended the temple stairway.

It was the practice of both Mayan and Aztec people to make individual offerings of blood. This was taken from the tongue by drawing across it a cord set with sharp thorns; ears were gashed, or bodies pricked to draw blood.

The gruesome sacrifices at the stately temples were staged with pageantry of music, chants and dances, with brilliant costumes and garlands of flowers. When the victims had been escorted up to the altar before the shrine each one was stretched over the stone, arms and legs held by minor priests while the high priest plunged his sharp stone knife into the breast. He tore out the quivering heart to offer to the god in his blood-stained shrine. Then the body was tumbled down the steps, to be dismembered and parts of it eaten by the priests, as a means of communicating with the deity. The smoke of copal incense and burning human hearts rose up to appease the grim idols decked with jewels. Since they accepted blood and death as part of religion, the people found relaxation from their disciplined lives in the excitement, music and dance of the great festivals.

Beauty and horror were sharply contrasted elements in Aztec life. The people were accustomed to cruelty and bloody sacrifice, yet they were sensitive to the beauty of nature and intensely fond of flowers. Everything that was made for daily use or ceremonial purposes had beauty of form and design. The colors of jade, precious stones and gold, the soft brilliance of bird feathers, the patterns of mosaics and textiles were appreciated by a beauty-loving people.

Some of the priests and nobles were capable of expressing their thoughts about the universe in poetic imagery. It was only these men of the upper ranks who were educated in the astrological learning, history and ritual of their race. They could interpret the calendars, a sacred one for feasts and fasts, another for the sun year. Aztec calendars and time counting were similar to those of other Middle American people. They had a sun year of eighteen months, consisting of twenty days each, with five unlucky days at the end, like the Maya. Time was reckoned in cycles of fifty-two years. Each day, month and year had its symbolic sign and religious significance.

The end of a fifty-two-year cycle and beginning of a new one was a time of great solemnity and fear. People believed that life came to an end and they could only hope and pray that it would be renewed. The crucial hour of change was celebrated with the thrilling New Fire ceremony.

During the last five days of the final year the people were given up to fasting and penance. All fires in homes and temples were extinguished and household possessions were destroyed. Then as the fatal hour of night approached a gorgeous procession of priests went from Tenochtitlán to the temple on the Hill of the Star behind Culhuacán, a town on Lake Texcoco. The hill was a sharp volcanic cone, visible for miles over the valley.

With deep anxiety the priests watched the star-studded sky, waiting for the Pleiades to cross the center of the heavens. As soon as that occurred the high priest took a fire drill and, in the open breast of a victim stretched on the altar, kindled new fire for all the people. Priests of every town lit their torches at the flame and hurried through the darkness to their temples to light the fire for the new cycle. Householders ran from the temples with blazing torches to set fire glowing again in every Aztec home. When the sun rose as usual the people felt safe once more and busied themselves joyously with the renovation of the temples and the manufacture of new utensils.

The Aztec symbols of days and years, with signs representing the ages of the world's history, were carved around the face of the Sun God on the enormous sculptured disk called the Calendar Stone. Carved in the reign of Axacayatl in the fifteenth century, the symbolic disk stood before the temple of the Sun in the Tecpán.

The cosmic myth of the Four Suns, carved in symbols on the stone, was common in various forms to Mayas, Toltecs and Aztecs. In the Aztec version Tezcatlipoca gave light to the world during the first Sun, Four Ocelot. He transformed himself into the sun, while inhabitants of the earth were devoured by jaguars. Quetzalcoatl ruled the second Sun, Four Wind, in which the world was destroyed by hurricanes and men were turned into monkeys. Four Rain, the third Sun, was ruled by Tlaloc and ended in a rain of fire. The Water Goddess presided over the fourth Sun, Four Water, an epoch brought to an end by floods when men were turned into fishes. The Aztecs were living in the fifth Sun, Four Earthquake and they expected it to end with earth upheavals. In this interesting myth one may sense the experiences of primitive men with the violence of nature, in a land subject to hurricanes, torrential downpours and volcanic eruptions.

The complex mythology and astrological lore, accumulated through centuries, was part of the inheritance of Montezuma II who became "chief of men' about A.D. 1503. He was trained as a priest and was steeped in their superstitious beliefs. Montezuma was the war chief of a powerful kingdom but he was a very different person from the vigorous warriors, his ancestors. He was the fine flower of Aztec aristocracy, luxurious and fastidious, surrounded with ceremonious attention. His people regarded him as semi-divine, and even the proudest chiefs removed their rich mantles and ornaments before entering his presence. They stood before him barefoot, with downcast eyes, addressing him as "Lord, great Lord."

Despite reverence and adulation offered to the ruler, the

great war lords and chiefs of the tribal council had their say in the administration of the empire. In addition to this check on his actions Montezuma never made a move without consulting his soothsayers.

Portents of disaster, signs in the heavens, troubled the people during the first years of Montezuma's rule. Their chief was haunted by the prophecy of a diviner that strangers would come to overthrow the Aztecs. Montezuma believed that Quetzalcoatl would return as he had promised. His fatalistic Indian mind foresaw the doom of his race when the god or his emissaries came to rule the world once more.

Then scouts from the coast of Yucatán brought reports of strange beings who came across the sea in ships as large as houses. They were white of skin, had fire in their hands, and some of them were four-legged monsters, half animal, half human—the first Indian reaction to horses and riders.

Quetzalcoatl, the deified hero, was associated with the year Ce Acatl or One Reed in the Mexican calendar, and diviners had prophesied that the god would return to the world in the year Ce Acatl of some fifty-two-year cycle. The year 1519, in the Christian calendar, corresponded to One Reed in the Mexican count, and in that year Cortés landed on the coast of Mexico. It was not strange that Montezuma brooded over the fate of his empire when scouts brought him the report of that landing.

CHAPTER 5

SPANIARDS DISCOVER MIDDLE AMERICA

ON A summer day in A.D 1502 four battered, worm-eaten Spanish caravels approached verdant islands in waters heretofore unexplored. They were the Bay Islands off the coast of Honduras, and the ships were those of Christopher Columbus, making his fourth and last voyage of discovery. Ill and disheartened, obsessed by visions, the old explorer was still searching for the treasures of Cathay, hoping to find a strait leading to the fabled Orient.

While anchored off one of the islands a large canoe paddled by many men approached Columbus' ship. The sailors looked down in astonishment at natives different from others they had seen. Their experiences so far had been with the primitive Indians of the Caribbean Islands. These men wore cotton shirts, and their chief, sitting with his family under a canopy of palm leaves, was evidently on a trading voyage. In the canoe were cotton shirts and mantles, flint knives, copper bells and hatchets, baskets of cacao beans.

That was the first contact of Spaniards with the Mayas, for the traders came from Yucatán. The wily merchant saved his land from immediate exploitation by encouraging Columbus to

55

take the opposite direction, saying that lands to the east contained gold.

The Spaniards sailed on, skirting the coast of Honduras. Columbus is supposed to have gone ashore at a point near the present Trujillo where he took possession of the land for Spain with the usual ceremonies. His men named it Higueras from the quantities of calabashes floating on a river, but it soon became known as Honduras, depths, because of the deep waters off shore.

Battered by hurricanes which tore the sails to ribbons and nearly destroyed the rickety ships, the Spaniards took refuge in the lee of a headland. In gratitude for its shelter Columbus named it Cabo Gracias á Dios. He continued the voyage, keeping in sight a coastline densely forested, with misty mountain ranges in the distance. He was passing the coast of Nicaragua and Costa Rica. The ships were beached for repairs on an island in a Costa Rican bay, now the harbor of Puerto Limón.

Along the Isthmus of Panama Columbus explored the bay named for him, Almirante Bay, and the lagoon of Chiriqui. Here he found a prosperous Indian land called by the natives Veragua. The Indians lived in grass-roofed huts amid cornfields, and Columbus' eyes were gladdened by the sight of their ornaments and crowns of gold. They told him that the gold was obtained from mines in their mountains.

Columbus built a fort to hold the land for the King, but this first attempt to settle on the mainland of America was soon destroyed by Indian attacks. Many men were lost and one ship wrecked on sand bars, but with what remained the explorer continued his voyage, investigating various bays with the hope of finding the mythical strait. One harbor he liked well enough to name it Porto Bello, and there another rotten ship was abandoned on the shore. Giving up the search then, Columbus returned, after many hardships, to Spain. Within a few years the great discoverer died, heartbroken over the failure of his dreams and the ingratitude of a King for whom he had opened a new world.

The navigation charts and records made by Bartolomé de Colón on that voyage were not forgotten, nor the Indians of Veragua with their golden ornaments. The record was added to the information accumulated through various Spanish voyages. Columbus and other navigators had explored the coast of Venezuela and found a wealth of pearls among the Indians on islands off shore. In 1501, the year before Columbus' last voyage, Rodrigo de Bastidas, with the famous pilot Juan de la Cosa, had found the Bay of Cartagena and the Gulf of Urabá, or Darien. On that voyage went an alert young hidalgo, Vasco Nuñez de Balboa. It was his first glimpse of a land where he was to find both glory and death.

The decade between 1500 and 1510 was a time of expanding Spanish exploration. Their first settlements on islands of the Caribbean Sea had been disappointing. There was little gold, the gentle Arawak Indians and the fierce Caribs were certainly not subjects of exotic Oriental potentates as had been hoped. The Spanish conquerors were obliged to become planters.

In return for their services Queen Isabella allotted them *encomiendas* of land with *repartimientos,* or groups of Indians, for labor. Encomiendas were not gifts, but were for the use of the *encomenderos,* who were supposed to undertake the conversion of the natives entrusted to their care. In practice, both lands and Indians were exploited for the benefit of the encomenderos, and after the death of the good Queen no one interfered with the cruel enslavement of the Indians.

Reports of navigators who had seen the coast of northern South America and that of Central America convinced the geographers of the Casa de la Contratación in Seville that this great land mass was a continent. The pearls of Venezuela, the gold of the Veragua Indians, the belief in a strait by which to reach India and Cathay, turned Spanish attention from the islands to exploration of the continent. King Ferdinand decided to plant colonies on Tierra Firme, as the mainland was called, before some other nation took the prize from his grasp.

In Spain adventurous men were all agog over discoveries across the Ocean Sea. Hundreds of soldiers, released from long wars to rid Spain of the Moors, were eager for more adventure. Soldiers and vagabonds of the toughest character, as well as impecunious hidalgos, besieged the Casa de la Contratación for permission to go to the New World.

King Ferdinand chose two gentlemen of good family to colonize and govern Tierra Firme. Alonso de Ojeda, who was already acquainted with the coast of Venezuela, was to have the territory east of the Gulf of Darien, to be called Nueva Andalucía. Territory west of the Gulf as far as Cabo Gracias á Dios was to be the domain of a gay, accomplished courtier, Diego de Nicuesa, and was to be called Castilla del Oro.

The rival governors set sail from Santo Domingo on the island of Hispaniola within a few months of each other, in 1509, but the high hopes of both ended in disaster. Most of Ojeda's men were killed by the poisoned arrows of Indians when they landed on the coast of future Colombia. Diego de Nicuesa rescued his rival and deposited him with the survivors on the east side of the Gulf of Darien. There they built a fort named, appropriately, for the saint who was shot full of arrows, San Sebastian. Nicuesa continued his voyage in search of Veragua, trying to follow the charts of Bartolomé de Colón.

The pitiful group at San Sebastian waited anxiously for a ship which was to come from Santo Domingo with supplies, in charge of the Bachiller Enciso. When their situation became desperate Ojeda decided to sail to Santo Domingo for help, leaving a young captain, Francisco Pizarro, in command. If Enciso did not arrive the men were to try to escape. Ojeda never returned, for after suffering shipwreck on the coast of Cuba he finally made his way back to Santo Domingo, only to die, broken in health and spirit.

The starving men at San Sebastian preferred to risk their lives in the rotten boats remaining to them than to die on the shore from hunger or poisoned arrows. Fortunately for them they had not gone far to sea when they were picked up by Enciso's ship. He was searching for the colony and forced the unhappy men to return to the deserted fort.

Bachiller Enciso had on board a stowaway who had roused his resentment by emerging from a cask when the ship was safely on the high seas. This was the enterprising Vasco Nuñez de Balboa, adventuring once more. He had been so determined to go along to explore the land he had seen before that he adopted the ruse of the cask to escape his creditors.

It was this intelligent young man who saved the miserable settlers of San Sebastian by suggesting that they move to the other side of the Gulf. He remembered from the former voyage that the Indians of that region did not use poisoned arrows, and that they grew plenty of corn.

A new fort was built on the west side of the Gulf, named Santa María de la Antigua de Darien. Antigua was the first permanent settlement on the mainland of America. Chief Cemaco, whose lands they invaded, tried to resist the strangers, but one encounter with terrifying firearms and men in armor defeated him.

Bachiller Enciso, who took command as the lieutenant of the lost Ojeda, tried to impose strict regulations which were ridiculous among adventurers on a primitive shore. The men, bitterly resentful, took matters into their own hands, aided by Balboa. He reminded them that by removing to the west side of the Gulf they had left the jurisdiction of Ojeda and did not have to obey his lieutenant. In the democratic fashion of Spanish townfolk in that century, they organized themselves into a municipality, deposed Enciso and elected Balboa and Martín Zamudio to serve as alcaldes.

Soon thereafter a ship appeared, commanded by Rodrigo de Colmenares, who was searching for Diego de Nicuesa's colony to deliver supplies. After putting heart in the men by distributing food, Colmenares set sail again to find the lost governor of Castilla del Oro. Meanwhile, what had become of Diego de Nicuesa and his ships?

His expedition had fared worse than that of Ojeda. Storms and winds strewed the wreckage of the ships along the inhospitable shore of Panama. Nicuesa and part of the company found themselves stranded among lagoons and swampy jungles with a few small boats. Sailors in these boats followed along shore while Nicuesa and his companions struggled onward among the swamps, beset with heat, fever and poisonous insects, garnering roots and shellfish to keep themselves alive.

The survivors reached an island in the Chiriqui lagoon, where they were finally found by the pilot of the expedition in the only ship to escape destruction. He had continued the search for Veragua without success. Although they had been rescued from death by the pilot, Nicuesa accused the man of trying to explore for himself and put him in chains. Disaster had soured the once gay courtier, and the men hated him for his harsh unreasonableness.

On board their worm-eaten ship the forlorn company retraced their way down the coast until they reached Columbus'

Porto Bello. The anchor of his abandoned ship lay in the sand. Exploring beyond that point they came to a fertile region of Indian villages. *"Detengámonos aqui, en nombre de Díos!"* Nicuesa is said to have exclaimed. "Let us stay here, in the name of God!" Thus the little fort which was to become Spain's gold port was christened Nombre de Díos.

The Indian villagers fled, leaving the invaders to die slowly of fever and starvation, cursing their commander. It was there on the desolate shore that Colmenares found the lost governor, a gaunt emaciated man in rags. His companions were yellow with fever and half dead of starvation.

The poor wretch, Nicuesa, learning that a settlement was ready made for him to govern, plucked up spirits and put on arrogant airs. Nevertheless, the men who had suffered from his harshness in the wilderness prepared to undermine him. When the ship anchored off Antigua the messenger sent ashore by Nicuesa to announce his arrival warned the settlers against their tyrannical commander.

Those rough, independent men took the hint. When Nicuesa's boat approached shore a reception committee waded into the water, not to welcome him, but to forbid him to land. The disconcerted governor slipped ashore next day only to be set upon and chased into the woods. Balboa rescued the poor fellow, but could not persuade the men to accept him. With unfeeling cruelty they sent him to sea with a few companions in a leaky ship, with orders never to return. He never did, nor was he ever seen again. Probably the ship was wrecked and the men perished on some deserted island.

Antigua or Darien—it was known by both names—was a forlorn settlement of huts and fort on a hot, unhealthy shore. Illness, hardship and loneliness so worked on men's tempers that they quarreled continually over their petty town offices while all joined in hatred of the pedantic, interfering lawyer, Enciso. Occasionally ships came from Santo Domingo with supplies and in one of these Enciso was sent away. In a letter to the King asking for reinforcements Balboa begged him not to send any lawyers, for they are all nothing but devils, stirring up controversy. Despite his failure as an administrator Enciso did a service to Spain in the good book he wrote on natural phenomena in the New World.

Balboa was now in charge of the settlement and set to work with all his skill and energy to make something of it. He knew that Enciso would go to Spain as soon as possible to denounce him and the colonists for illegal acts. If he could show a thriving colony and a good harvest of gold he might hope for royal clemency.

Much against their will the men were set to work planting cornfields to help the food supply, and building more commodious huts. The main occupation of all was to hunt for gold in the interior. There Balboa's skill in handling the Indians served them well. If they attacked the Spaniards they were beaten by terrifying gunfire. Once they had learned that lesson Balboa treated them kindly, respected their possessions and made them his allies. The Indians were willing to make presents to this powerful white chief of heaps of golden ornaments and gold dust washed from their streams. Careta, lord of a semi-civilized tribe near by, became Balboa's friend and offered him not only gold but his gentle daughter for wife. Balboa loved the Indian girl and never deserted her. His Indian father-in-law used his influence with other chiefs to bring them into friendly relations with the Spaniards.

Going far afield to collect gold, they made the most painful journeys through steaming swamps and jungles and over mountains. Balboa described some of these trips to the King:

"Your Royal Highness must not imagine that the swamps of this land are so light that they can be crossed easily, for many times we have had to go a league and two and three leagues through swamps and water, stripped naked with our clothes carried on a shield above our heads, and when we have come to an end of one swamp we have had to enter another, and to walk in this way from two to three to ten days."

Always Balboa marched at the head of his company, scouting for the best way to take, watching for danger, cheering them on. When they returned, the gold was scrupulously divided among the men after setting aside the King's fifth. This just treatment, his courage, and his care for the welfare of his men, won for Balboa the allegiance of the rough fellows he commanded.

Once when they were visiting a very wealthy chief, Comagre, who had presented a heap of gold, the Spaniards heard a tale that stirred their imaginations. While the gold was being weighed out the greedy men began to quarrel over it. Scornfully the chief's son dashed the scale to the ground. If these white men cared so much for the yellow metal, he said, he could show them a country where they could get their fill of it. Six days' march across the mountains would bring them to a sea on which were boats with sails, and to a country where men ate from dishes of gold. So for the first time the Spaniards had definite word of an unknown ocean and the empire of the Incas. Not only Balboa, but Francisco Pizarro, who was present, tucked away that information for future use.

To find that mysterious ocean became a consuming desire in Balboa's mind. He must get about it quickly before Enciso's enmity disturbed his command of Antigua. Balboa selected the strongest men of his garrison, firing them with his own enthusiasm. Careta's people were willing to help with provisions, guides and carriers for their supplies and arms. From Careta's village the party set forth on their arduous adventure. There were swamps to cross, dense jungle vegetation to struggle through, mountains to climb. All the way they were hampered by fever, heat and hostile Indians.

One day, as they made camp on a forested mountainside, the guides told them that from the summit the ocean could be seen. Commanding his men to wait, the leader went on alone— if the tale was false he wanted no one to witness his disappointment. Scrambling up to the highest point Balboa looked eagerly forward. Far away beyond the jungle-clad hills veiled in blue mist he saw the glitter of the distant sea. It was true! Balboa fell on his knees, crying out his thanks to God.

Summoned by their leader, the band of ragged Spaniards gazed with awe at the Pacific Ocean, called by Balboa the South Sea. They knelt around the priest singing a Te Deum of triumph. Then the notary, who always accompanied exploring expeditions to make records, drew up a certificate of discovery with the names of the sixty-seven Spaniards who were present.

Balboa spoke proudly to his men: "You see here, gentlemen and children mine, how our desires are being accomplished and the end of our labors. Of that we ought to be certain, for, as it turned out that what King Comagre's son told us of this sea was true, so I hold it to be certain that what he told us of there being incomparable treasure in it will be fulfilled. God and His Blessed Mother, who have assisted us, so that we should arrive here and behold this sea, will favor us so that we may enjoy all it contains."

On the bark of a tree they carved the arms of Castile and the date, September 25, 1513.

Days of difficult travel followed before they had descended

to the shore, which was not that of the ocean but a bay, named by Balboa San Miguel. Beyond lay the Gulf of Panama. Balboa took the banner of Castile and waded into the water, proclaiming in a loud voice that he took possession for the Crown of Spain of the South Sea, its islands and firmlands and all shores washed by its waters.

In Indian canoes with guides they explored the bay and the Gulf of Panama. On shore they reassured timid Indians and made friends with a rich chief, Tumaco, who gave Balboa a treasure of gold and a whole basin of pearls. Tumaco told them that the chief of the Pearl Islands, his enemy, had quantities of pearls. It was the Indian custom to roast the oysters to eat, which discolored the pearls, but the Spaniards showed them how to open the shells with knives.

Laden with treasure and overjoyed with their success, the adventurers began to trek back to Antigua, a desperately hard journey of four months. They went by a different route, exploring more of the wilderness, fighting hostile Indians despite their weakness from fever and forced marches. Each Indian chief was won to respectful submission and the Spaniards rested in their villages, receiving more gold to add to their store.

On January 19, 1514, the worn company reached Antigua, triumphant over their discovery and their wealth in gold and pearls. Balboa was a hero, fêted with the best the little settlement could devise in the way of celebrations. The beautiful handiwork of Indian goldsmiths was melted down to send the King, and Balboa hastened to despatch a ship with his messenger on board, commissioned to deliver the King's share of gold and a letter announcing the discovery. The discoverer asked for the governorship of the land he had explored.

Vasco Nuñez de Balboa looked forward to a future of glory

and success. He had given Spain the South Sea and the route by which to reach it. By his tact the inhabitants of the wilderness between Antigua and the South Sea were ready to coöperate with the Spaniards. The star of the conquistador's destiny was at its zenith but his triumph was short-lived.

In faraway Spain Enciso's enmity had done its work. His biased account of Balboa's high-handed activities roused the anger of King Ferdinand. Enciso accused Balboa of defying the lawful governor, Diego de Nicuesa, and of sending him off to die at sea. The fact that Balboa had kept the colony alive did not weigh with the King against usurpation of power, and he issued an order stripping Balboa of all authority. It was to be delivered by a new governor, Don Pedro Arias de Avila, a proud old hidalgo who had won fame in Spain's wars. In Central American history this man has been known as Pedrarias Dávila, the evil-hearted governor. King Ferdinand commissioned him to search for the unknown sea and rich lands, rumors of which had reached Spain. Ships were expensively equipped and a noble company of courtiers and soldiers assembled to accompany Pedrarias to the New World.

Too late, after the expedition had set sail, Balboa's messenger arrived with the announcement of the discovery of the South Sea. The messenger had been many months on the way, and many more elapsed before a ship reached Antigua, in 1515, bearing the King's congratulations and the royal commission for Balboa. He was to be Adelantado of the South Sea and Governor of the province on its shore. By that time things had gone badly for the discoverer.

Pedrarias Dávila and his imposing fleet reached Antigua in the summer of 1514. A crowd of shabby, hard-bitten men, old hands at wilderness life, greeted Pedrarias' elegant company as they made a stately entry into the crude settlement.

Pedrarias led the way with his wife, Doña Isabel, and Bishop Juan de Quevedo, followed by soldiers in mail, nobles and their ladies in silks and plumes. Doubtless the aristocrats from Spain were as dismayed at the rough town and its inhabitants as the settlers were scornful of their dress and haughty airs.

Balboa received the Governor with every courtesy, despite his deep disappointment at being superseded before the King knew of his great discovery. Soon, however, there began a bitter contest between arrogant, ruthless Pedrarias and Balboa, who had the loyalty of the men and succeeded in handling them when Pedrarias failed. It was a hard thing for Balboa to have his plans blocked and to see his good work with the Indians undone. Pedrarias was furious that the honor of discovering the South Sea had been snatched from him, he was intensely jealous of the younger man whose popularity and prestige overshadowed him.

Pedrarias' soldiers were sent out after gold armed with muskets and the fierce dogs employed by the Spaniards in the islands to hunt Indians. Their method of forcing gold from the Indians was the usual one of beating, torturing, setting the dogs to tear the Indians to bits if they did not deliver gold. Sometimes, when Indians captured these soldiers, they poured molten metal down their throats crying, "Eat, Spaniards, eat gold." Indian captives were forced into slavery in the settlement. The result was that whole tribes retreated to the mountains where they lived unconquered for generations, while others hid their ancestral treasures and went on the warpath against the Spaniards.

There was no gold to melt down for the King, Pedrarias' people sickened and died from the primitive food and deadly climate. As his failures mounted the Governor's hatred of his rival grew. Balboa, bitter also, did his best to undermine the

Governor. By every ship to Spain he sent letters complaining of Pedrarias' cruelty and mismanagement.

Bishop Quevedo tried to reconcile the two leaders by bringing about the betrothal of Balboa to the Governor's young daughter, then in a Spanish convent. With this prospective relationship established the rivals became more cooperative. Since Balboa's commission as Adelantado of the South Sea had arrived, Pedrarias could not prevent him from making settlements on the Gulf of Panama, or from advancing his plans to go in search of the rich empire on the shores of the South Sea.

At a new settlement, Acla, Balboa set hundreds of Indians to work cutting timbers and hewing them to make a few small brigantines. Timbers and ironware were carried on Indian backs through the humid jungle and over mountain trails to a river on the Pacific side where the craft were to be assembled. Hundreds of hapless natives died from the unaccustomed labor and hardship. Balboa had no more concern for Indian lives than other Spaniards when he wanted something done. He was consumed with ambition to explore the South Sea and find that golden kingdom.

The timbers of the little vessels were so worm-eaten from the steaming climate that they did not survive the voyage across the Gulf of Panama to the Pearl Islands. Balboa had to set up a shipyard on the islands to build more. He was so busy with work on the ships, equipment and plans, that he was absent from Antigua for a year and a half.

Then a friend came to him with news that the King was sending a new governor, Lope de Sosa, to replace Pedrarias Dávila. Once Balboa would have rejoiced, but now, reconciled to Pedrarias, he feared that a new governor would forbid him to make his voyage.

There was a consultation in the leader's quarters, in which

Balboa discussed with his officers the possibility of sailing at once before the new governor arrived. Failing that, Balboa declared he would defy orders, if necessary, to make the voyage. Outside the window a malicious soldier overheard the conversation which he could distort into a plot on Balboa's part to revolt against Pedrarias. He hastened away to report to the Governor. Another enemy added to the fire of Pedrarias' anger by declaring that Balboa never intended to marry his daughter, as he loved only the Indian girl.

Pedrarias snatched at the longed-for opportunity to get rid of his rival. A friendly letter was sent, asking Balboa to come to Acla for important consultations. Suspecting nothing, Balboa set off with his most trusted officers. On the trail they were met by Francisco Pizarro with a guard of soldiers. Without a word of regret Pizarro arrested his leader, by order of the Governor, on charges of treason.

In the small settlement of Acla was played out one of the blackest scenes in Pedrarias' evil career. Against the angry protests of the people, reluctant judges were forced to bring to trial the man who was a popular hero in Castilla del Oro. Pedrarias imposed his will on the judges, so that the farcical trial resulted in a death sentence for Balboa and his officers.

The discoverer who had opened a whole new realm for Spain was ignominiously beheaded in the plaza with four companions. That day in 1517 was a dark one in the history of the Spanish conquest. Vasco Nuñez de Balboa was the most intelligent and accomplished, the most honorable, of the leaders who, so far, had labored for King and glory in America.

Pedrarias moved quickly to entrench himself in Balboa's domain on the Gulf of Panama before the new governor arrived. Most of the settlers and equipment of Antigua were moved across the Isthmus to the Indian village of Panama. In

1519 a city was founded and the surrounding land divided into encomiendas. Men hungry for gold were forced, temporarily, to become planters; but Panama City, from its first days, was a town of restless adventurers, always plotting to hunt for treasure by land or sea.

When Lope de Sosa died soon after reaching Antigua, Pedrarias was free to tighten his grip on Castilla del Oro. The province suffered under his greed and tyranny, while the brutality of the settlers so decimated the Indian population that Negro slaves were imported for labor. Antigua was gradually abandoned to the jungle, as Panama City became the seat of government for Castilla del Oro.

Nombre de Dios and Panama City were the termini of a trail built through forests and by river to be the route to the Orient. When Francisco Pizarro, one of the reluctant planters of Panama, had conquered the Inca Empire, the gold and silver of Peru poured into Panama and across the trail to be shipped to Spain from Nombre de Dios.

In the year Panama City was founded, 1519, Magellan began his famous voyage through the straits named for him and across the Pacific. He discovered the Philippines and, although he was killed there by a native, one of his ships reached Spain after circumnavigating the globe. The Pacific Ocean, or South Sea, became a Spanish ocean on which sailed the galleons, garnering the treasures of China for Spain.

While the restless men of Castilla del Oro fixed their minds on the boundless ocean and unknown lands to the south, the settlers of Hispaniola and newly conquered Cuba turned their attention to the Caribbean shores of Central America.

Under the conqueror of Cuba, Diego de Velasquez, encomiendas were allotted to deserving soldiers of fortune and hidalgos from Spain. Since few gold mines were found most of these gentlemen made money from their plantations of sugar cane, tobacco, etc., worked by Indian slaves. And since they had no heart for farming they were always ready to listen to rumors of gold to be found in unexplored lands.

Only a few voices, those of Fray Bartolomé de Las Casas and other Dominican friars, were raised in protest against the barbarous treatment of the Indians. The Crown, through the Council of the Indies, made laws forbidding enslavement of the natives, but young King Charles and Bishop Fonseca, head of the Council, did not investigate too closely so long as profits came from the Indies.

The natives died in such numbers that slave-hunting expeditions among the islands, to obtain more laborers, were popular. On these voyages Spaniards widened their knowledge of the Caribbean Sea, and the desire grew to explore the mainland.

In 1517 a group of ambitious gentlemen pooled their resources to buy a few ships, and obtained permission from Governor Velasquez to make a voyage of discovery. Hernandez de Córdoba was their commander and one of the young captains in the expedition was Bernal Diaz del Castillo, who was to write the most absorbing account of Spanish exploits in Mexico. Through his descriptions we may visualize the first meetings of Spaniards with American aborigines who had a civilization of their own.

After sailing for several days beyond the known islands, the adventurers came to a flat land of barren coast and dangerous reefs—the peninsula of Yucatán. To their amazement they saw above the rocky coastline a white-walled town with towers and pyramids. Natives dressed in cotton shirts and mantles came out to meet them in large canoes. After receiving presents of green-glass beads the Yucatecans invited the Spaniards to come ashore. Once they had been lured inland they were attacked from ambush by warriors painted red and black, who fought with lances and two-handed wooden swords edged with obsidian. The Spaniards beat a hasty retreat to their ships, but continued their exploration of the coast.

They made a few other landings to obtain water and food and to investigate the interesting towns. Each time they were beaten back by gaudily decked warriors. Nevertheless the Spaniards had had a glimpse of Indians who lived in towns with stone houses and temples, who worshipped idols in the lofty shrines. They also managed to collect some loot in golden ornaments. Two natives were taken home with them to be taught Spanish so there would be interpreters for future voyages.

The discoveries made by Hernandez de Córdoba and his comrades caused great excitement in Cuba. Governor Velasquez wrote to his friend Bishop Fonseca, claiming credit for what had been done, asking permission to organize another expedition. Diego de Valasquez was an avaricious man, ambitious to win easy wealth and fame by the work of explorers sent out under his orders.

In 1518 the Governor received the desired permission and chose his relative, Juan de Grijalva, to command the expedition. Adventurers and planters eagerly contributed money toward outfitting the ships, to win a share in the expected treasure. On that voyage went future conquerors—Pedro de Alvarado, Francisco de Montejo, Bernal Diaz del Castillo.

Juan de Grijalva found the island of Cozumel off the coast of Yucatán. The men explored shrines of ancient Mayan gods in a town from which the inhabitants had fled in terror. Farther on, they went ashore at Champoton, where Córdoba's men had been worsted in a fierce battle. These Spaniards were also driven back to their ships by ferocious warriors.

As the ships sailed on, the navigators made useful charts of the coast and noted winds and currents. A great bay was called Boca de Terminos because the navigators thought it separated Yucatán from the mainland. Farther on Juan de Grijalva anchored the ships to explore, in small boats, a river flowing through lush tropical country.

This was the territory of a chief called Tabasco. His people were milder than the Yucatecans, willing to talk with the strangers through the interpreters, Julian and Melchor. Successful bartering went on, the Spaniards receiving food, ornaments and little images of wrought gold in return for the green-glass beads which the Indians prized for their color, that of sacred jade. In answer to the usual inquiries for gold the Tabascans said they had little of it. Farther on, however, in the great kingdom of Culua or Mexico, there was abundance of the metal.

With that good news to spur them on, the Spaniards continued their exploration of the coast of Mexico. Juan de Grijalva was the first to explore the bay from which Mexico would be entered, the first to go ashore among the sand dunes to claim the land for the Emperor Charles. Exploring inland, the Spaniards were delighted with the tropical luxuriance they found—fruits, flowers, cultivated fields. They visited towns where they were received with homage and heard the name of a fabulous ruler, Montezuma.

On the return voyage they went ashore to explore a native river town, Guazacualco. There the greedy soldiers thought they had made a fine bargain when they traded green-glass beads for six hundred golden hatchets with painted handles. Back in Cuba they discovered that the hatchets were only copper mixed with gold, and were well laughed at. At Guazacualco, also, Bernal Diaz and some companions slept in a temple to get away from tormenting mosquitos. Near by they sowed orange seeds which they had along just in case they founded a colony. After the conquest, when Bernal Diaz del Castillo received this province for his estate he found flourishing orange trees grown from the seeds, tended with care by native priests. They were the ancestors of the orange groves of the region.

When Grijalva's ships reached Cuba the news brought by the explorers caused great jubilation. Men's imaginations were fired by a tale of wealth and civilization heretofore unknown in America, and of an empire in Mexico, ruled by the great lord, Montezuma.

Governor Velasquez promptly sent an account of the voyage to Bishop Fonseca with a present of gold for the King. He asked permission to send out an expedition of trade and exploration to Mexico.

The stage was set for the vivid drama of Hernán Cortés the Spaniard, and Montezuma, lord of the Aztecs. Hernán Cortés was there in Cuba, ready to seize his opportunity for fame. He was one of the gentleman planters, a spendthrift and gambler like most of them, popular with his fellows and irresistible to women. With his vigorous manly spirit, his skill in arms and horsemanship, he was the perfect example of sixteenth-century hidalgo; and he had the twin loyalties of his age—to his King and his Church. But the frank, friendly manner that won people to him concealed a crafty mind and ambitious spirit.

Santiago de Cuba seethed with excitement as ships were made ready and stored with cassava bread, pork, artillery and munitions, trade goods and water casks. Planters sold their lands and soldiers their possessions to buy a share in the expedition. Sixteen precious horses were bought by the most prosperous captains.

Intrigue agitated the town as relatives of Governor Velasquez contended with popular Hernán Cortés for the post of commander. Cortés won, by clever scheming and the backing of the most audacious captains. Immediately, however, Velasquez regretted having given him the appointment. He suspected that this ambitious man would not be loyal, but would work for his own glory, rather than for the Governor.

While keeping up an appearance of friendship and subservience to the Governor, Cortés hastened preparations for departure. The ships were moved to the port of Trinidad, then to La Habana, to take on more recruits and supplies. Other vessels were to join the fleet when Cortés gave the word. Velasquez sent officers to rescind the appointment and bring Cortés back to Santiago, but they were won over by fair promises.

Before the Governor could make up his mind what to do the chance to act was lost. The ships set sail from La Habana to make rendezvous with the rest of the fleet outside on February 10, 1519.

With their sails given to the wind the Spanish fleet turned westward, toward glory and adventure beyond the fondest dreams of the bold conquerors. On their crimson banner, embroidered in gold with the Royal Arms and the Cross, Cortés had had inscribed their watchword: "Brothers and companions, follow the sign of the Holy Cross with true faith, for by that shall we conquer."

CHAPTER 6

HERNÁN CORTÉS IN MEXICO

ONE OF THE most dramatic adventures in all history began on that April day in 1519 when Cortés and his intrepid Spaniards disembarked on the sandy tropical shore of Mexico. They had anchored the ships in the bay discovered by Juan de Grijalva. Disregarding the prior claim the conqueror planted the banner of Castile among the dunes and took possession of the land for the Emperor Charles.

With sixteenth-century devoutness the adventurers dedicated their enterprise to the Blessed Virgin, Cortés' special patroness, as they knelt around an improvised altar on Easter Sunday. The clump of palm-thatched shelters among the sand dunes was named Villa Rica de Vera Cruz because they had disembarked on Good Friday.

Among the mailed soldiers were ten demure Indian girls in straight-hanging huipils and wrapped skirts. They had been among the presents given to Cortés by Tabascan chiefs after their warriors had been subdued by the Spaniards. On their way to Mexico the Spaniards had tried to explore Grijalva's river and had nearly come to grief in fierce battles with the Tabascans. These people, who had traded with Grijalva, had been taunted with cowardice by Yucatecans and were redeeming their reputation by resisting the second invasion of white strangers. The maidens presented as tribute had been promptly baptized by the priest, Fray Olmedo, and distributed by Cortés to his captains.

One of them, however, soon became the commander's mistress and constant companion, an acquisition beyond price in his enterprise of conquest. Doña Marina, as she was baptized, told Cortés that she was the daughter of a Mexican princess who had married a second time and wished her son by that marriage to inherit the kingdom. The unnatural mother gave her little girl to the Xicalango Indians who traded her to the Tabascans, and so, in her adolescence, she came to the Spaniards. Doña Marina had the pride of lineage and great intelligence, in addition to the soft brown beauty of a high-class Mexican girl. Without her knowledge of the language and psychology of the Aztecs, and her steadfast devotion, Cortés' task would have been twice as difficult. The conqueror, as lord of the Indian princess Malintzín, was known henceforth to all the natives as Malinche.

While they settled in their rude camp on the shore, neighboring Indians brought them food and gifts of flowers and gentle brown women came every day to grind maize and bake corn cakes for them. Through Doña Marina, Cortés learned that the great lord Montezuma had ordered his vassals to serve the strangers. Mysterious, glimmering in excited imaginations, was the kingdom the invaders heard of from their visitors. How were they, a few hundred Spaniards, to penetrate the dense forests, the great mountains that rose before them fold upon fold; how win to their goal without losing their lives?

Spring and early summer passed as Hernán Cortés, the astute and quick-thinking adventurer, matured his plans and maneuvered every event to his advantage. First there were exchanges of guileful messages between the Aztec lord and the representative of the Emperor Charles.

Montezuma's messengers slipped soft-footed from the green depths of the forest, like tropical birds in their colored mantles and feather headdresses. Their slaves spread reed mats on the sand at the feet of the white-skinned *teule,* or godlike being, whom Montezuma feared. Each time the emissaries arrived, with evasive messages couched in reverential terms, the gifts were more gorgeous. The Spaniards admired rare mantles woven of bird feathers and fans of green plumes with golden handles, but their eyes glittered greedily at the sight of great gold and silver disks etched to represent the sun and moon, and many exquisite ornaments of wrought gold. Every attempt of Montezuma to appease the mysterious ruler across the ocean with splendid gifts only strengthened the determination of his vassals to win this wonderful kingdom.

Cortés soon learned from the neighborhood people of the prophecy that worried the Mexicans; a prophecy foretelling that beings who came from the sun's rising would overthrow the Aztecs. Skillfully he played up to their fear that he and his mailed companions were teules, perhaps emissaries of the hero-god Quetzalcoatl. On the first visit of Montezuma's messengers he sent the horsemen to gallop up and down the wet sands, displaying the power of their rearing steeds to the awestruck Indians. Cannon were fired with spurts of flame, sending echoes reverberating through the forest.

Montezuma sent his artists to make picture records of everything they saw. Spanish soldiers were vastly entertained as they watched these brown artists swiftly sketch on their sheets of amate-fiber paper little pictures of ships, horses, guns, soldiers, even a portrait of Cortés. When the messengers humbly unfolded these record sheets before their lord, Montezuma shivered. These must be the beings come to rule over Anáhuac, as the prophecy foretold.

While gifts were heaped before Cortés and courteous messages were translated by Doña Marina, the soldiers grew impatient. After weeks of negotiation they were unable to move inland from the sand dunes and tormenting mosquitos. Montezuma firmly refused to receive the emissary of the Emperor Charles in his kingdom, and Cortés as firmly refused to leave without presenting the Emperor's greetings in person.

Partisans of Governor Velasquez among the men demanded that Cortés return at once to Cuba with the treasure before the Mexicans destroyed them. They were frightened because the neighborhood people had deserted them and it looked like preparation for war. Cortés would be exceeding his authority if he invaded the country without first reporting to Governor Valasquez, they declared.

The commander knew that most of the soldiers were as eager as he to continue the adventure; only a hint to the captains was necessary for them to handle the situation themselves. Their arguments prevailed, and in a town meeting Cortés was elected to lead the men as captain-general, responsible only to the King. He had won what he wanted, and the soldier vote gave him a show of legality for flouting Governor Velasquez' authority.

The die was cast, they were going to invade Mexico, and already the leader's astute mind had planned the next move. The provinces between the coast and Anáhuac hated the Aztec overlords, as Cortés learned from messengers of the Totonac people. Heavy tribute was exacted from them and their youths were seized for sacrifice to the blood-hungry gods.

Cortés led his soldiers inland to win allies among the discontented people. They passed through villages surrounded with cultivated fields, and through deep forest trails where exotic flowers hung from the trees and bright-plumaged birds flew before them. At every town they were received with gifts of food, flowers and gold, while long-haired priests "fumigated" them, as Bernal Diaz del Castillo wrote, with aromatic copal incense.

The fat old Totonac chief, nicknamed El Gordo, received them with honor in his beautiful white town, Cempoal. It was not difficult to convince El Gordo and his people that the marvelous strangers who had come across the sea in ships like houses were teules. That belief was confirmed when Cortés smashed the images of their gods without being struck down by a thunderbolt from heaven. The people watched, awestruck, as an image of the Virgin was set up in one of the temples on an altar heaped with flowers.

Soon El Gordo was thrown into a panic by the arrival of Montezuma's tribute collectors, who threatened him with dire punishment for harboring the strangers. The chief appealed to his new friend, Cortés, for advice. Throw the officers in prison, said Cortés, and send word to other chiefs to refuse tribute, for the Spaniards would protect them. In the morning the Mexican officers were gone, on their way to report El Gordo's defiance to their lord. The chief did not know that during the night double-dealing Cortés had released the men, assuring them with smooth words that he had nothing to do with their imprisonment. They would report the Spaniards' growing influence, and El Gordo's only hope was to throw in his lot with the invaders against his own brown race.

Next the Spaniards moved their camp from the sand dunes to a more comfortable place. Villa Rica de Vera Cruz was formally organized as a Spanish municipality. Spaniards and

Indians worked with a will to make adobe bricks and collect stone for a fort and church. They now had a base for operations, but before moving inland both Cortés and his captains wrote letters to the King explaining all they had done.

These letters, and the King's fifth of treasure trove from Montezuma, were sent in care of Francisco de Montejo in one of the ships, with orders to go directly to Spain. That gentleman, however, wishing to visit his estates in Cuba, went ashore on that island, and the tale of the ship and its errand reached the Governor's ears. By the time Montejo reached Spain Bishop Fonseca had heard from Velasquez of Cortés' defiance. The Bishop turned a cold shoulder to the messenger from Mexico, and as the Emperor Charles was in Flanders it was long before he received the letters and gifts.

Meanwhile there was more trouble with the men of Velasquez at Vera Cruz, when they saw the ship depart for Spain. They clamored to return to Cuba and Cortés let them take a ship, knowing that they would not get far in the leaky vessel. When they returned he hanged the ringleaders to show all grumblers who was master. The man of destiny was ready to move, but he had one more drastic plan to carry through.

Bernal Diaz del Castillo, in his chronicle, complains of other historians who claimed that Cortés scuttled the ships without consulting his men. On the contrary, says Bernal Diaz, he had the support and cooperation of his captains. One reason for the daring act was that the mariners, more than a hundred, could be added to the little army. Also, with the ships out of commission, no disgruntled men could desert their comrades.

All the fittings, sails, ropes and ironware were removed and stored in the fort. Then the ships were scuttled, and retreat was cut off. It was a solemn moment. Cortés addressed his comrades with dramatic fervor, exhorting them to go forward with him, having only their stout hearts and the help of God to rely on. Cheers answered him, as the men swore to follow him faithfully. When was a Spanish soldier ever ready to turn back, comments Bernal Diaz.

In August, 1519, the conquerors, not more than five hundred men, were on their way to invade Anáhuac, the realm of the powerful Aztecs. Totonac chiefs accompanied them, with slaves to carry supplies and artillery. By well-worn Indian trails they proceeded through the luxuriant lowlands, welcomed and fed by friendly people, glad to honor the teules who promised to free them from the Aztecs. Up they went from the hot lowlands through steep rough passes of the mountains. It was painful work getting horses and cannon up the steeps, while the change from tropical heat to icy winds and storms further exhausted the men.

Cortés had accepted the advice of El Gordo to proceed by way of the mountain kingdom of Tlascala because the people were friends of the Totonacs and bitter enemies of the Aztecs. For generations the fierce Tlascalans had resisted all attempts of the Aztecs to subdue their kingdom.

On the Tlascalan border the Spaniards camped, while Totonac messengers went ahead to ask permission of the chiefs to cross their territory. They expected no trouble, but the Tlascalans suspected Mexican trickery in any body of armed men. They would not risk their safety by allowing these foreigners to enter the country. Of no avail were the Totonacs' glowing descriptions of the teules and their mission, or the gifts and messages of Cortés. The Tlascalan nation marched out to fight the invaders in their high mountain country.

A few hundred Spaniards, aided by horses and artillery, contended with hosts of warriors. Many chiefs were killed and their bands dispersed, but the Spaniards lost precious horses and soldiers. Freezing, hungry and wounded, the Spaniards considered their desperate situation. Even the boldest lost heart and many begged Cortés to turn back before they were all destroyed. If the Tlascalans were so invincible, what would happen to them when they met the hosts of Montezuma?

It was a test for the conquistador's courage and belief in himself. Well he knew that they might be going forward to death, but his determination did not falter. Gently, like a good comrade, he reasoned with the soldiers. They could not turn back now, he pointed out. Not only would they lose the great prize so nearly in their grasp but their prestige as beings above human weakness would be gone. If the Indians saw that they could be beaten in war like other men then indeed they would be destroyed.

Just when they most needed hope came messengers from the Tlascalan chief, Xicotenga. He was convinced, now, that the teules were those destined to overthrow the Aztecs, therefore he invited Cortés to confer with him. The stout Tlascalans could well appreciate such prowess as the Spaniards had shown against overwhelming odds, and they took the battle-weary soldiers to their hearts. Xicotenga and his fellow chieftains offered their aid for the *entrada* into Anáhuac and from that time forth, through all the events of the conquest, the Tlascalans remained faithful friends. Xicotenga wished to mingle the blood of the teules with his race by marrying his daughter to Cortés, but the leader skillfully evaded, presenting Pedro de Alvarado as worthy of the honor. The Tlascalan princess, baptized Doña Luisa, went with Alvarado through many trials and their daughter Leonor was always his favorite child.

In long parleys through Doña Marina the Spaniards learned things that excited both cupidity and fear. The Tlascalans declared that the Aztecs were cruel and treacherous, mighty warriors, who had collected wealth beyond belief from subject peoples. Their chiefs lived luxuriously in beautiful towns, but most magnificent of all was Tenochtitlán, the city in the lake. Montezuma's capital was impregnable, said the Tlascalans. The causeways leading to the shores had bridges that could be opened, the streets were canals, and every rooftop a fortress.

After a few weeks Cortés was ready for the great entrada into Anáhuac, choosing the route past Cholula, a beautiful city of many temples. Accompanied by two thousand Tlascalan warriors the company descended from the pine-clad mountains of Tlascala to a beautiful valley. The invaders marched over good roads between fields of maize and blue-green spiky maguey cactus.

From the city of shining temples splendidly dressed chiefs came to meet Cortés, with haughty reserve in their manner. While the Tlascalans made camp in the country, the Spaniards marched into the streets, watched by excited crowds assembled on the flat housetops.

The visitors were housed in spacious rooms around a great walled court. Slaves brought them food, nobles bowed before them, but Cortés did not like the atmosphere in the city or the subtle insolence scarcely concealed by polite gestures. Xicotenga had warned him to beware of the treacherous Cholulans. Then Doña Marina was visited by a Cholulan lady who had taken a fancy to her. She begged the Mexican princess to join the people of her own race and thus save her life, for all the Spaniards were to be killed. Doña Marina pretended to be pleased with the proposal, but carried the tale immediately to her lord, Cortés. He had heard the same thing from priests whom he had forced to confess the plot. They told him Montezuma had ordered the Cholulans not to let the Spaniards escape alive.

Cortés had deliberately led his men into a hostile city, but he could match Montezuma in treachery in order to escape. After calling upon the priests and nobles to assemble in the great court next morning, Cortés faced them on horseback surrounded by his cavalry, with soldiers stationed at the gates. He berated the Cholulans harshly for daring to plan the death of subjects of the greatest ruler in the world. Then, giving a signal to his soldiers, he instigated a brutal massacre, as they fell upon the unsuspecting people with their swords, while the horsemen trampled them in the constricted space. Slaughter spread over the city, for the Tlascalans streamed through the streets, wreaking their hatred in indiscriminate killing. Hundreds of Cholulans perished, their proud city was humbled, and Cortés swore he would raze every temple before he was through with them.

The conqueror had signed his entry into Anáhuac with blood and put fear into the heart of its lord. When messengers from Cholula brought Montezuma the terrible story he shut himself up with the priests to learn the will of the gods. Although he was lord of unconquered armies he feared this handful of strangers who circumvented all his plots and won their way against the greatest odds. His war lords advised him to allow the invaders to enter Tenochtitlán, appeasing them in every way. Once trapped in the maze of canals and bridges, it would be easy to destroy them.

So, as the Spaniards with their train of wild Tlascalan warriors advanced toward their goal, they were met by various splendid chieftains bearing gifts and messages of welcome from Montezuma. Triumphantly Cortés led the way over the mountain passes and down into the Valley of Mexico.

In the translucent atmosphere it was a picture fair beyond belief. They saw vast shimmering lakes with beautiful cities framed in verdure on the shores. Lakes and gardens and a great cultivated valley were held in the embrace of mountains, while over all hung the snowy shapes of the great volcanoes, Popocatépetl and Ixtaccíhuatl. The soldiers marched on as though in a dream to Iztapalapa on the lake shore, a town of enchanting terraced houses, canals and gardens. They could not believe their eyes, and felt as though they were among the wonders described in old Spanish romances.

At Iztapalapa they were met by Montezuma's nephew, Cacamatzín, lord of Texcoco. He came in a rich litter to escort them to the city. They marched out in close formation on the broad causeway leading to Tenochtitlán. Throngs of canoes filled with wondering brown people darted about in the lake near the causeway, following their progress. Outside the city Montezuma himself appeared in a litter resplendent with gold, jewels and green plumes. Attendants spread mantles for his gold-shod feet to tread upon, as he descended from the litter and, supported by chieftains, advanced to meet the Spaniards. It was the eighth day of November, 1519, a fateful date for Indian Mexico.

At last Spanish conqueror and Aztec lord were face to face. The haughty Spaniard in velvet and plumed cap dismounted from his horse to greet the slender, dignified Indian, richly dressed and crowned with a diadem of green plumes. Cortés would have given Montezuma a Spanish *abrazo* but the chiefs thrust him back, to keep him from touching the sacred person. Doña Marina, beautiful and gracious, was the link between the two, as she translated their courteous greetings. Then Montezuma returned to his litter and preceded them to the city in regal state. Slaves with golden staves and feather banners cleared the way, while people stood against the walls with downcast eyes, not daring to look upon their great lord.

Bernal Diaz del Castillo, looking back years later on the marvelous adventure, asked, was ever in the world such audacity? That the Spaniards, so few in numbers among hosts who wished their death, should dare to enter the lake city from which there was no escape! The soldiers commended their souls to God and marched on.

Cortés and his company were comfortably housed in the spacious palace of Montezuma's father where they were served with respectful attention. The "chief of men" sent gifts and frequently received Cortés with his escort of captains in his own palace. In long interviews, when Doña Marina acted as interpreter, Spaniard and Aztec studied one another. Cortés admired the gentleness and intelligence of the Indian, while Montezuma, although he realized that white-skinned Malinche was not a god, fell completely under his influence.

The beauty of this city of canals, gardens and terraced houses impressed the soldiers mightily. They were shown stately plazas where lofty teocalli, or temples, rose high above the rooftops. The coming and going of canoes in the canals, the huge market place of Tlaltelolco, where quiet throngs bartered all the produce and riches of the empire, were observed with amazement and admiration.

Montezuma's pleasure palaces, his dancers and musicians, the luxury and reverence with which he was surrounded, made him seem like the potentate of a legend. Apparently the Spaniards were honored guests among these remarkable people, but they were uneasy and watchful. Bernal Diaz says they went always "with their beards over their shoulders," fully armed and ready for trouble.

Before long Cortés suggested a visit to the immense teocalli that soared above the market place in Tlaltelolco. Reluctantly Montezuma consented, provided the priests gave permission.

He sent nobles to escort Cortés and a few chosen captains to the temple, where he would meet them. An almost perpendicular stairway of a hundred and fourteen high narrow stone steps led up the face of the pyramid to the shrines. Those steps were built for small, flexible Indian feet, not for the feet of Europeans shod in leather. Refusing the aid of their escort, the Spaniards scrambled clumsily up to the broad platform on the top where there were altars, the huge ceremonial drum, and the stone temple roofed with thatch.

Montezuma came to meet them and taking Cortés by the hand led him to the edge of the platform. The whole beautiful valley and its shining lakes lay before them in its frame of mountains. Swarms of canoes darted over the lake and were gathered in the canal beside the market place below. Small colorful dots on the three broad causeways were people passing to and fro. Other white-walled terraced cities stood on the shores of the great salt lake and the smaller fresh-water lagoon. What a kingdom to win for God and Spain!

Cortés turned from the view to ask if he and his companions might enter the shrine, and Montezuma led them in. It was dark after the bright sunlight. In the gloom the visitors could see the dull gleam of gold and jewels, the rich color of painted beams. Two enormous idols with ferocious countenances loomed out of the shadows, wreathed in golden serpents and decked with jewels. The place stank with the fetid odor of blood, mingled with the fumes of copal incense burning in the braziers. Walls and altars were encrusted with dried blood and Bernal Diaz thought the place smelled like a butcher's shop. The horrified Spaniards bolted for the clean air and sunshine outside.

At the time the Spaniards made their acquaintance, the Aztecs' cult of blood sacrifice had risen to a frenzy. Hundreds of victims were sacrificed every year in Tenochtitlán alone. Huitzilopochtli and Tezcatlipoca, gods of war and darkness, had superseded Quetzalcoatl, god of learning and civilization. When the Spaniards explored the great market place they saw dreadful things; racks of skulls, heaps of bones, a temple with a yawning serpent mouth for entrance, where cooking pots were ready to boil human legs and arms for sacrificial feasts. The soldiers were disgusted, also, with the black-robed priests whose long unkempt hair under miter-shaped headdresses was matted with dried blood.

On this occasion Cortés could not contain himself. He and his companions were descendants of crusaders who had battled for the Faith against the Moslems in Spain, and the crusading spirit lived on in the conqueror. How could it be, he said to Montezuma, that a prince so wise and intelligent as he believed in those horrible creatures which were not gods but demons. He suggested that a shrine to the Virgin be set on the platform next to the temple of the Aztec gods. Deeply offended, Montezuma drew back and reproached Cortés for dishonoring the gods of his ancestors, who gave the people food and wealth and victory in war. The Spaniards were hurriedly sent home with an escort, while Montezuma expiated his sin in bringing them to the temple by more sacrifices.

Cortés did win permission, however, to have a chapel built in their own quarters. While preparing a wall for the altar, workmen broke through a sealed door and discovered in a compartment the treasures of Montezuma's ancestors. Cortés and his officers stood and gloated over that wealth; gold and silver, rare jades and precious stones, exquisite costumes, feather fabrics, headdresses, fans, shields and masks, some inlaid with turquoise and shell. Then the wall was sealed up again until the time was ripe for Cortés to demand tribute from Montezuma.

The soldiers were increasingly uneasy over their dangerous situation. Doña Marina, who mingled with the people, reported hostility in the city. The chiefs of the war council were urging Montezuma to make an end of the white strangers at once. The lords of the lake towns were rebellious against their weak overlord, each one plotting to grasp the rule over Mexico. If once they united, it meant death for the Spaniards. Further anxiety was caused by news brought by a messenger from the coast, who reported that Mexicans had stirred up the coast people to attack the fort at Vera Cruz.

The captains came to Cortés with a daring plan. They were accustomed to speaking their minds to the commander and he, a wise leader of men, listened to their counsels and generally consulted them on important moves. They demanded that Cortés capture Montezuma and bring him to their quarters where he could be watched. It seemed an impossible thing to accomplish and Cortés demurred, but finally consented.

One day the leader and his most trusted officers, all in full armor, appeared with Doña Marina at the palace, requesting an interview with Montezuma. There was nothing in this to rouse suspicion, for the guards were accustomed to visits from the Spaniards and they always carried their arms. When they were alone with the ruler Cortés turned on him with flashing eyes and his most haughty manner. He knew of the trouble on the coast, he said, and such duplicity in his friend shocked him. That came well from Cortés! He demanded that the chiefs responsible be brought to Tenochtitlán and given to him for punishment.

Cortés knew by this time how to deal with Montezuma, doubtless aided by Marina's suggestions. He knew how to play on his superstitions and vacillating will. Now, as hostage for his people's good behavior, Cortés demanded that Montezuma take up his residence with the Spaniards.

For a moment the Aztec flared into his old arrogance and angrily refused, but he was soon cowed by Cortés' commanding words and Doña Marina's persuasions. With sighs and lamentations he agreed to go with them.

What happened to the proud ruler who was accustomed to being treated as semi-divine? He had only to raise his voice to call the palace guards and the nobles who were always in attendance. The presumptuous strangers would have been killed and the kingdom freed from a menace. But Montezuma did not make the move. He believed that these were the beings of the prophecy, destined to rule the Aztecs, and he accepted his doom. He called for his golden litter and with outward pomp proceeded to the Spanish quarters. To his anxious chiefs he said that he went of his own accord, that the gods wished him to reside for a while with the teules. The Spaniards had made a terrific gamble and won.

While Montezuma transacted the affairs of the empire with chiefs under the watchful eyes of Spanish guards, he was treated with the utmost respect and affection by his captors. Nevertheless, the resigned Aztec became as wax in the ruthless hands of Malinche. Whatever Cortés asked for was done by Montezuma's orders, even to the imprisonment of chieftains who demanded death for the white men. Finally the humbled "chief of men" was brought to the act of submitting himself and his people as vassals to the King of Spain.

Weeping, the loyal chiefs obeyed his order and gave their submission to Cortés as emissary of the great lord of Spain. The treasure of Montezuma's ancestors was given up as tribute to the Emperor Charles, even to the exquisite carved jade pieces, more precious to the Aztecs than any amount of gold.

Beautiful specimens of the goldsmith's art were broken and melted down into bars of gold and silver. Soldiers were sent with escorts to get more of the metal from the country's mines. Mexican craftsmen were set to making chains, ornaments and vessels of gold for the Spaniards.

The division of the treasure naturally brought mutterings and dissension, as the soldiers accused Cortés of keeping more than the rightful share for himself and favored captains. Cortés placated the men with smooth promises to reward them all with wealth and lands when the conquest was completed, while the most vociferous were shut up with secret presents.

Now the conqueror dared to move against the religion of the Aztecs. When it came to idolatry Cortés the crusader lost his usual wisdom and diplomacy. Wise Fray Olmedo had already restrained him several times from smashing idols, arguing that it was better to wait until the people had some understanding of the Faith.

The final humiliation for Montezuma was the order forced from him by Malinche to have a shrine for the Blessed Virgin built on the great teocalli where Huitzilopochtli was worshipped. Triumphantly Cortés gathered his men to pray to the Blessed Lady of his devotion under the very shadow of the heathen gods. By this insult to their deities the conqueror roused the fury, not only of the powerful priesthood, but of all the people.

Montezuma told Cortés, with tears, that the gods were angry over the desecration of their shrine, that Huitzilopochtli and Tezcatlipoca threatened to desert the Aztecs unless the sacrilegious strangers were killed. Malinche and his men must leave the country at once, declared Montezuma, for he could no longer save them from the wrath of his people. Cortés pretended to yield, but said that they had no ships. If Montezuma would provide workmen he would have the ships rebuilt and depart. Thus he played for time while he thought up some new way to hold his control.

Six months had passed while the conqueror played his astute game to win the Aztec kingdom without war. Now, at the beginning of May, 1520, the Spaniards' fate hung in the balance and the scales were tipped against them by a challenge from other Spaniards.

Diego de Velasquez, Cortés' enemy, had sent a fleet to the coast in command of Pánfilo Narvaez, who claimed to have orders from the King to take over Mexico and send Cortés to Spain. These rivals must be won over or crushed. Cortés was obliged to leave the capital for the coast with a large company of soldiers. Pedro de Alvarado was left in command with orders to watch Montezuma and at all costs to keep the peace.

Two groups of Spaniards fought furiously among the coastal towns and woodlands, as Narvaez refused to treat with Cortés. The veterans of Mexico, though greatly outnumbered, had the advantage of knowing the country well, and Cortés sent spies into his rival's camp to grease the palms of soldiers with gold so many were ready to desert. There was a wild battle during a rainy tropical night in Narvaez' own camp in which he was wounded in one eye and was captured. He was shut up in the fort at Vera Cruz while most of his men joined Cortés, avid for the wealth he promised. Reinforced with men, horses and artillery, the conqueror hurried back to Tenochtitlán.

He had need to hurry, for disaster awaited him. Before they reached the Valley messengers came with the terrible news that the Aztecs had risen and besieged the Spaniards in their quarters. As the conqueror marched through Texcoco and other lake towns late in June no chiefs came obsequiously to greet

Malinche, no Indians brought gifts of flowers and food. There was no triumphal entry into Tenochtitlán, but a hurried march through the streets while warriors jeered at them from the housetops. It was embarrassing for Cortés, who had boasted to Narvaez' men of his power and prestige in Mexico.

Called to account, Alvarado told the tragic story. The people had asked permission to celebrate the great festival to Tezcatlipoca when a youth was sacrificed with ecstatic dancing and singing. After consenting, Alvarado had become convinced that the feast would end with an attack on the interlopers by Indians exalted with drink and emotion. He determined to act first and put fear in their hearts. While the great courts were thronged with dancers and worshippers the horsemen and soldiers rushed in among them, slaughtering hundreds of helpless people. Since the massacre, food had been refused to the Spaniards and they were attacked every time they ventured from their quarters.

Very likely there was danger of an Aztec uprising but the massacre roused Cortés to fury. With one impetuous, cruel deed Alvarado had undone all his painstaking work and skillful maneuvering. Brushing everyone aside with angry words, the leader shut himself up to brood over the catastrophe.

In the anxious days that followed it seemed there was no way out for the beleaguered Spaniards. They were short of food and water, the flat housetops around the palace were filled day and night with shrieking enemies who hurled stones and flaming arrows into their courts. Every sally in search of food ended in hasty retreat. Hunger and wounds weakened their resistance.

As a last resort Montezuma appeared on the roof to plead with his people. Stories differ as to this episode. The Spanish chroniclers say that Cortés ordered the captive monarch to make the plea, while the Indian story is that Montezuma was already dead, slain by the Spaniards; that his body was held up by soldiers while some other Mexican spoke in his name.

It appeared to be Montezuma, at any rate, who begged his people for a truce to let the Spaniards leave the country. He was answered with yells and reproaches. For the first time the gallant young chief, Cuauhtémoc, appears in the story. He was Montezuma's nephew and lord of Tlaltelolco. Answering Montezuma's plea he shouted, "What is this that the deceitful Montezuma, woman of the Spaniards, says. For with womanly soul he surrendered to them out of pure fear. He is no longer our King." With that, Cuauhtémoc raised his bow and shot several arrows at his uncle. Stones followed, and the Spaniards reported that one of them hit the unhappy Montezuma, who died in a few hours. His body was delivered to the people who had repudiated him and his brother was elected "chief of men" in his place.

No hope remained for the Spaniards but to try escape by night. The bridges over the big canals had been removed, they knew, but they constructed a crude one of planks to carry along for the crossings. Horses and Tlascalan Indians were loaded with the best of the treasure, then the rest was heaped on the floor and the commander told the soldiers to take what they liked. Greed outweighed prudence with some of the men, who stuffed their clothes so full with gold that they were unable to swim when thrown into the canals, and drowned in that terrible night.

In the rainy night of June 30, 1520, always thereafter to be known as the Noche Triste, the escape began. Cortés, with some of the horsemen and laden beasts, got across the im-provised bridge and hurried on to the mainland at Tacuba. Almost immediately shouts and blasts from conch-shell trumpets told those who followed that they were discovered. In rain and darkness, made horrible with yells and booming drums, hordes of Indians fell on the hapless men, pulling them into the water, jabbing at them from all sides. Horses and men fell into the canals and drowned, while others scrambled over the struggling mass to safety. All night the Aztecs pursued the fleeing soldiers, until they reached a little temple on a hill which provided protection.

A despairing, exhausted band took account of their situation in the dawn light. Many soldiers and Tlascalans were lost, all who survived were wounded, only twenty-three horses escaped, and powder and shot were gone. Cortés rejoiced to find Doña Marina and Alvarado's princess, Doña Luisa, among the survivors.

After binding up their wounds as well as possible the beaten men hurried on toward the shelter of Tlascala. Then, to their horror, scouts reported that a plain ahead was filled with warriors. The chiefs of the lake towns had gathered with their armies to make sure that no Spaniards escaped.

Exhausted as they were, the soldiers determined to go down fighting. Cortés told the twenty-three horsemen to ride into the ranks from all directions aiming for the chiefs, who were distinguished by plumed headdresses. Then, with their stirring battle cry, "Santiago and at them!" the Spaniards charged into the mass of warriors. Bernal Diaz wrote, "Oh, what a sight it was to see that fearful battle, how we moved all mixed up with them foot to foot, and the cuts and thrusts we gave them, and with what fury the dogs fought and what wounds and death they inflicted on us with their lances and swords." Cortés rode straight for the gold and silver plumes of the supreme chief and killed him. Many other chiefs were downed, causing such disorganization that the Indians fled in every direction.

The battered Spaniards rescued their dead and staunched their wounds. They were reduced to the number with which they had entered Anáhuac—four hundred men; they had only twenty horses, twelve crossbowmen, seven musketeers, all maimed and lame.

When they reached the Tlascalan capital old chief Xicotenga received them kindly, although he reproached Cortés for having trusted the treacherous Aztecs. While the men rested, Cortés the indomitable began to work out his strategy for regaining Mexico. Survivors of Narvaez' company cursed him and demanded that he leave the country, but his own valiant veterans stood by him.

Cortés learned that the garrison at Vera Cruz was intact and that ships had arrived. When he had received from the coast men supplies and artillery, he began his campaign to win the people of the Valley by persuasion or force. The winter was spent in raiding parties against hostile towns, or in protecting friendly chiefs from Aztec attacks. The soldiers thought there was no end to hardships and battles, but they continued to follow their commander. A man of such daring, who shared the privations of his men, could hold the loyalty of those hardened soldiers.

The conqueror's trump card was the audacious idea of building small vessels to besiege the city from the lake. All winter the Tlascalans cut timbers in their pine forests and shaped them for the building of thirteen brigantines, under the direction of a Spanish shipbuilder. Pitch for the seams was made in the forest, while sails, ironware and other fittings were brought from the stores at Vera Cruz on the backs of Indian porters.

Meanwhile, young Cuauhtémoc had become ruler in Tenochtitlán. He was the finest type of proud, intelligent Aztec, the only one who understood the necessity of Indian unity to drive out the invaders. This he strove to achieve among the lords of the Valley, hoping by rich gifts, appeals to their pride, or threats, to hold them to his cause. Thousands of the best warriors were assembled in the city. He would not yield to the Spaniard like weak Montezuma.

Texcoco, finest of the lake cities, must be won so that the brigantines could be launched from its canals. When Cortés with his escort rode in to confer with the chief, he found the city strangely empty. Most of the inhabitants had fled and their lord had gone to join Cuauhtémoc in Tenochtitlán. Priests told Cortés that this ruler had taken power illegally and they presented a young prince as the rightful chief. This youth was promptly baptized with Cortés' name and as Don Hernando was appointed a puppet prince to rule Texcoco for the Spaniards.

The Indians of Tlascala had done their work and now, over the mountains, came an amazing procession. Eight thousand Indians bore on their backs the timbers and fittings for the ships, protected by marching throngs of warriors, brave in plumes and mantles. In an unbroken line they streamed into Texcoco, shouting and blowing their trumpets, crying, "Viva, viva, for the Emperor our lord and Castile! Tlascala and Castile!" The Tlascalans were burning to get back into the fight to avenge their fellows who had perished in the Noche Triste.

When all was ready Cortés reviewed his troops and gave each commander his orders. They were to make camp at the three towns leading to the causeways; Pedro de Alvarado was sent to Tacuba, Cristóbal de Olíd to Coyacán, Gonzalo de Sandoval to Iztapalapa. Each commander had a company of Spaniards as well as hundreds of Indian warriors. Word was sent to friendly chiefs to have their armies ready to march.

On Corpus Christi day, near the end of May, 1521, Mass

was celebrated beside the canal where the thirteen brigantines rode at anchor with cannon mounted on their decks. With Cortés in command they sailed proudly into the lake. The other companies fought their way to their positions against Mexican resistance. Smoke signals rose from hills and lake towns—Cuauhtémoc's signal to loyal chiefs to assemble their canoes and warriors for attack.

Nearing the city, the brigantines with wind-filled sails bore down on swarms of canoes filled with warriors, crushing them under the prows while the cannon fire from the decks killed those who did not drown. As the first Spanish troops marched out on the causeway from Iztapalapa the little vessels cruised alongside, scattering the canoes before them.

So began that memorable siege. Day by day soldiers from the three camps forged ahead on the causeways—narrow battlegrounds filled with warriors—while they were attacked from canoes alongside. The brigantines scattered the canoes and helped with their cannon fire. Gradually the causeways were secured but the soldiers made no progress in capturing the city. Each day they fought their way in through swarms of defenders, filling in canal crossings, tearing down barricades, only to retreat to their camps. Each night the Indians opened the crossings and built more barricades.

For twenty days the fruitless struggle went on. War canoes were penned up in the city by the brigantines, others trying to sneak in with food from shore towns were driven off, but still there was no slackening of the fierce resistance. It seemed hopeless until the Spaniards secured a camp inside the city.

Cortés and his captains decided on a tremendous three-way attack from the camps, to force their way to the market place. Street by street and canal by canal they advanced. Cortés had cautioned the soldiers to fill in every waterway they crossed with stones, to provide a path of retreat, but one hasty troop crossed a wide canal on bundles of sticks and reeds thrown in. Cortés found the weak spot too late to repair it, as a troop of horsemen and soldiers came rushing toward him in full retreat. They tumbled headlong into the water, a milling mass of men and horses, hounded on every side by triumphant demons. The Indians had their hands on Malinche, a prize victim for Huitzilopochtli, but companions rescued him. Spaniards were dragged from the water by Indians who paddled off with them to the sacrificial altars.

Above the fury of battle reverberated the horrifying boom of the great war drum on the teocalli which rose above the housetops. Battling soldiers could see the figures of their comrades dragged up the temple steps to have their hearts torn out on the altars. Bleeding Spanish heads were thrown from roofs on the soldiers fighting toward the market place. "Thus will we kill you as we have killed Malinche and all who were with him," shrieked the Indians.

Terrified, bleeding, assaulted on all sides, the soldiers fought back to their camps. There they huddled for days, fending off attacks day and night, their nerves beaten on by the unceasing din of yells, trumpet blasts and the menacing roll of the great drum. They knew that comrades were dying on the altars and each soldier said to the next, "Thank God I am not being carried off today to be sacrificed."

Cuauhtémoc sent to chiefs of the surrounding towns flayed bearded skins from Spanish heads, arms and legs, and heads of horses. Thus had he dealt with the teules, and thus would he punish those who helped them. Naturally, Indian allies began to melt away from the camps, but the Tlascalans stood firm.

Cortés' only recourse was to tighten the blockade of the

brigantines around the city, and this was so successful that the people were cut off from food and water. They were starving, many died from drinking the salt water of the lake, but Cuauhtémoc's proud spirit would not yield. He refused to treat with Cortés.

If the Spaniards were not to give up and leave the country their only course was to pull the city down stone by stone. Reporting to the King later on, Cortés wrote: "Seeing that the people of the city were so rebellious and displayed such determination to die as no race has ever shown, I knew not what means to take to relieve our dangers and hardships, and to avoid destroying them and their city which is the most beautiful thing in the world. It was useless to tell them that we would not raise our camp, or that the brigantines would not cease to war on them, and that nowhere in the country was anyone left to help them, or that they would not obtain maize or fruits or water, nor any provisions anywhere. The more I spoke of these things the less sign of yielding did we see in them; rather we found them more courageous than ever in their fighting and scheming. Seeing that things went on in this way, and already more than forty-five days had been spent in this siege, I determined to take means towards our security and to further straiten the enemy. This latter consisted in our gaining the streets of the city and demolishing all the houses on both sides, so that henceforth we would not go ahead without levelling everything, so that which was water should be made dry land, no matter how much time it took."

"Scorched earth policy" worked well, even in the sixteenth century. Every day Spaniards and their Indian allies advanced into the city, fighting off defenders, tearing down and burning houses, filling the canals with stones and earth, leaving desolation behind them. The Aztecs jeered at the Indians working so hard to help the Spaniards destroy the city. "Pull down, destroy," they cried. "It is you who will have to build it again." The taunt came true when, in their days of servitude, the Indians built the Spanish city on the ruins of Tenochtitlán.

The Spaniards made their camp in the market place, having driven Cuauhtémoc and his people into a small quarter where all the houses stood in the water. Starving people crept out at night hunting for food, pestilence spread from rotting bodies heaped in streets and canals, but Cuauhtémoc spurred his warriors to continue the fight.

Cortés was deeply distressed by the suffering and destruction. Many times he sent messengers proposing peace, promising that Cuauhtémoc should be respected and remain a chief over his people. The only reply of the proud Aztec was that he did not believe Malinche's words, and he did not wish the fate of Montezuma.

Finally, one day, Cortés saw from the top of the teocalli that many canoes were assembling in Cuauhtémoc's quarter and he realized that the prince was planning to escape. Quickly he sent word to the captains of the brigantines to scour the lake and head off the canoes. García Holguin was the lucky captain who captured the lord of Mexico. Among the fleeing canoes he recognized that of the ruler by its rich canopy and decorations. Steering close by he threatened to shoot unless the rowers stopped. Cuauhtémoc accepted his fate and went aboard with his wives and chieftains.

The proud eagle had done his best to save his people and now wanted nothing but death. Brought before the white conqueror he resisted Cortés' embrace and brushed aside his words of praise for the valorous defence of the city. "Malinche, take that dagger in your belt and kill me at once," he begged. But Cortés tried to reassure him with blandishing words. Let his spirit be at rest, said Malinche, for he should rule his people as before.

Cuauhtémoc was captured on August 13, 1521. The beaten people submitted, for only his indomitable spirit had kept resistance alive. A startling silence fell over the city of ruin and death, after long weeks of nerve-shattering noise. Bernal Diaz wrote it was as though a man had stood in a church tower with all the bells clanging, and then they had suddenly ceased.

The mighty conflict between Spaniard and Aztec was over and the Indians were servitors in their own beautiful land. The wonders of Tenochtitlán became a theme of legend, for nothing was left to remind Spaniards of the next generation of what it had been. The great pyramids of the Aztec gods were pulled down and their stones went into the building of Christian churches. The center of the Spanish city was built over the ruins of the Tecpán, the central court surrounded by palaces and temples in the Aztec city. Cortés took over Montezuma's palace for his residence. Stones of the razed teocallis went into the Palacio Municipal and the great church which was to become the Cathedral.

Cuauhtémoc, the captured eagle, was not surprised to find that Malinche's fair words meant little. Although he was appointed Indian governor of the city, Cortés kept him always under supervision, fearful of the homage he might receive from his people. In the furious search of the Spaniards for Montezuma's treasure, lost in the Noche Triste, Cuauhtémoc and other chiefs were not spared from torture. Their feet and hands were cruelly burned in the effort to make them reveal where treasure was hidden. To his everlasting shame, Cortés permitted this torture of the man he had promised to honor.

As Franciscan friars came to build monasteries and convert the people, the sons of Aztec nobles were educated in church schools. Their best friend and the most sympathetic interpreter of ancient Mexico was a Franciscan, the scholarly Fray Bernardino de Sahagún. He not only spoke the Aztec language fluently, but composed an alphabet and grammar for the use of priests. Endlessly he questioned his loving pupils, as well as elderly aristocrats who remembered the symbolism of Aztec religion and all the ways of life in the Aztec realm. They painted the story for him in picture symbols, telling him in Spanish what they meant. Out of the mass of pictures and notes assembled, Fray Bernardino wrote, both in the Aztec language and Spanish, his great history of ancient Mexico. Fray Gante was another great teacher and friend of the Indians. Various educated Indians made picture records of the conquest and wrote chronicles, so that the story of Aztec Mexico was preserved.

Within an amazingly short time Spanish civilization was changing the face of Mexico, blending with but not destroying the life and character of the native race. The realm of the Aztecs became a new kingdom—Nueva España.

CHAPTER 7

CONQUERORS CLASH IN THE WILDERNESS

THE CONQUEST of Mexico revealed to the Spaniards riches and wonders such as they had dreamed of since the discovery of the New World. It gave a tremendous impetus to the ambition and imagination of these vigorous men, as they forged on to win more kingdoms for God, the Emperor Charles and their personal fame.

Immediately after the downfall of the Aztec kingdom, the restless conquerors in Mexico, and the men of Castilla del Oro, turned their attention to the unexplored territory between those regions. Cortés' comrades deserved honors, and their ambitions might clash with those of their commander if their energies were not employed in further exploration. Therefore the commander sent out his most distinguished captains in every direction, some to pacify distant tribes of Mexico, some to explore the Mexican coast of the South Sea. Pedro de Alvarado was sent southward to conquer strong Indian kingdoms in Guatemala. Cristóbal de Olíd had orders to go by sea to the coast of Honduras, there to establish a foothold under Cortés' jurisdiction.

The territory which now engaged Spanish attention lay between the two oceans, a narrow land of the most rugged mountainous terrain and fire-spitting volcanoes, sheathed on both coasts in jungle lowlands. The Spaniards had exaggerated ideas of rich mines to be found and were convinced that somewhere in the territory they would find the long-desired strait to provide an easy passage from sea to sea.

Men of Panama who were ambitious to explore were generally blocked by old Pedrarias, still governor of Castilla del Oro. He had the ships built by ill-fated Balboa but would permit no one to use them. His price for permission to make voyages was so exorbitant that few could deal with him. The governor had sent navigators to chart the Pacific coast north of Panama as far as a large bay, now called the Gulf of Nicoya. And several expeditions had penetrated the mountainous territory of Costa Rica, without success because of the resistance of a valiant warrior chief, Urraca. To keep a foothold a fort, called Borica, had been built on the coast.

Two determined explorers outwitted Pedrarias by going directly to the King. They were a distinguished gentleman, Gil Gonzales de Avila, already acquainted with the island colonies, and a veteran pilot in New World waters, Andrés Niño. When they arrived in Panama with the royal commission Pedrarias could not prevent the voyage, but he could hinder it by refusing to deliver Balboa's ships despite the King's order to do so. At great cost of time and labor Gil Gonzales had to assemble vessels at the yards of the Pearl Islands.

Finally, early in 1522, the explorers set sail with four vessels but had gone no farther than Borica when they were obliged to beach the ships for repairs. Gil Gonzales set off by land with a small company, leaving Andrés Niño to oversee the work on the ships and to sail to a gulf farther north for a rendezvous with the soldiers.

The land party had a miserable time, for the downpours of the rainy season swelled the rivers and soaked the country so that the men plowed on through mud and drenched vegetation. Gil Gonzales fell ill from exposure and was sheltered by a chief of river Indians in his cane house on an island. While the wretched soldiers huddled under forest trees or in Indian huts the deluge continued for fifteen days without cessation. The river rose, flooding the island, and Gil Gonzales barely escaped with his life when the thatched roof of the chief's house collapsed on the inmates. Indians told them that the river would lead them to the gulf, so in Indian canoes tied together they made a precarious trip down the wild stream, to find their comrades with the ships awaiting them.

The commander was anxious to explore the coast with Andrés Niño, sending soldiers to follow inland, but this they refused to do without their leader. Andrés Niño, then, took one ship for exploring, leaving the others anchored in the gulf with their crews to guard them. Gil Gonzales, with horsemen and soldiers, marched off to discoveries that repaid him for the unlucky beginning of the journey.

They paused to visit in the territory of a kindly chief, Nicoya, whose simple people welcomed the strangers with gifts of food and gold. They even listened meekly to the exhortations of the priest who accompanied the expedition, and permitted themselves to be baptized by hundreds. Next to the search for the strait this earnest explorer made it his duty to convert the Indians.

The expedition passed through a part of present-day Costa Rica and entered the narrow, hot strip of land between the Pacific Ocean and Lake Nicaragua. These Castilians were the first white men to gaze upon that vast yellow-green sheet of water, an inland sea. Gil Gonzales rode his horse into the water, claiming the Mar Dulce, as he called it, for the King and Castile. Surely so large a body of water must have an outlet to the North Sea (the Atlantic) and provide the water passage so eagerly sought. In Indian canoes he explored part of the lake, but found no outlet.

It was an interesting land inhabited by kindly semi-civilized people, this realm of a great chief Nicaragua. Large cacao plantations, fields of maize, cotton and the spiky plant from which they obtained fiber, showed the industry of the people. Several volcanoes thrust their imposing bulk into the sky, one of them sending up a column of smoke that glowed red at night. The natives worshipped the god of this volcano, sacrificing a maiden to him each year.

Nicaragua and his people were descendants of tribes of the Nahua race who had migrated into the region ages before, from Mexico. They were skilled in weaving cotton for garments and in making rope and baskets from the fibrous agave plant, pita. These goods and the produce of their fields were bought and sold with cacao bean currency in village markets.

The strangers who appeared so mysteriously, wearing shining helmets and riding powerful animals, were received as honored guests by Nicaragua. Unusual conversations took place in the airy cane-walled chief's house between the mailed Spaniard, his missionary priest and the barbarically decked Indian. Nicaragua was a remarkable personality, thoughtful and intelligent, an Indian philosopher. Through Gonzales's interpreter he posed questions that astonished the Spaniards. What kept the sun, moon and stars in their places in the heavens, and would they always shed their light on the earth? Did the Spaniards believe that the souls of men lived after their bodies died? Were their great king and the priests of their god immortal, or would they die like ordinary human beings?

Finding Nicaragua so receptive, the missionary gathered the people around him to tell them of the True God. He urged them to give up worship of the golden idol housed in a stone temple on a lofty mound. Perhaps out of curiosity the natives listened attentively to the preaching and permitted the priest to place a wooden cross above their golden idol. The Spaniards did not know that to the Nicaraguans, as to other pre-Columbian people, the cross was a familiar symbol. It represented to them the gods of rain and those of the four world directions. Gil Gonzales' missionary spirit was thrilled to see hundreds of the brown heathen submit to baptism.

Gold, as well as converts, interested Gil Gonzales. He asked Nicaragua about the mines of his country and expressed so much admiration for the lovely necklaces and other ornaments of gold worn by the important men that Nicaragua presented a heap of treasure from his ancestral store.

Leaving behind, as he thought, a nation of converts, Gil Gonzales marched on through other villages, collecting gold and souls. While they rested in one of these places they received a visit from another great chief, Diriangen. Slaves carried him in a handsome litter, musicians beat their drums and blew on their trumpets and flutes, demure young women decked with gold bore gifts, and a procession of slaves laid offerings of wild turkeys at the feet of the strangers.

While listening politely to missionary preaching Diriangen took note of the white warriors' strange weapons and animals, but observed that though their weapons were alarming they were only a small company. The wily chief asked for three days in which to decide whether he and his people would accept baptism, then marched away to his village.

The soldiers, feeling secure, relaxed in the enervating heat while they confidently awaited the return of Diriangen.

Stripped of their arms they were taking siestas in their huts when swarms of yelling warriors descended on them. Diriangen's answer to proselyting was war. Leaping for their arms the Spaniards fought furiously against overwhelming numbers, escaping only because the Indians finally fell back before the fire of muskets and crossbows.

The soldiers demanded that Gil Gonzales return at once to the ships. They had no mind to leave their bones in this Indian land, they had collected great treasure, they could not proceed against so many enemies. Reluctantly their leader consented. By night the battered company slipped away, marching in close formation with their few horsemen guarding the flanks. Hurriedly they passed through Nicaragua's territory, fearing that he would follow the example of Diriangen. Some warriors did attack them and more battles were fought before they reached the safety of the gulf and the welcome sight of the ships riding at anchor. Andres Niño, while they were gone, had followed the whole coast of Nicaragua and explored the great bay which Gonzales named Gulf of Fonseca for his patron, the Bishop of Burgos.

In 1523 the explorers were back in Panama. Gonzales was not at all discouraged by the battles they had sustained. He gave a glowing account of the fine land and fresh-water sea he had found, and of the great harvest of souls won for the Church. Pedrarias demanded that the King's fifth of the gold be turned over to him, but Gil Gonzales refused. He knew better than to let the treasure fall into the hands of the rapacious Governor. Secretly he crossed the Isthmus to Nombre de Díos where he took ship for Santo Domingo. From there his account of his discovery and the gold could be sent safely to Spain. The Audiencia of Santo Domingo gave him permission to go in search of the outlet of his Mar Dulce on the coast of the North Sea.

With Gonzales out of the way Pedrarias moved quickly to take over the fine territory he had discovered. Fernandez de Córdoba was sent with a large number of ships and men to found settlements and claim the land as part of Castilla del Oro.

Following the route of Gonzales, the new invasion of Spaniards, accompanied by many slaves carrying supplies, reached the immense lake. Apparently Nicaragua let them pass, for Fernandez de Córdoba explored the shore and chose a site near the head of the lake for a settlement. Granada was the name given to the church and fort surrounded by a few huts. Plots were allotted to settlers and a Spanish municipality organized.

Marching on with the rest of his company, Córdoba found another large body of water, Lake Managua. In a fertile valley between the lake and the Pacific he founded another town, León. This was in the year 1524, just when the rightful discoverer was landing on the wrong part of the north coast.

Fernandez de Córdoba had brought along in his ships the timbers and fittings for a small brigantine. From the landing place on the gulf to the Mar Dulce these heavy burdens were carried on the backs of Indian slaves. The Spaniards thought nothing of carrying vessels around piecemeal, since they could always pack them on their human beasts of burden. Córdoba's carpenters assembled the little craft and in it he cruised the great lake. He found the outlet, the Desaguadero or Rio San Juan, and explored it until stopped by rocks and rapids.

While Córdoba explored the lake, Gil Gonzales had bad luck in his search for the mouth of the river on the Atlantic side. It was unfortunate for the future settlements that he did not succeed, for men of as good character as he were rare among the explorers of Nicaragua. Instead of turning southward from Santo Domingo, the ship of the explorer skirted the coast of Honduras until storms forced the mariners to take shelter in a lagoonlike harbor. There some dead horses were thrown overboard so that Indians might not know that these sacred animals were not immortal, and from this episode the harbor was named Puerto Caballos. It is now Puerto Cortés.

Exploring still farther north, Gil Gonzales landed his men and built a fort on a sandy point, Tres Puntas, now in the territory of Guatemala. It was named San Gil de Buena Vista. The Indians of the neighborhood, hoping to get rid of the intruders, told them that there was much gold inland. In search of this, and of his river, Gonzales marched off with part of his company into the interior and into the mountains of Honduras.

There, in the primeval wilderness, they came upon a few Spanish soldiers, scouts of a party sent out by Córdoba, under Hernando de Soto to explore the interior. The territory between the lake country of Nicaragua and the coast of Honduras is of the wildest character; from the air today it appears to be one rumpled mass of mountains and ravines. Yet those tough Spaniards thought nothing of it. Through forests and over mountains, through gorges of rapid rivers, bands of adventurers roamed, before long, in every direction. Some were piratical groups hunting for gold and slaves, others were soldiers who fought fiercely for the claims of rival captains. Their endurance was amazing.

The meeting of Gil Gonzales' men with those of Hernando de Soto was the first of many clashes in the wilderness. They fought it out in the forests and de Soto was defeated. Gil Gonzales sent the party back to Nicaragua with the message that he acknowledged no other conqueror's claims to this territory. Gonzales then hurried back to the coast, for scouts had brought him word that Spanish ships had been seen.

These were the ships of Cristóbal de Olíd's expedition. Cortés had made the mistake of sending his trusted captain to Cuba to buy horses and supplies, and to collect recruits for his colonizing venture. Cristóbal de Olíd was a valiant soldier, one of Cortés' best captains in the conquest, but like others he was ambitious for individual success. In La Habana Governor Velasquez, Cortés old enemy, worked on him with flattery and with promises of royal aid if he threw off allegiance to Cortés and proclaimed himself governor of Honduras. He was, of course, to share the profits of his venture with Velasquez. Some of Cristóbal de Olíd's men were disgruntled fellows who felt they had been cheated of just rewards for their work in the conquest of Mexico. They also urged him to defy his commander.

With ambitious schemes in his mind Cristóbal de Olíd reached the coast of Honduras not far from Puerto Caballos. He named his crude settlement on the shore Triunfo de la Cruz and claimed the land in the name of the King and Cortés. He waited a more favorable moment to show his hand.

The men had scarcely had time to build their huts and raid Indian villages for food when another Spanish ship appeared on the horizon. Olíd's guilty conscience warned him that the ship brought a messenger from his commander, and he was right. About a year had elapsed since he had sailed from Vera Cruz for Cuba and there was frequent communication between that island and Mexico. Friends of Cortés had sent letters to inform him of the plot cooked up by his captain and Governor Velasquez. The conqueror lost no time in sending a young relative of his, Francisco de las Casas, to find Olíd's settlement and discover what was happening.

Francisco de las Casas intended to go about his mission in a diplomatic way, but Olíd sent out two caravels of armed men to prevent him from landing. Spaniards fought each other from their ships until nature took a hand. The dreaded storm of that coast, the Norte, swept down on them with howling wind and rain. Las Casas' ship was wrecked on the shore and when he and thirty soldiers scrambled out of the water they were arrested. Olíd freed the soldiers after making them swear allegiance to him, but Las Casas was a prisoner.

Triunfo de la Cruz was a forlorn, barren settlement; food supplies were running low, Indians were hostile, the men and their wives suffered as usual from hunger and fever. Cristóbal de Olíd decided to move inland to a fertile valley of prosperous Indian pueblos called Naco. The fields of growing corn, the villages, and avenues of fruit trees between them, were a goodly sight to the hungry invaders. They settled in Indian houses and persuaded the natives to supply them with food.

Gil Gonzales, marching in search of invading Spaniards, found his rival, Olíd, at Naco. The two leaders parleyed for a while, but when Gil Gonzales refused to relinquish his claim to Honduras, he was arrested by Olíd. The two captives, Las Casas and Gonzales, made the best of the situation by pretending sympathy for Olíd's ambitions. Thinking that he had won over his rivals, Olíd gave the two men liberty in the settlement and lodged them in his own quarters. Secretly, however, his false friends were plotting his downfall.

One evening the three captains sat chatting over the supper table after the pages had cleared away the meal and left the room. They talked of the great days of the conquest and of Cortés' exploits. Suddenly Las Casas rose, and grasping Olíd by the beard, thrust a knife at his throat. Gonzales also leaped on him with a knife. The strong man struggled free of his assailants and rushed out toward the forest, calling for help. Some soldiers answered his call but Las Casas stopped them, declaring that he was master and it was time to put a stop to tyranny. Death was threatened to any soldier who helped Olíd to hide so the unfortunate man was soon captured. Double-crossing was not unusual among these conquistadores. Olíd had betrayed the trust put in him by Cortés who, himself, had double-crossed Governor Velasquez. Now Olíd's rivals had played the same game on him. They held a farcical trial and had him beheaded as a traitor.

While adventurers roamed and fought in the wilderness of Honduras and a bloody drama took place in a lonely Indian village, Hernán Cortés was on his way to the new battleground of conquerors.

It is strange that Cortés, usually so wise and farsighted, left the scene of his magnificent success at that time for a long and hazardous journey. His firm hand was greatly needed in Mexico. The chiefs of distant provinces were far from pacified, Spanish government had to be consolidated, soldiers and gentlemen were clamoring for the lands promised them after the conquest. Enemies were working against him, as he well knew, and by going away he gave them every opportunity to undermine his control of Mexico.

But ambition overruled wisdom in the spirit of the adventurous conqueror. He could not permit others to win this new territory when by acting quickly he might add it to Nueva España. Reports from Santo Domingo informed him of Gil Gonzales' voyage to Honduras, a land which the Spaniards believed to be rich in mines. He had received no word from his emissary to Olíd, Francisco de las Casas.

In October of that busy year, 1524, Hernán Cortés was ready to leave. Two officials of the Mexico City council—Estrada and Albornoz—were appointed to govern in his absence.

With pomp befitting a successful conquistador Hernán Cortés set forth on his most disastrous journey. The great company included his best veteran officers, soldiers and horsemen. There were priests to preach the Gospel, pages to serve his table on dishes of gold plate, musicians with sackbuts and clarinets for entertainment. Indians guarded a herd of pigs for food, many Indian warriors and carriers accompanied them. Doña Marina was with her lord, as well as the melancholy Aztec chieftains, Cuauhtémoc and the chief of Tacuba. Cortés did not dare leave them behind for fear they would start a rebellion in his absence.

The march to the coast and on to Guazacualco, the domain of Bernal Diaz del Castillo and other veterans, was a triumphal progress. Indians and Spaniards received Malinche at every town with music and floral arches, eager to kiss his hand. At Guazacualco Bernal Diaz and his companions put on a great show to welcome their leader. Days were passed in fiestas with feasts and Spanish sports. There Doña Marina, faithful companion of so many adventures, was married to one of Cortés' gentlemen, Juan Jaramillo.

Cortés' satisfaction was marred by a message from Mexico that the government was not going smoothly, but he would not turn back. Two officials who had warned him of trouble were sent to the capital to keep an eye on Estrada and Albornoz. These men, Salazar and Chirino, were sly, treacherous fellows, only too glad to gain power for themselves while the chief was away.

When Cortés ordered Bernal Diaz and other captains to join the expedition they grumbled and complained. They were rest-ing from the exertions of conquest, just beginning to enjoy their estates. Soldier loyalty prevailed, however, and they followed their commander into tribulations exceeding anything they had yet experienced.

Cortés led his hosts through the hot, alluvial plains of Tabasco, all rivers, swamps and jungles. Streams were crossed in Indian canoes when they could catch the Indians; otherwise rude wooden rafts or bridges were constructed. Weeks passed while the soldiers floundered on in a maze of bogs, streams and forests, through unexplored and totally primitive country. There were no trails, for natives of the region were river people who traveled by canoe and did not know their way through forests. The few natives captured for guides escaped in the night.

The forests of immense trees were so thick that no gleam of sky showed between their spreading crowns of foliage. Even when men climbed high trees to get their bearings they could see nothing. Hopelessly lost, the soldiers hacked their way through impenetrable jungle growth with swords and knives. Cortés had a cloth map made by Indians of Guazacualco on which the situation of pueblos was indicated, but it was impossible to follow it. Cortés knew the general direction they should take, and finally led his men forward by means of a ship's compass.

Indian villages were found in clearings or on stream banks, but their inhabitants had fled into the forests. Sometimes the scouts were able to rob cornfields or collect food from houses, but the gnawings of hunger were added to exhaustion from the terrible struggles through swamps and jungles. Cortés had his musicians play at night to cheer the men, but they said forlornly that it sounded like the howling of demons and they preferred a sack of corn to music. Once when Bernal Diaz and some soldiers returned to camp with a load of maize and fowl they had collected from a large village, the soldiers snatched the food and devoured it. Not a scrap was left for Cortés and his captains.

They came to a river so wide and deep it could not be crossed by their usual makeshift methods. Then Cortés cheered his men on to superhuman efforts. Indians and Spaniards cut down trees from which they constructed a solid wooden bridge, and on this the company passed safely over the river. Immediately they were plunged into bogs so deep and quaking that the horses sank to their bellies and it seemed that horses and men would all be drowned or stifled in mud. Men and beasts struggled through, however, and soon they reached a more populated country where food could be obtained.

There in a native village a tragic event took place. One of the Mexican soldiers came to Cortés with the tale that Cuauhtémoc and the lord of Tacuba were plotting to kill all the Spaniards and return to Mexico to start an Indian war. The truth seems to be that it was only talk, such as men in their sad situation might indulge in. Cuauhtémoc and his companion mourned over their servitude and discussed the possibility of winning back Mexico if Malinche and his soldiers died in the wilderness.

Despite their protestations of innocence Cortés took the opportunity to rid himself of the Mexican lords whose influence he feared. He ordered them to be hung from a great ceiba tree in the village. Cuauhtémoc reproached Cortés for his perfidy, saying, "Oh, Malinche, I have known that you would cause my death for I know your false words; God will require it of you, for you kill me unjustly."

All the soldiers were shocked by this ruthless act, muttering among themselves that it was cruel and unjust. It is said that

Cortés was pensive and gloomy for days, unable to sleep at night. Well he might be disturbed after betraying all his fair promises to a valiant opponent. His entire treatment of Cuauh-témoc is a stain on the conqueror's record. In Mexican history Cuauhtémoc, the Aztec eagle, holds a place of honor beside later heroes of mixed race or Spanish blood; a man of pride and valor who loved his land and tried to save it from invaders.

At last, after months of suffering, the adventurers came out of the deadly forest into fine grassy plains full of game, which they hunted joyfully to fill their empty bellies. They had come into El Petén, a wild northern region of Guatemala. Before long they reached a lake, in its midst was an island crowned with a white-walled town. This was Tayasal, city of the Itzás who had migrated from Yucatán in ages past.

These Mayan people, although a little fearful of the strangers, were inclined to be friendly. Ragged and emaciated as they were after many months in the wilderness, the Spaniards could still make an impression. The chief of Tayasal sent a delegation of nobles in canoes, inviting Cortés to visit the island town, and he went off with them, much to the distress of his men. They need not have feared, however, for the white lord was treated as a being worthy of homage in the town of stone houses and temples.

The traders of the Itzás traveled over trails through the primitive country ahead, and down rivers to the seacoast. There they had seen white-skinned bearded men in armor like their visitors. This was joyous news indeed to the Spaniards. There was hope that their arduous trek was drawing to an end, and they looked forward to finding settlements on the coast.

At Tayasal Cortés left his favorite horse which had a sore foot, instructing the people to care for it until his return. They did so to the best of their understanding, worshipfully offering the animal flowers, birds and honey, as they would to a god. Naturally the horse died, whereupon its image, carved in stone, was set up in a temple. The people revered it as a god of thunder because Cortés, its master, had thunder and lightning in his hands. A century or more later, when Franciscan friars journeyed through this wilderness, they found the image of the horse god and smashed it in religious rage.

Hurrying on by Indian trade trails, the Spaniards found that their troubles were not yet over. They crossed steep sierras, painful with sharp rocks, and passed through tangled forests. At long last, they reached the river designated by the Indians as their route to the coast. Natives they met told them that two days' journey would bring them to the seacoast and their countrymen.

Gonzalo de Sandoval was sent with a few soldiers and Indians in canoes to find them. When they reached the seacoast they paddled along shore, seeing Indian traders in canoes with oars and sails. On the bank beside the mouth of a river, Sandoval spied two thin ragged men, browned by the sun, climbing *zapote* trees to gather the fruit. Overjoyed were these poor wretches to learn that the great Cortés himself was on his way to the coast.

The two men were taken back by Sandoval to the camp up river. Then Cortés learned the story of events in Honduras; he heard of Gil Gonzales' settlement, Olíd's treatment of Las Casas and the death of Olíd at Naco. He learned that Las Casas and Gonzales had gone to Mexico and that the settlers left by the latter at San Gil de Buena Vista had moved to an Indian trading village called Nito. The two men found by Sandoval were living in this village. They told Cortés that the Spaniards, not knowing how to grow food for themselves, were on the verge of starvation. Cortés packed his men into a fleet of canoes tied together, and with Indian paddlers and the horses swimming alongside, they made their way down the river to Nito.

Scouting bands were sent into the interior to find native villages and food. Cortés set his carpenters to work repairing Gil Gonzales' old brigantine. When it was ready he set out with the vessel and a fleet of canoes to explore the river Gonzalo de Sandoval had found. They passed into a mysterious tropical stream twisting and turning through deep gorges, intensely green with luxuriant vegetation and trailing lianas. Alligators leered at them from the banks, monkeys chattered from the trees, and flocks of little green parrots flew screaming across their path.

The river led them into a large beautiful lake framed in woodlands. Few villages were found in the forest, but by exploring another river in canoes large towns were found. There a load of maize, fruit and wild fowl was collected. With tremendous labor this store was brought to the brigantine in the lake and thence to the starving settlement. The Spaniards had found and named beautiful Rio Dulce and Golfo Dulce in the present republic of Guatemala.

Cortés next sent Sandoval with a troop of soldiers to find Naco and pacify the country. The journey was made without trouble by Indian trails, as there was much trade between the valley of Naco and the coast. Meanwhile Cortés embarked the rest of the company in the brigantine and followed the coast to Puerto Caballos, and then on to find the fort built by some of Las Casas' men at Trujillo.

The half-starved, deserted men of Trujillo could not believe their eyes when the ship appeared bringing the famous conqueror of Mexico. They flocked to the shore to kiss his hands and render homage. With great energy Cortés went to work on improvements that Trujillo might become a port for Honduras and headquarters for the exploration of the country. His Indians were detailed to chop down a grove of trees between the settlement and the shore to give the *vecinos,* or settlers, a clear view out to sea.

Not content with Mexico, and Guatemala won by Pedro de Alvarado, Cortés was determined to add Honduras to Nueva España. Soon he was able to include Nicaragua in his plans. Soldiers from Naco appeared at Trujillo with Spanish prisoners and a letter from Gonzalo de Sandoval telling of Spanish depredations in the interior. Indians had come to Sandoval at Naco, complaining of Spaniards who stole their food and carried off women and girls in chains. Sandoval had set off at once, had captured the Spaniards and released the Indian women.

These invaders, he learned, had been sent by Fernandez de Córdoba from León. The lieutenant of Pedrarias had done well in the land of lakes and volcanoes. His towns of León and Granada were growing, the soil was productive and the natives submissive. Panama was far away, so that Córdoba's ambition to rule the province for himself seemed feasible. He had sent the men captured by Sandoval to treat with the Honduran colonists for an alliance.

Cortés received the prisoners sent by Sandoval with his most blandishing words, for he saw the opportunity to ally himself with Córdoba against Pedrarias. The soldiers were given iron to shoe their horses and other useful things, and sent back to León with a friendly letter from Cortés.

Plots and intrigues thickened in the new territory, but Córdoba's ambitions were soon crushed and Pedrarias won Nicaragua from Cortés. The old Governor, learning of Córdoba's disloyalty, set sail for Nicaragua on the pretext of inspecting the province. Soon after reaching León he ordered the arrest of Fernandez de Córdoba and had him tried as a traitor. He was beheaded in the plaza of León, the town he had founded. Pedrarias had been replaced in Panama by a new governor, but he won from the King permission to govern Nicaragua. The province suffered for three years under his tyrannical rule, until death removed him from the scene in 1531, at the ripe age of approximately ninety.

To return to the year 1526, and Cortés at Trujillo. He had been near to death from tropical fever, an affliction which laid low many settlers in that unhealthy spot. As strength returned, he gave thanks to the Blessed Virgin for saving him to continue his conquests. Then, in his weakness, his plans were given a staggering blow by a letter which arrived by ship from Cuba. It was from one of his officers in Mexico, who had been driven out by intriguing enemies of the conqueror. This man had sent a letter to Trujillo, hoping to reach the lost Cortés. After reading it, Cortés shut himself up in his hut and the vecinos were startled to hear his sobs and groans. When he had recovered from the shock of bad news, the commander sent word to all his captains to assemble and discuss the alarming situation in Mexico.

For two years Cortés and his stout veterans had been absent, lost in the wilderness for all Mexico knew. Enemies took advantage of his absence to spread the rumor that the great Malinche and all his men were dead. Rapacious men, each out for himself, involved the affairs of Mexico in dangerous intrigues and quarrels. Encomiendas belonging to the captains were seized and their wives forced to marry the usurpers. Even the conqueror's own houses and possessions in the capital were taken. Albornoz and Estrada had schemes of their own, but they were outdone in villainy by the two men Cortés had sent to keep an eye on his officials.

The captains were all for embarking at once to punish the traitors and recover their lands, but Cortés demurred. He vacillated and delayed, hoping somehow to continue his ambitious schemes in Honduras. First he agreed to march overland with his troops, then changed his mind and told the soldiers they might go overland while he returned by sea. Three times he set sail from Trujillo and each time had to return because of storms or accidents. He chose to regard these happenings as a sign from heaven that he was to remain in Honduras.

Finally Cortés sent most of his soldiers overland by way of Guatemala, while he once more set out by sea. The soldiers were overjoyed to escape from two years of hardship to the civilized comforts of Mexico.

Before venturing, himself, into the rebellious capital, Cortés sent a messenger to land secretly on the coast and take letters to trusted friends in Mexico City. The mission was carried out successfully, and in the capital Cortés' friends were called to a secret meeting in the Franciscan monastery. So overjoyed were these men to know that their leader was alive and on his way, that they danced about, shouting and embracing each other, even the sober friars joining in. Cortés' impending arrival was announced, causing dismay among the usurpers in office. Some of the plotters scurried into hiding, while others hastened to set their affairs in order, and Cortés' friends clashed with rival factions in street battles.

No sooner had Cortés landed at Vera Cruz than the news spread like wildfire that Malinche was alive. On the journey to the capital rejoicing Spaniards and weeping Indians came to meet him and kiss his hands. To the Indians, the return of Malinche gave them hope that they would be relieved of the abuses inflicted on them by other Spaniards. The capital, too, gave him an ovation, while envy and hatred were concealed under a show of loyalty.

Before plunging into the intrigues of Mexico the weary conqueror retreated for prayer and meditation to the Franciscan monastery. He had need to make his peace with God and gain strength for the bitter struggle with his enemies.

Men whom he had overruled and others who hated him for his success laid serious charges against Cortés before the Council of the Indies. A royal official was sent to Mexico to investigate his administration. When this man died of some tropical ailment soon after his arrival, enemies added the accusation of poisoning to other charges against the conqueror.

In 1528 Cortés went to Spain to present his case in person to the King. From Palos to Toledo, where the Emperor Charles was in residence, Cortés marched with splendid display, cheered as a hero by throngs of excited people. They stared in wonder at the Indian chiefs in colorful costumes and headdresses; at the wild animals, such as jaguars, and the brilliant-feathered birds Cortés had brought as exhibits.

At Court, honored by the Emperor Charles, and surrounded with the adulation of courtiers, Cortés basked in the sun of royal favor. For his King he brought exquisite feather tapestries as well as carved jade and beautiful things of wrought gold. He scattered rich gifts also among powerful friends and won an aristocratic wife, Doña Juana de Zuñiga.

The Emperor rewarded him with the large estates he asked for, the title of Marqués del Valle, and the position of Governor-general. This did not mean much, however, since a Real Audiencia and a Viceroy were sent to govern Nueva

España. Charles was suspicious of a conqueror who followed his own will and flouted authority so ruthlessly as Cortés had done.

After returning to Mexico Hernán Cortés built a palace for himself and his family at Cuernavaca and occupied himself in developing his lands. He introduced cattle and sheep, sugar cane, wheat and silkworm culture. Such activities could not satisfy him, for he was a conqueror without a job and a restless man. His wealth was spent in futile expeditions, ending in failure, to find the Spice Islands or explore the peninsula of Baja California. This land, recently discovered, was thought by the Spaniards to be an island.

The star of Hernán Cortés was waning, while that of Francisco Pizarro, conqueror of golden Peru, was rising to take the attention of the Emperor Charles.

CHAPTER 8

PEDRO DE ALVARADO IN GUATEMALA

AFTER THE FALL of Tenochtitlán, Cortés' favorite captain was one of the men most in need of an opportunity to satisfy his ambition for personal success. During the two years of hardship and battle ending in glorious conquest, Pedro de Alvarado had shown his distinctive qualities, good and bad. He had been one of the best soldiers among Cortés' companions, brave and impetuous. His ruthless cruelty and impatience had been revealed in the massacre of the people during the feast of Tezcatlipoca. Before that happened the Aztecs had so admired the handsome, winning captain with reddish hair and beard that they gave him the reverential name of Tonatiuh, the sun.

Cortés recognized the insatiable ambition of his friend, so gave him a task in which he might win fame for himself far from his commander's own field of operations. It may be that scouts of the Cakchiquel nation had come to Mexico to see what was happening and to bring gifts to the great Malinche, or it may be that strong Indian kingdoms had been reported by chiefs of southern Mexico who traded with them.

In December, 1523, bright-haired Tonatiuh marched out to

127

conquest with a goodly company of cavalry and foot soldiers, as well as hundreds of Tlascalan and Mexican auxiliaries. They proceeded southward through the civilized country of the Zapotecs and Mixtecs, who were being won to submission. The lush tropical lowlands of Tehuantepec Isthmus were crossed and then the expedition followed the narrow coastal plain to the river Suchiate, part of the boundary between Mexico and Guatemala.

When they had maneuvered horses and baggage across this stream they turned inland over the sloping fertile land below the mountains. It was a hot country of luxuriant woodlands and cacao plantations with many Indian villages. Warlike people hindered their progress at times but Alvarado gave them a lesson in the power of Spanish arms and marched on.

The mountains they must penetrate to reach the highland kingdoms rose abruptly from the lower slopes, fold upon fold, topped by the sharp cones of volcanoes. Horsemen and foot soldiers followed the Indian trail into deep wooded gorges, their precipitous sides hung with rich tropical vegetation. Wilderness did not dismay these hardened veterans, but they had never met such difficulties for horses and armor as they found along the rough, rock-strewn track winding around these mountainsides. Horses stumbled and fell and had to be pulled along over rocks to save them from falling into the abyss.

High in the pass they found the bodies of a woman and a dog laid across the trail—a sign of defiance, Alvarado was told by his Indian guides. The highland lords knew of the invaders and gave them warning to keep out. Mountains rose steeply from the narrow pass and over them loomed the vast bulk of Santa Maria volcano.

When they reached the crest Alvarado looked down over a

jumble of hills and ravines to see the feathered crests and painted shields of warriors waiting for him.

In the rugged highlands of Guatemala the Spaniards were up against different people from those subdued in Mexico. The most powerful tribes—Quichés, Cakchiquels, Tzutuhils—were people of Mayan stock who had lived for centuries in this mountain country of ranges, plains and mesas, broken by deep barrancas or ravines. Some of the migrants from the cities of the Maya Old Empire may have joined them when those cities were deserted. Archeologists believe that there was a migration into this region of Nahua-speaking tribes from Mexico about the twelfth century of the christian era. They were completely amalgamated with the mountain people by the time the Spaniards arrived.

The tribes of Mayan stock were a semi-civilized people. They used a calendar similar to that of the Mayas and kept records in hieroglyphic characters. They worshipped many gods whose diviner priests had great influence on the people. The women were expert in spinning, weaving and dyeing of cotton for their garments—a skill their descendants have never lost. These Indian highlanders were sturdy, independent people, mountaineers bred to fighting by generations of intertribal warfare. Their cities were fortresses perched like eagles' nests on inaccessible crags or hills. The warriors who waited for Alvarado's army were men of the Quiché nation, at that time the most powerful of the kingdoms.

Skirmishing with Indians who attacked them on the trail, Alvarado cautiously made his entrada into the lofty cold country of the Quichés, 8000 feet in altitude at the first town they came to. He was glad to see the broad plain below the town where he could maneuver his cavalry to attack the host that awaited the invaders. Weary as they were, Alvarado did not hesitate, but led his horsemen and soldiers pell mell into the Indian ranks. At first they were overwhelmed by the sheer mass of fierce fighters attacking with arrows and lances. Gradually the Spanish weapons, which seemed like thunder and lightning, and the terrible animals, had their usual stunning effect. The Indians fell back to the foot of some hills, the Spaniards at their heels. Alvarado used his favorite strategy, pretending to retreat so that the Indians were drawn out to the open plain where the horses could gallop. Suddenly the little army turned and fell upon the advancing warriors, mowing them down by the hundreds.

The Quichés retreated to their stronghold, Gumarkaaj, while the Spaniards nursed their wounds in the abandoned town of Xelahuh. It was christened Quezaltenango by Alvarado's Mexican warriors. Many place names of the Guatemalan highlands are Mexican, the Spaniards having replaced the old Mayan names with those given by their Nahua-speaking auxiliaries. Gumarkaaj they named Tecpán-Utatlán, tecpán meaning residence of the king. The Cakchiquel capital, Iximché, was called Tecpán-Quahtemallán and the lake citadel of the Tzutuhils, Tecpán-Atitlán.

Tecúm-Umán, king of the Quichés, called on all his chiefs and their armies to come to the defence of the kingdom, while bribes brought him the temporary support of some other tribes. An army of seventy thousand fanatical warriors marched out to meet the Spaniards on the plain, braving the horrifying weapons and animals in their determination to free their land from the invaders.

At the head of his hosts, says the Indian legend, marched Tecúm-Umán while over his head soared his nahual or familiar spirit, an enormous quetzal bird of brilliant green plumage.

Bitter indeed was that conflict and terrible the slaughter as masses of fierce warriors leaped on the Spaniards, clinging to the manes and tails of the horses until Spanish lances and iron hoofs crushed them. Tonatiuh the terrible Spaniard and Tecúm-Umán were locked in hand-to-hand combat. The king was run through by Alvarado's sword, just as the spirit bird fell wounded from the sky.

With their king gone and thousands of warriors dead, the Quichés fell back to their citadel. Their unflinching courage and great army had failed but they still had their fortress. Utatlán or Gumarkaaj was built on top of a steep-sided mesa entirely surrounded by deep barrancas. The only access was by steps cut in the rock sides and by a narrow stone causeway across the ravine.

The Quiché nobles rallied around Tecúm-Umán's successor while they plotted to destroy the Spaniards by guile. They would sue for peace, inviting Alvarado to Utatlán to receive their submission. Then they would set fire to the city, break down the causeway and kill the invaders like rats in a trap. Firewood was stored in the houses and their women and children sent to the mountains before the messengers went to Alvarado.

Obsequious nobles met the conqueror as he made an impressive entry into the citadel, riding across the causeway at the head of his cavalry, followed by foot soldiers and Mexicans. They passed through steep, winding streets, so narrow that two horsemen could not ride abreast, between the thatched adobe huts of commoners and the stone palaces of the nobility. Alvarado's strategic eye took in at once the dangers of their situation. He wrote Cortés afterwards that the place was more like a robbers' stronghold than a city. He observed that the causeway had been partly broken and he realized that horses and men would be helplessly trapped in the restricted alleys in case of attack.

Refusing the chiefs' offer of food, Alvarado told them that his horses were sacred animals unused to being shut up. He must return at once to make camp on the plateau so the horses could move about and find grass for fodder. Back went the whole Spanish procession to the deep disappointment of the plotting chiefs.

They were so foolish as to be lured by Alvarado's gifts and fair words to visit him in the camp. Once in his power the conqueror put them in chains and dragged from them by torture a confession of the plot. Reporting to Cortés by letter, Alvarado said: "And seeing that by fire and sword I might bring these people to the service of His Majesty I burnt them and sent to burn their town and destroy it." Thus Alvarado reveals his ruthless spirit and the typical attitude, that resistance to the conquerors was treason against the King of Spain, who claimed all these natives as his subjects by royal decree. For their courageous defence of their land the Quiché chiefs were burned alive and their citadel reduced to heaps of stones.

The disorganized Quichés continued guerrilla fighting without the aid of other tribes. The Cakchiquel king, to his own undoing, decided to make friends with these awe-inspiring strangers. Propitiatory messengers had visited Alvarado, and at his request a troop of Cakchiquel warriors were sent to aid him against the Quichés. Thus the proud Quichés were reduced to submission. Alvarado branded his captives, like cattle, with a hot iron and kept them to be sold as slaves to add profit to his enterprise. Even Cortés was guilty of this cruel practice. The King's mark was branded on Indian faces, so that if they escaped from their masters they would be known as slaves.

After building a fort near ruined Utatlán, called Santa Cruz Quiché, the conquerors marched on to visit the king of the Cakchiquel nation in his capital, Iximché. This was the place called by the Mexicans Tecpán-Quahtemallán, the origin of the name given by the Spaniards to the whole province, Guatemala.

Iximché was situated in a high valley surrounded by irregular pine-clad mountain ridges. Alvarado observed that the valley, like the Quiché country, was covered with cornfields. Patches of maize probably patterned the steep hill slopes as they do today.

The king received Alvarado with many attentions, housing him and his officers in one of the stone palaces. The Cakchiquels thought themselves lucky to have these godlike strangers for allies in their wars, but they soon learned their mistake.

After the conquest Cakchiquel priests wrote in their hieroglyphic characters a chronicle of their people in which they described the Spanish invasion and related the dolorous downfall of their nation. The manuscript was found during the nineteenth century in an old monastery of Guatemala and has been translated by various scholars.

"Good was the heart of Tonatiuh when he entered the city with the chiefs," says the chronicle. "Thus did the Castilians enter of yore, oh, my children; but it was a fearful thing when they entered; their faces were strange and the chiefs took them to be gods."

The Cakchiquels were at war with the Tzutuhils of Lake Atitlán and asked the Spaniards to aid them. Alvarado was more than pleased to make his next conquest with the help of the natives. If these valiant highland tribes had united, sheer numbers might have driven the Spaniards from the country. They did not understand this until too late, when the invaders were firmly entrenched. Age-old hatreds led some tribes to join the Spaniards, thus bringing about the subjection of their race.

Even rough Spanish soldiers must have been impressed when they looked down from the cliffs on Lake Atitlán, a gleaming jewel set in a bowl of mountains and somber volcanoes. Indian towns dotted the shores, and fortified crags, jutting into the lake, protected the strong city of the Tzutuhils at the foot of the volcano San Pedro. Never yet had this citadel been taken. The farming people lived on the rich volcanic land where the village of Santiago Atitlán stands today. The Tzutuhils were a prosperous nation, ruling a fertile territory cultivated in corn, cotton and cacao. Trade around the lake was carried on by dugout canoes.

To reach the shore the Spaniards, cumbered with their armor, had to scramble down from a volcanic ridge which descended precipitously to a narrow piece of flat land. There the Tzutuhil army awaited them. Crossbow and musket fire did their deadly work among the inexperienced Indians, so that the Tzutuhils fled for their fortress, pursued by the Spaniards and by Cakchiquels in a fleet of canoes. The hill was taken in hand-to-hand battle, after which the terrified people abandoned their strong city on the slopes. The Tzutuhils submitted to Spanish rule, remaining peaceful in the next two years when other tribes revolted.

The fame of godlike Tonatiuh was great among the Cakchiquels, but he soon revealed his true character to the people with whom he should have cemented friendship. Cortés had given Alvarado strict instructions to treat the natives well and make alliances with them. Such skillful strategy was not in the nature of this impatient and avaricious man. Gold he must have and he had seen little of it in this bleak country. He demanded that the chiefs bring him all they had, jars full of gold, even their gold drinking cups and crowns.

Says the chronicle: "Tonatiuh became angry and said to the chiefs, 'Why have you not given me the metal? If you do not bring me the precious metal in all your towns, choose then, for I shall burn you alive and hang you.' Then Tonatiuh cut from three of them the gold ornaments they wore in their ears. The chiefs suffered keenly from this violence and wept before him. But Tonatiuh was not troubled and said, 'I tell you that I want the gold here in five days. Woe to you if you do not give it. I know my heart.'"

While the gathering of treasured ancestral ornaments and raw gold was carried on by the resentful people a priest of their gods was seized with a vision. "I am the lightning, I will destroy the Castilians," chanted the Priest of the Demons to the chiefs. "I will destroy them by fire. When I beat the drum let the chiefs come forth and go to the other bank of the river."

In their despair the people listened to the Priest of the Demons. With chants and throbbing drums they deserted Iximché on the appointed day, while Alvarado was away on a raiding expedition. Across the river they waited for the fire of heaven to strike the hated invaders. Instead, fire from Spanish muskets laid them low when Alvarado's returning army fell upon the rebellious people. After fierce battles they fled to the mountains for safety, deserting forever their city of Iximché. Henceforth the Cakchiquels were bitter enemies of the Castilians. Stones from their empty palaces were used by the Spaniards in building their settlement.

During his first adventurous year Pedro de Alvarado founded

this settlement of huts and a fort near Iximché, christening it Santiago in honor of the Spaniards' saint of victory. The usual *regidores* and *alcaldes* were elected and for a short time this crude village was the Spanish headquarters in Guatemala. Alvarado's troops, with Mexican and Guatemalan warriors, continued their expeditions. More fortified mountain eyries were captured and their people enslaved. Coastal tribes were fought as the invaders explored the slopes below the mountains.

Southward they marched into the land of Cuscatlán (El Salvador) meeting fierce resistance from some tribes while others took refuge in remote mountains. It is believed that at this time Alvarado built a fort in Cuscatlán named San Salvador, on the site of the modern capital of El Salvador.

Bogged down by mud, cold and heavy downpours of the rainy season, in July and August, Alvarado retired to Santiago to await better weather. He wrote Cortés full accounts of the land and the exploits of the conquering army. They were in the wildest country they had ever seen, he wrote, among the most warlike people. He told of a terrifying volcano that spewed incandescent rocks from its throat as big as a house, rocks that made living flame of the mountainside when they fell. Another volcano sent a towering column of smoke into the sky. Sulphurous rivers flowed down these mountains, one so hot the men could not enter the waters, but it flowed into a cold river to make a temperate stream.

Indians told him of great countries inland, of cities of stone and mortar. (Perhaps they were those of Yucatán or some of the ruined Mayan cities.) The land was so great and thickly populated that much time was needed to conquer it. Alvarado begged Cortés to order a procession of all the friars and priests of Mexico City to ask God's aid for the task. They were so far away that if God did not help them, no one else could.

Alvarado was no administrator. He was impatient with the quarrels of the town officials and men who had received allotments of land and Indians. Cooped up in this wilderness he was not receiving the praise he wanted for his exploits, and was convinced that Cortés was not giving him full credit in his letters to the King. Then, in 1526, he received word from his commander from Honduras.

Cortés was then planning to accompany his army overland to Mexico and wrote that he would visit Guatemala to see what Alvarado had accomplished. This did not please the conqueror of Guatemala. He did not want Cortés to see the miserable settlement of Santiago, or to hear the complaints of soldiers and the tale of abuses inflicted upon the natives. Taking a troop of soldiers, Alvarado set off through Cuscatlán to meet his commander. As we know, Cortés was not with his army. Alvarado met the soldiers in the wilderness and they all marched back to Guatemala together. The province, they found, had flamed into rebellion.

Pedro's brother, Gonzalo, left in charge of the settlement, had been even more cruel and greedy than the conqueror. Indians were driven to wash the gravel of river beds and to dig mines in search of gold. Two hundred Cakchiquel children, nine and ten years of age, were forced by their masters to deliver, each one, a reed full of gold the size of a little finger every day. The threat of being sold into slavery was held over the poor little creatures if they did not deliver the required amount. Quichés and Cakchiquels united with other tribes in a concerted effort to drive these cruel masters from the country.

Every soldier was needed for the punitive expeditions with which Alvarado tried to crush the rebellious natives. With the fury of desperation they fought, preferring death to slavery.

They had no chance of success against Spanish arms, but they would not submit. No sooner was one uprising settled than another tribe attacked the Spaniards.

For two years Pedro de Alvarado had marched and fought and squeezed gold from the Indians without receiving from the King the reward he considered his due. Now he would wait no longer, although it was the part of wisdom to consolidate Spanish control in the province. Against the will of his soldiers and officers he turned over to his lieutenants the task of pacifying the natives and made off to Mexico with Cortés' soldiers. Two gentlemen, Portocarrero and Carrillo, were appointed alcaldes to govern in his absence.

Having made an ostentatious entry into Mexico City, Alvarado was received with friendship by Cortés, who was trying to regain control of the government after his return from Honduras. Jorge de Alvarado was appointed to govern Guatemala while Don Pedro paid a visit to Spain. He sailed from Vera Cruz in February, 1527.

Indian wars, dissension and discontent beset the forlorn colony Jorge de Alvarado found in Guatemala. He and the officers of the *cabildo,* or city council, immediately set about finding a good site for the capital of the new kingdom. They chose the peaceful valley of Almolonga, Place of Gushing Waters, at the foot of the volcanoes Agua and Fuego. It was a valley of delightful, mild climate and fertile soil, well watered by streams from the mountains. Some of the men were worried about the volcanoes, but they were quiescent at that time and seemed harmless.

On the slopes of the Volcán de Agua the city was founded with solemn ceremonies on November 22, 1527. It was given the resounding title of Muy Leal y Noble Ciudad de Santiago de los Caballeros de Guatemala. Some years later the Emperor

Charles gave the city its coat of arms, Santiago on his white horse above three pointed volcanoes.

Streets and plots were laid out on the rectangular pattern of the Spanish town around a central plaza. There land was alloted for a church, a jail and a building for the cabildo. At the highest point of the town it was planned to build the governor's palace. The vecinos set to work with a will directing Indian laborers in the building of cane and mud huts with thatched roofs. By the time Alvarado returned to his "city" most of the huts were replaced by stone buildings and Santiago de los Caballeros was a well-established Spanish town.

Encomiendas of land and the services of Indians living thereon were assigned by Jorge de Alvarado to the gentlemen and captains of the conquest. The best lands had river frontage for crops, pasture land for cattle and a plot of woodland for timber. In this pleasant, peaceful spot, with Indian farmers to cultivate the land, the vecinos soon settled down to civilized life. The valley of Almolonga looked like a prosperous farming community under the serene bright sky, watched over by the two beautiful volcanoes.

There was no harmony in the city of Santiago, however. Most of the vecinos were greedy for gold and land, or ambitious for profit from municipal offices. Jorge de Alvarado was accused of giving the best lands to his favorites and of tucking away more than his share of gold obtained from the mines. Soon officials of the cabildo were sending letters to the Audiencia in Mexico City, complaining of their governor's actions. There were also Indian uprisings to contend with as the natives rebelled against hard work in fields and mines.

Meanwhile Pedro de Alvarado, who should have been governing his province, was enjoying himself in Spain. His arrival had not been happy, for enemies had reached Spain before him to present charges against him before the Council of the Indies. He was accused of atrocities against the natives and, worse, of holding for himself some of the gold due the King.

Accusations only roused the fighting spirit of this arrogant cavalier. Alvarado applied all his skill and charm of personality to win friends in high places. Francisco de los Cobos, secretary of the Council of the Indies, became his supporter, and the handsome hidalgo further entrenched himself by winning the hand of Francisca de la Cueva, niece of the powerful Duke of Albuquerque. Since Alvarado had such backing, Charles V received him with high praise, honoring him with the coveted Cross of the Order of Santiago. The conqueror was appointed Adelantado, Captain-general and Governor of Guatemala. Instead of hastening back to take over his governorship, he lingered with his bride to enjoy his distinction and the luxuries of court life.

When he arrived at Vera Cruz in July, 1528, he came ashore with his aristocratic bride, a splendid suite and a distinguished ecclesiastic to preside over the religious life of Santiago. Francisco Marroquin was to be the first bishop of Guatemala and a power for good in that turbulent province. Trouble immediately darkened the bright picture of Alvarado's future. His bride died of tropical fever before they reached Mexico City, and there Alvarado was brought to trial by the Audiencia.

The Audiencia was a governing council and high court appointed by the King to sit in every capital of colonial government as his representative. It was the monarch's scheme for preventing governors from achieving too much power and independence. The Audiencia had great power under the King's orders. Any official could be brought to trial before this court.

This time there were no powerful friends to save Alvarado from the consequences of his high-handed actions in Guatemala. Cortés, his commander and friend, had gone to Spain to defend himself from enemies and to present his own case before the sovereign. Alvarado was tried on many charges, among them concealment of the King's treasure, neglect of his government, abuse of the natives. He fought the case with all the energy and skill at his command and emerged triumphant once more.

Hastening back to Guatemala, in 1530, the Adelantado found his capital seething with intrigues and controversies. His brother, Jorge, had been dismissed from office by the *Visitador,* or judge, sent by the Audiencia to investigate his administration. This Visitador, Orduña, had rescinded the grants of land made by Jorge de Alvarado and redistributed the encomiendas to his friends. The encomenderos clamored for their lands, the vecinos hated Orduña, but wanted none of the Alvarados. Some of the councillors hoped to prevent Don Pedro, their legal governor, from ever ruling again.

It was, then, a very hostile cabildo which received from their arrogant governor the announcement that he had the royal commission to rule as Adelantado and Captain-general. Sullenly the councillors kissed the document and placed it on their heads, the usual token of submission to the King's will. Then Alvarado dismissed the whole quarrelsome lot and appointed new councillors. For a time he applied his energies to bringing order into the distracted province and imposed his imperious will on all the factions. During his absence Pedrarias, from Nicaragua, had sent a troop of soldiers into Cuscatlán to claim that province for his domain. Guatemalans had chased them back, but now Alvarado made expeditions to establish forts and pacify the natives, so that the territory could be held for Guatemala.

The Adelantado had been active enough since his return, but

governing could not satisfy his restless spirit. He had won favor with the King by proposing to make a voyage in search of the Spice Islands. Spain was then trying to edge in on the Portuguese empire in the Pacific, hoping to win some of the wealth of spices and other luxuries on which Portugal had a monopoly. All the money Alvarado could lay hands on was poured into the enterprise of building and equipping ships at a little port on the Pacific coast of Guatemala. His five hundred Indian slaves were driven to wash gold from the rivers on his lands. Discontented men of Guatemala were roused to go off on new adventures.

Just when everything was ready for departure the Spanish world was thrown into a new fever of excitement by the conquest of Peru. The wonders of the Inca Empire were on every tongue and every restless adventurer wanted to join the new "gold rush." Pedro de Alvarado longed for a share in such a rich conquest. He wanted to take his fleet to Peru instead of to the Spice Islands, but both the King and the Audiencia forbade it.

Nevertheless, as soon as he was safely at sea, Alvarado directed his ships southward to invade Ecuador. It was a terrible and disastrous adventure in which most of his men were lost and he was bribed to leave the country by Pizarro, who paid a large price for the ships in order to get rid of such a famous rival. Alvarado returned unabashed to Guatemala minus ships and men but rich in castellanos to repay him for what he had spent.

Once more the Adelantado's absence and the quarrels of ambitious men had disorganized the administration of Guatemala. Once more a judge was sent from Mexico to straighten out the government and investigate Alvarado's actions. The proud governor would not submit to the judge, and his affairs would not bear investigation. Just then an appeal from Honduras gave him an excuse to get away.

The Honduran settlements were in a turmoil owing to the conflicts among three men, each claiming the right to govern. The settlers begged the famous Adelantado to bring Honduras under the jurisdiction of Guatemala. Nothing loth, Alvarado went busily from place to place in the wilds of Honduras, settling controversies and making deals to insure his rule over the province. He founded San Pedro Sula in a fine fertile valley to be a way station on the trail between Guatemala and Puerto Caballos.

The settlers of Guatemala were isolated in their highlands. Goods and passengers from Spain had to reach them by the tremendously long, difficult journey from Vera Cruz, through Mexico and over the mountains to Santiago. If ships from Spain could unload at Puerto Caballos it would be much easier to keep the province supplied.

After thus strengthening and enlarging his domain, Alvarado sent a casual message to the outraged cabildo in Santiago that he was going to Spain. It was necessary to make his peace with the King for having disobeyed his orders in the costly voyage to Peru. He sailed forthwith from Puerto Caballos.

Maldonado, the judge sent from Mexico, was a conscientious, businesslike man. Under his firm rule Guatemala settled down to orderly life. In Santiago de los Caballeros gentlemen who prospered from their haciendas and mines had good stone houses with furnishings from Spain. The pioneer settlement had become a town of Spanish architecture, with several stone churches and solid buildings with arcades and balconies surrounding the plaza. High on the slope of the volcano stood the two-story palace of the Captain-general. Alvarado had managed, in his brief periods of residence, to make it a home worthy of the Governor. Its large stone rooms were rich with tapestries, velvet hangings and carved furniture from Spain.

Among the officials of the cabildo were men busy with intrigues, hoping to take over the government when Maldonado departed. They fully expected that the Adelantado would be dismissed in disgrace, as Maldonado had brought judgment against him for mismanagement and confiscated his lands.

On a September day in 1539 these plotting councillors were startled to receive a letter from the absent Adelantado, announcing his arrival at Puerto Caballos. It was not the letter of a man under a cloud for his misdeeds, but rather that of a triumphant and successful lord. He announced that he came with a large company and a new wife, Doña Beatriz de la Cueva, sister of Francisca who died at Vera Cruz. So high in favor was Alvarado that King Charles himself had obtained a dispensation from the Pope permitting him to marry his sister-in-law. Doña Beatriz had with her twenty maids of honor of noble family; merchandise, wrote Alvarado, that he was sure would soon be off his hands. He ordered the cabildo to prepare a reception for the company and to send many Indian carriers for the trip to the capital.

The aristocratic Spanish ladies must have found the rough trip up the mountains a wild experience, but they took such things in their stride in the sixteenth century. Horses and mules had been brought in the ships for the service of the ladies, the Adelantado and his gentlemen. Accompanied by marching soldiers and Indian carriers loaded with baggage, the Governor's court proceeded through many weary days of travel to Guatemala.

Pealing church bells and shouts of the inhabitants welcomed

the Adelantado and his noble company. The picturesque governor was popular with the common citizens and they were overjoyed to have the splendor of Spain come to their town with haughty Doña Beatriz and her entourage of ladies.

Alvarado's first act was to make clear to the cabildo who was master. Well he knew their disappointment over his success and he took pleasure in presenting a royal cedula from the King confirming him as governor for the next seven years. Slyly he watched the men's faces, noting which councillors protested that he could not govern while under trial. Then he produced another cedula in which the King ordered Maldonado, the judge, to dismiss the charges against the Adelantado and to release his lands. Alvarado knew, now, who were his enemies. He embraced them all with expressions of friendship, while they hid their chagrin under respectful attention.

Santiago welcomed the Governor and his bride with days of fiesta. Spanish sports were staged in the plaza while Doña Beatriz and her ladies watched from balconies hung with silks and velvets. The crowning event was a tournament in which all the caballeros, beautifully mounted, in knightly armor, tilted with one another. Doña Leonor, the Governor's favorite child by the Tlascalan princess, was queen of the tournament. Masqueraders reveled in the streets by night, the common citizens were pleased spectators and had their share in the festivities. The Governor was his most winning self as, with his handsome bride, he received the aristocrats in the palace.

Despite ugly intrigues under the surface it seemed that Pedro de Alvarado was riding the crest of the wave, but he was not content. Once more he must go in search of the Spice Islands. The King had ordered him to make the expedition, in which Don Antonio de Mendoza, new Viceroy of Mexico, was to have a share. Alvarado put all his wealth and all he could borrow from friends into the building of thirteen ships, well equipped with soldiers and supplies.

If that impressive fleet had sailed out into the Pacific Alvarado might have added another exploit to his successes, but the tide of his good fortune was ebbing. The ships were anchored in a port of the province of Jalisco in Mexico while the commander went inland for a conference with Don Antonio de Mendoza. On his way back to the port the Governor of the province appealed to the famous soldier for aid in a great uprising of the Indians.

Always ready to fight Indians, Alvarado disembarked soldiers and horsemen for the assault on a mountain stronghold, Nochtistlán. The Indians were hidden in deep trenches on the mountainside from which they hurled arrows and great stones on the attacking Spaniards. Impatient to finish the task, Alvarado led the assault straight up the cliffs over holes and rocks and spiny cactus. Avalanches of boulders sent men and horses tumbling back down the slope in disorganized retreat.

Alvarado leaped from his horse, and had rallied the men for another attack, when a frightened scribe on a runaway horse bore down on him. The horse slipped on the rocks and fell, pinning Alvarado, in his heavy armor, beneath its body. Soldiers rushed to rescue him, but he was badly crushed. It was his last Indian battle. Broken and dying, he was carried on a shield to Guadalajara, not far away. When a captain asked where he felt the most pain, he muttered, "In my soul." His brilliant, restless life and great exploits were ended by a stupid accident in 1541

When the staggering news reached Santiago the city was overwhelmed and Doña Beatriz was inconsolable. She ordered the palace to be painted black inside and out and draped with black velvet. In a darkened room she wept and wailed. The people whispered that she uttered blasphemous reproaches against God for permitting the catastrophe.

Grief did not prevent Doña Beatriz from thinking of the future, however. Somber and haughty in black velvet she appeared before the bishop and city council, and forced them by her imperious will to elect her governor in Alvarado's place. Such a thing as a woman governor had never been heard of. Reluctantly the officials consented until they could appeal to a higher authority.

The first act of Doña Beatriz was to sign an order for the arrest of the men who had been plotting against Alvarado. She wrote on the document the simple signature, *La Sin Ventura,* the Hapless One. So, in history, has the only woman governor of Spanish America been known, La Sin Ventura.

In those early days of September, 1541, it seemed that the very heavens wept for the dead Governor. Torrents of rain descended night and day, thunderstorms darkened the sky and fierce lightning frightened the people. Roofs leaked and rivers of water ran in the streets.

On the night of September 10th, an earthquake added to the terrors of the storm, toppling walls of houses on the inhabitants, killing with falling roof tiles those who rushed into the streets. Suddenly the diapason of the storm was deepened by a terrifying roar. A solid wall of water rushed down on the town from the volcano Agua, carrying trees and boulders in its wake, filling the streets and lower floors of the houses with a raging flood. Terrified people caught in its tide were swept away and drowned. Doña Leonor was among these but she was caught in some bushes outside the town and rescued next day.

Doña Beatriz and her ladies fled to the chapel on the roof of the palace. La Sin Ventura ciung to the crucifix with her companions about her, begging God to save them. Some say that just then the neighboring volcano, Fuego, burst into eruption, lighting the darkness with a wild red glare. Horrified rescuers, struggling to reach the women, saw the walls of the chapel collapse. La Sin Ventura and her companions were buried in the ruins.

The town was swept clear of jealousies and intrigues by the catastrophe. It was a mass of fallen walls, mud and debris. The people declared that Doña Beatriz' blasphemy had brought the calamity upon them and they wanted to throw her body in the river. Bishop Marroquin prevented them and La Sin Ventura was buried in the cathedral, one of the few buildings that was intact. The ruins of Guatemala's first capital still stand on the slopes of the volcano, known as Ciudad Vieja.

Santiago de los Caballeros would be rebuilt on another site, to become the stately capital of the Kingdom of Guatemala. That kingdom, and the Viceroyalty of Nueva España, were, by 1541, organized Spanish provinces. Yucatán, by-passed in the tide of conquest, remained to be won before all Middle America became part of the Spanish Empire.

An epic period of great deeds came to an end. The vivid, lusty figures of the conquest were superseded by townsmen and landowners, governors and municipal officials. Pedro de Alvarado, the picturesque and reckless conquistador, was gone. Doña Marina, after her adventurous years, settled down in Mexico to finish her life as a pious, respected Spanish lady. Gonzalo de Sandoval died in Spain. Bernal Diaz del Castillo, the valiant soldier, spent his old age as a vecino of the rebuilt Santiago. There he looked back on the grand old days of adventure, hardship and glory and wrote his chronicle.

Speaking of Hernán Cortés, he says the conqueror was always the "gran señor" and the great captain. Although he had vast estates and the title of Marqués, he did not need a title. He was always known just as Cortés, like the great conquerors of the Old World. Hernán Cortés, the most worthy of honor among the Spanish conquistadores, died in Spain, his wealth spent in fruitless expeditions, his services forgotten by the monarch to whom he had given Nueva España.

CHAPTER 9

THE CONQUEST OF YUCATÁN

THE Land of the Pheasant and the Deer, as the Mayas called Yucatán, continued its native life unmolested, save for the landings of Hernandez de Córdoba and Juan de Grijalva, while adventurers rushed to Mexico and adjacent territory. The people farmed their lands and worshipped their gods while nobles and warriors involved rival clans in local wars. The once prosperous empire had become a poor land, harassed by disasters and wars. No glitter of gold, such as that of Mexico, lured Spaniards into the peninsula.

Yucatán was finally invaded by a man who had tried his luck in various Spanish settlements without winning glory. Francisco de Montejo was a man of no special ability, but of an envious disposition. He had come with Pedrarias to Darien, passed from there to Cuba and gone along on the voyage of Juan de Grijalva. He had been one of the band of captains who accompanied Hernán Cortés to Mexico. Cortés had sent him to Spain with the first letter to the King and the first gift of treasure. There he lingered, taking no part in the labors of conquest. When he visited Mexico after the kingdom had been won he was exceedingly jealous of Cortés' success and determined to try a conquest of his own. He remembered the prosperous towns he had seen on the coast of Yucatán.

In Spain he married a lady of wealth who was willing to help him in his ambition. She sold jewels and land to provide funds for an expedition, when the Emperor Charles gave Montejo permission to conquer Yucatán at his own expense.

With the title of Adelantado and Captain-general of Yucatán granted him for life, Francisco de Montejo left Spain in 1527, his ships loaded with supplies for settlement.

The explorers landed at the island of Cozumel where the peaceful people received them kindly. Moving over to the mainland, the commander tried to settle in a swampy region which was disastrous to the men's health. Francisco de Montejo then marched inland, searching for good towns such as he had seen on the voyage with Grijalva. He was, however, on the wrong side of the peninsula for those. At first the natives were so terrified by the weapons and horses that they were submissive. So impressed were they by the wonderful animals that they placed dugout canoes along the roads and filled them with thousands of jugs of water for drinking troughs. These attentive natives soon gave way to hostile warriors who drove the invaders back to the coast. Montejo tried another landing on the east coast of Yucatán but was driven to retreat by the fierce warriors of Chetumal.

For the time being the conquest of this rough, unpromising land was given up. Francisco de Montejo went to Mexico and obtained the governorship of the province of Tabasco, next door to Yucatán. There another expedition was prepared.

This time the would-be conqueror landed on the west coast and made his way to the ruins of Chichén Itzá. The stately city of temples had long been deserted, although pilgrims still came to make offerings to the Rain God at the Sacred Well.

The inhabitants found by the Spaniards lived in a village on the outskirts. It was a hot, dry, scrubby land around the ruins, the territory between cornfields covered by tall bush, thick and thorny. The trails were rocky footpaths, cut through the brush, made for pedestrians and very difficult for men on horseback.

Montejo set up his headquarters among the ruins and proceeded to allot adjacent lands and their inhabitants to his soldiers. One wily chief took advantage of the Spaniards' cry for gold to tell them that across the peninsula they would find mines. Thus the camp was weakened, as a large number of soldiers set off on a fruitless search which cost them many lives. The survivors took canoes in the Bay of Chetumal and followed the coast to Honduras.

Montejo's soldiers were the worst kind of Spaniards, brutal and cantankerous. They so abused the natives, who were forced to provide food from their fields of corn, beans and chili, that soon the whole countryside was in revolt. The Spaniards were hemmed in among the great mounds on which the temples stood by bands of savage warriors.

It is believed that the Spaniards had their camp in the vast plaza between the tall round temple called the Caracol and the cluster of beautiful buildings set on enormous terraced platforms which they named Las Monjas. They concluded that the buildings had been a nunnery because they found so many stone metates, or grinding stones. Only a large company would have needed so much equipment for cooking, they thought. It is more likely that the buildings were palaces and dwellings of priests who studied the stars in the round astronomical observatory.

The Spaniards could defend themselves with muskets and crossbows in the shelter of the huge grass-grown mounds surrounding their camp, but they were soon desperate for food and water. Howling Indians lurked in the forest all about, sending showers of arrows into the camp, pouncing on the men when they made sallies in search of food.

Montejo was in the habit of calling his men to Mass every day by the ringing of a small church bell. The besiegers came to recognize this ringing as a sign that the Spaniards were occupied and would not be coming out on forays. Montejo realized that and traded on it when the men decided on a desperate attempt to escape. Before they left, in the middle of the night, a dog was tied to the church bell, just out of reach of a piece of bread. Every jump he made to reach the food set the bell to ringing. Cautiously the Spaniards crept along the forest trails in the darkness while the tolling bell protected them.

Before long the Indians became curious about the continuous tolling. Scouts crept in between the mounds and found the camp deserted, with the poor dog still jumping for his piece of bread. At once all the warriors went in full cry after the Spaniards. They attacked from every side as the weary soldiers struggled along through thorny thickets and over rough trails. At last, more dead than alive, they reached a friendly coast town and gradually drifted back to Mexico.

Francisco de Montejo did not have the makings of a conqueror and he was through with inhospitable Yucatán. He was governor of Honduras for a few years while his son, Francisco de Montejo, the Younger, took over his father's rights and completed the conquest of Yucatán in 1540.

His expedition had little trouble with the coast towns of Champoton and Campeche where the people were used to the Spaniards. There Montejo lingered, making forays into the hostile country. Finally they marched inland, meeting the most stubborn resistance as they battled on over rocky ridges and through narrow trails in the bush. Strong palisades of logs had been built across trails and these had to be torn down while Indians attacked them savagely from the forest. Wells were few in that land of subterranean rivers, and those the Spaniards found were filled with stones and dirt by their enemies. Beset with hunger, thirst and heat, the invaders fought their way on to the town of Tiho beyond Chichén Itzá.

Tiho had been a beautiful city in the past, but its terraces and temples were ruins, overgrown with vegetation. The inhabitants lived in a village on the outskirts, as at Chichén Itzá. Skirmishing with these people, Montejo led his men into the grass-grown plazas and made his camp on one of the high temple mounds.

After a few days the invaders were alarmed to see a great company of warriors approaching, their feather headdresses, colored mantles and shields brilliant in the sunshine. They were escorting their chief who reclined in a handsome litter. He was Tutul Xiu, lord of the old, powerful Xiu clan.

This time it was a visit of peace. Tutul Xiu knew enough of Spanish success in Mexico to realize that his people could not hope to conquer the white men and he decided to make an alliance with them. He would then have their aid against his implacable enemy, Nachi Cocom, lord of the Cocom clan.

The Xiu ruler descended from his litter to speak with Montejo, while his warriors laid their shields and weapons at the feet of the white lord and bowed themselves in submission. Tutul Xiu offered the allegiance of all his people, the most powerful in Yucatán, to the King of Spain, and promised to urge other chiefs to submit.

With such a strong ally to aid in subduing the country, Francisco de Montejo, the Younger, set about founding his capital.

On January 6, 1541, the conquerors gathered for the ceremonies. They named the future city Mérida because the empty palaces and temples reminded them of the massive Roman ruins at the Spanish town of Mérida. Streets were laid out and thatched huts built among the temple mounds. Later on, the stones of Mayan buildings went into the construction of cathedral, monasteries and governor's palace, as Mérida became a Spanish city.

These first Spanish settlers in Yucatán were cruel conquerors who made up for their disappointment over the lack of gold by demanding heavy tribute from Indian towns. The farming people were driven to hard labor in the fields of their encomiendas. The temples of the gods were broken down and the people punished for worshipping at the ancient shrines. Nachi Cocom, who had never submitted, gathered all the rebellious clans to make an end of the invaders. Thousands of warriors swarmed into the village of Mérida. The Spaniards had retreated to one of the highest temple mounds with cavalry and musketeers ranged at the foot. All day the battle raged with unremitting fury, but in the end the Indian spirit was broken and they fled. It was the last attempt of the Yucatecans to save their land.

Within a few years the conquerors had trampled over the northern part of the peninsula, the most populated section, subduing the people, founding towns and quarreling over allotments of land. Spanish architecture and Spanish government were imposed on the old towns of Champoton and Campeche. With plenty of native labor at hand it did not take long to raze the temples and platforms of Tiho to make of Mérida a typical Spanish town. It lay on the flat plain within twenty-four miles of the coast. The Montejo family had a handsome mansion on the plaza, built around interior gardens. On its façade was a sculptured escutcheon depicting two Spanish knights with their mailed feet on the heads of kneeling Mayan natives. Gentlemen encomenderos and town officials had their stone houses with tiled roofs, great wooden entrance doors and tall windows protected by wrought-iron *rejas* or grilles. Within, the families spent most of their time in the cool roofed corridors around airy garden patios. Before the end of the sixteenth century the cathedral of yellow stone on the plaza was finished. In colonial Yucatán, little Mérida, the capital, was the center of Spanish civilization and sociability.

Soon after the founding of Mérida, Franciscan friars came to Yucatán to undertake the religious teaching of the natives. The encomenderos had no concern for the conversion of the Indians alloted to them. They were simply creatures destined to serve their masters and to labor in the fields. These masters were not anxious to have their human beasts of burden taught and did not welcome the friars.

The humble farming folk of Yucatán were accustomed to supporting their nobility by work in the fields and at crafts, and by paying tribute to local chieftains. But never had they experienced such harsh driving or such heavy demands for tribute as the Spaniards inflicted on them. Frequently they revolted. Some fled to the forests to exist in misery, but most of them fell into a state of sullen acquiescence.

At first the coming of the friars only added to the suffering of the natives. The missionaries were good men who honestly thought they were saving souls by the fanatical zeal with which they tried to stamp out idolatry. Images were smashed, temples torn down, severe punishments were inflicted on the people who clung so stubbornly to their intimate deities of earth, sky and rain on whom they and their ancestors had always relied.

Baptism they accepted, having a baptism ceremony in their own religion. When the natives had outwardly submitted to the new faith the friars undertook to protect their charges from the abuses of encomenderos and townsfolk. The controversial atmosphere of the colony increased as friars and gentlemen attacked each other. The Dominicans and other orders followed the Franciscans, and all built massive stone churches and monasteries, some erected on the platforms of ancient temples.

Outside the towns the friars gathered their flocks of rural Indians from their scattered habitations to live in villages, where they might more easily be instructed in Christianity and the Spanish language. Great fortresslike churches were built, raised on broad platforms of earth and stone like Mayan buildings of distinction. Lifted thus above the level the churches loomed as landmarks over the flat countryside and dominated symbolically the villages of thatched houses huddled around them. In these villages the friars established schools for Indian children in which a good many sons of the nobility received education.

The religious orders had an intelligent scheme for their missionary work in Spanish colonies. Before going out among the Indians, young priests lived in the monasteries to be instructed in the native languages and the heathen customs and religious practices they must combat.

The Franciscans immediately began the study of the Mayan language, learning from the Yucatecan priests and nobles. They were the guardians of the learning and religious symbolism of their race, so that eventually the Spaniards tried to exterminate the priestly class in their effort to destroy the culture of the conquered people. Fortunately, due to the work of the early friars, a record was preserved. The man most responsible for it was Diego de Landa, despite the fact that he destroyed many of the sacred Mayan books.

He came to Yucatán as a young Franciscan missionary in 1549 and retreated to one of the monasteries to study the language. During his years in Yucatán he tried to work out an alphabet, an effort not very successful, as the Mayan characters represented ideas or phrases, not letters. The friars did, however, learn to write the language using the Spanish alphabet and taught the young nobles they educated to do likewise.

The portrait of Diego de Landa, second bishop of Yucatán, hangs in the cathedral at Mérida. The tight-lipped, severe countenance reveals the character of the man who exceeded all others in his fanaticism. He abominated the native religion and resorted to the most severe punishments in his efforts to destroy what he considered devil worship.

As he went out among the villages, preaching and punishing, he became interested, despite his horror of idolatry, in the Mayan hierarchy of gods, the ceremonies and learning of the race. Everywhere he questioned the Indians about their old customs and observed their ways of life. Young nobles educated in church schools gave him a fund of information about the history of their people. Being a man of keen intellect, he was impressed by the astronomical learning of the priests, their complex calendars and time counting.

Gaspar Antonio Chi, son of a Xiu lord, and Juan Cocom, of the Cocom clan, were his most useful informants. From the beginning the friendly Xiu nobility had been a great help to the Spaniards in subduing the people and in spreading Christianity. The chief who submitted to Francisco de Montejo accepted the new religion and allowed all his people to be baptized.

Long before the Spaniards came, the Xius had deserted their wonderful city of Uxmal to migrate to another territory and settle around a town called Mani. Although the people were superficially Christian they were among those most guilty, in Bishop de Landa's eyes, of secret devil worship. Everywhere the people hid in their houses little images of their earth and fertility gods, or crept to the deserted temples to leave their offerings of flowers, birds and copal incense. Such stubborn idolatry filled the fanatical bishop with rage and he determined to make an example of Mani.

Although he had no authority to do so, he set up a court of the Inquisition to judge the guilty people. Search of the houses revealed many images which were brought to the plaza and smashed. De Landa discovered that the priests of Mani had hidden a precious store of Mayan books, the painted record of their learning. To the bishop these books, despite his intellectual interest in them, were works of the devil which prevented the people from becoming true Christians. These, too, were added to the pile in the plaza. Leaders of the people accused of idolatry were publically whipped and sentenced to hard labor, while priceless records of an ancient culture went up in a holocaust of flame. The people sorrowed with tears and groans, some committed suicide, but the bishop had no sympathy for them.

This time Diego de Landa had gone too far. Besides his severity to the Indians, he was a controversial person, always attacking Spanish officials and complaining of them to the King. He was called to Spain to give an account of himself and while living there in a monastery he wrote his famous *"Relación de las Cosas de Yucatán,"* prepared as his defence before the judges. That book has been one of the most reliable sources of information on Mayan life and history.

The Bishop and other scholarly priests were moved only secondarily in their studies by intellectual curiosity. The laborious work done by the friars was not undertaken out of respect for a great culture, but to provide a source of information for young missionary priests.

One good thing can be said for early Spanish administration in Yucatán. Although the people were abused and their culture trampled upon, the Spanish officials and home government respected aristocracy even in Indian races. The lord of a clan, called a cacique by the Spaniards, continued to direct the life of his people under orders from the colonial government. Every Indian town had its native governor and officers to manage local affairs. The towns paid tribute to the Spanish government, but the inhabitants were permitted to keep their traditional allotments of land, worked more or less in common. The people supported their governors from the produce of special fields, according to the old custom, and caciques were allowed several servants to wait on them. Native nobles wore Spanish costume, while some caciques won special privileges, such as the right to ride a horse or own a musket. Among the common folk, white cotton shirt and drawers replaced the breechclout and mantle for men. Women wore a long white skirt with a straight garment overhanging it, trimmed with colorful embroidery. Country folk in Yucatán wear the same type of costume to this day.

Bishop de Landa wrote that the Indian towns were like orchards, each house having its garden patch and fruit trees. Mayan houses were built with walls of poles lashed together with thongs, surmounted by a huge steep roof of thick palm thatch hanging low over the walls. More prosperous people had oval-shaped houses of whitewashed stone walls with the same great roof. Replicas of these Mayan houses are found carved in stone on the façades of ancient temples, and Yucatán villages now are picturesque with the same type of dwelling. Yucatán is indeed a land of stubborn tradition.

In those early colonial times sons of caciques were taught in the friars' schools and those who showed special ability received the same kind of churchly education as Spaniards of their class. Some of these young men made a place for themselves in Spanish life—Juan Cocom, for example, but more especially Gaspar Antonio Chi. In him the ability and intelligence of his race were demonstrated. He proved that a young Maya could adopt Spanish culture without losing sympathy for his own people. He became proficient in Spanish and Latin as well as his own language and that of the Aztecs. As royal interpreter he was invaluable to the Spanish government, trusted and respected by officials. To the Mayan people he was a natural lord, their defender and the confidant of all their troubles.

Gaspar Antonio Chi helped to save their lands in controversies with greedy Spaniards. On the other side, he helped Spanish settlers work out the long questionnaires sent by the King, requiring information on climate, crops, mines, lands and other matters. Late in life he was commissioned by the governor to write a history of Yucatán, a work to which all early historians referred. In the colonial life of Yucatán this Mayan nobleman was an interesting figure; dignified, accomplished, very astute, respected and honored by all.

While towns grew and government was organized the encomenderos developed their vast tracts of land into thriving haciendas. Some of the gentlemen had within their grants the ruins of ancient cities, as at Chichén Itzá. Cattle grazed in the deserted plazas and Indians planted their cornfields on broad terraces. Northern Yucatán did not yield easy wealth.

The flat stony plain stretched in every direction, greenish-brown with its cover of dry forest and bush between the cultivated areas.

The Spanish landowners adapted themselves to the climate and the age-old Mayan activities of the agricultural year, best suited to the country. In the winter months, dry and pleasant, the farmers cut timber, built granaries and repaired the thatch of house roofs. During the hot spring months the brush on fallow fields was cut, dried and burned, so that a haze of heat and smoke hung over the land. Then the fields were cleared and prepared for planting. In spring the country was beautiful with the white and golden bloom of flowering trees, dear to the Maya. Summer was hot and wet, the growing season, when corn, beans, chili and crops introduced by the Spaniards quickly matured. The old Mayan clans never went to war during the growing season, and doubtless there were no revolts against the new masters in this period when life was concentrated on the precious crops. The northers and hurricanes of autumn were dreaded because of the damage they caused in the fields.

Spaniards augmented the native crops by the introduction of wheat and other grains. Plantains, brought from the islands, added another nourishing fruit to the breadfruit and zapote cherished by the natives. Horses, mules and pigs were raised and some landowners developed large cattle ranches.

Drought was always a menace, and the Spanish haciendas, like native villages, were always centered about one of the great natural wells called cenotes, or about an artificial one dug to reach the subterranean water.

The laborious native method of hauling water in clay jars by ropes was improved by the introduction of the old Arabic *noria* used in Andalucía. This was a great wheel hung with buckets, set in the well and worked by a sort of windlass. A horse or ox hitched to the windlass, walking round and round, kept the wheel turning and emptying its buckets into large stone tanks. A roof of palm thatch or poles sheltered the well and water tank. Village women and hacienda servants went to and fro between the well and the houses, with great clay water jars of classic shape poised on their shoulders.

The hacienda house was a solid, simple dwelling of stone set in a great compound surrounded by thick stone walls and entered through an arched gateway. In the compound wide-spreading ceiba trees offered shade to cattle and workers. Mules, horses and cattle came to the compound to drink from stone troughs. The laborers were called together by a farm bell and scattered from there to their tasks. The master and his family came to the hacienda for country holidays, but for the most part the work was directed by overseers, with resulting cruelty to the Indian laborers.

In the early colonial period quarrels and controversy were the rule in Yucatán. The religious orders intrigued against each other but joined in attacking the encomenderos for their abuse of the Indians. Francisco de Montejo apparently tried without much success to enforce the Spanish laws against slavery, but every kind of tribute and service was demanded of the Indians. As Diego de Landa said, "They received with sorrow the yoke of slavery." The friars came to be regarded by the people as their protectors, so often did they attack the abuses of the Spanish system. Their constant interference in civic affairs so enraged the colonists, however, that they frequently refused to go to Mass.

After Montejo's time officers were sent from the Audiencia de los Confines in Guatemala to straighten out affairs in Yucatán. They reduced taxes demanded from Indian towns, abolished some forms of slavery and ordered the Spaniards to acquire Spanish wives to lessen their cohabitation with Indian women.

The Maya were a strong race. Despite their subjection Mayan life and character persisted in Yucatán. The language lived on in monasteries and church schools, among the people of towns and countryside. Spanish children learned it from nursemaids and servants. It was spoken in many homes where Spaniards married Mayan women.

The isolation of Yucatán, its physical character and the customs of the natives, added to the blending of Spaniards with a race different from that of Mexico, created a people and way of life very distinctive in character. The conquest had been separate from others, and the colonial province, far away from the Viceroyalty of New Spain, lived its own independent life under governors nominally subject to the Viceroy.

CHAPTER 10

SPANISH RULE BEGINS IN
HIGHLANDS AND JUNGLES

THE CONQUEST of Central America had been a hard task, even for men of iron. They had not found abundance of precious metals or well-ordered native life as in Mexico and Peru. In tremendous marches through the most rugged wilderness, fighting Indians and their own countrymen, they had won the land for Spain. Soon after the conquest there were small settlements scattered through the highlands and a few on the coast. King Philip II ruled that thirty persons disposed to settle together, each to have ten cows, four oxen, one mare, one pig, twenty sheep, six hens and a cock, constituted a town. Few of these early "towns" had more than sixty vecinos, but each one had its municipal government.

Adventurers and first settlers had suffered hunger, destitution, sickness; they intended to compensate themselves for their labors from the products of fields and mines, or to win control of communities through municipal offices. They would endure hardships to win to their bright goal of wealth and prestige, but they would not work for themselves.

By the year 1536 natives near the Spanish settlements had submitted to their fate except for occasional outbreaks. Wherever mines or gold-bearing rivers were discovered hordes of Indian slaves were driven to extract the precious metals for their masters. Over rough trails in the primitive country all goods were carried on Indian backs. Native tribes living on lands allotted to encomenderos slaved for their masters in the fields and paid tribute of their produce and of gold when they had it.

One of the easiest methods of getting wealth was the sale of slaves to the island colonies where the native population had been decimated. Slave-hunting in Honduras and Nicaragua reached scandalous proportions. Those natives who were not serving Spaniards on encomiendas, in mines or households, were torn from their land to find misery and death far away.

Until 1536 encomenderos in the provinces of what is now Central America had exploited the natives without interference from Spain and with only the protests of Franciscan and Dominican missionaries to annoy them. In that year came a voice crying in the wilderness, a voice already known and hated in the islands—that of Fray Bartolomé de Las Casas.

For years he had preached against slavery and cruelty in Cuba and Hispaniola, aided by other Dominican friars, and had exposed before the King and Council of the Indies the brutalities of the encomenderos. He challenged the convenient theory of the colonists that the Indians were sub-human creatures of no intelligence, therefore it was permissible to treat them like animals.

In Guatemala the good priest, Francisco Marroquin, soon to be Bishop of Guatemala, was an ardent missionary. He was deeply concerned for the conversion of the natives but had few friars to help him. In 1536 he invited the radical Padre de Las Casas, then preaching in Mexico, to found a monastery of the

Dominican Order in Santiago where missionaries could be trained.

Gladly the Protector of the Indians came to Guatemala. He saw the opportunity to put into practice his belief that the natives could be won to the True Faith by gentleness, persuasion and sympathetic teaching, rather than by battle and murder. For this demonstration he prepared to enter the Tierra de la Guerra, so called because the Spaniards had been defeated in every attempt to invade the territory of fierce tribes of the Quiché race. It was a northern section of Guatemala, now included in the provinces of Alta and Baja Vera Paz.

Fray Bartolomé proposed to the King and the Audiencia of Mexico to undertake the peaceful conquest of Tierra de la Guerra, on condition that the natives were not to be given into servitude to any Spaniard. They were only to pay a moderate tribute to the King as his vassals. Fray Bartolomé also stipulated that no Spaniard was to settle in the country for five years. When the proposals were accepted he and three Dominican companions prepared their ingenious scheme of conquest.

After perfecting themselves in the Quiché language, they set to work on simple stories of the Christian faith, written in the native tongue. A long narrative poem in stanzas was composed, and set to tunes which could be sung to the accompaniment of native instruments.

For months the missionaries worked with four native Christian merchants who were accustomed to trading their goods in the land of Tzulultlán, the Indian name for Tierra de la Guerra. The Indians learned the whole long poem and its music by heart. To their store of trade goods the friars added mirrors, knives, copper bells and other Castilian trinkets to attract the untamed people.

Through the forested wilds of Tzulultlán the traders came to Zameneb, Indian city and capital of the great lord, or Ahau of Rabinal. They spread out their goods in the market place as usual and began to chant their story. Crowds gathered to finger the fascinating trinkets and to listen to this legend of strange gods. Curious to know what so attracted his vassals, the Ahau invited the traders to the palace. There he kept them eight days while he listened over and over to the chant and asked questions. The traders assured the Ahau that the good men who had sent them were different from the brutal Spaniards who had tried to invade his territory. They were men of simple life, kind and compassionate to the Indians.

The Ahau of Rabinal was so impressed with the traders' story that when they returned he sent his young brother and a barbaric retinue to visit the Spanish city and test the truth of what he had heard.

People in Santiago were kind to their visitors, and the friars made such a good impression that the Indian lord invited one of them to return with him to Zameneb, to tell the Ahau more of this new religion. Fray Luis Cáncer set off, alone, with the Indian company to the land so dreaded by the Spaniards.

In Zameneb the Ahau received his visitor with respectful attention and offerings of flowers. The populace was invited to the palace to observe the ceremonies for the stranger's god, as Fray Luis chanted a Christian service before a candlelit altar. So sympathetically did the good friar reason with the chief that he accepted the new religion. When Fray Luis promised that his people would not be enslaved, the Indian chief agreed to become a vassal of the Spanish King. The idols were destroyed by his order and a chapel built for Fray Luis' preaching.

Padre de Las Casas himself visited the Ahau at Zameneb,

preaching to a large concourse of curious people. For several years the Dominican friars continued their work in Tierra de la Guerra, going alone or in pairs through the wild country, baptizing, building chapels, preaching their message of gentleness and peace. The Spanish promise was kept so that the converted people became peaceful subjects of the King. The friars who lived among them were regarded as friends and protectors, and the Tierra de la Guerra was renamed Tierra de la Vera Paz.

It was a great triumph for Bartolomé de Las Casas. The peaceful conquest gave point to his arguments as he went up and down the Spanish possessions from Mexico to Peru, defending the rights of the Indians. With his fiery denunciations of abuses he made himself a hated nuisance to authorities and encomenderos.

Many other noble friars, during the first century after the conquest, went from their headquarters in Guatemala to win over scattered tribes who had retreated to the remote wilderness to escape the Spaniards. Barefoot, in their rough robes, they went alone or in pairs through trackless country. Fearlessly they entered the territory of tribes who had received every white man with showers of arrows. Sometimes they were martyred, at other times they succeeded in bringing scattered Indian families together in villages to be instructed. The fame of the Padres Santos spread through every settlement in Central America.

Two Franciscans were among those most celebrated for courage and saintliness—Fray Antonio Margil and Fray Melchor Lopez. When they appeared out of the wilderness in the small town of Cartago in Costa Rica, chanting psalms, the people knelt before them in reverence. These two men did good work among the fierce Indians of Talamanca in Costa Rica, who resisted every attempt of Spanish settlers to enter their territory.

Fray Antonio Margil became a sort of Saint Francis about whom legends gathered. One of these tales relates how he and Fray Melchor once lost their pack mule in the forest. It was found next day, killed by a "tigre"—a jaguar. Fray Antonio commanded his Indian companions to take up the pack and follow the savage beast. When they found the animal Fray Antonio said to it, "now shalt thou carry the pack for having killed the mule." The "tigre" bowed its head humbly, accepted the burden and carried it to their destination.

The missionary friars were selfless, devoted men, but the Franciscans, Dominicans and other orders, as soon as they had built monasteries in the colonial capitals, became one of the most controversial elements in community life. The monasteries were assigned encomiendas for their support on which Indians worked for them, cultivating the fields and raising cattle. As they became wealthy the orders engaged in intrigues among themselves in their struggle for power. They were determined, particularly the Dominicans, to dominate the political life of the provinces. There was constant recrimination between men of the Church and municipal officers and encomenderos.

Meanwhile, Fray Bartolomé de Las Casas, soon after his triumph in Tierra de la Vera Paz, succeeded by his constant propaganda in bringing about a royal investigation of conditions in the Indies. That led to the promulgation of the New Laws of 1542 which fell on the Spanish colonists like a bombshell.

The principles set forth in the New Laws were eminently just and humane. Fray Bartolomé de Las Casas was largely responsible for them and the colonists knew where to lay the blame for what they considered their ruin. The most violent abuse was heaped on the head of the priest.

The New Laws forbade the enslavement of the Indians for any reason or by any method. They were to be well treated and to receive the same consideration as other vassals of the King. Those already enslaved were to be released. No Indians were to be forced to work in fields, mines or households against their will, and those who served were to be paid. The *tlamemes,* or carriers, were not to be sent far from their homes to carry burdens on long journeys without recompense. The excessive tribute paid to their masters by Indians of encomiendas was to be reduced. Worse yet, the encomiendas granted to conquerors, first settlers and their sons, were to be theirs for one lifetime only, after which the lands were to revert to the Crown.

The attempt to enforce the New Laws threw the whole colonial empire, from Mexico to Peru, into disorder and confusion. From the officers of cabildos and encomenderos of Central America floods of letters went to the King, protesting, beseeching the King not to ruin his subjects. Was it for this, cried the encomenderos, that they had spent their blood and strength in the service of Spain, to live in poverty, to see their sons and daughters reduced to beggary! The King had ordered them to marry and rear their families in America, but what was to become of those families?

Colonial existence was founded on the servitude of the native races. There were no other laborers, except imported Negro slaves, to work in the fields, mines and sugar mills. It was deeply ingrained in the Spanish character to despise manual work of all kinds. The colonists could not see themselves, or any Spaniards except the humblest peasants, working to grow crops, tend cattle or dig in mines. They had transplanted to the New World the feudal system of old Spain, and had a subject race to exploit with unbridled cruelty until the government stepped in with the New Laws.

The servitude of the hapless natives was unjust and wrought untold suffering. It could not be abolished, however, in one drastic sweep, as Las Casas and his friends tried to do in the enforcement of the New Laws. Some officers of the Audiencia, the Dominicans, and some few bishops, stood with Las Casas, but for the most part churchmen were as hostile as the secular men of the communities. Some acknowledged the justice of the laws but believed their enforcement would ruin the colonies. Others, who had great wealth in lands and Indians, joined in reviling the troublesome revolutionist.

Fray Bartolomé de Las Casas was appointed Bishop of Chiapas province and, although a man in his seventies, threw himself with zeal into the work of enforcing the laws. Open warfare raged between the inhabitants of Ciudad Real, seat of the bishopric, and the Dominicans. The Bishop ordered his friars to refuse confession and absolution to encomenderos who had not freed their Indians. He hurled the dire threat of excommunication against the highest officers who opposed the enforcement of the decrees. When he appeared with his denunciations before the Audiencia, enraged officers shouted, "Throw out that lunatic!"

After a few years of fruitless struggle in Chiapas, the Bishop resigned his office and returned to Spain, to spend the rest of his life speaking and writing in defence of the native races. He was a man so violent and intense in temperament that he was often led into exaggerations, and his fiery intolerance hindered the advancement of his ideas. Few men roused such hatred in the Spanish colonies, yet history has proved that Fray

Bartolomé de Las Casas was one of the great characters of his age. He was a man far in advance of others in humanity and ideas of social justice. He even had the temerity, in some of his writings, to question the absolute right of the Spanish monarchs over the lives of their vassals, white or brown.

For a time the New Laws were rather strictly enforced in Guatemala, Honduras and Nicaragua. Many colonists lost their lands or were in desperate straits for laborers to continue their enterprises. Some householders complained that they were left with no one to carry firewood and water, or to grind maize and make tortillas. In Peru, the resentment of the encomenderos led to the open revolt of Gonzalo Pizarro, who tried unsuccessfully to make himself monarch of Peru.

Before many years had passed it was easy for colonial authorities to ignore the laws. The old system of servitude continued, with slight improvement; the encomenderos became hereditary landowners, passing on their estates to their descendants. On the whole, however, the Indian races of the Spanish possessions profited from the just scheme of government, planned to incorporate them into the life of the colonies. It meant that they were not exterminated, or driven on before the advancing tide of settlement, as happened in the English colonization of North America.

The friars of religious orders were instructed to gather Indians of scattered pueblos into towns where they could be converted and taught Spanish ways of life. Fields of maize were planted at new sites, and when the harvest was ripe the priest led the Indians of chosen villages to the place with chants and banners. The reaping of the harvest and building of huts, with cane and mud walls and thatched roofs, was celebrated with fiestas and dances. Native alcaldes and *regidores* were appointed to manage local affairs. Chiefs, or caciques, remained as heads of their tribal life. From these settlements grew Indian towns, dominated by large handsome churches, built by Indian labor under the direction of the friars.

The Indians suffered from this system in the loss of land for their sustenance, for in the old villages they had had large tracts cultivated in common. In the new towns people gathered from numerous villages were confined for their crops to one *ejido,* established by law as one league in extent. Nevertheless, in their Indian town government the natives had recourse in law from the injustices of encomenderos.

In Guatemala, where natives have clung stubbornly to their customs and beliefs, the system of Indian government endures to this day. Mountain towns with mixed population have two sets of municipal officers, Indian and white, each concerned with the affairs of their own people.

The cruelties imposed on human beasts of burden were slightly alleviated after 1542. Foot trails were widened and improved so that mules, imported and raised by the Spaniards, could be used for transporting goods. Many Indians became *arrieros,* driving the long strings of pack mules over the trails which were the only highways in colonial Central America.

People who had never known a beast of burden were easy prey, however, for their new masters. Abused and poorly paid though they were, Indian *cargadores* were human pack animals throughout the colonial period. To this day mountain Indians of Guatemala trot over miles of trails carrying great loads on their backs to town markets.

The blending of two races began with the conquest, as Spaniards took Indian women for companions or married them. The conquerors themselves—as for example Cortés and Alvarado—set the example by taking Indian princesses for

companions and treating their children by these native aristocrats with the same consideration as their legitimate sons and
daughters. Intermarriage was not frowned upon and, despite
the later pride in white blood, Spanish American life was
founded on a racial tolerance unknown in English-based North
America.

Indian craftsmen soon found opportunity and a place for
themselves in trades. Spanish artisans were brought to Guatemala and other centers with the first settlers, and with them
the Spanish system of trade guilds. The services of shoemakers,
iron workers, leather workers, carpenters and masons, were
much needed in the towns. Soon, however, master craftsmen
became more interested in getting land and making money
from Indian labor than in pursuing their trades. In order to
have a supply of skilled workers, Indians, mestizos, even
Negroes, were taken into the guilds and trained. Anyone except a slave could become a master craftsman if he had the
ability. During early colonial times, before the caste system
became rigid, there was democratic mingling in the guilds.

After the imposition of the New Laws of 1542 there was, in
Nicaragua, an echo of Gonzalo Pizarro's revolt. There, too,
angry reckless men planned to seize Spain's colonial possessions
and set up an independent monarch.

The province had its first chance to recover from the tyranny
and greed of Pedrarias and his successor with the good governor, Rodrigo de Contreras. He was a gentleman from Spain,
intelligent and just.

Under his direction the Rio San Juan, outlet of Lake Nicaragua, was finally explored. Three small craft were built at
Granada, and while they were navigated among the rocks and
sandbars of the river two hundred men marched along the
shores, pacifying the Indians and exploring the country. The

vessels came through and sailed to Nombre de Díos. This potential route from ocean to ocean was to be the dominating factor in the history of Nicaragua.

A few settlers, occupied with fishing and shipbuilding, started the little port of Realejo on the Pacific. There began a limited trade by ship from Granada through the Rio San Juan to Nombre de Díos, and from Realejo to Panama on the Pacific.

León had been a turbulent place since its foundation. There had been violent controversies between the Dominicans and secular leaders, intensified by the preaching of Padre de Las Casas. Bishop Valdivieso of Nicaragua, friend and supporter of Las Casas, had employed his power for the enforcement of the New Laws. Since his concern for the Indians had not prevented him from amassing wealth he was hated on two counts by most of the citizenry.

Many gentlemen, including Governor Contreras, were ruined by the confiscation of their lands and Indian slaves and, being unruly men, were ready to fight for their rights. Rodrigo de Contreras went to Spain to plead his cause, but his wife and sons thought up a mad scheme of revenge, directed first against the Bishop whom they blamed for their troubles. Contreras' lady was a daughter of old Pedrarias, a true child of that violent man. She it was who aided and abetted her young sons, Pedro and Hernando, in their ambitions and instigated Hernando's brutal attack on Bishop Valdivieso.

Nicaragua, wild and sparsely settled, was the haunt of the worst vagabonds and adventurers who roamed Central America in search of fortune. These men, ready for anything that promised them loot, were enlisted by the Contreras sons and other defrauded encomenderos in a fantastic plan of conquest. The ringleader, with Hernando Contreras, was Juan de Bermejo, a man who had taken part in Gonzalo Pizarro's revolt. Their wild scheme was to capture Panama, sail to Peru and rouse resentful men there to join them in seizing that rich country. Then Hernando de Contreras would be proclaimed monarch of an American empire.

Pedro de Contreras, who was only nineteen, was sent with his mother to Granada to manage the revolt from that point. The first act of the drama was played in León, where Hernando de Contreras gathered his followers in his house and made them an oration about their wrongs. Then he led them into the street in fighting mood, hands on swords, shouting, *"Viva el principe Contreras, libertad, libertad!"*

Bursting into Bishop Valdivieso's house, Hernando stabbed the prelate before anyone could come to his aid. Leaving him bleeding on the floor, the desperados rifled his coffers of silver and gold, then rushed to the treasurer's house and took fifteen hundred pesos of gold. Horses and arms were demanded at the sword's point from other citizens. Hernando sent to his brother in Granada the dagger with which he had stabbed the Bishop, as signal that the deed was done.

Gathering more desperados, the rebels marched to Granada and took the place with the aid of Pedro working within. Then they marched to Realejo and seized two ships lying there. A handful of adventurers sailed off with full confidence to capture Spain's empire.

The crews of ships at anchor in the Bay of Panama were taken by surprise and surrendered. Pedro was left in charge of the ships while Hernando and Juan de Bermejo, with their rabble, went ashore to take Panama City. They advanced with banners flying to shouts of, *"Viva Contreras, principe de libertad"!*

Totally unprepared for attack, the citizens could do nothing.

The bishop and treasurer narrowly escaped hanging by swearing allegiance, which of course meant nothing. The rebels sacked houses, swaggered around the streets in fine clothes stolen from wealthy merchants, seized a store of gold awaiting shipment to Spain.

Contreras learned that the royal officer, Gasca, who had been restoring order in Peru, had just left for Nombre de Díos on his way back to Spain, escorting a load of Peruvian silver. Hernando and Bermejo, with their rabble of adventurers, set off to capture Gasca and the silver, leaving only two soldiers on guard in Panama.

No sooner were they gone than the vecinos rang the church bells to summon the militia to go after the rebels. From his post in the harbor Pedro thought the bells were ringing for a triumph of his brother and sent men ashore to investigate. These were promptly captured. That night, under cover of darkness, the Panameños sent soldiers in small boats to board Pedro's ship, forcing one of the captured men to give the password. They had no luck, for the defenders threw down large jugs of wine which capsized one of the boats, drowned many men and sent the rest scurrying back to shore. Pedro raised sail and made off to the safety of the open sea.

Hearing the tocsin of the bells in Panama, Juan de Bermejo turned back with his company to meet the Panameño soldiers in a fierce battle, in which he and other captains were killed. Some captured men were hung or tied to a post in the Bishop's house and stabbed by Negro slaves. Panameños manned a ship and set off in pursuit of Pedro de Contreras. He and his men escaped capture by beaching their vessel and running into the mountains, where Indians made an end of them.

Hernando, *"principe de libertad,"* learning of these disasters, fled into the wilderness pursued by Gasca's soldiers. Some of them found in a swamp the drowned body of a man whom they recognized as Contreras by his cap with a gold medallion. The head was cut off and exhibited in a cage in the plaza of Panama City. Thus, in 1550, the madman's dream of conquest ended in blood and death.

Men were unruly and passionate in Nicaragua, but they lived in a land where nature was violent. The uneasy earth destroyed towns by earthquake, fiery volcanic eruptions and lava flows terrified the people. In the early days the volcano of Massaya, near the shores of Lake Nicaragua, was very active. The Spaniards named it El Infierno, for frequently fountains of flame shot from its crater lighting up the country-side, visible far at sea.

The Indians had a legend that a powerful witch lived in the molten lake at the bottom of the crater; a witch whom they consulted and propitiated with human sacrifices.

The tale of the molten lake came to the ears of a greedy renegade friar, Blas del Castillo, and he became convinced that under its crusted surface was molten gold. He and several adventurers plotted secretly to get this treasure. They prepared iron pots, pulleys, and a sort of cage with a derrick in which they might descend to the bottom of the crater.

Indians were forced to carry the stuff up the mountain, but when they saw the friar prepare to go over the edge of the crater they fled in terror. With a crucifix in one hand and a flask of wine in the other, Fray Blas entered the cage and was lowered by his companions into the crater. Frightened to death, choked by sulphurous fumes, Fray Blas nevertheless took a good look at the crusted lake and exorcised its demons with crucifix and wine. He and his fellow plotters dug up several pots of the stuff, sure that they had a fortune. Of course they were disappointed, but the legend of gold in the crater of El Infierno was slow in dying.

There was gold in the mountains, but the settlers had not the means for working mines. They continued slave-hunting for profit and turned to trade by lake and sea.

In the sixteenth century Granada prospered as the lake port for trade by ship with Nombre de Díos. The business was small and the prices of commodities brought from Spain to Nombre de Díos and thence to Nicaragua were scandalously high, but it provided livelihood for merchants living in Granada. Other prosperous inhabitants were encomenderos who had their field crops and herds of cattle in the countryside. Well-to-do vecinos had houses with adobe walls and tiled roofs, but altogether the town had only two hundred house-holders.

Thirty settlers kept the small port of Realejo alive and León, near the sea, had fallen into a dilapidated condition. The inhabitants had so many troubles that they believed the place was under a curse because of the murder of Bishop Valdivieso. In 1610 they decided to move to a site midway between the ocean and Lake Managua, in a fertile Indian valley. Carrying banners and led by their priests, the vecinos marched to the new site and founded León for the second time. The town grew rapidly and became one of the finest cities in Central America.

While conquerors tramped up and down subduing Indians and founding towns, the territory which was to be Costa Rica remained almost untouched. The precipitous mountains, thick forests and wild rivers rushing down from the mountains through gorges made it even more difficult of access than primitive regions already conquered. The Spaniards were convinced that the mountains held great mineral wealth, so hopefully named the future province Costa Rica—rich coast.

Fruitless attempts were made to gain a foothold by building forts at the mouths of rivers on the Caribbean coast, or on the other side on the Gulf of Nicoya. The settlements melted away under Indian attacks or were deserted because of hardship and lack of food.

It was from Nicaragua, finally, that permanent settlers came to Costa Rica. In 1561 Juan de Cavallon, the *alcalde mayor* of Nicaragua, led a pioneer company of soldiers and settlers over the sloping plains between Lake Nicaragua and the sea, on into the mountainous territory beyond. They marched like pioneers, driving their flocks and herds—horses, cattle, pigs and goats— the first domestic animals to reach Costa Rica. Although a few miserable settlements were started, and exploring bands penetrated the fine highland valleys called the Meseta Central, Juan de Cavallon gave up his attempt at colonizing.

The task was taken up by Juan Vasquez de Coronado in 1562. He was a Spaniard of noble birth and fine character, who was already experienced in American life. He had been an alcalde in various Honduran and Nicaraguan towns. Juan Vasquez de Coronado may be considered the founder of Costa Rica. In a high valley rimmed with mountains called Guarco from its Indian chief, he traced out the first town of Costa Rica, Cartago. Settlers were allotted land and town life began in 1564.

Other settlements were reinforced, other exploring bands followed on the heels of Coronado into the new territory. Painfully they made their way through forests, river gorges and over mountains. From some mountain heights they could see both oceans at once, so narrow was the land. They found one river with gold-bearing sands which stimulated their hopes of wealth. Gradually they explored the land from sea to sea until it was considered conquered and formally added to the other provinces. Yet at the close of the sixteenth century Costa Rica had only a few straggling settlements and two towns—Esparza and Cartago.

The Indians of the mountainous territory were small tribes hostile to each other and fierce in their resistance to the invading Spaniards. Every settlement had to contend with Indian uprisings and every new region was won after hard battles with the natives. The Padres Santos did much to reassure and pacify the wild people, but it was well into the seventeenth century before they became part of colonial life.

From the beginning of Spanish settlement the character of life in Costa Rica was different from that of the other provinces. The first settlers, from Nicaragua, had among them many men of good family, natives of Andalucía and Castile; some were *criollos,* or Creoles, American-born of Spanish parents. All were men of pioneer spirit, accustomed to life in a new, unsettled country. They went about the business of colonizing with vigor and intelligence.

The expectation of wealth was disappointed—there was no gold. Indian labor was scarce, so that the settlers, if they were not to die of hunger, had to work with their own hands, a new thing for Spaniards. Lands in the good highland valleys were fairly distributed among the settlers and they became cultivators of the soil rather than feudal lords. They lived from their fields of wheat, maize and beans; from their herds of cattle, pigs, and the mules and horses raised for sale.

The tendency of Spaniards to concentrate in towns was counteracted by the necessity of depending on agriculture for existence. Social life developed around country activities and farm homes. There was a more democratic spirit in social relations than elsewhere and independence in the management of civic affairs.

It was not until the eighteenth century that other towns besides Cartago were founded in the fertile valleys of the Meseta Central. Alajuela, Heredia and San José began their existence as market and church centers for the farming population of the surrounding valleys.

Spanish settlements in the neighboring Isthmus of Panama continued to exist chiefly because the Isthmus was the route between Peru and Spain. Over the trail from Panama City went the long trains of pack mules laden with wedges of silver and bars of gold from the mines of Peru, to be shipped from Nombre de Díos. That town was a poor unhealthy settlement of only sixty houses with a bad harbor exposed to storms. It had no life at all except when the ships came from Spain to be loaded with treasure and to bring Spanish merchandise to the colonies.

Surveys were made to find a new port, but it was not until 1597, when raids of buccaneers were terrifying the Spaniards, that the treasure port was moved to Porto Bello. There the fine harbor was protected by three strong fortresses, and fertile land in the vicinity gave a means of subsistence for the inhabitants between the visits of the treasure fleets.

The city of Panama, though small, had dignified stone churches and monasteries. Houses of wealthy merchants were built of fine cedar and set in gardens. The people suffered from the climate, tropical diseases and scarcity of provisions. Save for crops grown in their fields all provisions and merchandise came from Spain. As the King supported the monopoly of Seville merchants they set high prices on a limited supply of goods.

Some colonists profited from mines in mountainous Veragua,

but Indian and Negro laborers died off from hardships and the region remained unsettled. Until the pearl-oyster beds were exhausted from overuse, pearl fisheries were a source of wealth. On the whole, however, life was not prosperous on the Isthmus.

Conquerors and first settlers of the Isthmus killed off the Indian population by cruelty and hard labor, except for tribes who escaped to the mountains and kept their freedom. They were replaced by Negro slaves brought by Portuguese slave traders from the Guinea coast of Africa. Householders had their retinues of slaves, the labor in towns and on plantations was done by the black people.

The abuses of their masters led them to run away in great numbers to the jungles and mountains. There they lived in savage freedom, often joining wild Indians in raids on settlements and trails. The *cimarrones,* as the runaway slaves were called, became a menace to planters and travelers. They swooped down on the treasure trains, killing with poisoned arrows, cutting in pieces the men they captured. Bands of cimarrones raided plantations, and merchants dared not travel on the trails without large escorts. When corsairs and buccaneers turned their attention to the Isthmus they found the cimarrones ready and eager to help their raids.

Panama might have lost the trade route between Peru and Spain if the King had favored the scheme proposed by Francisco de Montejo during his few years as Governor of Honduras. He wrote the King in glowing terms of a possible route from Puerto Caballos across Honduras, by way of the mountain valley of Comayagua, to the Gulf of Fonseca on the Pacific. It would pass through territory of good soil and climate, and harbors on both sides were safe and easily accessible. In preparation for this road Montejo founded the town of Comayagua in a fertile highland valley. He failed to consider the length and mountainous character of such an overland route, but it might have made quite a difference in the history of Honduras if the King had approved the plan.

Honduras, with a tropical forested coast and very mountainous interior, was difficult to civilize. Settlements were harassed by frequent Indian attacks. The natives found a great leader in the chief Lempira, Lord of the Mountains. He told the tribes it was a disgrace for them to be in subjection to a handful of strangers, and under his leadership they terrorized Spaniards in town and country.

When Francisco de Montejo mustered his soldiers to march against them, Lempira and his warriors retreated to a mountain stronghold near the town of Gracias á Díos. For six months the Spaniards besieged the rock-bound fortress without success and only conquered in the end by a base trick. A horseman was sent to call Lempira out to parley for peace. Behind him was hidden a soldier with arquebus ready to take aim as soon as Lempira came within range. The chief came out on his cliff, was shot instantly and his body tumbled down the rocks. His panic-stricken people fled into hiding but were finally persuaded to return to their villages.

The Spaniards were right in their conviction that the mountains of Honduras were rich in minerals. Early explorers found gold in the river beds, and were able to scratch out large quantities from the hills with no tools but stirrup irons. Gracias á Díos was founded and prospered high in the mountains because of mines in the surrounding hills. The mountainous region with the Indian name Teguzgalpa, Hill of Silver, became a symbol of wealth to Spaniards, but it was long before the indomitable tribes of the region were subdued. The mountain town, Tegucigalpa, was founded when rich mines of silver were opened in the vicinity.

In its early days the province of Honduras was indeed a place of hardships, Indian wars and bad government. The coast towns were far from the trade route to Spain, the interior settlements were isolated from each other. Their only communication was by rough trails through primitive country.

Guatemala had been the spearhead of conquest and settlement, and it remained the center of government. It was first the seat of the Real Audiencia and later the residence of the governor and captain-general of the Kingdom of Guatemala.

After the destruction of Santiago de los Caballeros by flood and earthquake the surviving inhabitants moved to a new site in the nearby valley of Panchoy. On Corpus Christi Day, 1543, a solemn procession of priests bearing the Sacrament and the treasured Virgen del Socorro brought to the country by Alvarado, led the vecinos to the new site. The Virgin was placed in the little hermitage of Santa Lucia.

The people still had the beautiful but dangerous volcanos, Agua and Fuego, framing their view. They had fertile lands, good streams, and were blessed with a delightful climate. The second capital, Santiago de los Caballeros, soon became a handsome city built in the stately architecture of the Spanish renaissance. It was to become the third in magnificence among Spanish colonial capitals.

In 1560 the King appointed a governor and captain-general for the Kingdom of Guatemala, composed of six provinces—Guatemala, Honduras, Nicaragua, El Salvador, Costa Rica and Chiapas. The Audiencia remained as the high court of justice for the whole region.

El Salvador was a tiny province, an adjunct of Guatemala. It was more isolated than most of them, having no outlet to the Caribbean Sea and only one tiny port on the Pacific. The inhabitants occupied themselves with agriculture and cattle raising. Their best town, San Salvador, suffered disaster during the sixteenth century from the first of many earthquakes.

As settled families, townsmen and artisans replaced conquerors and adventurers, the vigor and drive of the conquest period were lost. Bureaucratic government and trade restrictions stifled initiative. The provinces managed a small trade among themselves by trails or by vessels from their little ports, but even that was hampered by the Spanish government. When, in 1556, the King forbade trade with any nation but Spain, he dealt a blow to the prosperous development of the colonial empire.

The Spanish monarchy conceived of its overseas possessions as the source of profit from minerals and excessive taxes for their European enterprises. It never entered the heads of the kings who succeeded the Emperor Charles V that colonies prospering from agriculture, trade and industry would strengthen the empire.

The Spanish Americans lived shut away from the world behind walls of exclusion; no foreigners were permitted to live in the colonies, there was to be no trade with outside nations. As we shall see, those walls were soon penetrated from the ocean.

CHAPTER 11

THE COLONIAL KINGDOM OF GUATEMALA

ONE OF THE few foreigners to get within the Spanish walls, a century after the conquest of Mexico, was Friar Thomas Gage. He was an English Dominican, sent from Rome with other friars in charge of a superior, to take ship from Mexico for missionary work in the Philippines.

Reaching Mexico City in 1625, the missionaries were so dismayed by tales of hardship in the Philippines that Friar Gage and one or two others decided to run away from their superior. They escaped from Mexico City on horseback, hoping to find a ship in some port of the Kingdom of Guatemala to take them to Spain and thence to their homes.

The story of his adventures, written by Thomas Gage and published in England in 1648, is one of the most engaging travel books in the world. In picturesque language, the tale of "the English American, his travails on land and sea," gives a vivid picture of life within the Spanish walls during the early part of the seventeenth century. To know how people lived we can do no better than to follow the keenly observant Englishman in his travels.

He and his fellow runaways rode southward, through Oaxaca

188

and the Isthmus of Tehuantepec, staying with plantation owners in the country and with priests in towns. Thomas Gage marveled that towns on rivers and the seacoast were not protected by fortifications. Looking back on his adventures while writing the book, he observed that all the small seaports on the South Sea from Acapulco to Panama were "open doors to let in any nations that would take the pains to surround the world to get a treasure." It was not long before nations were doing just that to Spain's colonial ports.

Proceeding to the luxuriant tropical province of Chiapas, Friar Gage and his companions lived with the Dominicans for some time. The good friar enjoyed the conserves and cups of chocolate offered to him by the sociable ladies, but he was critical of their self-indulgence and doubtful virtue. They insisted that they had not the strength to stay through Mass unless their maids brought them cups of chocolate and bits of sweetmeat. When a Dominican friar forbade the practice, and later died from drinking a cup of poisoned chocolate, the vengeful ladies were suspected.

By the time the traveling friar reached Santiago de los Caballeros he had decided that the Spanish Americans had a more varied and plentiful diet than the English. They had wheat and maize, beef and mutton from their herds, all kinds of fruits, both European and native. Everybody was addicted to drinking chocolate many times a day, that gift of the New World to the Spaniards.

Santiago de los Caballeros had not reached its full glory when Friar Gage visited there, but he was impressed with the fine monasteries and nunneries richly endowed with golden altars, statues, gold and silver plate. There were wealthy merchants and aristocrats in the town and the people, he thought, were given over to ungodliness and gambling.

The symmetrical shape of the Volcán de Agua, destroyer of the first capital, looked very innocent, its green sides patched with Indian milpas, or cornfields. Volcán de Fuego was roaring and spitting fire, occasionally making the earth tremble. The people were so accustomed to living in the shadow of volcanoes that they disregarded them, except when a big quake sent them running to the churches to confess their sins.

In his travels about Guatemala Friar Gage saw great cattle *estancias* and plantations of indigo on the hot Pacific coast, worked by Negro slaves. The Indians had used the dye obtained from the wild indigo plant, *jiquilite,* to dye their cotton fabrics. After the Spaniards had cultivated it on a large scale it became one of their most profitable exports.

In the seventeenth century Guatemalans were receiving and exporting goods by way of a little port called Santo Tomás de Castilla, at the mouth of the Rio Dulce. Once a year in the summer, a few Spanish ships, after stopping at Puerto Caballos, sailed on to the Rio Dulce and Santo Tomás. The goods were shipped by pack mule from the Golfo Dulce over the trail to the capital. Thomas Gage says this road was the most used in the country, for over it passed the goods from Spain, while the produce of the country was transported by mule to the warehouses at Santo Tomás to await shipment.

Visiting that lazy, sleepy little port Friar Gage commented: "O the simplicity and security of the Spaniards who appoint no other watch over these their riches save only one or two Indians and as many mulattoes who have for their misdemeanors been condemned to live in that old and ruinated castle of Santo Tomás de Castillá." José Milla, Guatemalan historian, says that not only did the King fail to appoint a royal officer for this important post, but the commissionaire who undertook the receiving and transporting of goods was obliged to pay the King four hundred pesos annually for the privilege.

The Indians were harshly treated, in the opinion of Friar Gage. The poorest and most abused were rounded up every week by an officer and parcelled out, without pay, to Spaniards who needed laborers. Others had to be on hand in towns to serve travelers as burden-bearers. Some Indians were free to farm their bits of land and sell their produce in markets. Indian towns, he observed, had native officers subject to white superiors, and the officer most respected and always obeyed was the priest. Those Indians who served the church and priest were exempt from the weekly round-up of laborers and from serving travelers. Indian children were gathered in schools by the priests to be taught Spanish, church doctrine and singing.

By 1637 Thomas Gage had wandered on to Nicaragua. He called it the Paradise of America, so fertile, so abundant in the fruits of the earth. Life in León he thoroughly enjoyed. It was a city "very curiously built, for the chief delight of the inhabitants consisted in their houses and in the pleasures of the country adjoining and in the abundance of all things for the life of man, more than in any extraordinary riches which are not so much enjoyed as in other parts of America. They are contented with fine gardens, with variety of singing birds and parrots, with plenty of fish and flesh which are cheap, and with gay houses and so lead a delicious, lazy and idle life; not aspiring much to trade and traffic although they have near unto them the lake which commonly every year sendeth frigates to the Havana by the North Sea and from Realejo on the South Sea."

Granada was a town of larger population than León, with fair houses and churches. Some of the inhabitants were wealthy merchants sending produce from the provinces to Cartagena by the North Sea. Thomas Gage gives a good picture of the trade passing through Granada from all over the kingdom.

In one day he saw enter six *requas,* or pack trains, of mules from San Salvador and Comayagua, laden with nothing but indigo, cochineal and hides. Two days later came three requas from Guatemala bringing the King's tribute of silver and indigo and sugar as well.

It had been Friar Gage's intention to take ship from Granada to Cartagena, but what he heard of the voyage down the Rio San Juan, and at sea, disheartened him. Sometimes the passage of the river took two months owing to the fall of the waters and many rocks. At dangerous places the frigates were unloaded and goods packed on Indian backs by land to the next safe place, while the vessels maneuvered through the rapids. In addition, voyagers were plagued with clouds of gnats and heat so intolerable that some died before they reached the sea. The voyage on to Cartagena was likely to be interrupted by attack from corsairs.

Thomas Gage did not have to try his fate, for the governor forbade the frigates to sail that year because of reports that English and Dutch ships were lurking about the mouth of the river to attack merchant vessels. The friar says this news "caused the merchants of the country to fear and sweat with a cold sweat and the President to be careful of the King's revenues."

The few who had planned to make the voyage from Granada wondered how they were to get out of the country, no easy matter in the seventeenth century. The ports of Honduras were terrorized by corsair raids, so the travelers decided to go overland by mule to Cartago in Costa Rica, and thence by trail to the small port of Matina near the mouth of the Rio Suerre (now the Reventazón). There they might catch a trading vessel going to Porto Bello and get passage on one of the galleons, returning after the great trade fair of Porto Bello.

The travelers set out on muleback with Indian guides for the long painful journey to Costa Rica. After leaving the "Mahomet's Paradise" of Nicaragua they passed through rough and craggy ways and came at last to Cartago after surviving a thousand dangers.

Cartago was not so poor as the richer Guatemalans and Nicaraguans had given the friar to understand. The city had four hundred families, good houses and churches. Some well-to-do merchants carried on trade in the produce of the country by sea to Porto Bello on the North Sea and with Panama on the South Sea.

Governor Gonzalo Vásquez de Coronado, son of the founder of Cartago, had opened in 1601 a pack road through the wild mountains of Veragua to Panama. Over this road there was a great trade in mules raised in all the provinces of the kingdom. They were driven over the trail to Panama to be sold at high prices for use in the transport of merchandise and treasure over the gold trail to Porto Bello. Learning of the hardships of this journey and the frequent attacks made on pack trains by barbaric Indians, the travelers decided against trying to reach Panama overland.

They took the trail from Cartago down to the port of Matina on the North Sea, the Caribbean. It was a rough journey but on the way Friar Gage passed through some good valleys planted with corn where Costa Ricans lived on prosperous farms.

Setting sail on a trading vessel from Matina, they were soon held up by a Dutch corsair ship commanded by a mulatto of Havana. The passengers were robbed of their money and

Thomas Gage lost his precious store of pearls and pieces of eight. Provisions destined for Porto Bello—fowls, bacon, honey —were taken before the vessel was allowed to return to port.

Back in Cartago the much-traveled friar took the trail down to Nicoya on the South Sea, or Pacific, whence trading vessels sailed to Panama. Here again he ran into trouble, for the ship was beaten by winds and carried by currents all the way to the equator and back north. Water and food gave out and the passengers were in pitiful condition when the ship finally made the Bay of Panama.

Thomas Gage set out to reach Porto Bello by way of the gold trail. It had become a well-worn road paved with stone to Venta de Cruces, where travelers and goods were transferred to flat boats to go down the Chagres River. Pack trains with gold and silver took another trail through the forests to Porto Bello. It took Friar Gage twelve days to reach the sea by the Chagres River. The boats manned by "blackamoors" were grounded on sand bars or driven by the swift current close under the banks to be caught by overhanging trees and bushes. The Englishman marveled again at the carelessness of the Spaniards who relied on the poor navigation of the river to protect their treasure trail. They had allowed the fort of San Lorenzo at the mouth to fall into disrepair.

Rowed along the coast by "blackamoors," Thomas Gage finally reached Porto Bello. He saw requas of mules arrive from Panama laden with wedges of silver which were heaped up in the market place like so many stones. Then the merchants from Panama and Peru arrived, and the fleet from Spain—eight galleons and ten merchant ships. The forlorn town was crowded with merchants; food prices rose outrageously and every mousehole and hovel was rented.

For fifteen days, while the merchants traded and the galleons were loaded with silver, there was furious activity. Merchants sold their goods not by the yard but by piece or weight, exchanging them for wedges of silver instead of coin. In the hot, steamy, insanitary town men sickened and died; "what with much eating of fruit and drinking of water and other disorders hundreds of merchants, soldiers and mariners died of the flux." The friars, in their hospital, were kept busy tending the sick and burying the dead.

When the galleons sailed Thomas Gage went with them and eventually reached England. He renounced Catholicism and took part in the religious wars between Catholics and Protestants. Cromwell read eagerly his travelogue with its description of the unprotected Spanish ports, and so did other nations who were envious of Spain's riches. Cromwell had a bold Western Design for attack on Spain's colonies, but it got no farther than the capture of the island of Jamaica in 1655. Gage went along on that expedition and died in Jamaica.

Spain's security on the high seas and in colonial ports was given a rude jolt during the seventeenth century, but late in the preceding century other nations first challenged her exclusive possession of the wealth of America and her control over the Caribbean Sea and the Pacific Ocean.

In the reign of the great Emperor Charles V, Spain, with her vast possessions, dominated Europe. Late in the sixteenth century, Charles, weary of the world, left the burden of the empire on the shoulders of his young son, Felipe II, and retired to a monastery. During the reign of this absolute monarch, his attempt to keep all the threads of the great empire under his personal control, and his entrance into religious wars as the champion of Catholicism, weakened Spain's power.

Protestant Elizabeth of England was his chief enemy and she had to help her in the bitter contest her bold and lusty sea rovers—Sir John Hawkins, John Oxenham, Francis Drake. They harried the towering clumsy galleons on the high seas in their swifter ships, captured treasure on the way to Spain, raided the Spanish ports around the Caribbean Sea. Sir John Hawkins gave England the beginnings of a navy when he designed a new type of ship and set out to find trade as well as loot in Spanish ports.

John Oxenham led a band of marauders, aided by wild cimarrones, across the Isthmus of Panama and actually captured a treasure-laden galleon in the Bay of Panama. The Spanish recovered the ship, John Oxenham and several others were captured and executed, but they had proved that the gold trail could be invaded.

The name of Francis Drake became a byword of terror throughout Spanish America. In 1578 he broke into Spain's private ocean through the Straits of Magellan, raiding ports of South America. He accosted little trading vessels between Mexico and Guatemala, took everything of value, entertained the officers aboard the *Golden Hind,* then set them ashore to spread fear of his name in the Kingdom of Guatemala.

Twice Francis Drake raided Nombre de Díos; the second time he and Sir John Hawkins, in 1595, sacked and burned the town. Drake planned a raid on Porto Bello but he died of a fever and was buried in the waters where he had won renown.

The religious wars disrupting Europe were echoed in the Caribbean as English and Dutch Protestant sea rovers and French Huguenot corsairs lurked with their light swift ships in coves and among islands. They darted out from hiding to attack Spanish galleons and coast settlements. Spain was their common enemy; they hated the Popish Spaniards and their Inquisition, and were greedy for the gold and silver of the Indies. To the Spaniards they were all *corsarios luteranos,* ungodly heretics, and hatred was added to the fear they inspired. When France, England or Holland was at war with Spain their sea rovers gave open aid by their attacks on Spanish shipping; in times of peace between the nations the home governments skillfully ignored the exploits of their privateers in the Caribbean Sea.

So many silver-laden galleons were captured by raiders that the Spanish government, in the seventeenth century, sent the annual fleets of galleons and merchant ships under the convoy of war vessels. One "flota" went to Vera Cruz for the trade fair with New Spain; the other, after stopping at Cartagena to trade with the merchants of New Granada, went on to Porto Bello to collect the gold and silver of Peru and trade with the merchants of Panama and Peru. With luck the flotas returned safely to Seville or Cadiz with the wealth of the Indies.

Journeys of thousands of miles by land and sea were made by colonial merchants to bring the produce of the colonies to the trade fairs and to buy Spanish merchandise. They were helpless under the exactions of the Seville merchants who kept goods scarce and prices high. Heavy taxes and export duties made trade even more difficult.

Under such circumstances it was easy for Dutch and English sea captains, slipping into Spanish ports, to build up a lively smuggling trade. Governors of towns looked the other way or accepted presents as illegal transactions went on, bringing to the colonists the manufactured goods they needed and could not obtain from Spain. These bold captains were the advance guard of rising maritime nations, England and Holland, sending their sea-borne commerce around the world.

The first to edge in, soon after Spanish towns were growing, were the slave traders. The Portuguese came first, then were supplanted by English and Dutch slave traders. Spain allowed a certain number of Negroes to be imported each year, but so great was the need of slaves for labor that the traders built up a lucrative smuggling business in their human cargoes.

In 1641 a Portuguese slave ship was wrecked on the Mosquito Islands off the coast of Honduras. Slaves who escaped drowning swam to the mainland and made a place for themselves among the primitive natives, Indians of Carib race called Missikis; a name distorted by Spaniards to Mosquito.

The Guinea Negroes mated with Indian girls, and the mixed breed soon grew into a large population of strong, active, lawless people called zambos. They inhabited, with Indians, what was known as the Mosquito Coast, partly in Honduras, partly in Nicaragua. It was a vast hot region of tropical swamps and rain forests. Innumerable streams and lagoons provided communication for primitive people in canoes. The territory extended back into the foothills of the mountains and the forests were full of valuable timber, as the English soon discovered. Spaniards had given up the attempt to conquer the savages of this region, which was so hot and inaccessible. They were too much occupied with their life in the highlands to realize the danger to them from the large population of lawless zambos.

Soon after the capture of Jamaica by the English in 1655, adventurers from that island penetrated the Mosquito Coast. They made friends with the zambos, taught them English, and took them on as allies for attacks on Spanish settlements, particularly those of Costa Rica.

By mid-seventeenth century the Caribbean Sea had become the resort of rogues, adventurers, piratical criminals of many nations. They had their hideouts among the small cays or islands, and their first rendezvous was on a neglected part of the island of Hispaniola or Santo Domingo. There they joined descendants of Spanish settlers who existed by hunting wild cattle, selling the hides and smoking the meat. The Carib Indian method of curing meat, called *boucan,* was employed, and the drying establishments were called *boucaners;* hence the name buccaneer applied to many of the variegated pirates who infested the sea.

Soon the island of Tortuga, off Santo Domingo, became the lair of pirates under French leadership, while Port Royal on Jamaica was the rendezvous of those who followed English captains. These two places were hellholes, dens of iniquity where the raiders gathered to spend the loot of successful attacks in riotous debauches.

These rogues of many nationalities were worse than the early sea rovers. They acknowledged loyalty neither to God nor nation; their sole object in life was plunder won by daredevil exploits. Leagues of cutthroats under ruthless leaders called themselves Brethren of the Coast. The names of captains such as the Frenchman L'Olonnois, the Englishman Mansfield and the Welshman Henry Morgan, struck terror to the hearts of Spanish colonists.

These Brethren of the Coast invaded the Pacific by way of the Straits of Magellan to harass South American ports, and the little settlements of Central America. Isla del Tigre, in the Bay of Fonseca became a hangout from which they invaded Honduras. The captains were determined to find a way from the Caribbean Sea across the narrow land of Central America to increase their depredations in the Pacific.

In 1640 and 1649 Dutch pirates made excursions into Nicaragua by the Rio San Juan to Lake Nicaragua, sacking and terrorizing Granada, seizing ships so that trade from the lake was practically paralyzed. That route across Nicaragua, almost all by water, attracted the attention of the Brethren of the

Coast and of the English who were seeking a foothold in Spanish territory rather than loot.

Mansfield and Morgan, in 1666, invaded Costa Rica by the Bay of Matina, the Costa Ricans' access to the sea for trade with Caribbean ports. They believed they would find a road to lead them across to the Pacific and that rich loot would be taken in Costa Rican towns. The trail to Cartago was a rough scramble up mountains, through deep barrancas. The invaders reached the high valley of Turrialba, but an Indian had hurried up the mountains ahead of them to warn the governor of Cartago of their landing. The hardy people of the highlands gathered every man and musket for defence and marched against the pirates. They attacked from the shelter of forests with such ferocity that the invaders thought a large force was after them and retreated down the mountains.

Henry Morgan, most ruthless of the pirate captains, made Porto Bello his goal in 1668. The men landed up the coast and sneaked on the town overland, to capture and blow up one of the forts. The governor, besieged in the strongest castle, refused to surrender, even when Morgan forced monks and nuns to mount scaling ladders ahead of his men to give them cover. With dead lying all around him, in the midst of flames and destruction, the staunch governor faced the pirates and was killed. Drunken marauders sacked the town, robbed the citizens and stripped the churches of treasure. Morgan held the place until the governor of Panama paid a ransom of a hundred thousand pesos.

Fabulous Panama City was a prize Morgan determined to have. In 1671, with a gang of desperadoes, he crossed the Isthmus, through the deadly jungles where his men nearly died of hunger and fever. Exhausted though they were, they could beat the frightened Panameños. Much of the hoped-for treasure escaped the pirates, as monks, nuns and wealthy citizens got away by ship with their riches to hide among the islands. After his troops were routed the governor set fire to the wooden houses, so that the raiders entered a city in flames. By hunt and torture, Morgan collected a load of treasure and departed with captives and loot, leaving Panama in ruins. The city was rebuilt on a better site with stronger fortifications, but Spain's commerce with Peru had been dealt an irreparable blow.

Meanwhile English adventurers were entrenching themselves on the Mosquito Coast through friendship with the zambos. From that coast mixed bands of marauders harassed the hardworking Costa Ricans for more than a hundred years. Entering by the Bay of Matina they overran the cacao plantations of the lowlands, seizing the crop, burning houses and killing planters whose livelihood came from the export of cacao. They had a poor little fort on the bay from which to ship their produce and to trade with merchant vessels. Cargoes were seized by English and zambo raiders; once the governor of the fort was carried off and killed. The Costa Ricans avenged this by murdering zambos and Englishmen who had been allowed to come ashore for contraband trading.

On the Mosquito Coast adventurers went up the rivers in the dry season to cut dyewood and mahogany, floating the rafts of logs down stream in the rainy season. Along the shore, settlements of huts were inhabited by thieves and rascals of all sorts. The Spanish government protested in vain to England, and one year Spanish frigates attacked the settlements. Adventurers soon filtered back, protected by the Governor of Jamaica, who flattered the zambo chiefs into acceptance of British rule. In 1740 a fort was built on the coast from which an English superintendent controlled Mosquitia.

England had come to stay in the Caribbean Sea and Spain was too weak to prevent it. With a base on Jamaica the English could strengthen their hold on Mosquitia and keep an eye on the desirable interoceanic route across Nicaragua.

Late in the eighteenth century, when England and Spain were at war, an English squadron, guided by zambos, came to the mouth of the Rio San Juan. Soldiers and mariners were transferred to small boats to go up the river for an attack on Fort Imaculada Concepción. It was built on a cliff at the outlet of Lake Nicaragua. The commander was a soldier of renown, Don José de Herrera y Sotomayos, whose wife and eighteen-year-old daughter Rafaela lived with him at the fort. As she was brought up in a garrison with no girl companions Rafaela amused herself by learning from her father how to load and fire the cannon. Just before the English came up the river Don José died, leaving only a sergeant in charge of a garrison mostly composed of scared Negro and mulatto soldiers.

Valiant young Rafaela took charge of the defence, urging the men with spirited words to be worthy of their dead commander. When the English officer appeared across the moat to demand surrender a proud slip of a girl faced him defiantly and refused to yield. The amazed officer argued with her, pointing out her hopeless position, but Rafaela was unmoved. For five days the English besieged the fort while Rafaela directed the defence and fired the cannon herself. One of her shots penetrated the English officer's tent and killed him, causing such confusion among his men that the siege was abandoned. The Nicaraguans, delirious with joy, gave the young heroine and her mother a great ovation in Granada.

The defeat was avenged when, in 1780, an expedition from Jamaica captured Fort Imaculada Concepción after a hard siege. Among the English naval officers was a young man of future fame, Horatio Nelson. In the peace treaty signed by England and Spain the fort was returned to Nicaragua, but England won concessions for cutting dyewood and colonizing on the Mosquito Coast. She remained there, ready to take a hand in Central American affairs whenever it suited her.

During the seventeenth and eighteenth centuries, the inhabitants of the Kingdom of Guatemala, with the exception of the small privileged class of landowners and merchants, had rather a thin time of it. Spanish restrictions on trade and excessive taxation hindered the development of agriculture and industry. Taxes were imposed on all produce of plantations or goods made in workshops. The King had a monopoly on the profits of the tobacco industry and many other things. Colonials were forbidden to develop traditional Spanish industries, such as wine, olive oil, linen and silk weaving, because they would compete with Spanish producers. Only Indian cotton fabrics were exported.

The small ports and coastwise vessels were continually menaced by pirate attacks. When a man ventured to undertake a voyage to Spain he made his will and said a final farewell to family and friends. In some years the seas were so dangerous that no ships came from Spain. The colonists resorted more and more to contraband trade, to sell their produce and buy merchandise from English and Dutch smugglers. Townspeople did their best to defend themselves from pirate attacks with colonial militia, but powder and arms were scarce.

Spanish monarchs neglected the interests of their subjects in the Kingdom of Guatemala, since the provinces were poor in precious metals compared to Mexico or Peru. Only in Honduras were there exceedingly profitable mines producing a wealth of silver and some gold. Spanish colonial mine owners grew rich despite heavy tribute paid to the King and squandered their

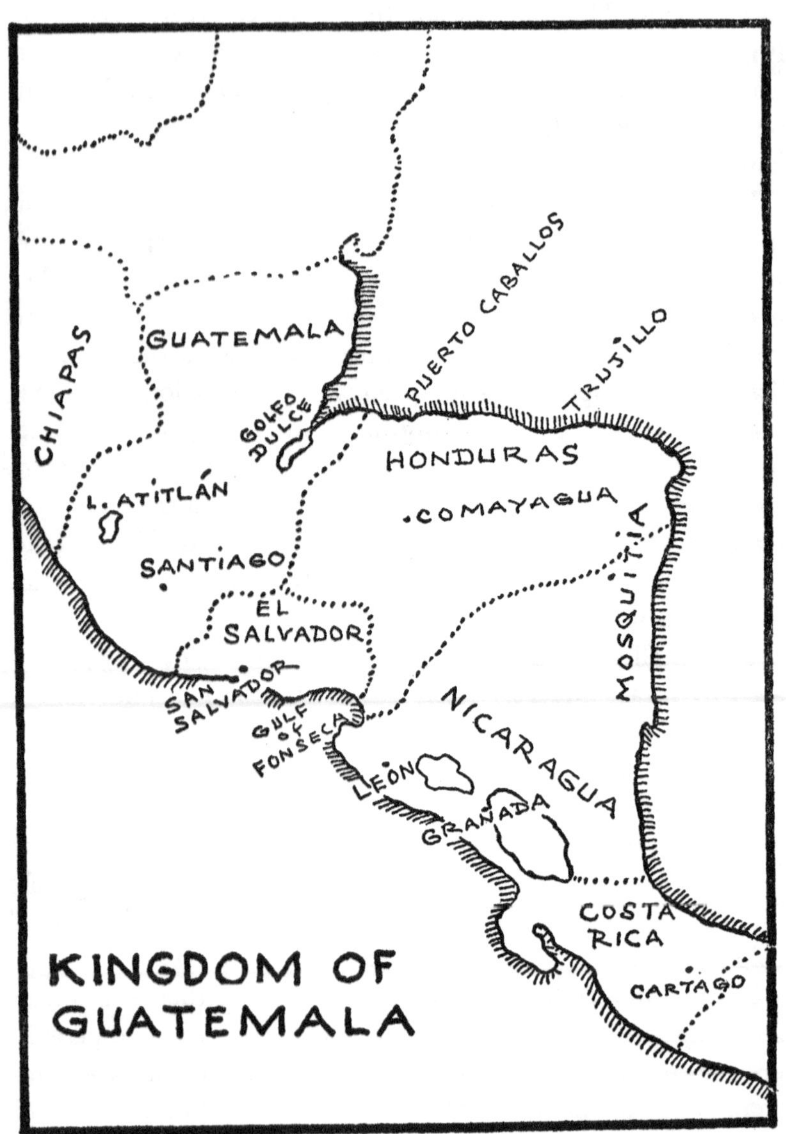

CHIAPAS
GUATEMALA
PUERTO CABALLOS
TRUJILLO
GOLFO DULCE
HONDURAS
COMAYAGUA
L. ATITLÁN
SANTIAGO
EL SALVADOR
MOSQUITIA
SAN SALVADOR
GULF OF FONSECA
NICARAGUA
LEÓN
GRANADA
COSTA RICA
CARTAGO
KINGDOM OF
GUATEMALA

wealth lavishly. Rich men of the gold mining town of Olancho not only furnished their handsome horses with silver-mounted bridles, stirrups and saddles, but shod them with gold to enjoy the ring of the metal against cobblestoned streets. One proud Don of Tegucigalpa, when he made his annual visit to church in Lent to confess his sins, had his servants lay a path of silver blocks from his house to the church. He wanted his horse's hoofs to touch nothing but silver from his mines when he went, in the sight of his neighbors, to perform his religious duty.

On the whole, the provinces of the Kingdom were the step-children of the colonial empire, always the last to be considered or helped. Natural resources would have brought general prosperity if producers had been aided rather than hindered by the mother country. There were native products such as tobacco, balsam, sarsaparilla, gums and resins. Merchants and landowners who did make money prospered from sugar cane and cacao plantations, for sugar and chocolate were in great demand in Europe, and from the shipment of hides and dyestuffs. Indigo was the most profitable export, and next in value was a red dye made from the dried bodies of cochineal bugs. The insects lived on the leaves of the nopal cactus, of which there were large plantings in the highlands.

People lived in towns of pastel-tinted houses, as Spanish as those of the mother country, set in tropical or highland surroundings. Always the central plaza was the focus of social and civic life. Stately buildings of municipal government, and the façade and towers of the principal church, framed the plaza. There the Indians brought their produce on market days. In the afternoon promenade, called a paseo, citizens exchanged greetings as they strolled round and round, ladies and their daughters in one stream, passed counter clockwise by the *caballeros*.

Houses of well-to-do citizens were built around a series of patios open to the sky. Rooms of the master's family opened on a garden patio delightful with flowers, singing birds, the tinkle of cool water flowing continually into a tile-faced tank called a *pila*. Kitchens, stables, servants' quarters were grouped around other courts. This open-air style of living was transplanted from Andalucía and was perfectly suited to the springlike climate of the highlands or to the hot lowlands.

The dull round of daily life was cheered and provided with drama by great festivals of the Church, or celebrations for the arrival of a new governor from Spain or for the King's birthday. Indians, with music and pageantry in their blood, joyfully took part in processions. Beautiful statues of saints were borne on the shoulders of devout worshippers when the glittering processions wound through the streets.

In Guatemala the Indians contributed dance spectacles to fiestas, mingling native and Spanish stories. A favorite drama was that of the conquest and the epic battle between their hero Tecúm Umán and Alvarado.

There were always fireworks at night during festivals, when castles, serpents and other fantasies bloomed against the sky. The swish and bang of rockets, mingled with the clanging of church bells, celebrated every saint's day—a custom that has never been abandoned.

It was in the musical accompaniment of life that the two races best understood one another, and each contributed. Indian drums and flutes were added to Spanish violas and guitars for festival music. Marimbas, which may or may not have originated in Guatemala, contributed their thin, tinkling notes. In folk songs Indian themes were blended with those of Spain.

Indians and mestizos sang in church choirs, the common folk sang in street fiestas and in their homes. Music was the social art of the upper-class señoritas, with which they entertained parties in the stately homes.

The small provincial capitals copied their social life from that of Santiago de los Caballeros, as the wealthy of that city patterned theirs on the aristocratic society of Spain. Santiago, city of wealth and licentious living, was regarded with both jealousy and criticism by people of the other provinces.

It was the seat of the governor who ruled the whole kingdom, nominally subject to the Viceroy of New Spain. Under the governor the *intendentes,* or local governors, and cabildos of provincial cities managed their own affairs rather independently, due to the great distances and lack of roads between them and Santiago. The provinces resented the domination of Guatemala in government and business, so that jealousies and a separatist spirit were already strong before the provinces became nations.

In the early eighteenth century Santiago de los Caballeros was outshone only by Mexico City and Lima as a splendid colonial capital. There the wealth of the aristocrats and the Church was concentrated. The huge monasteries, convents and churches were structures of solid dignity enriched with the sculpture and decoration of Spain's finest artists. There were streets of thick-walled mansions, each a treasure house of rich furnishings, each beautified with secluded patio gardens. On the Plaza de Armas handsome buildings framed the square; the Cathedral, the beautiful Palace of the Captains-general with double arcaded corridors of graceful arches; the Casas Consistoriales or Real Cabildo, seat of city government; the Portal de los Mercadores with shops of merchants.

In the Plaza were held the ornate colonial festivals, and

every afternoon the ladies and gentlemen of society made their promenade around the square on foot or in sedan chairs and coaches.

The cobbled streets were dark at night, lit only by candles burning before statues of saints in niches. Citizens found their way about by candlelight, and nobles were preceded by lackeys with flaming torches.

Bells of innumerable churches rang their messages to the populace from dawn to dark. Government edicts, or important events were announced by a *bando,* an officer accompanied by a trumpeter, who read his document at various corners after a trumpet blast had collected a crowd. Once or twice a year, when mail arrived from Spain, the postmaster with officers and knights in full dress rode out to receive it at La Cruz de Piedra, a stone cross on the outskirts.

The monastic orders and sisterhoods had grown immensely wealthy from their great estates, from tithes, gifts and the dowers of those who entered the orders from rich families. Rivalry for power was so intense that quarrels between monks sometimes came to open conflict in the churches. Through the bishop and the powerful orders the Church dominated politics and controlled the moral and social life of the inhabitants; not without protest, however, in the defiance of godless ones, and interference from civic authorities.

Many sons and daughters of the aristocracy, through piety or boredom, joined the orders to live in seclusion. The most talented people of the city, those with the best education, were in the monasteries and convents. They studied weighty religious and philosophic volumes in monastic libraries and sometimes wrote books themselves. The only schools were those of the Jesuits, Dominicans and Franciscans. Santiago attained a leading position in scholarship when the Dominican College became the University of San Carlos Borromeo in 1678.

Judging by the stories which have come down from that age, young people of the nobility did not renounce worldly comforts or ambitions when they entered the orders. They lived well on the fat of the land. The flowery cloistered gardens, with fountains and fish pools, were places of peace. There were music rooms and libraries for study. The churches were filled with the finest works of art and craftsmanship of the period in silver, brocades, wood carving, sculpture, painting.

In the convent of La Concepción and other sisterhoods young nuns of noble families became expert in cookery and fine needlework, learned to play the harp and organ and were trained in singing. Their voices added to the beauty of the solemn church music.

Few among the rich, ambitious monks had the devoted spirit of the early friars. One humble brother of the Third Order of Saint Francis, however, was beloved by the people as the Servant of God. A man of saintly spirit and simplicity, Hermano Pedro de Betancourt devoted his life to the sick and poor.

In a thatched hut of a humble suburb he started his hospital and a school for poor children. Poverty-stricken sick people were brought there, often on his own back, to be nursed back to health. Hermano Pedro's work attracted the attention of devout men who became his helpers. Funds were raised to build a chapel and hospital for him. He chose the symbol of Bethlehem, for love of the Christ child and all children, and called his helpers the Bethlehemites.

Every year Hermano Pedro's chapel was crowded with worshippers for the midnight Mass of *La Noche Buena,* or Christmas Eve. The scene of the Nativity arranged in the church, called the *Nascimiento,* was particularly beautiful. After the service there were games, dances and gifts for all poor children, with Hermano Pedro leading the fun.

The Servant of God was distressed over the gambling, extravagance and general loose living of the wealthy. In his brown robe he went through the dark streets night after night, ringing his bell and calling on the people to pray for their souls' salvation.

One night a richly dressed gentleman rushed from a house and fell on his knees before the friar, begging to be saved from a terrible predicament. He was Don Rodrigo Arias de Maldonado, one of the gayest and most popular of the caballeros in Santiago's extravagant society. He had fallen in love with the wife of a high official, and that night, her husband being away, he was visiting the lady when she suddenly fell lifeless in his arms.

Don Rodrigo ran out at the sound of the friar's bell, promising to devote the rest of his life to Hermano Pedro's work if the lady was saved. The good friar restored her from the strange collapse into which she had fallen and Don Rodrigo kept his word. He entered the hospital, devoting himself to the poor, no matter how menial the task. Often promenading aristocrats in the Plaza were scandalized to see their former companion carrying raw meat on his back to the hospital. Offers of honorable positions were refused by the reformed gallant who took the name of Hermano Rodrigo de la Cruz. When Hermano Pedro died his assistant received permission from the Pope to found the Bethlehemite Order, inspired by the good Franciscan friar.

The volcanoes beyond the handsome city were dangerous neighbors. Often Volcán de Fuego's scarred crest was crowned with smoke and flame and its rumblings shook the city. As the eighteenth century advanced disastrous earthquakes became frequent, toppling down houses, weakening foundations and causing great cracks in the solid walls of churches, and 1773 was a year of terror, as tremors increased from month to month. Panic-stricken people camped in the fields, some of the nobles spent their nights in their coaches.

On July 29 came a terrific shock, sending householders screaming into the streets. It was followed by a rending and swaying of the earth so appalling that houses collapsed in heaps, walls of churches fell in, and as the towers crumbled the bells tolled wildly like a warning of doom. To the uproar of crashing walls was added the confusion of people and animals running about in panic, shrieking with fright. Choked by clouds of dust, people rushed for their priests, kneeling around them amid the ruins to confess their sins.

The beautiful city was a mass of ruins with gaunt walls and some church façades rising above heaps of rubble. Countless bodies of people and animals were buried under the stones so that the stench of death filled the streets and decay brought pestilence. To this was added hunger, and lack of water as the aqueducts were broken. Still the people clung to the city which had been their pride.

For two years a struggle went on between the Captain-general and civic officers who were determined to move away from the volcanoes, and the ecclesiastics who were equally determined to stay with their great properties and rebuild. Some people followed the civic officers when they moved to a hermitage on a hill, La Ermita, in the Valle de las Vacas. It was a fine site in a wide valley broken by deep barrancas. Mountains separated it from the dangerous volcanoes.

In 1775, by the King's decree, the inhabitants of the ruined city were moved to the new site. Streets and houses spread out from the foot of the hill, La Ermita. The new city was given the name Nueva Guatemala de la Asunción, present-day Guatemala City.

Old Santiago, now called Antigua, was never wholly abandoned. For some years the monks and bishops refused to move, rebuilding as much as possible of their ruined structures. Common folk moved into tumble-down houses and monasteries, raised vegetables and pastured their cows in great enclosures which had been cloisters and gardens. Antigua today, a lovely, dreamy place, is the haunt of artists and tourists who come to study the magnificent colonial architecture, ruined though it is.

One year after the earthquake at Santiago, in 1774, the English colonies of North America declared their independence of the mother country. Winds of liberty were blowing across America, and the ruin of Santiago was a symbol of the cracking walls of Spain's colonial empire. The inhabitants within were soon to awake from their lethargy to demand freedom.

THE VICEROYALTY OF NEW SPAIN

CONQUERORS, explorers and missionaries extended Spain's grasp of America northward from central Mexico in the time of the first Viceroy, Don Antonio de Mendoza. Fantasies of mysterious glittering cities—golden Quivira, the Seven Cities of Cibola—shimmered in credulous Spanish minds, aided by Indian romancing. The tales sent conquerors exploring through the mountains and deserts of northern Mexico, Arizona, New Mexico. Even as far as Kansas went Francisco Vásquez de Coronado in search of the mythical Quivira. Juan de Oñate subdued the Pueblo Indians and made the first settlement at Santa Fe in what was to become the province of New Mexico.

By sea, navigators explored the Pacific coast, along the arid mountainous strip of Baja California, northward to found San Diego, Monterey and Yerba Buena, which was to become San Francisco.

Missionary padres were the vanguard of settlement. They accompanied the soldiers, preaching to the Indians and founding missions. Their converts were persuaded to live in compounds close to the simple but beautiful mission churches.

Tucking up their robes, the padres, by their own labor, taught their charges blacksmithing, carpentry, masonry and fruit culture. Indian labor built the churches under the direction of the friars, and as they painted the interiors Indian ideas were sometimes mingled with Spanish design. Near the missions were built presidios, military posts for protection against Indian raids. The mission-presidio settlements became the outposts of Spain's empire and, through the work of the friars, little islands of civilization.

Missions were also founded in Texas, and from Arizona intrepid friars such as Padre Kino, who were explorers as well as missionaries, made their way overland to California. On their heels came bands of soldiers and settlers. That distant province of New Spain became a land of thriving mission settlements, sleepy little towns and ports, great cattle ranches where life was easygoing, expansive, hospitable. The land was held for Spain against the encroachments of Russian fur traders moving down from Alaska.

The vastly extended Viceroyalty of New Spain ranked with the Viceroyalty of Peru in importance.

Herds of wild cattle roamed the plains of northern Mexico, progeny of animals escaped from explorers' expeditions. Spaniards soon had Indians and mestizos on horseback, rounding up the wild cattle to slaughter them for the hides. The hard-riding *vaqueros,* expert with horses and cattle, served the owners of enormous ranches in the later colonial period.

Descendants of conquerors and of hidalgos who came early to New Spain became hereditary landowners, lords of huge domains, the haciendas. These families, the founders of Mexico's aristocracy, grew rich from their sugar cane, corn, cotton, tobacco, and the brewing of pulque, the fermented liquor made from the sap of the agave cactus plant, maguey. The downtrodden Indians became addicted to this liquor of the Aztec nobility. It was one of the means by which their masters kept them in bondage.

Hacienda headquarters were like fortresses for protection against Indian uprisings. Workshops, granaries, stables, the master's spacious house and the chapel were enclosed in a great compound surrounded by thick stone walls. A large gateway with wooden doors was the entrance. Major-domos administered the estates and since their job was to produce profits the Indian laborers were exploited without mercy.

During the eighteenth century the landowning families enjoyed expansive sociability on the haciendas where they came for country holidays, fiestas, and parties with neighboring hacendado families. For the most part, however, they were absentee landlords, preferring luxurious existence in their stately town mansions to country life.

Before a century had passed Spanish ways of life and the magnificent architecture of Spain had changed, but not obliterated, Indian Mexico. In the social pattern the native people were fixed in their position of servitude.

They were superficially converted by earnest friars, accepting the pageantry of Catholic worship with its festivals and images of saints in place of their ancient ceremonies. The wise fathers did not interfere with the fusing in Indian minds of attributes of the old gods with those of some Catholic saints.

In the sixteenth century the miraculous experience of a humble Indian, Juan Diego, gave the people their special patroness. On the hill of Tepeyac at Guadalupe, near Mexico City, the Holy Mother herself appeared to Juan Diego. He was to tell Bishop Zumárraga that she wished a church erected on that spot. The Bishop dismissed the Indian's story impatiently— he required a token from the Virgin.

When Juan Diego returned to Tepeyac the Virgin appeared again, commanding him to gather roses from the barren mountaintop to show the Bishop. Although it was December, the roses were there and Juan Diego carried them in his coarse cotton *tilma,* or mantle, to the Bishop. Reverently the Indian opened the tilma and out tumbled the fresh flowers before the startled prelate. Even more amazing was the image of the Virgin, imprinted on the coarse fabric. There she was against a starry background, smiling sweetly, surrounded by an aura of golden rays.

Bishop Zumárraga and his councillors decided to call it a miracle and a beautiful church was built at Tepeyac for the Virgin of Guadalupe. From that time forth she was the special protectress of the Indians and all poor or oppressed people. Eventually the Virgin of Guadalupe became the patroness of Mexico.

Don Antonio de Mendoza established the right of Indian caciques to govern their villages and to retain the communal tracts of land where the villagers grew corn, beans and chili peppers for their families. This tract, the ejido, was generally about ten square miles in extent. Haughty Spaniards, however, could not grow rich without the labor of Indians in mines, fields and shops. The Spanish government, by the New Laws, forbade absolute slavery, but the forced labor of Indians on the haciendas was slavery in another form.

Worse off were the Indians compelled to work in mines and in the *obrajes* or weaving shops. Silver mines of inexhaustible, fabulous wealth were developed in the provinces of Zacatécas and Guanajuato. Mining methods were crude and thousands of Indians suffered and died under the hard labor. The ore was brought from the deep shafts on Indian backs, each man carrying from two hundred and fifty to three hundred pounds as he crawled up steep ladders in the sweating darkness.

Other men and women, skilled in weaving, were rounded up to work in the obrajes which were like jails with guards at the gates. The work day was from sunup to sundown and workers were often forced to sleep in the obrajes, going out to see their families only on Sundays. Their tiny wages were frequently withheld on one pretext or another, so that the workers, like the Indians on haciendas, were bound to their masters. The Council of the Indies sent successive decrees to regulate working conditions in the obrajes, imposing fines for infractions, but the laws were generally ignored or circumvented.

It was in crafts and building that Indians found a happier life, for their skills were useful. As masons, as carvers of wood and stone, Indians and mestizos produced the architectural splendor of colonial Mexico under the direction of Spanish master craftsmen. Spain, in her most creative period, sent her artists to beautify New Spain, and a deeply artistic Indian race eagerly contributed its talents.

Guilds of master craftsmen trained native workers in their skills—the production of leather goods and wrought iron, blown glass, jewelry and silverware, weaving and pottery. From the pottery works at Puebla came beautiful dishes and jars for the homes of the wealthy. *Azulejos,* painted tiles, were also made at Puebla. This Hispanic-Moorish art was transplanted to adorn buildings and grace patio gardens or public parks with tiled fountains, benches, pavements. Aristocrats had the façades of their houses decorated with soft-colored azulejos; monasteries and convents had the walls of cloisters lined with them. Tiled domes of churches—blue, green, yellow—bloomed delightfully against the background of Mexican mountains

Indian village craftsmen adopted Spanish designs and some techniques to mingle with their own ideas in traditional crafts. From father to son, in some villages, the workers were weavers, in others makers of sandals and saddles, or pottery, or weavers of fibers and reeds into mats, baskets, hats and hammocks. Tarascan Indians, in certain villages of Michoacán, were famous in colonial times as they are today for beautiful lacquered ware, done by a process which is still their secret. Carved and lacquered chests and feather tapestries, a continuation of the old Indian art, were prized in many homes.

The wealth of the powerful Church was largely responsible for the colonial baroque architecture, so massive and dignified, so ornately rich in exterior sculpture and inner decoration. Church interiors glowed with color and the sheen of gold leaf, immense monasteries and graceful bell towers dominated the landscape. Native stone of creamy, gray or dull-red tones gave color to church buildings and stately towns where the aristocrats had their spacious mansions.

The easy life of privileged people in the cities was in sharp contrast to the poverty of the submerged classes. In towns and villages the dull existence of the poor was brightened by colorful church processions and fiestas. Indians, in village fiestas, performed their traditional dances, sometimes mingling with them Spanish themes and costumes. Spanish influence helped to create the regional songs and dances which make Mexico such an enchanting land.

Travelers jolted over rough roads in coaches or made journeys on horseback, always on the alert for the bandits who infested the countryside. From town to town and from coastal ports to the highlands, went long trains of pack mules loaded with goods, driven by the arrieros.

From Acapulco on the Pacific trading vessels sailed to ports of Central America, and once a year a galleon arrived with Chinese goods. New Spain was the only kingdom permitted to carry on the China trade. The galleon sailed to Manila in the Philippines laden with silver and with missionary friars— *plata y frailes*—and there silver was exchanged for Chinese silks, porcelains and beautiful shawls embroidered with brilliant flowers. The galleon brought not only Chinese goods but laborers and girls to go into service.

Over the mountains by a stone-paved trail pack mules carried the goods to Mexico City, thence to Vera Cruz to be shipped to Spain. Colonial merchants had their share, however, and wealthy ladies of Mexico City eagerly awaited the arrival of silks and porcelains from China.

New Spain suffered from the same excessive taxation and restrictions on trade as the rest of the colonial empire; there was no incentive to develop native industries as most of them were for home consumption only. From merchandising to the topmost government posts men from Spain had the advantage over American-born, or creole, aristocrats and merchants, so that hatred of the *gachupines,* as the Spaniards were called, increased from year to year.

Late in the eighteenth century King Carlos III sent a visitor-general, José de Valdes, to reorganize administration and trade in New Spain. On his recommendation trade restrictions and taxes were lightened somewhat but it was too late to make contented subjects of the colonials. They were already thinking of managing government and trade for themselves. The administrative system Valdes organized, dividing the viceroyalty into districts with local governors or intendentes, was useful to Mexicans after independence as a framework for local administration.

As time went on the class divisions of colonial society became fixed. At the top were the haughty Spanish nobility, resented by the Mexican-born aristocrats, the Creoles, who in turn lorded it over those beneath them. The large mixed-blood population, the mestizos, unstable and frustrated, resented the Creoles and hated the Indians who were at the bottom of the social scale. They, in turn, despised the mestizos. There were also Negro slaves and mulattoes who were still worse off.

The whole vast realm of New Spain, from California and New Mexico to Yucatán, was ruled by the Viceroy, living with pompous luxury in Mexico City. He was directly responsible to the King, but the monarch was thousands of miles away, giving the Viceroy the opportunity to rule like a minor king. Some few of these men were good administrators, but most of them were Spanish noblemen who cared only for power and the wealth they could accumulate to take back to Spain.

All the best positions in viceregal and city government were in the hands of gentlemen from Spain who obtained them by appointment or purchase. Municipal officers—alcaldes and regidores—were creoles for the most part. Ambitious men with a tinge of Indian blood sometimes managed to advance themselves by buying certificates of whiteness, thus becoming eligible for office.

The top-heavy, cumbersome bureaucracy was ridden with corruption and bribery from top to bottom, for most officials used their posts to make money for themselves, aping their superiors in unscrupulous methods. At first colonials had some small opportunity for self-government in the cabildos of towns, but this lessened as gentlemen bought their positions and held them for life. Nevertheless, it was in the cabildos of cities scattered over the country that colonials had some local control and were leaders in the movement for independence.

As Tenochtitlán was the pride and glory of the Aztec kingdom, so viceregal Mexico City, built on its ruins, was the pride of New Spain. It grew in dignity and splendor with amazing rapidity from its sixteenth-century beginnings. Great churches, monasteries, government palaces and mansions of the nobility gave the city an air of harmonious richness. The life of powerful ecclesiastics and aristocrats was similar to that of Santiago de los Caballeros, but on a much grander scale.

Homes of the wealthy were furnished with the most luxurious products of Spain in mirrors, hangings, soft carpets, carved and inlaid furniture. Families had table services of embossed silver as well as fine Chinese porcelains. They dressed with ostentatious richness and exquisite jewelry made by master craftsmen. Elegant ladies went abroad in the streets in coaches or in sedan chairs, painted and lined with Chinese silk, borne on the shoulders of Negro slaves. These slaves, and Indian or mestizo servants, were dressed in gaudy costumes to enhance the prestige of their masters. Gentlemen prided themselves on their horsemanship and decked their pure-bred animals with silver-mounted bridles, saddles and stirrups.

In the lovely Alameda, a place of trees and flower-sprinkled meadows, fashionable society made the daily paseo to see and be seen. Round and round they went, the ladies in coaches and sedan chairs, escorted by caballeros on horseback and Negro slaves. The "bosque" of Chapultepec, once Montezuma's pleasure ground, was a country resort of cool woodlands and ancient *ahuehuete* trees where horsemen rode and families came for holiday excursions. The viceroys had a summer palace at Chapultepec, and the city received pure water from its springs by an aqueduct.

Until late in the eighteenth century there were many canals and bridges in the city, with one broad waterway leading from shrunken Lake Texcoco. Traffic by canoe was picturesque, but householders threw into the canals all sorts of refuse, even dead animals, so that the stagnant waters were breeding places for epidemics which frequently swept the city.

The old causeway to Tacuba, lined with trees, passed between cultivated fields on land reclaimed from the lake. In the watery regions of Xochimilco and Chalco, Indians lived in their ancestral way, growing fruit, flowers and vegetables for the capital. Paddling their dugout canoes heaped with blooms and garden produce they passed through the city canals, crying their wares. Canoes of fruit and flower venders huddled about the steps of the Portal de Las Flores in the Plaza Mayor, now called the Zócalo, where householders and servants came to buy.

All sorts of venders had their shops under the arcades of the Portal de los Mercadores in the Plaza Mayor and on market days the whole great square swarmed with people. Reed mats supported on sticks sheltered the *puestos,* or stands, from the sun. In their shade Indian women sold tamales, dulces and village wares. The animal market of calves, pigs, burros, poultry, added to the uproar and dirt of the disorderly Plaza.

Indeed, the colonial Plaza Mayor, built on the ruins of the Aztec Tecpán, was not a well-kept place until late in the eighteenth century. To be sure, it was surrounded with handsome buildings—the Cathedral, the Palace of the Viceroys, the Municipal Palace. Despite dust and filth underfoot it was a place of vivid life and varied spectacles.

On the stone-paved atrium before the Cathedral were played religious dramas called *autos,* and comedies of Spanish playwrights. Gorgeous processions, on great Church festivals, emerged from the Cathedral with richly dressed images borne on platforms in the midst of priests and choristers. Chanting mingled with the clangor of the great bells in the Cathedral towers. There were worldly festivities as well, such as bull-fights and street fairs; and on San Hipolito's day Masses and fireworks commemorated the conquest of the Aztec city by Cortés.

In the Plaza Mayor the populace gathered to welcome a new Viceroy, as with pomp and splendor and a great retinue he passed through to the Palace. Until the canals were filled in, the Viceroy and his family, when going to theatrical performances in the Coliseo Viejo, stepped into canoes with sumptuous canopies at the palace door to proceed by water to the show.

Life for both rich and poor, in the seventeenth century, was steeped in superstitious piety. People believed in the miraculous intervention of the saints in their affairs, feared the work of demons, told stories of witches who sold their souls to the devil.

The translucent atmosphere above the mountain city was filled with the calling of bells, from the Ave Maria at dawn to the Angelus at evening. Bells deep and booming, or thin and sweet, rang for innumerable services, regulated the activities of monks and nuns in their retreats, announced in solemn strokes the death of viceroys, bishops, or others of high rank.

The judges of the dread Inquisition pried into the actions and thoughts of all inhabitants. Unfortunates accused of heresies or witchcraft were tried by the court. Those who escaped with penances were obliged to walk through the streets wearing robes called *sambenitos* painted with flames and devils, carrying green candles in their hands. Dangerous heretics were burned alive in the awful ceremony of the *auto-da-fé*.

During daylight hours the streets hummed with colorful life. In the variegated crowd were monks in the robes of their orders, gaudily dressed slaves and servants, mestizos in picturesque costumes bargaining at shop doors where merchants displayed their wares. Horsemen and painted coaches clattered over the cobblestones, itinerant venders chanted their wares, the bando blew his trumpet and read decrees, men cried the announcements of bullfights, cockfights or street fairs. Sometimes university students on the way to receive degrees were escorted by riotous bands of masked companions. In addition to processions for saints' days there were those of the penitents in *sambenitos,* or of the religious brotherhoods called *cofradías,* or parades of the guilds celebrating the day of their patron saint.

These guilds were close corporations, each with rigid control over its particular craft. Silversmiths, leatherworkers, ironworkers, all had their shops in certain streets. Master craftsmen who ruled the guilds had an honored position in the social system. They must be of white blood, and have attained their position through skill, so that all craft work was of a high order.

The capital of New Spain had the best of Spanish culture insofar as the mother country permitted it to reach the colonies. Mexico City had the first printing press in the Americas, and the first University founded in 1551. In the eighteenth century the press was publishing books of devotion or lives of saints. Booksellers displayed also theological volumes, Greek and Latin studies, and knightly romances brought from Spain in the "flota." Eighteenth-century citizens had a newspaper, the *gaceta,* from which they might glean bits of Spanish news, learn of the arrival of ships, or read wondrous tales of sea monsters, comets, or the doings of witches.

Upper-class youth studied in the religious colleges, or attained knowledge of law, Latin, medicine and theology in the University, and for the most ambitious readers there were libraries attached to the University and Cathedral. Before the close of the viceregal period the Academia de Bellas Artes was giving instruction in sculpture and painting. The population as a whole, however, went without even elementary education.

In the monasteries scholarly monks studied and wrote volumes, or taught in the Jesuit, Dominican and Franciscan colleges. Mexico had two literary lights whose fame spread beyond its borders. One was the remarkable poet nun, Sor Juana de la Cruz, whose poetry won her the title of Muse of the Western Hemisphere. The Mexican-born dramatist, Juan Ruiz de Alarcón, had his plays honored in Spain.

At times the easygoing life of the city was disturbed by floods from the lake, epidemics, clashes of political factions, or riots when hunger and oppression roused the people.

Friar Thomas Gage witnessed one of the most violent upheavals during his visit in mid-seventeenth century, when the viceregal government was especially corrupt. A Spanish nobleman, Don Pedro Mexia, became the first speculator of Mexico. He cornered the Indian wheat and corn, selling it for outrageous prices so that famine conditions resulted. In their despair the people appealed to their priests, and the Archbishop took up their cause. He exposed the scandal and excommunicated Don Pedro Mexia. When the Viceroy tore down the notices on church doors and refused to punish the speculator, the Archbishop excommunicated the Viceroy and closed the churches in protest.

The scandal grew when the Viceroy dared to send an officer to arrest the Archbishop in the sanctuary of the Cathedral. Defiantly the prelate faced the officer before the altar, holding the sacred Host. Most men would have been cowed by that, but the officer avoided sacrilege by ordering a priest to take the Host while he carried through the arrest.

These insults to their religion, added to the desperation of hunger, roused the population to furious rioting. Creoles joined mestizos, Indians and black slaves as they roared through the

streets, shouting, *"Viva el Rey y muere el mal gobierno"*—
"Long live the King and death to bad government." It was a
cry that was to ring through the years as colonials protested
against the evils of their government. Angry crowds set fire
to the palace while the Viceroy, Don Pedro Mexia and other
grandees escaped in disguise.

Although Spain tried to keep her colonial subjects sealed off
from all outside influences, the echoes of new ideas stirring
Europe filtered in through smuggled books and a few travelers. Groups of Creoles, men and women, including some
scholarly priests, met secretly to read the works of eighteenth
century French philosophers and to discuss the right of men
to free themselves from tyranny. They were beginning to think
of themselves as men of the New World rather than Spaniards.

When Napoleon invaded Spain in 1808, set his brother Joseph
on the throne, and kept the Spanish King Ferdinand VII in
exile, the discontent smoldering under the drowsy surface of
colonial life flared into action.

In Spain itself the people rose against the usurper; juntas,
or governing councils, sprang up in cities to manage affairs
until their rightful king was restored to his throne. The confusion and disorder in the mother country were reflected in
New Spain.

Loyalty had been given to an absolute monarch rather than
to the mother country. He had been the fountainhead of all
authority. Without that royal personage, to whom were government officials responsible? The Creoles did not intend to
permit the ambitious Viceroy to become ruler of Mexico. Unworthy King Ferdinand was eulogized, juntas of church and
municipal officials declared their unswerving fealty to him.

Their idea was to establish a Mexican kingdom governed by
Creoles, but acknowledging loyalty to the Spanish monarchy.

Even the most conservative Creoles were urged on by a desire to win Mexico for the Mexicans, to get rid of the gachupines. To the groups of men imbued with republican spirit, who were inspired by the French Revolution and the new republic of the United States, the formation of governing juntas was only the first step toward true independence.

CHAPTER 13

NEW NATIONS ARE BORN

AS DAY was dawning on September 16, 1810, the people of the Mexican village of Dolores were wandering toward their church to attend early Sunday Mass. The church bell was clanging with unusual urgency, a rumor was passing from group to group that something had been happening in the village during the night. At the church the people's expectancy was confirmed. Their good friend and priest, Padre Miguel Hidalgo, addressed them with earnest fervor. The hour had come, he declared, to strike for freedom. Were they ready to follow him, to overthrow Spanish rule, to win liberty and the lands taken from their forefathers by the Spanish conquerors?

"Viva la Virgen de Guadalupe! Viva America!" cried Padre Hidalgo.

The answer to his call was a mighty shout. His words were not entirely new to the villagers. For a long time, as he ministered to them and directed their industries, he had been preparing them. He had spoken of their right to free themselves from servitude to the Spaniards, the right of the humblest to have land and a good life. The most trusted men had been taken into the group Padre Hidalgo was organizing in Dolores to take part in a revolt against Spanish rule.

The news of Padre Hidalgo's *grito* or call spread rapidly that Sunday morning in Dolores. Men streamed in from the countryside and came from village houses to gather around their *cura* and a couple of patriot army officers.

They were a motley band with an odd assortment of weapons —clubs, machetes, a few guns seized from the barracks. Their brown faces solemn with the exaltation of the moment, they marched out of the village, led by Padre Hidalgo on a black horse, in his clerical robe. The banner of the Indian Virgin of Guadalupe floated over their heads. It was the first move of the dispossessed folk of Mexico in their long struggle for land and liberty.

Miguel Hidalgo y Costilla was a man of vigorous, independent mind and great heart. With his theological training he might have been rector in the College of San Nicolás in Valladolid where he studied, but he chose to be a simple village priest. To the people of Dolores he was a father, beloved for his sympathy and for his schemes to lessen the hardships of their lives. Under his direction the villagers planted vineyards, learned beekeeping and silkworm culture. He taught them to make good clay pottery, tan hides, weave textiles and make wine from their grapes.

Even these simple village industries were frowned upon by the Spanish authorities. Mexicans were forbidden to produce anything which would interfere with the business of Spanish merchants and this priest, who tried to help his flock to be self-supporting, was looked upon as a dangerous person.

Padre Hidalgo was frequently called to account by church authorities as well because of his independent thinking and unorthodox utterances. He refused to have his mind stifled by the rules of the Inquisition. He read the forbidden works of the French philosophers and dramatists, and although the French ideal—*Liberté, Egalité, Fraternité*—had gone down under Napoleon's rule, Padre Hidalgo dreamed of applying those great principles to Mexico.

In the nearby town of Querétaro, Padre Hidalgo joined a group of Creole townsmen and army officers in a club they called a literary society. Secretly they discussed the revolutionary ideas of the French and talked of Mexican independence. Their plans went no farther than to achieve a Mexico freed from Spanish rule, perhaps an independent monarchy, but such ideas were revolutionary in viceregal New Spain.

In Miguel Hidalgo's mind independence meant a free nation with land and prosperity for all the oppressed, Indian or mestizo. A young Creole army officer, Captain Ignacio Allende, took the lead with Padre Hidalgo in plans for a revolt. The group in Querétaro was in touch with other Creole clubs who intended to make a joint declaration of independence in December, 1810.

Then their schemes were betrayed to government officials in Querétaro. The mayor's wife, Señora Dominguez, a member of their society, learned of the danger. She sent a servant posthaste to warn Captain Allende, who galloped off in the night with another officer to consult with Miguel Hidalgo.

Their idea was to escape before they were arrested, but that did not suit the valorous priest. No, he said, now was the moment to strike. Once they had given the call for independence the country would rise to join them.

The three conspirators went out into the sleeping village during the night of September 15 to seize the officers in the barracks and capture muskets. On the historic morning they marched out with their company of peasants.

News of the revolt spread quickly from village to town over the countryside. Creole officers with their troops came to join Captain Allende and Padre Hidalgo; the Indian campesinos came in hordes, in their ragged cotton suits, with clubs and knives for weapons, to fight under the banner of Guadalupe.

The Spanish authorities, amazed at such an insurrection, were slow in assembling troops. In many small towns the rejoicing people captured the barracks and received the rebels with open arms. Even when they met Spanish artillery fire and disciplined troops the Indians fought through bloody battles to win important towns in northern Mexico. As the little army swelled to a hundred thousand, Spaniards and bishops fled before them, priests exhorted their people not to listen to the renegade cura from Dolores.

At Valladolid a short, stocky young priest, José Maria Morelos, joined the rebel army. He was a former pupil of Miguel Hidalgo at the College of San Nicolás, and a devoted follower of the good priest. Morelos was a mestizo of the humblest birth. He knew from youthful experience the tribulations of the Mexican poor and was heart and soul with Hidalgo in his quest for liberty and justice.

Miguel Hidalgo sent him with a few men to stir up rebellion in the south. Morelos organized guerrilla companies and, in 1811 and 1812, won many victories in the mountains between Acapulco and Taxco.

As the Spanish General Calleja gathered his forces the war became a ferocious, bloody conflict. The Indians fought with fanatical fury, dying in shoals before Spanish cannon fire. Poverty-stricken campesinos and the lowly folk of towns, bursting out from the oppression of their lives, took revenge on wealthy masters, whether Spaniard or Creole.

Haciendas were raided and burned, town houses looted, as the peasant army got completely out of hand. The insurrection took a turn most alarming to wealthy Creoles who had no intention of giving up privileges or land to the common folk. Many deserted the rebels to return to Spanish allegiance.

The viceregal government set a price on Padre Hidalgo's white head, the Inquisition and powerful bishops thundered against him and declared him excommunicated. Nothing daunted, the Captain-general of America, as he was styled, led his army on. Though thousands of poorly armed Indians fell before Spanish artillery, more came to swell the ranks. The Creole officers tried to discipline the Indian bands, but it was more a rabble than an army of many thousand men that finally drew near to Mexico City.

The Spanish nobles and officials shook in their shoes. Masses were said in the Cathedral and the treasured Virgen de los Remedios was paraded through the streets. The rebels might have won the city if they had taken advantage of Spanish terror to strike quickly. Hidalgo's officers urged attack, the rebels were full of confidence, but for some reason the Captain-general of America refused to follow up his victories and thus lost the revolution. The order for the army to turn back north checked the fiery sweep of the revolt, caused desertions of disgusted Indians and soldiers and a rift between Hidalgo and Allende.

While Captain Allende with a diminished army suffered many defeats in the north from General Calleja, Miguel Hidalgo retired to Guadalajara to organize his government. He was a reformer, not a military man; he believed the cause would triumph despite defeats and that his work was to set up the framework of the new order. With serene confidence he issued decrees and made plans for the free Mexico he dreamed of. All slavery was to be abolished, land was to be distributed to the Indians, crafts and industries were to be stimulated for the prosperity of the people.

Later on Hidalgo joined his army in the north, where it was being rapidly decimated by Spanish soldiery. The end came through the treachery of one of Hidalgo's own officers. Captain Allende and Hidalgo were trapped in a small village and arrested by this traitor, Colonel Elizonde. Ignacio Allende was shot and Padre Hidalgo was taken to a northern town for trial. After being degraded and stripped of his priestly position by church authorities, Miguel Hidalgo was condemned to death. He faced the firing squad with calm dignity, July 30, 1811. The heads of the two patriots, old Hidalgo and young Allende, were exposed on the wall of Guanajuato where they remained, desiccated by weather, until 1821.

It was not until that year, 1821, that Mexico actually won independence, but it was the patriot priest of great vision, with his army of campesinos, who gave Mexicans their *patria*. September 16 is Mexico's independence day. Every year the president of the Republic appears on the balcony of the National Palace in Mexico City to give the *Grito de Dolores,* commemorating that historic day in 1810 when the valiant priest led his brown children out to fight for liberty.

José Maria Morelos, who was very successful in the south, became the leader of the revolution after Padre Hidalgo's death. He was a man of tremendous energy and intelligence, with more military ability than the older leader. Realizing that untrained Indian mobs could not oppose professional Spanish soldiers, he trained small disciplined units, arming them with muskets taken from Spaniards. Bands of horsemen and some

Creole landowners were drawn to his leadership and many cities were captured. One of the best of Morelos' lieutenants was an uneducated mestizo peasant, Vicente Guerrero, who was to keep the flame of liberty alive after Morelos had been killed.

Morelos, like Padre Hidalgo, was so anxious to set up government that he could not wait for the war to be won. A congress of delegates was called together at Chilpancingo in 1813, to discuss his plans and write a constitution for a Mexican republic ruled by the will of the majority. The young mestizo priest, so close to the dispossessed people of his land, carried on the ideals of Miguel Hidalgo. He formulated revolutionary principles for which Mexicans would be fighting again a hundred years later in their Revolution of 1910.

In sweeping proposals Morelos planned to break up the political and social system of Spanish-ruled Mexico. He advocated racial equality and the distribution of wealth for the general welfare and public works. All special privileges of army officers, clergy and landowners were to be abolished. He proposed that the great estates be divided into small holdings for the campesinos. Thus the rigid caste system would be broken up and the chasm bridged between wealth and poverty. Although Morelos was a priest and sincere Catholic he wanted the funds of rich church institutions confiscated for the benefit of the people.

The laws written into the constitution at Chilpancingo were anathema to the clergy and landowners. They did not want independence on such terms and Morelos lost many adherents from the upper class. His concentration on lawmaking gave General Calleja the opportunity to augment his forces and win back northern Mexico.

Morelos marched his soldiers to take Valladolid, his birthplace, where he intended to set up his government. Later the city was to be renamed Morelia in honor of its patriot son. In the struggle over that city the rebels were defeated by a fellow townsman of Morelos, a dashing young cavalry colonel who was to crush the revolution.

He was Agustín de Iturbide, an officer and member of a well-to-do family. He had joined other wealthy Creoles in favoring independence until he saw that the priests' rebellion meant the abolition of privilege. Then he offered his services to the Spanish general and rose rapidly in favor through his ability, popularity with the soldiers and ruthless execution of prisoners.

Under Iturbide's command, the Spanish troops defeated and scattered the rebels. Morelos was captured at Tehuacan in 1815. He was taken to Mexico City and shot secretly without a trial, lest a public execution should cause a new uprising.

The revolution of patriots and Indians was over. Two peasant leaders held out in the mountains with their guerrillas—Vicente Guerrero and a man of Vera Cruz province who took the name of Guadalupe Victoria. A few Creole insurgents with small companies were pursued by royalist troops and shot without mercy when captured. Men who still dreamed of independence kept silent, but took hope from the revolution in South America, under the leadership of Simón Bolívar and José de San Martín. Life for the poor was worse than ever in a country devastated by years of war.

Mexican patriots had tried to win freedom but what they got, in the next move for independence, was an emperor. Separation from Spain was talked of in the most conservative salons in 1820 as the powerful classes became alarmed over the turn of events in Spain. In the mother country liberals were in revolt against despotic King Ferdinand, and a liberal Spanish government would soon curb the privileges of churchmen and landowners in Mexico.

The conservatives talked of separation from a liberal Spain in order to invite King Ferdinand or some other prince of the reigning house to become monarch of Mexico. In this movement the ambitious officer, Agustín de Iturbide, saw his opportunity for power.

He was a recklessly extravagant man, a clever demagogue. Mexican conservatives approved of him, remembering his war record in defeating Morelos. Iturbide made himself solid with wealthy churchmen and aristocrats who were talking of separation from Spain. After failing in a campaign ordered by the Viceroy to capture the rebel Guerrero, Iturbide decided to change sides. He sat down in the Indian town of Iguala to write his Plan of Iguala, to which his soldiers swore allegiance.

It was a shrewd document, calculated to win both patriots and conservatives to follow him as the liberator of Mexico. "Liberty, Union and Religion," was his misleading slogan. Mexico was to became an independent monarchy ruled by some prince of the Spanish royal house. Reactionaries were won by this and by the promise that church organizations and great properties would not be disturbed.

Mexican patriots were attracted by the declaration that former rebels would be pardoned and that Creoles would have equality with gachupines, while Spanish officials who did not accept the Plan would be dismissed. There was not a word of hope in the Plan of Iguala for the campesinos who had fought so courageously for liberty. Nevertheless Vincente Guerrero was won to support Iturbide as the only chance to get rid of the hated gachupines.

Creoles of every shade of opinion flocked to Iturbide's banner. Some royalist officers and their troops joined him, city after city declared for independence. In 1821 the royalist army and Spanish officials marched to Vera Cruz to return to Spain. The self-styled liberator made a triumphal entry into Mexico City, magnificent on a black charger. Mexico had won independence from Spain, but the people had merely exchanged one set of masters for another.

At first Agustín de Iturbide governed as head of a Regency of Five, while a congress was elected by a farcical process that made sure no man of liberal tendencies would get in. The plan to choose a Spanish prince for ruler was discarded as the liberator's ambition swelled. Soon Iturbide hired some of his soldiers to make a demonstration before his house, demanding that he become Emperor of Mexico. Appearing on his balcony, Iturbide graciously accepted the call, after a becoming show of reluctance. The submissive congress elected him on May 18, 1822.

In the Cathedral, with pomp and display befitting royalty, Agustín de Iturbide and his wife were crowned Emperor and Empress of Mexico. A new aristocracy was created by handing out titles of nobility to Iturbide's relatives and friends. The capital was treated to the spectacle of an upstart emperor and a comic-opera court, as the nation's funds were squandered on pretentious display and festivities.

Emperor Agustín I dreamed of ruling a great American empire, to which end he tried to gather in the newly-independent provinces of the Kingdom of Guatemala. When the legislators refused to vote more funds for his extravagancies, Iturbide dismissed the congress and ruled as a dictator, depending on the support of the army. Officers were loyal, however, only so long as they had plenty of money, and the treasury was empty.

The defrauded liberals began plotting for the overthrow of

Agustín de Iturbide and the establishment of a republic. To lead the revolt came a handsome young Creole officer of Vera Cruz province, Antonio López de Santa Anna. He had not been sufficiently favored by Iturbide to suit his ambitions, and now prepared to topple him from the throne that he might be known as the liberator of Mexico from an emperor. Santa Anna was a man of great personal magnetism, popular with the soldiers and common people of his province. His flare for dramatic action at the right moment was soon to make him the popular hero of Mexico.

In his yearning for glory, his unscrupulous ambition and skillful opportunism, he was a dangerous leader for confused Mexicans. Now, at his eloquent call, Vincente Guerrero and Guadalupe Victoria took the field once more while officer after officer declared for a republic.

Before he had been emperor for a year Iturbide's day was over. On March 29, 1823, he offered to abdicate and the congress sent him into exile in Italy. The legislators kindly voted him an annual allowance of twenty-five thousand dollars but he was declared a traitor to his country.

Unaware that there was a price on his head and believing that the reactionaries would flock to him, Iturbide returned in disguise the following year. Before he could make contact with the anti-republicans he was captured and shot without ceremony. Those who hated republican ideas called him a hero and bewailed his ignominious end.

At last Mexico was a republic, after a fashion. The liberals, taking the young United States for a model, organized a federal republic with president, vice president and congress, supposedly elected by the people. A constitution was written and Mexico was started on the path of republican government.

Guadalupe Victoria, intrepid rebel, was elected the first

President of Mexico. He was followed, after several years of storm and stress, by the other peasant leader, Vicente Guerrero. They were both honest men, devoted to liberty for the people, but they could not cope with the powerful forces of the church, army and aristocrats, or the individual generals who wanted to rule.

Spanish American patriots, in all Spain's colonial empire, tried to impose a republican form of government on a feudal society with no experience in self-government. The North American colonists had an inheritance of British parliamentary procedure, they had their own colonial assemblies and town meetings before they declared their independence from England. Not so the Spanish Americans who, totally inexperienced, tried to organize republics. It was only in the municipal councils, the cabildos, that leading colonials had obtained some slight practice in self-government.

The Creole upper class had been largely responsible for separation from Spain, and they wanted independence in order to rule for the benefit of that class. Elections could mean nothing in countries where the submerged classes—Indians, Negroes, mestizos, mulattoes—were illiterate and subject to upper-class masters. The feudal pattern of society remained intact and government, though republican in form, was government by powerful leaders, the caudillos.

The caudillos were usually military leaders, men who through dramatic personality, ambition, cleverness and control of the army seized and held power. Sometimes they were the power behind the throne, or they ruled despotically in the guise of presidents while legislative assemblies and cabinet ministers had little influence.

All Spanish America, after independence, passed into the age of the caudillos. The principle of *caudillismo* has been a leading factor in politics even up to modern times. It has been slow to die and is not yet eliminated.

In Mexico, Antonio López de Santa Anna, who helped to overthrow Iturbide and to place Guadalupe Victoria in the presidency became the supreme caudillo. He and less successful men of the same type led unfortunate Mexico into a long period of turbulence, corruption and bad government.

The struggle for independence in Mexico, and in South America, came as a distant echo to the isolated people of the Kingdom of Guatemala, but roused them from apathy. They were urged in the same direction as other Spanish colonials by thorough discontent with their situation.

Individual provinces had their complaints against the rule of the Captain-general in Guatemala and citizens of local capitals sometimes demonstrated against the tyranny of their governors or intendentes. Hatred of the haughty, dominating Spaniards called *chapetones* in Guatemala, was as universal as in the other colonial kingdoms.

Distance from the seat of government, and poor communications, encouraged a spirit of independent action in the separate provinces. There were, in the provincial cities, small groups of Creole gentlemen, not the most wealthy, whose thoughts turned to republican ideals. Central America, too, had its patriot priests of the same fine type as Miguel Hidalgo and José Maria Morelos.

Liberal thinkers secretly discussed the right to self-government and freedom from Spain; propaganda was carried on, anonymous pamphlets distributed from town to town. Liberal Creole friars, protected from suspicion by their robes, were among the most active in this dangerous work. One of these patriots was a native of Nicaragua, Fray Miguelena of the Merced Order in León. He went so far as to hide arms for rebels in his cell. In San Salvador there were three brother priests—Manuel, Vicente and Nicolás Aguilar—who were leaders among the thoughtful citizens.

The spirit of independence was particularly strong among the townsfolk, both white and mestizo, in El Salvador and Nicaragua. There the ringing call to liberty given by Padre Hidalgo and Simón Bolívar in 1810 did not go unheeded.

In León, in 1811, citizens rose against their city government, gathering before the cabildo in angry crowds, armed with sticks and knives. Oust the chapetones, give us a government of Creoles, was their cry. Creole juntas were formed in other Nicaraguan towns in the next few years, and there were several revolts of mestizos and Indians. Battles took place when the Captain-general sent troops to pacify the towns and punished leading citizens by imprisonment, exile or death.

There was an uprising in the city of San Salvador in 1811, in protest against the imprisonment of the three Aguilar priests for their subversive preaching. It is said that Padre José Matías Delgado, who later on was a republican leader, rang the bells of La Merced monastery to start off that revolt. The people were pacified when the patriot priests were released and the bad governor removed.

Once again, in 1813, the sturdy Salvadoreans rang their church bells and demanded freedom from oppression. They wrote to Morelos in Mexico, assuring him that they were fighting for the same principles as he, and asking his aid when he should have triumphed in Mexico. The revolt was soon put down with cruel reprisals.

So, in their widely separated towns, before 1821, the Creole groups spoke up for self-government. In some towns juntas with both Spanish and Creole members were administrative bodies ready to take over when the time for separation from Spain arrived.

It was Iturbide's call for independence and his Plan of Iguala that set off the declaration of independence in Guatemala.

The Creole aristocracy of Guatemala City were the most conservative and wealthy people in the kingdom. They were determined to rule the country themselves, while retaining loyalty to King Ferdinand VII who was such an unsuitable figurehead for the first move toward independence. Thanks to the sympathetic attitude of their Captain-general, Don Gabino Gainza, the Creoles had formed a Provincial Junta. Under cover of this the men of republican spirit awaited their chance.

When the news of Iturbide's revolt reached Guatemala the city was thrown into a fever of excitement. The Bishop from the pulpit warned his flock against disloyalty, the Captain-general also urged the Creoles not to act, but he permitted them to illuminate the city in honor of Iturbide. Some citizens wanted to declare independence immediately, others urged their fellows to wait and see how things went in Mexico.

Don Gabino Gainza, realizing how strong was the feeling for separation, called together the ecclesiastical, civil and military officials at the Governor's Palace to consider the question of independence. Hastily the Creole leaders sent word of the meeting to various quarters of the city, urging the people to come, for they thought the backing of the populace would strengthen their declaration of independence.

On September 15, 1821, the Junta and highest officers of church and state gathered in the great salon of the palace. Crowds of townsfolk pushed through the corridors outside and peered through the windows. Don Gabino Gainza read the news from Mexico and announced that the province of Chiapas had seceded to join Mexico. Creole leaders and Spanish officials plunged into a lively discussion. Even the Spaniards believed that separation from Spain was inevitable. The question was, should they wait, or declare independence that day.

One by one the Creole leaders rose to make eloquent pleas and cast their votes for immediate independence. Applause and shouts of approval came from the people crowding outside the windows. Only eight men voted against the declaration. The meeting broke up in tumultous excitement, while in the plaza outside the band played, rockets were set off, and the crowd shouted with joy.

An Act of Independence was drawn up and signed by twelve leading Creoles. They persuaded the Captain-general to throw in his lot with them and sign the document by offering him the presidency of the new state. During the next few months the other provinces made separate declarations of independence, but September 15 remained for all Central Americans their independence day. Panama also separated from Spain, but as the province was too weak to stand alone, the leaders voluntarily joined Simón Bolívar's Gran Colombia, composed of Venezuela, Ecuador and New Granada.

The old Kingdom of Guatemala separated painlessly from the mother country. Don Gabino Gainza advised the King not to oppose it, and that monarch could not have spared troops to discipline Central Americans had he wished to, overwhelmed as he was with a liberal revolt in Spain and revolution in South America.

Soon the rejoicing over liberty was darkened by dissension, as the Emperor Agustín I sent his emissaries to Guatemala to urge the new states to join his empire. In the furious discussion and armed clashes over this issue the lines of future political thinking were sketched out. The republicans of that time became the liberal party, while the top-ranking churchmen and aristocrats became the nucleus of the conservative party.

In Guatemala the influential families, headed by Don Gabino Gainza, were all for joining the Empire of Mexico, and the protests of republicans were ignored. Although the governing junta gathered votes in the provincial cities, it announced adherence to Iturbide without waiting to learn the result of the vote. Liberal Salvadoreans rose in arms to resist the troops sent from Mexico and Guatemala to force them into the empire. The people of El Salvador asked to be annexed to the United States but were refused. Nicaragua, Honduras and Costa Rica were divided by cities into imperialist and republican factions, fighting one another.

Before the battle clouds cleared the short-lived Empire of Mexico toppled and Iturbide went into exile. In July, 1823, delegates from all the provinces but Costa Rica met with the Constituent Assembly in Guatemala to declare Central America independent of Spain, Mexico or any other country. Chiapas decided to remain with Mexico, thus becoming a subject of boundary disputes in years to come.

The ideal of a federation of the sister states in a republican government had strong support among liberal-minded Central Americans and the time had come to organize it. Delegates at the Constituent Assembly announced the formation of a federal government, Provincias Unidas del Centro de America. Although Costa Rica was not represented that state joined the federation.

During the next year, in an atmosphere of great enthusiasm, the National Assembly formulated its principles, established government and designed an escutcheon and banner for the Provincias Unidas. The escutcheon was a triangle framing five volcanoes, spanned by a rainbow and bathed by the two oceans, Atlantic and Pacific. Between two bands of blue on the flag the escutcheon was printed on a white band.

Liberal principles were written into the Constitution of the Provincias Unidas; slavery was to be abolished, also all titles of nobility and the *fueros,* or special rights and privileges of ecclesiastical bodies. Citizens were to be guaranteed freedom of thought, speech and press, but religious liberty was not included. The Roman Catholic Church remained the state church.

The patriots of Central America worked out the framework of their federated republic more or less on the model of the United States. There were to be a president and vice president elected for four years; a national congress composed of senators and deputies and a supreme court. Each state was to elect its own chief of state, congress and court of justice; and each state was obligated to contribute toward federal expenses and to provide troops for national defense. Don Manuel Arce of El Salvador, a leading liberal, was elected federal president.

The founding fathers of Central American independence were faced with the same problems as those of Mexico in trying to impose representative government upon populations living under feudal conditions. The colonial aristocrats were determined to rule and were far from republican in spirit. There was a small group of upper-class men imbued with the highest patriotism, but their impractical idealism could not cope with the problems before them.

There were also the old resentments of the provinces against the domination of Guatemala, and jealousies between provincial cities. It was to be expected that the Provincias Unidas del Centro de America would have rough going.

The Central Americans shouldered a mass of problems as

they set about building free states from the colonial provinces. Poverty was widespread; the plantations of cacao, sugar cane, tobacco, had decreased in productiveness under Spanish trade restrictions and heavy taxes. Indigo and cochineal were the chief products for export.

There were a few cart roads near cities, but aside from those communication was by mule trails. Travelers went on horseback or were carried in hammocks by Indian bearers. Goods for the highland cities must be transported on mule back from the dilapidated little ports. Owing to rough mountainous country, the mud and washouts of the rainy season, goods were sometimes months on the way to their destinations.

The merchants were at last free to trade with outside nations and England was right there on the doorstep ready to move in. Colonial merchants had long carried on a smuggling business with English traders. Now that it was open and aboveboard English merchants brought in a quantity of goods and commercial officers were installed in various cities.

The British government had kept a firm grip on a strip of the Guatemalan coast, the colony of Belize, profitable for the mahogany taken from the forests. A few white officers governed a population of Negroes who cut the mahogany. Soon after Central America became independent England moved to strengthen her protectorate over the Mosquito Coast, that primitive unexplored region along the coast of Nicaragua and Honduras.

British officers staged a farcical ceremony in which a big Negro chief was made King of Mosquitia. Bursting out of a major's uniform with glittering epaulets on the shoulders, and childishly pleased with his finery, King Robert was solemnly crowned by an English bishop. At the time, Central Americans were too busy to notice what was happening in Mosquitia, but the irresponsible, British-controlled black "kings" were to be a useful instrument for British plans for a long time to come.

The building up of trade and communications were tasks overwhelming enough for the small white upper class of Central America without the difficulties of a new kind of government. Released from Spanish absolutism they fell into a turmoil of conflicting ideas and ambitions. Those who believed that their salvation lay in a federation fought those who advocated separate national states. City was arrayed against city.

In Nicaragua León became the stronghold of the liberals. It was the center of a large farming region where mestizos and some Indians had a sturdy spirit and added their voices to the discussions of Creole townsmen. Granada was the home of the wealthy merchants and aristocrats, ultra conservative in spirit. The battles between the parties of these two cities tore the land asunder. In Honduras the conservatives of the old capital, Comayagua, contended with the liberals of Tegucigalpa, chosen for the capital of the new state.

The state of Guatemala was divided between the wealthy conservatives and churchmen of the capital and the mountain region called Los Altos, almost wholly Indian and mestizo in population. At one time the whites and mestizos of the mountain towns seceded from Guatemala to form a separate state with the capital at Quezaltenango.

Costa Rica, protected by geographical isolation, remained apart from the conflicts between states, but had internal troubles between cities. The Costa Ricans were steadier and more industrious than their neighbors, more homogeneous in population. Their attention was concentrated on their farms and the commerce of towns, and their first chief of state, Juan Mora Fernandez, was a citizen of constructive ideas who did much to develop prosperity and orderly civic life.

It was jealousy among the four cities of the Meseta Central—Heredia, Alajuela, Cartago, San José—that caused conflict. For some years the capital rotated from city to city to satisfy the prideful spirit of the citizens.

Federation was a progressive principle which might have led Central Americans into an era of stability and prosperity if they had been able to maintain unity. As it was, provincial jealousies, the ambitions of caudillos, the struggle between liberals and conservatives, brought about years of disastrous conflict.

CHAPTER 14

TROUBLED YEARS

IT WAS an epochal period in the history of the Western Hemisphere when the colonies of England and Spain threw off their allegiance to the mother countries and proclaimed their right to live as independent nations. These American nations intended to prevent any further encroachments of European monarchies on the continents. The Americas began the long process of building nations eventually composed of many peoples and cultures.

The North American colonists led the way, thus making the newborn United States the example and model for the efforts of Spanish American patriots. The North American people gave their sympathy and support to the struggles of their Spanish American brothers and the United States was the first to recognize some of the new nations. Unfortunately that period of mutual friendliness did not last long in Mexico.

The colonial people of Spain's empire were Spanish in blood, customs and social system, but they were also men of the New World by their experiences and environment; their blood was mingled with that of the native Indians. Although they in-

249

herited a feudal order of society and the corruption of Spanish colonial government, they based their independent nations on new principles.

Diplomats from European nations and the United States functioned in their capitals, trade relations were established with foreign nations.

In the confusion and conflict that followed independence in Mexico and Central America, problems and behavior were similar, but everything was on a larger scale in Mexico, the former vast Viceroyalty of New Spain. The inherited practices of corruption and graft were more brazen, more money was squandered, as white aristocrats, generals and climbing mestizos scrambled for wealth and power. Generals "pronounced" against presidents and overthrew them, constitutions were made and unmade, while the people sank into hopeless disillusion.

Out of the turmoil, at every psychological moment for change, emerged the melodramatic figure of General Santa Anna with his charm and brooding black eyes, his talent for display, his consuming ambition to be acclaimed a military hero. He was the man on horseback, waving a sword and proclaiming the most high-flown sentiments in a flood of eloquence. Frequently he made presidents by his campaigns, and in 1832 the liberals elected him to the presidency. He allowed his liberal vice president, Gomez Farías, to rule until reform laws were enacted that roused reactionaries to angry protest. Then Santa Anna, the turncoat, dismissed Congress and became a dictator.

It was during this dictatorship that Texas was lost to Mexico. Colonists from the United States had been permitted by the Mexican government to move into the great empty plains on condition that they became Mexican citizens and embraced

Catholicism. Thousands of pioneers settled in Texas with or without titles to land.

They were rugged frontiersmen pushing westward to occupy new land, believers in the theory that it was the manifest destiny of the United States to dominate North America. They brought in slaves, which was contrary to Mexican law. Texan settlers resented laws imposed on them by a state alien to them, although they had accepted Mexican citizenship. They wanted to govern themselves according to the rules of North American communities. When the Mexican government tried to prevent further immigration, imposed customs duties and forbade settlers to bring in slaves, there were clashes between Mexican troops and settlers.

The Texans declared their independence in 1836. General Santa Anna with three thousand troops moved into Texas to put down the revolt with brutal severity. Besieged in the old Spanish mission, the Alamo, one hundred and fifty Texans held out to the last man. Their indomitable spirit, the slaughter of the entire garrison, roused Texans to fury. Under the leadership of Sam Houston, frontiersman of legendary fame, they began a campaign of vengeance against the Mexicans. While Santa Anna's troops were taking siesta in their camp on the San Jacinto River the Texans pounced on them from the woods, yelling their battle cry, "Remember the Alamo!" They more than avenged the deaths of their fellows in the Alamo by the slaughter of six hundred and thirty Mexicans, while the survivors surrendered. Santa Anna escaped, but was soon captured.

On May 14, 1836, in the Treaty of Velasco, Santa Anna signed away Texas. He spent some months in the United States, and at home the one-time hero who had surrendered Texas was decidedly under a cloud. The Mexican Congress refused to recognize Texan independence but the army gave up the fight. For some years the territory was the Lone Star State, until it was annexed to the United States. It was probably inevitable that when two cultures clashed in sparsely populated border territory the more vigorous of the two would win. From the Mexican point of view, however, Texas was unjustly taken from them by a powerful neighbor and resentment over its loss has not yet died among the Mexican people.

Before long the man on horseback retrieved his reputation with his countrymen in a battle called the Pastry War at Vera Cruz. A French fleet arived to collect payment for damages done to a French pastry shop and other little businesses ten years earlier. Santa Anna sprang to the rescue, had his leg shot off by a French cannon ball and, when the enemy fleet retired, proclaimed a great victory. For the rest of his life he played up the loss of his leg as a noble sacrifice for his country.

While these events were taking place in Mexico the Central Americans were sunk in struggles between federalists and nationalists, liberals and conservatives, led by caudillos, few of whom had any real patriotism.

The Provincias Unidas del Centro de America had no opportunity to establish order and build up prosperity. The seat of the federal government was in Guatemala City, where it was in constant conflict with the state government. Manuel José Arce, elected to the federal presidency by the liberals, tried to win the support of conservatives and clergy, with the result that he antagonized the liberals of the other states. Central America became a battleground as generals of the two parties with their troops fought each other in every state but Costa Rica.

The struggle to save the federation was led by a Honduran, Francisco Morazán, who was chief of state in his own country when he took the field against the forces of Arce in Guatemala. Arce was defeated in 1829 and sent into exile along with leading ecclesiastics. In 1830 Morazán was elected to the federal presidency by the liberals. The capital was moved to San Salvador to escape controversies with the state government of Guatemala.

Francisco Morazán was the great patriot leader of Central America, a man of integrity and true liberal spirit, devoted to the ideal of a federated Central American nation. The federal government, guided by him and the liberals until it was dissolved, tried to stabilize Central America. There was no end, however, to factional wars between states and within their own borders.

The bitter enemies of the liberals and of Morazán went to great lengths in their efforts to destroy the influence of their opponents. In order to discredit them, priests of Guatemala roused fanatical Indians and mestizos with the cry that the liberals were enemies of religion and intended to exterminate the Indians.

When taxes were imposed on church properties in Quezaltenango priests incited a mob of furious men and women to attack the officer who came to enforce the decree. He was pursued into a church, dragged out and beaten to death. When federal troops tried to enter Guatemala City from El Salvador another priest-incited mob drove them out.

The priests had stirred up a whirlwind, for out of Indian Los Altos came a popular leader who would master the cringing reactionaries through fear, and kill liberalism in Guatemala for many a long year. Rafael Carrera was a poor mestizo of the highlands—ignorant, with a fanatical piety, but a man of powerful personality. He came from poor people and announced himself as their saviour.

The Indians called him Nuestro Señor, Our Lord, and believed him to be the champion come to deliver them from centuries of subservience to hated white men. Indian villagers of Los Altos had changed little in character or customs since their ancestors fought Pedro de Alvarado, except that they had added a superstitious Catholicism to their ancient religion. All white men were foreigners to them, and Rafael Carrera started a race war when he called on the oppressed people to exterminate foreigners and enemies of religion.

The Indian army descended from the highlands on Guatemala City. Terrified townsfolk barricaded themselves in their houses as the mob choked the streets—a mass of ragged Indians and their women wearing straw hats with green branches stuck in them, carrying old muskets and knives on poles. Carrera on horseback, his straw hat adorned with pictures of saints printed on dirty cotton, led his host into the plaza to shouts of *"Viva religion y muerte a los extranjeros!"*—"Long live religion and death to foreigners." Indians thronged the handsome Cathedral, gazing with awe on glittering gold and painted saints, setting up their village saints among the resplendent images.

The citizens called on Francisco Morazán for aid and he came from El Salvador with federal troops, to drive out Carrera and his Indian hordes. The wild chief returned several times to attack the city, but was driven back to the mountains. Each time Carrera escaped capture and his men melted back into their villages and cornfields, looking like harmless peasants.

Carrera's revolt was the final blow to the brave new federal state which was torn apart by conflicts between federalists and nationalists. In every state but Costa Rica, Creole officers led their barefoot brown troops against each other. The soldiers simply obeyed the orders of their officers with no idea of what they fought for. Early in 1838 Costa Rica seceded from the federation and was followed by Nicaragua during the same year. In 1839 the National Congress formally dissolved the Provincias Unidas del Centro de America.

Rafael Carrera rose to power as the reactionaries of Guatemala supported him out of hatred for the liberals and their leader. Priests believed that church supremacy was secure under the fanatical chief, while the aristocrats, much as they feared him, placated him for their own ends.

The war became a personal conflict between the two men who represented the best and worst in Central America: Francisco Morazán, the high-minded patriot and liberal; Rafael Carrera, man of superstition and backward ideas. Morazán had some Honduran troops and the liberals of El Salvador to fight Carrera, who had the aid of conservatives of several states. In 1840 Morazán's troops were routed and he fled by ship to spend two years of exile in Chile.

Rafael Carrera soon forgot the woes of oppressed people whose champion he had been. He had the intelligence and will to rise, he learned to read and write, to move in polite society and wear elegant uniforms. The ignorant mestizo from the mountains became the absolute dictator of Guatemala for a long period.

In 1839 an observant North American visited the distracted states of Central America and gave to the world, in the book he wrote, a vivid picture of life in town and country. John L. Stephens was sent by President Van Buren on a mission to the federal government of Central America. Part of his assignment was to study the possibilities of a canal route across Nicaragua. From city to city Stephens searched for a federal government to which he might present his credentials, but there was no central authority. There were only military caudillos who had seized power in one state or another.

In the intervals of his search for a government Stephens followed his avocation, that of archeologist. He and his companion, the English artist Catherwood, explored ruined Mayan cities and were the first to visit some of them, lost and forgotten in the forests. Catherwood's beautiful engravings became classics in the study of Mayan sculpture.

Nothing fazed the intrepid Yankee traveler. On muleback he went up and down the mountains; he climbed volcanoes, and crossed the Gulf of Fonseca in a bongo, a primitive boat hewn from a large tree trunk. These bongos, manned by mulattoes and Indians, transported people back and forth on the Gulf between El Salvador, Nicaragua and Honduras.

Through his lively interest in people and his cheerful adaption to hardships, Stephens became well acquainted with the inhabitants of town and country. He found them simple, easygoing, hospitable, resigned and more or less indifferent to the tide of warfare that swept back and forth. Travel was decidedly adventurous, for bandits as well as undisciplined soldiers roamed the countryside. There were no inns even in the cities. Travelers lucky enough to have letters to leading citizens were graciously entertained in their homes. Others, after spending weary days on muleback, sought lodgings in towns and villages with the *cura,* or hung up their hammocks in a bare room of the cabildo while their mule drivers cooked for them over charcoal fires.

Stephens had an interview with Francisco Morazán shortly before he was driven from the country. He was impressed by the fine character of the federal leader and thought him the only general with a true love of country.

In Guatemala City, Stephens also met and studied Rafael Carrera, who, in 1840, was master of the battered city. The town was disorderly, few pedestrians ventured into its dark night streets, lit only by candles burning before the images of saints. Secure in their homes, upper-class families passed sociable evenings in the old colonial fashion, receiving guests in the large dignified *salas*. Pretty daughters entertained with songs to the music of marimba or guitar, while groups of men and women chatted or gathered eagerly about the gaming tables. The ladies, graceful and charming, their dark hair decked with flowers or jewels, lighted up their *cigarritos* nonchalantly, to join the men in smoking.

Life was indolent and rather dull, a monotonous round of Masses and saints' day observances. In the homes a bountiful midday meal was followed by a long siesta from which people roused themselves for chocolate drinking and gossip at four o'clock. Families came to life for the evening parties, called *tertulias*.

Cockfighting amused the men when they were not at war, and church festivals provided the chief entertainment outside the homes. Parties journeyed to Antigua for elaborate country picnics, with an entourage of Indian servants and pack mules to carry provisions and hammocks for the night.

These people were delightful in their own group, but their minds were set in traditional grooves. Any threat of change to their secure comfortable lives alarmed them, hence their hatred of the liberals.

The year 1842 saw a last attempt by Francisco Morazán to restore the federation of states. Liberal generals of El Salvador and Honduras then joined with Costa Ricans who were tired of their dictatorial chief, Braulio Carillo, to recall Morazán from Chile.

Costa Rica had been having an orderly, prosperous life under Braulio Carrillo. His encouragement of coffee growing, recently introduced, was bringing to small farmers and large landowners a dependable means of livelihood, but he kept down political quarrels with a firm hand. Citizens were restive under the dictatorship, deprived of their civic freedoms. Enemies of Carrillo thought it a good opportunity to join the plot for the recall of Morazán, and to invite him to invade Costa Rica.

In April 1842, four ships arrived at the Costa Rican port of Caldera, to disembark Morazán and his followers from Honduras and El Salvador. As they marched up to the highlands Carrillo sent troops to oppose them, but the general in command went over to Morazán, and the troops were ready to support the man who would free them from Carrillo. Francisco Morazán was therefore able to win Costa Rica with little opposition. Carrillo went into exile rather than subject his country to civil war.

The people welcomed Morazán as the restorer of liberty and elected him chief of state. The constitutional guarantees abolished by Carrillo were restored, his decrees annulled. The legislative assembly gave Morazán permission to attempt the desire of his heart, the restoration of the Central American federation. It meant war with the other states which had repudiated federation.

It was not long before the people turned against the man they had welcomed, as Morazán, the man of one idea, imposed heavy taxes for the proposed war and ruthlessly conscripted men for the army. Morazán became autocratic in his rule, issued decrees that angered the people. A revolt of Carrillo partisans was put down with severity. Morazán's soldiers from other states were undisciplined and caused trouble in the towns. The people had not taken part in wars outside their country and had no wish to become involved in conflict with sister states.

In September 1842, the city of Alajuela pronounced against Morazán. Those rebels were soon joined by people of San José in attacks on Morazán's headquarters in that city. The whole population took part in this revolt against the man they had admired. When all seemed lost Morazán escaped to Cartago where he was captured by Costa Rican troops and brought back to San José.

To calm the people and make an end of the war, the commanding officer ordered the death of Morazán. He was shot in the plaza of San José, together with the Costa Rican general who had aided him to win the country. Francisco Morazán, the best of Central American patriots, the man who had kept a clear vision of a progressive Central American nation, met his tragic death with calm dignity.

It was unfortunate that Costa Ricans, in a moment of political fury, should have been responsible for the deed. Francisco Morazán made the mistake of trying to impose war on an industrious people who were not averse to union with their sister states in principle, but who did not want to see their country ruined in a disastrous war. After the death of the federal leader turmoil and fratricidal war were the lot of Central Americans for many years.

CHAPTER 15

GENERAL SANTA ANNA AND MANIFEST DESTINY

THE PEOPLE of Mexico and the United States had little understanding of one another in the period when outlying, half-empty Mexican territory was being overrun by the westward surge of pioneers. Frontiersmen, dealing with poor Mexican villagers, dishonest officials and "Santy Anny's" soldiers, looked down on their neighbors as a lazy, inferior race. On the other hand, the American minister in Mexico during the trying times of the Texas controversies was a man calculated to inspire contempt rather than respect for his country. And the Mexicans who fought the Texans considered American soldiers a lot of adventurers without principles, religion or manners.

In the early 1840's, however, Boston intellectuals awoke to interest in Mexico as the land of ancient Indian civilization and dramatic history with the publication of William H. Prescott's fascinating *Conquest of Mexico*. Due to the urging of this historian the delightful letters of Madame Calderón de la Barca were also published in Boston and London.

This vivacious lady of Scottish birth was the wife of the first Spanish minister sent to the Republic of Mexico—

Don Angel Calderón de la Barca. Brought up in the United States, she moved in the intellectual circles of Boston before marrying the Spanish minister. Clever and talented, she became one of the young ladies with literary ambitions sometimes known as "blue stockings" in that period.

Don Angel Calderón de la Barca and his lady reached Mexico by sailing ship from Havana just before the close of the year 1839. During their two years' sojourn in Mexico Madame Calderón de la Barca, in letters to her friends, painted an inimitable picture of Mexican life.

Through their diplomatic position the Spanish minister and his wife were well acquainted with society in the capital. On visits to influential families in cities or on haciendas they traveled bravely over the highland and in the *tierra caliente,* by private coach, public diligence or on horseback. Madame Calderón de la Barca was an intelligent tourist, determined to see everything. Like thousands of visitors since then she was captivated by the varied, profoundly appealing Mexican landscape, by the color of dress, customs and fiestas. The romantic charm of life did not blind her, however, to the prevailing poverty and disorder, sharply contrasting with the luxury of the ruling class. With shrewd and often caustic humor she commented on the foibles of Mexican society and the hold of Catholicism, dressed in gorgeous ceremonials, over the lives of rich and poor.

With her aristocratic friends Madame Calderón de la Barca shared in the celebration of great holy days in the Cathedral of Mexico City. There alone all classes mingled as, from elegant gentlemen and ladies in mantillas to ragged Indians, they knelt together on the dirty bare floor of the Cathedral. Dirt and poverty rubbing shoulders with luxury, all eyes in the vast crowd were turned devoutly to the glitter of gold, silver, jewels, brocades around the great altar, softened by candlelight and seen through a haze of incense. The magnificence and wealth of the immense churches, monasteries and convents in the city amazed this Anglo-Saxon lady.

Society in the capital had at that time its diplomatic circle in the legations of France, Great Britain, with other European nations and the United States; the French and British ministers being the most influential. Great Britain was firmly entrenched in business and diplomacy, with France a close second. Aristocratic families were beginning to look to Paris for culture and fashion. French dressmakers and French restaurants were popular in the capital; before the end of her stay Madame Calderón de la Barca commented on the change in feminine dress from the Mexican costume, overloaded with jewels and frills, short of skirt and topped by the graceful mantilla, to more sophisticated Paris gowns and bonnets. Sons of the aristocracy were sent to Europe to be polished off in education and manners and the most intellectual men were European-trained.

Vast sums were squandered to support governmental society and the all-powerful army. Only a pittance went to feed and clothe the conscript soldiers, while fat salaries for the swarm of officers provided them with gaudy uniforms, mistresses and the pleasures of gaming and balls. When the treasury was bare, loans were arranged with French or British financiers; thus the binding of Mexico to foreign capital was well under way.

Social life in the capital was a round of resplendent masked balls, banquets, diplomatic receptions, evenings at the Italian opera, or great church festivals. There were bullfights, a glory of bright costumes and excitement under the cloudless sky. Every social function was an ostentatious display of uniforms, jewels, silks and satins. Diamonds and satin slippers must be worn even with the clear muslins, lace petticoats and silken *rebozos* of the morning costume.

Every afternoon, for the paseo, a stream of coaches and horsemen passed along the tree-lined road beside the broad canal, La Viga, leading to the Indian villages, Santa Anita and Xochimilco, with their canals and chinampas. Bevies of ladies, draped in mantillas or with flowers and jewels in their hair, fanned themselves and smoked their cigarritos as they received the greetings of the dashing *charro* horsemen. Poorly dressed pedestrians camped under the trees to watch the show, while on the canal Indian canoes glided by, each one like a flower garden, heaped with roses, lilies, poppies, sweet peas. Gay parties from the city frequently went in canopied canoes to Santa Anita to see the Indian market of flowers and vegetables. As they glided among native canoes on the canals they were entertained by the dancing of poppy-crowned Indian women to the strumming of guitars.

Watching these scenes, commented Madame Calderón de la Barca, one might think Mexico a happy and peaceful land; but she remarked shrewdly "there is hardly a link between the blankets and satins, the poppies and diamonds."

In the capital stark poverty could never be forgotten; it darkened the picture of gay, easygoing life in the great houses and in the streets. Everywhere swarms of *léperos,* the beggars, whined their appeal for alms, *por amor de Díos.* Ragged dirty Indians with loads on their backs trotted into market, driving their burros, pigs and turkeys. Multitudes of street venders filled the air with their varied, musical chants. Robbers preyed on the wealthy to such an extent that householders kept armed retainers in the courtyards of their mansions and it was unsafe to walk in the streets at night. Nowhere, in city life or on country visits, did Madame Calderón de la Barca find any evidence of republican spirit.

The *hacendados* were feudal masters, served humbly by Indian peons and mestizo villagers. The families visited their estates only for country parties, leaving administration to major-domos. The large fortresslike houses were bare and almost empty of furniture, for destructive soldiers of revolting generals looted them so frequently that families would not risk their fine furnishings. Gardens were neglected, fields only partially cultivated; dilapidated villages and roofless houses indicated what was happening to the country from eternal political unrest.

Travelers journeying in private coaches or public diligences over rough, rutted roads, choked in dust or bogged down in mud, were escorted by armed horsemen. Passengers kept guns pointed out the coach windows, on the alert for the ever-present bandits.

Country folk and Indians accepted with apathy the poverty and social injustices of their lives. Indolent and improvident, they raised sufficient corn and beans for subsistence, finding release from dull hardship in the color, song and dance of saints' day fiestas. The political circus going on continually in the capital was something beyond their ken. Peons and farmers saw their fields trampled by warring bands, and were dragged from their homes to fight under one general or another.

The Calderón de la Barcas witnessed two *pronunciamientos* in the capital, when ambitious generals tried to overthrow the *políticos* in power. Government forces barricaded themselves in the National Palace, cannon roared in the great Plaza, the Zócalo, cavalry troops galloped through the streets. Generals of each side issued appeals to the people in high-sounding statements, promising justice and reform.

Some hapless citizens became involved in forays of soldiers and were killed, but most of the inhabitants promptly shut themselves up in their houses; shops were closed and business came to a standstill. Many wealthy families piled their valuables into coaches to take refuge in neighboring villages or their country estates until the trouble was over. It was as though a furious storm raged through the city, something over which the people had no control and were concerned only to save their lives and goods from its destruction.

In Mexico, and most of the other Hispanic American republics, the mid-nineteenth century was the age of the caudillos, of whom Mexican Santa Anna and Rafael Carrera of Guatemala were striking examples. These leaders won support from some sections of the population by dramatic personality and demagogic pronouncements in favor of justice and the rights of the people.

The same period in the United States was the age of Manifest Destiny. The North American republic was a young nation of vigorous, conquering people, boastfully proud of their rapid advancement; the spirit of frontiersmen and ambitious politicians was responsible for the doctrine of Manifest Destiny— the conviction that North Americans were destined by superior race and energy to dominate the continent.

In the decade between 1836 and 1846, Manifest Destiny began its march. The Texans had carved out the Lone Star State from Mexican territory; in Oregon the clamor of American settlers had brought about a treaty with Great Britain by which Oregon became part of the United States. By land over the mountains and by sea at the ports North Americans were filtering into California. Traders' wagons had followed fur trappers over the Santa Fe trail to New Mexico and Yankee enterprise longed to have a free hand in that province of

Mexico. North Americans itched to develop the vast regions of good land which Mexico could neither populate nor govern successfully. To the Mexicans, naturally, each advance was an unwarranted invasion. The clash was bound to come between the men of Manifest Destiny and a Mexico weakened and corrupted by bad leaders who despoiled the country for their own gain.

The most melodramatic and most dangerous of those leaders was Antonio López de Santa Anna. He was living in retirement on his lovely estate, Manga de Clavo, when the Calderón de la Barcas were entertained there on their arrival in Mexico. While awaiting new opportunities for glory, the General nursed his health and devoted himself to cockfighting.

In 1844, Santa Anna sat for one of his frequent, but brief periods in the presidential chair, but his government was soon overthrown and he was driven from the country to Havana. From that retreat he sprang into the limelight once more as the evil genius of Mexico's war with the United States.

The Mexican government had never acknowledged the independence of Texas. The loss of the territory had been a blow to national pride, distrust of the northern republic was ably fostered by British innuendos and abetted by Yankee incursions into California.

The conflict which had been brewing a long time was precipitated by a boundary quarrel in Texas and the final annexation of that state to the Union. Ever since the Lone Star State won independence the controversy had gone on in Congress over the admission of Texas, which would come in as a slave state. At last in 1845 the battle was won and Texas was added to the United States. To the Mexican minister in Washington annexation was an act of aggression; he handed in his papers and went home.

In Texas the people claimed the Rio Grande as their boundary, while Mexico placed it at the Nueces River with a line drawn in a northerly direction. President Polk, elected in 1845, supported the Texan claim and also told the American consul in California that he would be backed up if he encouraged a local revolt. Manifest Destiny was in control; the President himself was determined to annex California by one means or another. Since negotiations to buy the territory had failed, only an "incident" was needed to precipitate war. This was supplied when President Polk sent General Zachary Taylor, "Old Rough and Ready" into the disputed zone in Texas, to defend American territory, according to the Texans, while Mexico denounced it as an invasion. In the spring of 1846 there was a clash between Mexican troops and those of General Taylor. Feeling ran high on both sides of the border. "War exists by act of Mexico," cried President Polk and sentiment in most of the country was with him.

There was opposition, particularly in New England, where the acquisition of new territory was involved in the slavery controversy. Some few members of Congress, among them Abraham Lincoln, denounced the war as an act of aggression against unoffending neighbor people and against American principles. In the press, however, the prevailing sentiment was expressed in the argument that Mexicans must be taught the superiority of the North American way of life and must learn to keep peace with the United States.

The advance of Zachary Taylor's troops into northern Mexico, winning victory after victory until Monterrey was taken, roused national spirit among the people of the region, who fought valiantly for their towns. In the capital it was another matter, as political rivalries continued and one general succeeded another from week to week. In dismay and confusion

Mexicans were ready to welcome their somewhat tarnished military hero, chafing in Havana.

General Santa Anna responded to the situation like an old war horse, more for his own glory than for his country. He got through the blockading American squadron at Vera Cruz by promising President Polk to bring about an early surrender if he were permitted to enter the country. Arriving in Mexico City with his usual bombast Santa Anna declared himself ready to defend his country "to the last drop of my blood," a pronouncement he was fond of making each time he became the chief actor on the Mexican stage. The fact that he came in with an American passport caused doubts of his sincerity, but Mexicans knew that he alone had the personality and skill to organize the army.

The man on horseback threw himself into the task with the energy and ability that made him a good leader in emergencies. Finally he headed his army north from San Luis Potosí to meet the advancing Americans, traveling in a mule-drawn coach with a crate of his pet gamecocks. He had good officers to lead an army of poorly clad, ill-fed conscripts accompanied by their *soldaderas*—the women who always went along with cooking pots and babies to take care of the men.

There were forced marches through desolate desert and mountain country. Worn down though they were by fatigue and hunger, the Mexicans made a surprise attack on General Taylor's camp. By numerical superiority and the stubborn fighting of weary men they sent the enemy running to the hacienda of Buena Vista. Through two days and nights of fierce, bloody fighting the Mexicans contended with stoical bravery against the superior skill and artillery of General Taylor's army.

Santa Anna's conscripts had fought without food or sleep,

they were exhausted, dying of wounds and dysentery, frightened by the efficiency of American artillery fire. Rather than face another battle against American cannon the General chose retreat. During the night cavalry and artillery began the backward march, deserting the wounded and women, leaving campfires blazing to deceive the enemy.

In the morning the Americans, who had expected to fight for their lives, were astounded and overjoyed to find that the Mexican army had vanished. While General Taylor sent a message announcing victory to President Polk, General Santa Anna, rolling through town after town in his coach, waving two captured American flags, proclaimed a great victory for Mexico. He generally managed to make people think his mistakes were victories. Although good in planning strategy he did not carry through campaigns with the ability of the really good general.

Meanwhile a second army under General Winfield Scott had been sent by ship to Vera Cruz to march on the capital. Political strife continued in Mexico City while the port was taken and the Americans started up the mountains, aided by disaffected Mexicans. Powerful ecclesiastics were opposed to the war because the Church had been taxed for its support; they and the conservatives wanted peace at any price. Ambitious generals intrigued against each other while patriotic men tried to gather money and troops for defense. Puebla, a Catholic stronghold, surrendered without a shot and welcomed the American army. Selfish strife within was more dangerous to Mexico than the enemy at the gates.

In and out of the confusion dashed General Santa Anna, now rousing the spirit of the people and organizing defenses, now pushed aside by rivals who hated him. He seemed to be playing two games at once; on the one hand calling for defense of the country and on the other dealing with the Americans. There was a truce while negotiations went on at General Scott's headquarters. Although no terms of surrender could be agreed upon, Santa Anna brazenly demanded and received from American authorities ten thousand dollars to aid his peace movement!

When General Scott's troops moved on relentlessly from Puebla, General Santa Anna fortified strong points, then fell back under attack, abandoning men and artillery. Whole companies of good soldiers eager for battle were wasted by withdrawing battalions when they should have advanced. Others were sacrificed needlessly by failure to give them sufficient support. A succession of failures killed the fighting spirit of the soldiers and disorganized resistance. After each disaster, Santa Anna raged against other officers or the troops, blaming everyone but himself. Whether or not his acts were deliberate treachery, his vacillations and mistakes eased the conquest of Mexico City by the Americans.

Chapultepec Castle, seat of the Military Academy, was bombarded, and the heroic boy cadets shamed their elders by the ardor with which they fought and died for the honor of Mexico. The people of the capital at last united to defend themselves; every man was armed, street barricades were thrown up, snipers fired from the houses on the advancing Americans. There was little they could do, but they tried their best to halt the invaders.

In September 1847, the American army was camped in the Zócalo before the Cathedral and the flag of the United States was raised over Mexico. Before the city was lost Santa Anna and some other leaders had escaped. While guerrilla bands of Mexicans, and American soldiers on the loose, fought and looted in the country the discredited hero sat in his retreat, planning to retrieve his reputation in more battles. Soon he became a fugitive, with a band of avenging Texans, still remembering the Alamo, on his trail. He made his way through the mountains to an American camp where the officers welcomed him and speeded him on his way to asylum in Jamaica.

The terms of the peace treaty, signed on February 2, 1848, were bitter for Mexico. In addition to acknowledging the loss of Texas, Mexico relinquished New Mexico, Arizona and California; in all, more than half her territory. The cancellation of long-standing American damage claims and the payment of fifteen million dollars were no consolation for such loss and humiliation.

Disunity and corruption among her own leaders made it impossible for Mexico to hold her distant undeveloped territory against the momentum of Manifest Destiny; nevertheless the war left a legacy of smoldering hatred among Mexicans for the aggressive northern nation. In the United States the acquisition of such a vast new territory intensified the struggle between the abolitionist North and planter South over slavery.

Of General Santa Anna his Mexican biographer, Rafael Muñoz, says: "Next to Ferdinand VII who lost a continent, no one in America lost so much as Antonio López de Santa Anna." Before Mexico could be free of him forever the country had to endure two years of his dictatorship, the most ruthless and spendthrift of his career.

In the hard years after the war, patriotic liberals, intellectuals and students of the provincial cities gathered their forces to discuss and publicize the reforms necessary to save Mexico, to make it a genuine republic. Through political clubs, oratory and journalism, they strove to arouse national spirit in the people.

Alarmed over this threat to their exclusive positions, the reactionaries of aristocracy and Church turned to their old friend Santa Anna. He was recalled from exile to become, by their aid, president with dictatorial powers.

Lucas Alemán, chief of his cabinet, was a conservative with constructive ideas for developing the country, but he soon died, leaving the dictator with no check on his actions. All liberals were ousted from the government and the most dangerous sent into exile. The aging hero was bored with affairs of state; he cared only for the adulation of his pseudo court, for the amusements of cockfighting and amorous adventures. Seldom in its fantastic history had Mexico City been treated to such a theatrical display of retinues, uniforms, jewels—the gorgeous show of mimic royalty. Santa Anna proclaimed himself Perpetual Dictator with the acclaim of the reactionaries; subservient society addressed him as Most Serene Highness. He outdid Iturbide in the gaudy pomp of his court. The tormented country was looted and neglected while the mad egotist had his last fling.

To replenish the treasury, stripped bare by his extravagances, Santa Anna, in 1853, sold to the United States territory which is now southern Arizona. Known as the Gadsden Purchase, this deal, by which ten million dollars was delivered into the reckless hands of the dictator, brought to a climax Mexican resentment against him.

In 1854 the liberals gathered sufficient strength to start a revolt. Defeated in battle, and frightened by the rising tide of patriotism and hatred for himself, Santa Anna hastily abdicated and fled. He took refuge in Venezuela, this time to remain in obscurity. Mexico was through with him.

For a quarter of a century he had played with spectacular effect the leading role in the Mexican drama. If he had had the character and convictions to match his personal magnetism he might have done much for his country. As it was, his over-weening ego and love for personal glory made his actions more destructive than those of any other caudillo of the period. The melodramatic hero on horseback was replaced on the stage by the austere, black-clad figure of Indian Benito Juárez, the man of incorruptible honesty and patriotism.

CHAPTER 16

MEXICAN PATRIOT VERSUS FOREIGN EMPEROR

THE MAN who was to be a tower of strength to Mexican patriots had his roots deep in the earth of his land and belonged to the native Indian race. Benito Juárez was a dark, full-blood Zapotec Indian, whose ancestors had been one of the most advanced of native peoples. Born of a peasant family he spent his hard-working childhood in a poor mountain village of the southern state of Oaxaca.

The boy who walked all the way from his mountain home to the old city of Oaxaca to seek his fortune found favor with the two kind men who employed him. Young Benito worked first as a houseboy in the family of an Italian gentleman, Señor Maza. Later he became the servant of a Franciscan friar who cared for the books of the monastery.

Fray Antonio taught the quiet boy whose mind responded so eagerly to knowledge. His two benefactors appreciated the strength of character and ambition in their young protegé, and determined to give him a chance for the education he craved. In the year when Mexico became an independent nation under Agustín de Iturbide of imperial ambitions, Benito was entered in the College of Santa Cruz in Oaxaca. It was a

274

religious college where sons of well-to-do Creoles received a narrow theological schooling. Among the upper class students Benito was the only Indian—a lonely, silent youth who pursued learning with stubborn persistence.

After the fall of Agustín de Iturbide the republican government established state schools for the education of all classes. The College of Arts and Sciences in Oaxaca became the nursery of ardent young liberals, white and mestizo. Benito Juárez entered the College and found stimulating friends among the students. Their minds awakened by study of European social and political theories, the young Mexicans threw themselves enthusiastically into discussion of Mexico's troubles and need for reform.

Benito Juárez won his degree as *licenciado* at the College of Arts and Sciences and hung out his shingle to practice law. It speaks well for the character of the young Indian lawyer and the liberalism of the townspeople that Juárez was able to establish himself in his profession, that he was received as a friend in the home of his former employer, Señor Maza, and married his lovely daughter, Doña Margarita.

Other poor boys of Indian or mixed race studied and shared ideas with their Creole fellow students in the College. Among them was Porfirio Díaz, a boy of humble mestizo family whose Indian blood was that of the other vital native race of Oaxaca, the Mixtec. Porfirio's mother wanted her boy to become a priest, but under the influence of the young republicans he turned from theology to politics and soldiering. Porfirio Díaz studied law under Juárez and for many years he had for the older man the admiration of the disciple for the master who formed his ideas.

In the stately colonial city of Oaxaca the young intellectuals, austere in their professional costume of stovepipe hat and black frock coat, brought progress to their city and state. Benito Juárez was a leader among them. Deep in his soul the Indian knew the helplessness of the masses of people in a Mexico ruled by greedy politicians and an all-powerful church. Justice and education for all, freedom from the political control of ecclesiastics, became his passionate ideal.

Liberalism was kept alive in Oaxaca during the turbulent years when presidents came and went, when one pronunciamiento followed another and Santa Anna was, at frequent intervals, the popular hero. Benito Juárez despised the vainglorious demagogue, symbol of the disorder and corruption he hated in Mexican life.

When the Indian lawyer went into politics, was elected to the state legislature and then to the governorship of his native state, he became more widely known as a man of uncompromising liberal convictions. He was a phenomenon in Mexican politics; the man of absolute integrity, who administered every office he held with scrupulous honesty.

After the war with the United States, Benito Juárez was an influential figure in the rising class of mestizo intellectuals and politicians who were planning reforms and gaining power. He was the man Santa Anna wanted out of the country when he returned for his last dictatorship and ousted all liberals from government. On a trumped up charge of plotting against the dictator, Santa Anna had Juárez arrested and sent into exile in 1853.

While Santa Anna was squandering the nation's funds, patriotic Mexicans were gathering strength to overthrow him. In the state of Guerrero the regional chieftain was an old Indian, General Alvarez, who had fought oppression since his youth, when he was one of Vicente Guerrero's followers. General Alvarez headed the liberals who were planning a revolt.

In New Orleans a small group of exiles were living in extreme poverty, making plans for joining the rebels in Guerrero. Benito Juárez was there, earning a pittance in a cigar factory. In the group were other liberal leaders, Melchor Ocampo and Ignacio Comonfort. These exiles gathered funds from American sympathizers and finally managed to reach Acapulco to join General Alvarez.

In 1854 the liberals served notice on the Perpetual Dictator with their Plan of Ayutla. The declaration called for the overthrow of Santa Anna, a new constitution and reform of government.

In vain General Santa Anna took the field to put down the revolt of liberals in Guerrero. Defeated in battle he fled before the rising tide of revolt and left the country with all the loot he could collect. Mexico City declared for the Plan of Ayutla and liberals all over the country supported it.

General Alvarez, appointed provisional president, made a triumphal entry into the capital with a bodyguard of fierce Indian warriors, a horrifying sight to upper-class society. It reminded them painfully of Padre Hidalgo and his Indian army.

Mexico had an Indian President and an Indian Minister of Justice, Benito Juárez. Other progressive ministers in the cabinet, Melchor Ocampo and Miguel Lerdo de Tejada, followed the lead of Juárez in the belief that Mexico's sickness could be cured only by drastic measures.

Benito Juárez wrote his *Ley Juárez,* abolishing special courts and legal privileges of the army and ecclesiastical bodies, instituting reforms to give all people the right to justice before the law. This caused intense opposition from the privileged groups and Juárez was accused of attacking religion.

Within a few months the old soldier, General Alvarez, gave

up the attempt to administer government. Elections were held in which Ignacio Comonfort was chosen for president while Juárez was elected vice president and head of the Supreme Court. Comonfort was a weak-kneed liberal, a compromiser. Through fear of the powerful clergy he tried to prevent the more aggressive ministers from enacting laws against clerical, as well as military, domination.

The reformers went ahead, however, despite his opposition. Miguel Lerdo de Tejada wrote his *Ley Lerdo,* more far-reaching than Juárez' law, which brought forth a storm of denunciation from the clergy. The *Ley Lerdo* prohibited corporations from owning real estate not used for purposes of worship. Tenants on such lands were to be free to buy parcels for reasonable prices.

The law struck at the great church institutions and monastic orders which were corporations owning huge tracts of agricultural lands. It did not confiscate property, and the orders gained wealth as the proceeds from sales of their lands were turned over to them. It was an attempt to free lands needed for farming from the dead hand of the church and provide opportunities for small farmers. It did not hinder the priests in their spiritual guidance of the people, but interference with the temporal power of the Church roused ecclesiastics to a violent campaign against the liberals, a crusade to save religion, in their words.

Meanwhile the Constituent Assembly had framed the Constitution of 1857. It was a noble document, containing the principles of Mexico's most progressive men. Based in a general way on the Constitution of the United States, it provided for the establishment of representative, popular, republican government. The President of the Supreme Court was to be also the

Vice President. Citizens were assured of freedom from forced labor, freedom of speech, press, petition and assembly.

The *Ley Juárez* and *Ley Lerdo* were written into the Constitution, thus confirming the restrictions on clerical and military privileges. The framers of the Constitution intended to lay the foundations for a modern political state. Although the laws were too advanced to be applied successfully to the chaotic Mexico of that period, the document provided the basis of constitutional rights for which Mexicans would fight in future struggles.

The Constitution became the law of the land on the day of the *Grito de Dolores*, September 16, 1857. The anti-clerical position taken by the government brought against it the full force of entrenched powers. The liberals themselves were weak, not sufficiently united or clear-cut in their convictions. Many could not free themselves from the old fear of the aristocracy and clergy.

Other laws were made to deprive priests of fees for marriage, baptism or burial by which poor people were exploited. Cemeteries were removed from church control to a department of government. Marriage was ordained to be a civil contract. All these reforms were flying in the face of established clerical control and increased the bitter opposition of ecclesiastical authorities. This mistaken, selfish attitude lost the Church support from the people and made them increasingly anti-clerical.

The tremendous influence of the priests over the people was brought to bear in the conflict. Public officials, required to take an oath of allegiance to the Constitution, were refused the sacraments if they did so. Threatened with the wrath of their priests, small farmers were afraid to buy lands from church properties when they were put up for sale under the *Ley Lerdo*.

The law failed of its purpose, for estates were bought up by newly rich Creoles and foreigners, creating a new class of landowners.

Ignacio Comonfort went too far in his efforts to conciliate opponents. He lost the confidence of his party and was driven from the capital by the revolt of General Zuloaga, proprietor of a fashionable gambling house. The liberals declared that Comonfort had violated his oath of allegiance to the Constitution and that Benito Juárez, the Vice President, was the legal successor to the presidency.

For three years Mexico was devastated as never before by the bloody fury of the War of Reform in which each side, soldiers and populace, fought with fanatical bitterness. Mexico had two presidents; in the capital the brilliant, ambitious officer, General Miramón who ousted Zuloaga, and outside in the country, Benito Juárez.

Juárez had escaped from Mexico City in a closed carriage on the pretext that it contained a sick family. Immediately Mexicans, with their love for political satire, named the Juárez cabinet "the sick family." The legal government did indeed lead a precarious existence, hunted from place to place by the conservative army. That old black carriage of the President became the symbol of the courageous patriot, as a prancing charger had been the symbol of the spectacular caudillos.

Benito Juárez and his cabinet retreated before their enemies from one part of the country to another, until headquarters were established in Vera Cruz, a liberal state which welcomed them. In that dark time when the liberals, or constitutionalists, had only a small foothold in the country, Benito Juárez and his ministers went ahead with their program of reform. They planned for schools, roads and railways, for the creation of a small farmer class by breaking up the huge estates. Miguel

Lerdo de Tejada issued a decree confiscating church lands for the nation and disbanding the monastic orders.

The destiny of both Mexico and the United States was involved in the struggle, as international powers lined up for or against republicanism in Mexico. The United States recognized Juárez as the legal President of Mexico but, as the nation was on the verge of the War between the States, nothing could be done to block the schemes of European powers.

England, France and Spain recognized the anti-republican Miramón, claiming the presidency in Mexico City. The three European nations hoped to see a monarchy established in Mexico to prevent the spread of democracy in America. They were agreed in their desire to block, commercially and politically, the expansion of the United States.

At the same period Mexico and the United States engaged in a life and death struggle for national existence. In the northern republic it was the fight to preserve the Union and abolish slavery, while in Mexico it was the fight of progressive men to free the nation from the deadening grip of reactionary privilege. It was also the age-old conflict between centralism and federalism. The anti-republicans wanted a strong central power to preserve their position, preferably with a monarch to keep the country in line. The liberals of the states, advancing in political consciousness, wanted a federal union like that of the United States.

Each nation had its leader of tremendous moral stature, the man of unflinching courage and great soul who represented the highest ideals of their people. Abraham Lincoln and Benito Juárez were single-minded, unassuming, imbued with selfless consecration to their nations. The stocky Indian and the tall gaunt Yankee respected and admired one another. In the hearts of their countrymen they would be forever honored.

The constitutionalists triumphed in January 1861, and Benito Juárez took office in Mexico City as President of Mexico. Within a few months Abraham Lincoln was inaugurated President of the United States, to lead his country in the deadly struggle between North and South.

The liberal government of Mexico inherited chaos, an empty treasury, a tremendous foreign debt incurred by predecessors. While sporadic fighting continued outside the capital, and many men in his own government were apathetic, Benito Juárez went ahead relentlessly with his program of reform. It was not in his stubborn Indian nature to compromise or delay.

The Archbishop of Mexico and other ecclesiastics were banished, the disbanding of monastic orders was carried through. Churchmen raged, the aristocrats hated the Indian President, while in Paris certain Mexicans of old families were plotting for a monarchy. They found a willing confederate in Napoleon III. That mediocre ruler tried to pattern himself on his famous uncle, and among other schemes, planned to restore French empire in America, lost long since in Canada. The Mexicans persuaded Napoleon that a monarch would be welcomed in Mexico and the French ruler had a prince in mind to be his puppet, the Austrian Archduke Maximilian.

The Juárez government, immersed in troubles, could not rehabilitate the country without money. In order to obtain funds President Juárez, with the approval of Congress, suspended payment for two years on the huge foreign debts.

That brought down on Mexico the European powers who wanted their money and were opposed to Juárez. In the spring of 1862 British, French and Spanish fleets arrived at Vera Cruz to collect payment. Juárez' explanations and promises of future payment were accepted by the British and Spanish commanders, who withdrew their ships. The French commander had orders to land troops if necessary to collect payment, an excuse for French invasion while the United States was too busy with civil war to interfere. Troops went ashore with the Mexican plotters from Paris and their General Almonte.

While this general called on Mexicans to support the French, the invading army, thousands strong, marched up the mountains to attack Puebla. With outmoded weapons and insufficient troops, General Zaragoza and young General Porfirio Díaz held the city against such odds that they could scarcely believe their victory when it came. The French discovered to their cost that Mexicans defending their land fought like lions. On May 5, 1862, the French withdrew, leaving a thousand dead on the field.

Wild with joy, the people of Puebla rang their church bells and hailed their heroes, Zaragoza and Díaz. Cinco de Mayo has been ever since a glorious date in Mexico, a day of national commemoration.

Napoleon sent thirty thousand troops to reinforce those in Mexico, to redeem French honor, while General Almonte gathered an army of anti-republican Mexicans. In the spring of 1863, from March to May, Puebla was again besieged, the defenders holding out until starvation forced them to surrender. Porfirio Díaz and a few other officers escaped from their captors to continue the fight with guerrillas of the mountains.

President Juárez, knowing that the capital could not withstand attack, moved his government to San Luis Potosí. Mexico City was decked in gala array by the anti-republicans to welcome as deliverers the French and Mexican troops. An Assembly of Notables was convened which declared in favor of a monarchy, headed by a Catholic European prince, to be called Emperor of Mexico. The crown was then offered to

Archduke Maximilian in accordance with Napoleon's scheme.

Archduke Maximilian and his wife Carlota were a young pair of royal romantics, unaware that they were mere pawns in Napoleon's ambitious schemes. In their appearance and aristocratic pride the tall blond prince with the fan-shaped golden beard and his high-spirited princess were well fitted to play the imperial role they dreamed of.

When their ship docked at Vera Cruz in May, 1864, the new Emperor and Empress expected to receive their kingdom from a people ready to welcome them with open arms. Napoleon and the Mexican notables had seen to that. Maximilian, after accepting Napoleon's offer and the invitation of the Assembly of Notables, demanded as well a call from the people through an election. He was a paradox among royalties—a prince of meticulous pride in royal state, yet of vaguely liberal spirit. French and Mexican officers had forced through a farcical vote in various cities, so that Maximilian believed he was the choice of the Mexican people.

Eagerly the young pair awaited the enthusiastic welcome of their subjects as the ship docked, but they saw only a drowsy tropical port, its streets empty and silent. No guns, no bells, no cheering crowd. Carlota burst into tears of disappointment. General Almonte, charged with giving them a royal reception, was late through some misunderstanding. Hours after the ship arrived he dashed into town to greet the forlorn royal pair, ordered the guns fired and tried to make up for the shock of the first impression. The people of Vera Cruz, however, refused to cheer for an unwanted emperor. On the trying trip up the mountains royal spirits were somewhat brightened by delegations of Indians bearing gifts to the tall fair ruler who seemed to them a reincarnation of Quetzalcoatl.

After they had been reassured by the adulation of the notables in the capital and had been crowned in the Cathedral, the Emperor and Empress began to take an enthusiastic interest in their kingdom. They fell under the haunting spell of Mexico; the flowers, the impressive landscape and translucent atmosphere, the unique ways of life so different from those in Europe, the Indians adding just the right note to New World scenes for romantic Europeans.

They were well-meaning, this deluded pair, who planned to be kindly rulers over an interesting people. Maximilian and Carlota did not understand that they had been imposed by a few unscrupulous schemers upon a population that regarded foreign rule with sullen hate. It was some time before they learned that to the people at large they were unwanted interlopers.

Benito Juárez, to be sure, had given a shock to Maximilian's complacency soon after his arrival, in a letter so scathing it was like a blow in the face. He wrote: "It is given a man, sir, to attack the rights of others, seize their goods, assault the lives of those who defend their nationality, make of their virtues crimes and of one's own vices a virtue, but there is one thing beyond the reach of such perversity—the tremendous judgment of history." Maximilian began to realize that this Indian, spoken of so scornfully by the notables, was a patriot. He would have liked to win Juárez to work with him for Mexico.

Maximilian made great plans for bringing European culture to Mexico and for beautification of the capital. Chapultepec Castle, aloft on its cliff among the woodlands, was rebuilt and decorated with European elegance for Carlota. An avenue was laid out from the park to the city—an avenue that is now the beautiful Paseo de la Reforma.

The Emperor went about the country visiting towns and

villages, accepting the staged demonstrations of welcome as a sign that the people liked him. He became interested in the Indians and determined to improve the miserable conditions under which they lived. Vaguely the royal idealist began to sketch out plans for reform.

For a time the aristocrats of the capital preened themselves in the European atmosphere of court life established with meticulous etiquette by Maximilian and Carlota. Soon, however, their Mexican sponsors and Napoleon in France discovered that their royal puppet had ideas of his own, ideas most displeasing to them. When a papal nuncio arrived to demand that the Juárez Reform Laws be annulled and Church lands returned, Maximilian refused and Carlota backed him up. The Emperor tried to persuade liberal leaders to enter his cabinet, to help him in reforms.

The experiment in empire seemed to be succeeding, nevertheless, in 1865. When Maximilian and Carlota felt the chill of disapproval in court society over the Emperor's liberal ideas, they tried to regain favor by staging extravagant parties at Chapultepec Castle. Society guzzled at banquets of fine foods and rare wines, or drowsed comfortably through concerts of Viennese music. Rich costumes, decorations glittering on handsome uniforms, made a satisfying display at balls and soirées.

The French army appeared to be winning the country from the republicans. Porfirio Díaz and his guerrillas were pushed back into the southern mountains and the President's black carriage rolled farther and farther north. Juárez set up headquarters at Paso del Norte, now Ciudad Juárez, across the Rio Grande from Texas. Thinking to break resistance by terror the French General Bazaine induced Maximilian to issue a decree ordering officers to shoot every *juarista* captured. Bloody executions resulted, which alienated Maximilian's Mexican friends and caused denunciations in the press of the United States.

When the War between the States ended with the triumph of the Union the United States was free to act, and the flimsy fabric of empire in Mexico began to fall apart. Sympathizers in the United States wanted Union troops sent against the French, but the government decided instead to give secret aid to Juárez with men, money and munitions slipped across the border to Paso del Norte. In 1866 the United States was sufficiently stabilized so that Secretary of State Seward could invoke the Monroe Doctrine. Napoleon was informed that French troops must leave Mexico.

The Mexican Empire had been a headache to the French ruler, Maximilian had proved intractable, Napoleon did not wish to become embroiled with the United States, and he was faced with a military Germany preparing for war. He dropped Mexico like a hot potato and told Maximilian that henceforth he would have to get along without French help, that the army would be withdrawn. It was a terrible blow to the ill-starred Emperor, for he felt the strength of national spirit opposed to him, and realized the bitter truth that he had not won the people.

Betrayed by his sponsor, repudiated by Mexicans, the Emperor vacillated between abdication and the desire to preserve his royal honor by remaining at his post. Carlota, the ambitious and strong-minded, urged him to remain, while she began her tragic pilgrimage around Europe pleading with royal relatives, with Napoleon and the Vatican, for aid to Maximilian. Frenzied by the frustration of her hopes, she babbled hysterically of poisoning and enemies, and went completely out of her mind. Her family shut her up in a quiet retreat and the tragic Empress of Mexico faded from the scene, to spend the rest of her life in the dream world of insanity.

In Mexico the French army began to embark for Europe, while republican troops moved in to take over the places they abandoned. Porfirio Díaz was winning victories in the south and republican troops, reinforced with an army of trained Indians, began to march from the northern border. Bad advisors, among them the notables who feared their fate at the hands of Juárez, played up to the Emperor's conception of royal honor. They urged him not to abdicate, but to win back the kingdom by heading his Mexican army in person.

Maximilian took up headquarters at Querétaro in February 1867. With him were four Mexican generals who, with him, came to be called the "five tragic Ms"—Mejía, Márquez, Méndez, Miramón and Maximilian. The town was soon surrounded by forty thousand *juaristas* and although General Márquez slipped away to bring reinforcements, they were beaten back before reaching the city. The *juaristas* settled down to starve out their enemies. Hunger, dysentery, corpses rotting in the hot spring sun, created terrible conditions in the city. Maximilian tried to encourage his troops by his sympathy and courageous spirit.

When republican troops penetrated the city one of the Emperor's officers tried to arrange for his escape, but Maximilian would not go. He joined a small company on the Hill of Bells outside the city, his tall figure making a conspicuous target as the enemy closed in around the hill. He hoped that a bullet would bring him death, but the *juaristas* held their fire while their officer made the Emperor his prisoner. Dignified to the last, Maximilian mounted his white horse and rode down the hill to present his sword to the commander.

General Méndez had been shot in the siege, General Márquez was not in the city, but Maximilian and the generals Mejía and Miramón were tried by a military court of republican captains. The Mexican generals were quickly convicted of treason, but there was more argument over the fate of the Emperor, lying wasted with fever in a bare convent cell. He was tried on charges of filibustering, treason, and the ruthless execution of prisoners. So intense was the resentment of Mexicans over the French invasion that none of the men had a chance of acquittal. The jury decreed execution for all three.

Benito Juárez, sitting in his headquarters at San Luis Potosí, with the fate of Maximilian in his hands, was the object of world attention. He was showered with cables and letters from every court in Europe and from sympathizers everywhere, urging him to spare the life of the Emperor. Emissaries, personal and official, visited him to plead for Maximilian. The implacable Indian seemed to be unmoved by all the pleas or the weight of world opinion. Justice must be done and the usurper must die, to teach other ambitious European princes that Mexico would not tolerate foreign rule.

On a beautiful summer morning, June 16, 1867, Maximilian, Mejía and Miramón faced the firing squad on the Hill of Bells. Calm in the face of death, Maximilian gave his final thought to the country he had come to love, praying that his blood might be the last to be shed for Mexico.

Porfirio Díaz had won the war in the south and taken Mexico City. He prepared a celebration for the President with floral arches, banners and pageants, but Juárez would have none of it. He rode toward the city with his family in the rusty old carriage which had taken him through so many retreats—a silent, black-clad figure as impassive in victory as in defeat. Díaz rode out on horseback to meet him, expecting to receive warm praise from his leader and an invitation to ride beside him into the capital. Instead, Juárez greeted him coldly and proceeded on his way alone. It was a blow to the vanity of the young general who had indeed done a great work in the war and wanted his share in the moment of triumph. Already Díaz had grown far apart in ideas from the man he had formerly admired, and this insult to his sensitive pride broke the last bond between them.

Other officers, and the soldiers who fought and suffered so long, felt the lack of human warmth in their austere leader, and needed the praise he did not think to give them. He had been a rock of strength in the war, but he could not relax to rejoice with them in victory.

The Mexican people had won through dark years of war and foreign rule to a deeper national consciousness than they had ever known. They were united, temporarily, by the tremendous struggle to free themselves from the French. They had as basis for a progressing nation the principles of their Constitution. That document would be ignored in times to come, but the people had a goal in their efforts to win freedom, their constitutional rights in the nation.

As vindication for having assumed leadership after Comonfort's downfall, Benito Juárez wanted to win the presidency in the next election. He received the vote of confidence he asked for and became the properly elected President in 1867. He continued to live with unassuming simplicity, devoting his whole strength to the tasks of reform. It needed a strong hand to advance the work and Juárez employed it, becoming so autocratic that some accused him of wanting to be a dictator.

The constitutionalists protested vigorously when he stood for re-election in 1871 against Porfirio Díaz, the war hero, and Sebastian Lerdo de Tejada, brother of the man who wrote the

Ley Lerdo. The liberals were the government party who could manipulate the votes of ignorant men. Although the result of the election was indecisive, Congress declared that Juárez had won.

Porfirio Díaz, thwarted in his ambitions, declared the election was fraudulent and raised the standard of revolt, on the principle of honest voting and no re-election. It was an ironic slogan indeed from the man who was to be the most absolute dictator for the longest period in Mexican history. The revolt was soon put down, but Díaz continued to lay the foundations for future power.

Porfirio Díaz, once the young patriot, was a military hero during the war, and developed into the despotic caudillo, the most constructive one, in some ways, in Mexico's history. He had the vanity and great ambition for personal power of the caudillo, but he was also an astute politician. He knew his Mexico and employed cynical skill in manipulating people as he climbed to power.

Benito Juárez had brought Mexico back to a respected position in the family of nations. He established friendly relations with European powers and was on the best of terms with the United States. He had not forgotten the friendliness of the northern republic during the dark years of war, and made public acknowledgment of the moral support given by the United States.

Under Juárez, Mexico came closer than ever before to having honest, constructive government. It would have been impossible, under the best of conditions, to carry through completely his great program of reform, but some progress was made. Roads and telegraph lines were built, the railway begun before the French intervention to connect Vera Cruz with the capital was almost completed.

The most important laws, having to do with breaking up of great land grants for the benefit of small farmers, failed of their purpose. The Church lost the lands but they did not go to the people who needed them. The reformers also made the mistake of breaking up some of the communal village ejidos, hoping to rouse incentive in the peons by making them owners of small plots. As a result, many ignorant Indians sold their parcels to hacendados for a handful of pesos, and a bad precedent was established for future exploitation of Indian villagers.

Enemies called Juárez a despot, but it was necessary to employ arbitrary methods to enforce laws in a nation of illiterate Indians and self-seeking politicians. He was stubborn and rigid in following his conception of justice. Juárez never forgot his deep desire to raise the Indian masses from their poverty and ignorance. He tried to improve living conditions and ordered hacendados and municipalities to build schools for Indian children. Several thousand little schools were built during his administration.

The man who had spent his life in devotion to his nation had his work cut short before it was finished, like his great contemporary, Abraham Lincoln. On July 18, 1872, Juárez was seized with a heart attack and died during the night. A great hush fell over the nation; civil strife ceased while high and low mourned the passing of the man whose courage and vision had preserved Mexican nationhood through difficult years.

In the spectacular drama of Mexican history, the blood and treachery and greed which mar so much of the story, Benito Juárez stands out—a simple, rock-hewn figure of quiet strength. He remains to the Mexican people a national symbol. Benito Juárez was, as Sebastian Lerdo de Tejada said when he died, "the soul of Mexico."

CHAPTER 17

ON TO THE PACIFIC

WHEN GOLD was discovered in John Sutter's millrace in California the destiny of Central America and the Isthmus of Panama was immediately affected. That momentous discovery, in 1848, coming while the war between the United States and Mexico was going on, made it inevitable that California would go to the North Americans. Gold, and the Pacific coast to develop, brought a tremendous westward rush by sea and the need for a more accessible route to the Pacific Ocean than the long perilous voyage around Cape Horn.

Because of their potential interoceanic routes, the small nations in the waist of the Americas became involved in the rivalry between Great Britain and the United States, for the two nations had long been competing in Pacific trade.

Even before the Wars of Independence of the Spanish colonials, English and Yankee whalers were sailing around Cape Horn to Pacific whaling grounds and Yankee traders were calling at the little ports of Spanish California. During the first quarter of the nineteenth century the rich furs of the northwest Pacific coast, to be traded for the silks and teas of

China, brought the stately clipper ships of England and the United States into the Pacific for the China trade.

With the introduction of steam navigation in the 1840's the pace of sea-borne commerce and passenger traffic was speeded up. Steamer service drew Europe and America together, bringing about changes as revolutionary for people of the mid-nineteenth century as the girdling of the globe by air is for the mid-twentieth century world.

Two little paddle-wheel steam vessels built in England for Chile were the first steamers to enter the Pacific Ocean. The *Chile* and *Peru* were built on the sailing-ship model with engine and paddle wheel in the middle. On their first voyage up the coast from Chile the odd little vessels, belching great clouds of black smoke, made a sensation. They were the first ships of the Pacific Mail Steam Navigation Company which was taken over in a few years by a British concern. Mail, cargo and passenger service was inaugurated in 1842 between England and the West Indies when steamers of the Royal Mail Steam Packet Company began their runs.

Increasing commerce between England and the west-coast nations of South America brought the old Spanish route across the Isthmus of Panama into use, to avoid the voyage around the Horn. Passengers and goods were unloaded from west-coast steamers at the port of Panama. Thence they were transferred by mule and river canoe across the Isthmus to Chagres. Since there was no harbor small boats, maneuvering through the rolling surf, carried goods and passengers between ship and shore. Travel across the Isthmus was as primitive as in the seventeenth century when Friar Gage made the trip and described it so vividly.

Life on the tropical Isthmus was shaken out of its colonial groove by separation from Spain. The small class of rich mer-

chants and old Spanish families in Panama City had, in colonial times, their indolent comfortable life in patriarchal
mansions with tropical gardens, served by many Negro slaves.
They had silks, satins and house furnishings from Spain; their
traditional social customs were adapted to life in a hot, damp
climate. Dependent as they were on the labor of the black
people, the abolition of slavery, which came with independence,
was more upsetting than elsewhere. Slaves, freed from their
masters, could work or not as they chose. Some became quite
prosperous in small trades while their former masters, having
lost slaves and money as well, had to reduce their style of
living.

The provinces of the Isthmus, Panama and Veragua, were
distant, neglected sections of New Granada. That state had
become a separate republic after the Gran Colombia of Bolívar's
time had split into the three states of Venezuela, Ecuador and
New Granada (present-day Colombia).

Panamanian delegates to the National Congress had before
them a fantastically difficult journey by ship, river boat and
mule to reach the capital, Bogotá, high in the Andes. Once
there, their pleas for consideration for their provinces were
generally ignored in the political struggles going on in New
Granada. So indignant were the Panamanians over neglect of
their interests that in 1840 the provinces of the Isthmus seceded,
only to rejoin the larger state within a year.

The only hope for prosperity lay in the development of an
effective route from the Atlantic to the Pacific. Delegates
pleaded for this in the National Congress, the government of
New Granada realized the potentialities of such a route but
did not have the means to finance it. At various times New
Granada tried without success to interest Great Britain or
France in financing the building of a road, railway or canal

across the Isthmus. Engineers who made surveys considered the project too difficult and expensive, European governments did not yet realize the importance of such a route, and the United States had not come definitely into the picture.

In 1846 it was Great Britain rather than the United States that was regarded by Latin Americans as an encroaching foreign power, because of her control of business, her tendency to intervene in internal affairs and her control over the Mosquito coast of Nicaragua and Honduras. It was in that year that the government of New Granada turned to the United States and signed a treaty giving the United States certain commercial privileges and the right to intervene if necessary to keep the transit of the Isthmus open. In return, the United States guaranteed the sovereignty of New Granada over the Isthmus. New Granada expected to obtain similar guarantees from England and France and to give similar privileges, but the governments of those nations did not respond. Unintentionally, the United States found itself possessed of exclusive rights and privileges over the Isthmian route. At the time, the treaty of 1846 did not appear to be very important but it was to have a vital bearing on the future of Panama.

The whole picture changed when gold was discovered in California. The spotlight of world attention was focused on that bonanza land and incidentally on the Isthmus of Panama, while the United States forged ahead as the nation with the most vital interest in the central portion of the Americas.

For some years, as we know, intrepid Yankee pioneers had been filtering across the mountains into easygoing, sparsely settled Spanish-Mexican California. Yankee trading ships had increased their barter of manufactured goods for hides, furs and lumber at the ports of San Diego and Monterey. Before California was lost to Mexico in the disastrous war of 1846–48,

Captain Frémont and his cohorts had raised the Bear Flag to declare California an independent state. The instant that news of war with Mexico reached the commander of American naval ships in the Pacific he seized Monterey and hoisted the Stars and Stripes over the custom house.

Into this atmosphere of change and turmoil, with determined Americans marching into a new promised land, came the cry of "Gold! Gold!" to send adventurers from every country rushing to California. By every transcontinental trail they trekked to the golden mountains, and by sailing ship to Chagres to cross the Isthmus and make their way to California by any kind of boat.

In 1849 the rush across the Isthmus began. Already, in preparation for the inevitable opening of California and Oregon to the United States, the government had authorized a wealthy promoter of New York, William Henry Aspinwall, to build three paddle-wheel steamers for the Pacific trade, and eventually to build a railroad across the Isthmus of Panama. The first steamer of the Pacific Mail Steamship Company, the *California,* started on her maiden voyage around the Horn October 6, 1848. Although the discovery of gold in California was known in the east, only the most enterprising adventurers had then started for the mines. Long before the *California* reached Panama City, however, the tide of gold-seekers had begun to surge upon the Isthmus.

By schooner, brig and steamer they came from New York to be disembarked upon the beach before the filthy, forlorn settlement of Chagres. Some men had tickets bought in New York to go aboard the *California* when she should reach Panama, but many more took this route to the land of gold under the delusion that they would find plenty of sailing ships to take them to San Francisco.

In a fever of excitement, laden with pickaxes, shovels, pans for washing gold, the adventurers at Chagres piled into cayugas, great dugout canoes with palm-leaf canopies, to go up the river to Gorgona, thence over the trail to Panama City. Every Negro or half-breed who had a cayuga or a mule found fortune dropped in his lap as he gouged the gold-seekers for transport to Panama. Tropical sun and tropical rain beat upon the adventurers, food gave out, they fell victim to the deadly fevers of the region. On foot with packs on their backs, or on mules when they could get them, the men passed over the terrible trail through the jungles, a trail worn into deep holes and knee-deep in mud.

Like a swarm of locusts the adventurers descended on the startled inhabitants of Panama City. It was a poor dilapidated town with grass growing in the streets and vines smothering the ruins of old churches. There were few shops, no food or accommodations for such a horde. The invaders filled every nook and cranny of the town and camped in swarms on the beach. When the *California* arrived in the Bay of Panama she was already well filled, for the news of gold had reached Peru, and Peruvians were aboard on their way to seek fortune. The ship was mobbed by frantic men, some with tickets, some without, demanding passage to San Francisco. The *California* finally sailed bulging with eager humanity, decks and cabins crowded to capacity. Panamanian shipmasters with brigs, schooners or even small sloops sold every inch of space on their crude vessels to transport the prospectors to their goal.

So began the fantastic saga of the crossing of the Isthmus. Various travelers, in those first years of the Gold Rush, described vividly and with humor the terrors of that journey. The Argonauts, as the first prospectors called themselves, slept in filthy native huts among animals, insects and babies, or on the ground exposed to rain and fever-breeding mosquitoes. They lived on tortillas and greasy stews of iguana lizard bought from natives, or foraged for food in the forest.

The trail, a deep tunnel of green through the jungles, was crowded with mules, with black, half-naked muleteers and men on foot, staggering on through mud and drenching rain. The narrow alleys of drowsy old Panama City, between bright-hued balconied houses, swarmed with alien life as the red-shirted Argonauts swaggered through them, adding their shouts and songs to the cries of native venders. Yankee saloons and eating houses, shops selling supplies for the mines, crowded out native shops. There were street brawls and killings among the rough men of many nationalities awaiting transport to California. Many a hopeful prospector died of fever and left his bones to rot in Panama without ever reaching his goal; others, yellow and gaunt, waited for months to get passage. From the crowded camps on the shore canoes darted into the harbor every time a sail appeared, surrounding the ship while the occupants fought with frenzied anxiety to get a foothold on board.

Within a year or two after the first stampede to the gold fields in 1849 steamers of the United States Mail Steam Company were bringing prospectors from New York and New Orleans to Chagres, and the three steamers of the Pacific Mail Steamship Company were transporting them from Panama to San Francisco. Sailing ships, large or small, added their quota to the hordes brought to the Isthmus and carried to California. Before long there was traffic from west to east as prospectors, successful or disappointed, returned. The steamship lines reaped golden profits.

From coast to coast, along the route of the new gold trail, the Isthmus awoke from lethargy to hectic life. Panamanians profited from the stream passing back and forth but they did not like the lawless swaggering adventurers among the more orderly travelers, who stirred up brawls and got into fights with the natives.

In 1849 William Henry Aspinwall began the heartbreaking project of building the first transcontinental railroad of America across the tropical Isthmus. The concession obtained from New Granada provided that the South American state might acquire the road after a course of years and the payment of some million dollars.

The contractors established their camp on Manzanillo Island in Limón Bay, planning to make this swampy piece of land, infested with mosquitoes, the Atlantic terminus of the railroad. So devastating were mosquitoes and sand flies that workers had to wear gauze veils over their heads while at work and were obliged to spend their nights on an old brig anchored in the bay. The settlement was called Aspinwall by the Americans, but as a town finally grew out of the swamp it acquired the Panamanian name, Colón. Another camp was built at Gatun, seven miles away on the Chagres River, where steamers brought machinery and supplies.

The road was under construction during the height of the Gold Rush, thus the demands of prospectors for boatmen, porters and mule drivers made it almost impossible to obtain native labor. Workers were brought from New Granada and from Europe; even from China the company imported a thousand coolies, with rice and opium to keep them happy. Unfortunately the Orientals were overcome with misery in the strange land and were seized with a mass suicidal mania. Hundreds walked into the sea to drown while many more killed themselves in other ways until only a few were left. Malaria, dysentery and yellow fever took a terrible toll of life;

the hospitals built by the company were filled and it was said in the United States that every tie laid cost a life.

Great sums were sunk in the project, as the contractors struggled to overcome the difficulties of railroad building in the tropics. A hurricane swept into Limón Bay, wrecking every ship at anchor. The roadbed had to be laid on rock fills or piles across swampy lowlands. Wooden ties rotted in the climate and the only wood hard enough to withstand it was transported all the way from New Granada.

When the track had been laid as far as Gatun the railroad received a bit of free advertising from two boatloads of prospectors who took refuge in Limón Bay from a fierce storm. The men insisted on riding to Gatun on flat cars. As they rolled along shouting and singing, they drew attention to the superior ease of riding across the Isthmus instead of making the transit by mule and canoe.

Eventually, despite disasters and expense, the Panama Railroad was finished. On January 27, 1855, the last rail was laid and the next day a locomotive chugged across the Isthmus from ocean to ocean.

American enterprise built the railroad; American steamship lines carried the bulk of traffic to and from California. The gold fields and the vast territory opened up on the Pacific coast made the sea route more vital to the United States than to any other nation until the first transcontinental railroad in the republic reached California in 1869.

Great Britain was also on the alert to protect her trade interests in the Pacific, and for this reason kept her control over the Mosquito Coast of Nicaragua and Honduras. She moved in on the settlement of San Juan del Norte or Greytown, at the mouth of the San Juan River, in order to have control over the potential route across Nicaragua.

Because of this route from sea to sea, Nicaragua, weak and distracted with civil war, became a pawn in the rivalries of two nations, Great Britain and the United States, for commercial advantages. British investors watched with concern the expansion of the United States through the acquisition of Oregon and California. Developments on the Pacific coast also stimulated North American schemes for a canal route across Nicaragua.

When that blustering genius in money-making enterprises, Cornelius Vanderbilt, obtained a concession from Nicaragua to run river and lake steamers and build a road or canal to connect with the Pacific, British alarm increased. The treaty with Nicaragua guaranteed its sovereignty over the route and did not give the United States exclusive rights; nonetheless Great Britain was concerned. Meanwhile, the proud expansionist spirit in the United States caused North Americans to regard Nicaragua as their domain, and British control over Greytown and Mosquitia was resented.

The two nations watched each other's moves in Nicaragua like two dogs maneuvering for a bone. Controversies led to the formulation of the Clayton-Bulwer Treaty, in 1850, between Great Britain and the United States. By its terms any canal built across Nicaragua was to be international and both nations pledged themselves not to fortify or colonize in Central America. Great Britain, however, insisted that these terms did not apply to territory she already held, the colony of Belize and the Bay Islands off Honduras, and the American minister, Clayton, acquiesced.

Vanderbilt's Accessory Transit Company was to pay Nicaragua ten thousand dollars annually and ten per cent of the profits for the privilege of transporting passengers by steamer and road or canal across the country. By contract the promoter was pledged to construct a canal from Lake Nicaragua to the Pacific but this was never done, and his accountants saw to it that very little profit was recorded to be shared with Nicaragua.

The rough, profane Vanderbilt, a filibuster with a check-book, was the first of the soldiers of fortune who were soon to overrun the strategic Central American country. He himself piloted the first small steamer through the rapids and shallows of the San Juan River to Lake Nicaragua. Before long he was cutting into the profits of the steamship lines serving the Pacific by running his own ships from New York and New Orleans to Greytown and from San Juan del Sur on the Pacific side to San Francisco.

Passengers, going up the river in small vessels, were transferred to lake steamers at San Carlos for the sail across the lake to Virgin Bay. For the thirteen miles of overland transit Vanderbilt constructed a macadam road, the only decent road in Nicaragua, over which travelers rolled in a string of gay blue-and-white coaches with the seal of Nicaragua painted on the sides. Crowds of merchants, settlers and red-shirted, slouch-hatted prospectors journeyed to California with more comfort than those who took the Isthmus route; as it was five hundred miles shorter, and Vanderbilt's fares were lower, the Accessory Transit Company was a great rival to the promoters of the Panama route.

Spanish colonials had made use of Lake Nicaragua and its outlet river for their limited shipping trade, but it was Cornelius Vanderbilt who demonstrated the feasibility of the interoceanic route across Nicaragua for the modern world of commerce. His Transit Company brought little profit to Nicaraguans; it was simply a means of passage for travelers from the east coast of the United States to California, and was to become in a few years an aid to exploitation of the country by the king of filibusters, William Walker.

Expansion to the Pacific brought both Panama and Nicaragua into the limelight. Henceforth both states were to be involved in the international politics of big nations because of their possession of interoceanic routes.

CHAPTER 18

FILIBUSTERS IN CENTRAL AMERICA

AFTER THE westward-rolling tide of pioneers had reached the Pacific, and international hordes of gold-seekers had taken the cream from California mines, adventurers looked about for new lands to exploit and found them in Central America. In colonial times Central Americans had been terrorized and their towns sacked by raiders from the sea. Some of these raiders were called by the Dutch *vrijbuiters,* by the French *flibustiers,* from which developed the English words filibusters and freebooters. In the 1850's a new kind of filibuster, not content to loot and depart, but with designs on the land itself, invaded Nicaragua.

The filibusters of the mid-nineteenth century were lawless men, soldiers of fortune, ready to invade the territory of harmless neighbors on the pretext of extending the blessings of Manifest Destiny to the downtrodden "greasers." This was a name given by frontiersmen to the lowly, brown-skinned Mexican settlers of border territories. To the arrogant filibusters the natives of small Spanish American countries were all "greasers" unable to manage their own affairs. The only hope for them was to have North Americans take control and eventually annex their lands to the United States. When filibusters plagued the Spanish governors of Cuba with their raids or advanced into Mexican territory, they cloaked lawless adventure under noble declarations that they came to free oppressed people from their bad governments.

Central America was ripe for exploitation by soldiers of fortune. Most of the time the republics, except Costa Rica, were distracted and hindered from development by political conflicts taking the form of armed revolts. Politics was a disease, the only means by which ambitious men, white or mestizo, could attain wealth and power. Party lines overran borders and the whole territory was divided between two parties known by various names, but usually designated simply as Liberals and Conservatives. The original distinctions in principle had ceased to count for much, although the Conservatives were traditionally the *calzados,* those who wore shoes, in other words the old ranks of the clergy and aristocracy. The Liberals were supposed to be a people's party, but they were no more democratic than their opponents.

Each party wanted power to run the country for the benefit of its own group of allied families, for politics was more a matter of personal relationships than of principles. The individualism inherent in their Spanish blood made it impossible for Central Americans to achieve national unity, or even to accept the result of so-called elections.

When the caudillo of one party lost an election he retired to a neighboring state and called on the leaders of his party in that country to aid him in a revolt to overthrow his opponent. The republics were not yet nations; rather, they were groups of selfishly contending parties, more concerned for their own gain than national welfare. The few patriotic, constructive political leaders could accomplish little in their terms of office.

Although Costa Rica had political troubles and overturns of government, that state was saved from the interlocking wars of her neighbors by isolation, by the industrious character of her people and their more homogeneous racial make-up. The few remaining Indians were negligible, the farmer and tradesman classes were more white than mestizo, and the republic was blessed more frequently than the others with honest statesmen who encouraged agriculture and business.

Coffee, introduced into Costa Rica much earlier than in the other republics, had become a source of prosperity and the life-blood of the country. Small farmers as well as wealthy proprietors had their plantations of coffee trees and profited from the crop. The transport of the coffee harvest from the highlands to the port of Puntarenas on the Bay of Nicoya was a picturesque affair, an occasion for gayety and fiesta.

Processions of laden two-wheeled carts drawn by placid bullocks crawled down the mountain road, the only good one in the country, from San José to the coast. Under the hooded tops women and children, families of the carters, rode on the sacks, merrily chatting and singing. They leaned out between the scarlet side curtains to greet friends in other carts. The road wound down from the highlands between great over-hanging trees draped with flowering vines. At intervals there were wayside cantinas where the carters cheered themselves with *aguardiente,* sugar-cane rum, camped for the night or stopped to cook a meal. Jolly family groups, gathered around the campfires, made fiesta of the evenings with food, drink, and singing to the strumming of guitars.

The industrious Costa Ricans did not want their prosperous farms and coffee *fincas* wrecked by disorders. Their attitude, commented on by an Anglo-Saxon visitor in the 1860's probably was the same in the 1850's. Frederick Boyle wrote: "If government must be overthrown, say the planters, Carajo! let's do it between crops. If anyone must be shot, say the merchants, Carai! get it over before the warehouses open."

The bright picture of prosperity in Costa Rica was a contrast indeed to that of next-door Nicaragua, backward and undeveloped because of perennial conflict between the Liberals of León and the Conservatives of Granada. In a richly fertile land most of the people lived in a primitive fashion, poor but indolently easygoing in the hot climate; subsisting from their patches of corn and plantains or the Indian crafts of weaving fibers into hats, bags and hammocks. Bullock carts with solid wooden wheels crawled over rough dirt roads, transporting produce. Travelers went on horseback over cart tracks or trails and hung up their hammocks at night in crude village inns.

There were Indian villages of bamboo-walled thatched huts nestled among tropical fruit trees, and small towns of simple adobe houses. The wealthy families of the fine old towns, León and Granada, had their pleasant social life in the intervals between revolts. When generals and their troops were on the march the families barred the great wooden doors of their mansions and waited for the storm to pass.

The beautiful lakes, luxuriant woodlands and plantations of cacao, indigo and sugar cane, presented to strangers a picture of tropical beauty and fertility, needing only peace and enterprise to make it a paradise. So it appeared to some of the California-bound travelers on the Accessory Transit Line. One of them, the New Englander, Byron Cole, stirred restless men in San Francisco with his tales of the great opportunities for vigorous adventurers in this fine but neglected land.

In William Walker, working on the newspaper owned by Byron Cole in gaudy San Francisco, the New Englander found a partner for the most ambitious filibustering scheme yet dreamed of. William Walker was the last man anyone would have picked to be a leader of tough adventurers. Small and slight of frame, with icy gray eyes, straggling tow-colored hair and a cold, impassive manner, there was nothing dramatic about his personality—yet he could make the wild men of the 1850's follow him on the most fantastic projects. His insignificant appearance concealed an iron will and insatiable craving for power.

Born and brought up in Nashville, Tennessee, the austere young William studied medicine, abandoned that career for law study, practiced law and tried newspaper work in New Orleans. Dissatisfied with these activities, William Walker followed the Forty-niners to California.

In San Francisco he mingled with the crowd of reckless, undisciplined men of various nationalities, looking, as he was, for new fields of exploitation. The chance for lucky strikes in the mines was diminishing; disappointed prospectors, vagabonds and riff-raff of all sorts were ready to follow filibusters to Spanish American lands.

It was among these men that the ambitious lawyer and journalist found companions for his first exploit, the crazy attempt to wrest Baja California and Sonora from Mexico, and to make himself president of an independent state as Sam Houston had done in Texas. The deserts and mountains, sparsely populated with poor peons, ranchers and bandits, were uninviting, but Sonora had rich mines.

William Walker, an odd-looking conqueror in a long blue coat with gilt buttons, a tall white-fur hat topping his grim face, led his gang of vagabonds on a blundering, disastrous trek. From the ports of Baja California the self-styled President of Sonora marched his men across the northern deserts, suffering hunger and hardship, meeting unexpected resistance from the "greasers." Mexican bandits chased the survivors to the border where they staggered into the fort at Yuma to surrender to the United States army. Walker and his officers were tried at San Francisco for violating the neutrality laws, but Walker himself was acquitted through the sympathy of the jury for such a bold schemer.

Nicaragua, described in glowing terms by Byron Cole, offered a worthy field for Walker's overweening ambition. He learned everything he could about the country and soon realized that the man who mastered Nicaragua and built a canal across it would indeed be a power. Cole reported that a Liberal revolt led by Don Francisco Castellon was having hard going and that Castellon had been responsive to his offer of help from North American adventurers.

Having had one brush with the neutrality laws Walker rejected the plan for an armed invasion and evolved a scheme to evade the law. Byron Cole obtained from Don Francisco Castellon a contract permitting three hundred American "colonists" to enter Nicaragua, to be given grants of land and to have the privilege of forever bearing arms. The filibusters threw themselves with enthusiasm into the work of gathering recruits and supplies for the expedition. Walker's reputation was such that his activities could not escape the watchful sheriff in San Francisco. Finally, in order to avoid arrest, the filibuster slipped out of the harbor by night in his one leaky brig, leaving half his supplies behind.

Walker had on board fifty-eight men; a few unemployed army officers and a mixed gang of prospectors, vagabonds and criminals down on their luck, who soon dubbed themselves The Immortals.

In June, 1855, Walker and his fifty-eight Immortals landed at Realejo to offer their aid, according to the filibuster's statement, in freeing Nicaraguans from oppression. Proud Nicaraguan officers looked askance at the drab, unimpressive liberator and his mob of bearded Californians in slouch hats, red shirts and high boots. The Immortals, for their part, regarded with contempt the brown, barefoot peon soldiers in ragged cotton suits, armed with ancient muskets.

Walker's men were sworn into the Nicaraguan army as the American Phalanx, becoming citizens by their own declaration. Castellon and his commanding officer did not like these Yankees whom they had permitted to come to their aid and were apathetic about the campaign. Walker, with cold determination, proceeded to act for himself. With his Immortals and a few Nicaraguans he sailed down the coast in his old brig and marched through rain-drenched jungles to attack the town of Rivas. The Californians were nearly worsted, but learned the useful lesson of house-to-house fighting.

From Rivas, Walker marched on to seize the warehouse of the Accessory Transit Line at Virgin Bay. A steamer, *La Virgen,* had just arrived from across the lake with a load of California-bound passengers. The hapless travelers were shut up in the warehouse while Walker put his men aboard the steamer, ordering the captain to sail for Granada, despite his protest that the ship was an American vessel.

They passed the fort of Granada in the night, landing farther on. As the filibusters marched along a country road at dawn they met country folk on their way to market with baskets of produce who told Walker that the Conservative garrison in Granada was sleeping off a night of drunken celebration over a victory. It was easy for the Americans to get through the sleeping town and gain the Plaza with only a few shots fired. Walker disarmed the Conservative soldiers and held the town.

The Granadinos, all too accustomed to having their town

sacked and damaged, were pleased with the strict discipline imposed on his rowdy men by the austere Walker. Soldiers patroled the town, looters were punished, and although the cantinas became Yankee barrooms, the filibuster kept strict control over the drinking bouts. Soon a shipload of recruits came from San Francisco by the Transit Line in the guise of colonists with guns in their hands. The American Phalanx marched them through the town in a torchlight procession with a band blaring *Yankee Doodle* and *Hail Columbia,* while the Granadinos hung over their balconies to watch the antics of the *yanquis.*

Nicaraguans were amazed at the speed of action and prowess in fighting of this handful of adventurers. William Walker issued proclamations declaring that he came to bring the people good government and democracy. For a time the farming folk and Indians believed him and gave him their support, while the influential families and clergy of Granada were placated by his polite behavior toward them. Castellon soon died of cholera, whereupon Walker assumed entire control of the campaign against the Conservatives, dictating from his headquarters in Granada.

Christmas Eve in the lake city that year was the strangest the Granadinos had ever known. According to tradition every householder arranged in his home the Nascimiento, or scene of the Nativity, and the populace visited freely from house to house to do homage to the Babe of Bethlehem. Among the ladies in mantillas, ragged Indians and half-naked children went the bearded Yankees, probably touched on the sentimental side by the spirit of the celebration. When at midnight the bells of the Cathedral pealed joyously and the people knelt in the plaza, the rough men from the north knelt with them.

At that time Walker was still keeping up his pretense that

he was working for the Nicaraguan people, but they soon began to understand what was happening to their country. The Conservative General Corral was persuaded to surrender, as Walker promised to organize a government, setting up a moderate Conservative, Patricio Rivas, as puppet president. General Corral was given the post of Secretary of War while Walker retained command of the army. Gradually, as streams of recruits came to swell the ranks of the American Phalanx, Nicaraguan soldiers were disbanded, leaving Walker free to control the country with his own men.

General Corral was a patriot, deeply distressed by the subjection of his country to the Yankee. He corresponded with chiefs in other states urging them to join him in an attempt to oust the invader. When the letters were captured by Walker's scouts, General Corral declared he had acted for his country and went proudly to his death before a firing squad by order of Walker. Deeply shocked by this highhanded act, Nicaraguans awoke to the fact that they were in the power of a foreign dictator.

In the cold, ruthless mind of William Walker dreams of power were growing. He planned to master all of Central America, perhaps Mexico as well. He would build a canal and control the trade of nations between the oceans. Central Americans feared and hated him, but they were involved in their own quarrels and did not come to the rescue of Nicaragua. When Walker issued a brazen proclamation inviting the other states to lay down their arms and unite under his rule, none deigned to answer him but El Salvador.

In order to win his empire Walker must control the Transit Line to have free movement of supplies and recruits. To this end he conspired with Vanderbilt's agents in San Francisco and New York, Morgan and Garrison. These financiers had already manipulated stocks to win control of the line from

Vanderbilt and they were glad to work with the filibuster. After studying the contract, Walker and the agents declared that Vanderbilt had not fulfilled the terms, since he had not built a canal or shared profits with Nicaragua. With a fine show of indignation over the cheating of Nicaragua, Walker seized the installations and steamers of the company. Then he forced his puppet president, Rivas, to sign a contract with Morgan and Garrison on such terms that he had complete control over the route. Walker made his worst mistake when he made an enemy of the financial filibuster with unlimited funds at his command. Vanderbilt swore he would ruin them all.

In July 1856, little over a year from the time when he entered the country with noble pronouncements, William Walker had himself "elected" President of Nicaragua. He seized the opportunity to become dictator when Patricio Rivas retired to León to start a revolt against him. The inauguration was a gala affair in Granada—the city decked with flags and flowers, free drinks for all, Yankee bands marching to Yankee tunes. After being blessed by the priest in the Cathedral, the new dictator-president appeared on the balcony of Government House to receive the plaudits of the American Phalanx and Granadinos. In that Latin American setting, looking totally unlike one of their own dictators, Walker was as much out of place as his Yankee soldiers; a grim small figure in black hat, frock coat and flannel shirt. He looked insignificant but he was more dangerous to Central Americans than any of their own caudillos.

The remarkable exploits of the little man with icy gray eyes and a mania for power were watched with intense interest from outside the country. British warships cruised off Greytown, as the British government awaited an opportunity to act against the man who would make Nicaragua an American possession. In the United States people cheered him on and rejoiced over the blocking of British interests. Walker was a hero to every adventurous Man of Destiny. Recruits flocked to the New York office of his unscrupulous promoter, Parker French, in answer to an innocuous advertisement in the *New York Herald;* "Wanted, ten or fifteen young men to go a short distance out of the city. Single men preferred. Passage paid."

Southern slaveholders supported the filibuster enthusiastically, believing that he would bring Nicaragua into the Union as a slave state with unlimited rich land for slaveholding planters. While Walker did intend to introduce slave labor into Nicaragua on plantations allotted to his men, he had no wish to turn over his empire to the United States. He planned to colonize the territory with North Americans and announced that he would exterminate the mestizos whom he considered the curse of the country.

The United States, at this time, was approaching the crisis in the struggle between slave and free states. The government vacillated as to the policy to pursue toward the lawless filibuster, hesitating to antagonize the abolitionist North by supporting Walker, or the slaveholding South by acting against him. The compromise was refusal of recognition to Walker's government.

Lost in arrogant dreams, the little dictator pursued a mad course, antagonizing every man he should have conciliated, blind to the powerful forces gathering against him. Men had poured into the country from both sides by Transit steamers and the horde, mostly scum of the cities, had to be armed, clothed and fed. The early friendliness of Nicaraguans turned to hate for the swaggering Yankees who treated them with contempt and took everything they wanted without payment. The farmers turned against Walker when he began taking their lands for his Americans.

The filibuster antagonized Central Americans who favored him, and other generals began raising troops to fight him even before he made himself president. Costa Ricans were incensed when he seized one of their schooners and made it a one-ship navy, christened *Granada,* with guns mounted on its deck. Under the command of Lieutenant Fayssoux, an old-time filibuster, the *Granada* cruised along the Pacific coast to prevent Central Americans from landing soldiers.

In the spring of 1856, Central Americans were at last rousing themselves, putting aside differences, in a united effort to oust the invader. The first move came from Costa Rica. The beloved statesman and president, Juan Rafael Mora, was the only chief who realized that all Central America would be lost if Walker were not stopped. He called on the other states to join him and led his peace-loving people to war against the Yankees. Walker's troops, invading Costa Rica by the peninsula of Guanacaste, were attacked and defeated at the hacienda of Santa Rosa. President Mora declared a war of extermination, shooting every prisoner captured.

The Costa Ricans moved on to seize San Juan del Sur, Virgin Bay and Rivas, cutting off the Transit road. There they were surprised by Walker's troops and would have been lost but for the brave action of a young soldier of Alajuela, Juan Santamaria. At the cost of his life he set fire to the large house where the Americans were entrenched, driving them out to be defeated by the Costa Ricans. Cholera was more destructive than cannon to each side. The men died in great numbers in both camps, and the Costa Ricans, retreating to their country, took the pestilence with them. Costa Rica was so prostrated by the loss of life that no further move could be made for some time.

Meanwhile, in the autumn of 1856, generals of Guatemala, El Salvador and Nicaragua formed an alliance and gave battle to Walker in the lake country, taking Masaya and laying siege to Granada. Then the Costa Ricans returned to action, capturing San Juan del Sur and the Transit road for a brief time.

Vanderbilt's campaign of vengeance against the presumptuous dictator brought new troubles. He removed his ships from the Transit Line and refused to disembark recruits from ships going to Panama. Then Costa Rica went into action once more to aid Nicaragua. Troops came through wild forested country and by way of a rapid river to the Rio San Juan. Sailing down that river, they captured four Transit steamers of Morgan and Garrison in the harbor of Greytown, while commanders of British warships cruising off shore refused to help the Transit captains. Using the steamers to get up the river, the Costa Rican general captured Fort San Carlos at the outlet of the lake and cruised the waters to prevent Walker's use of the lake for transport. Helpless passengers became involved in the war as steamers were seized by contending forces to engage in shooting forays.

Walker was cut off by Vanderbilt and the Costa Ricans from supplies or men coming from the east, and when Morgan and Garrison decided not to contest Vanderbilt's control any longer, it was a final blow. They notified Walker they could send no more ships from San Francisco. At last the filibuster awoke to his danger and realized that a trap was closing around him. Help from outside could not reach him; his men, dying of cholera and panicky over their desperate situation, no longer had the daredevil spirit of the early days.

While Walker made his headquarters at Rivas, his officer, Henningsen, was ordered to evacuate Granada, first destroying the city as a lesson to Nicaraguans who opposed him. Roaring drunk on liquor they found, the men ran amok in the fine three-hundred-year-old city, indulging in an orgy of burning and destruction. Before the work was finished the Central American allies attacked from all sides.

The siege of Granada was a ghastly business. Bit by bit the Central Americans fought their way into the town, from one crumbling house to another, from church to church, until the Yankees were barricaded in the Cathedral. Rotting corpses and unsanitary conditions spread the plague of cholera. Men dying of pestilence and festering wounds added their cries to the hell of battle and flame in the wrecked city. Walker, cruising near by in a steamer, managed to rescue a company which reached the shore. As a last note of defiance, Henningsen set up a wooden placard over the smoking ruins and heaps of dead: "Here was Granada."

With ruin and death on every side, brought about by his insane ambition, the filibuster fortified himself at Rivas, hoping to keep a way of escape open to San Juan del Sur and his one-ship navy. There the Americans were besieged for weary weeks by Costa Rican companies. The men, worn down by hunger, disease and panic, deserted in groups to the Costa Rican commander when he offered them protection.

Then the United States took a hand, in the person of the commander of the U.S.S. *St. Marys,* who kept his ship near San Juan del Sur. Commander Davis had orders to protect American lives and properties and to persuade Walker to surrender. When the filibuster saw nothing before him but death, he tried to evacuate his men to his ship the *Granada,* but Commander Davis prevented it. Walker had come to the end of the road. On board the *St. Marys,* he surrendered to Commander Davis on May 1, 1857. Within two years the bold schemer, with never more than a few thousand men, had made himself dictator of Nicaragua and lost his empire. Central America was freed from what was to all patriotic citizens the dishonor of subjection to a foreign filibuster.

The dramatic saga of Walker's attempt at winning empire made him a hero in New Orleans when he returned to that city. It mattered not to his admirers that he had illegally invaded a neighbor country to exploit it for his own ends, or that he had caused great destruction and loss of life in the process. Walker insisted that he was the legal President of Nicaragua, unlawfully deposed by Nicaraguan rebels and by the intervention of the United States. He found supporters to help him return, and despite the watchfulness of government officers, he slipped away in a schooner with some of his old Phalanx men. He intended to seize Greytown and the San Juan River, but British warships closed in behind his schooner. The commander of the American naval squadron joined the British and under the guns of the warships the adventurers were forced to surrender.

In 1860 the little madman made his last try to regain his empire. This time it was on the pretext of helping the English settlers of the Bay Islands off Honduras. These islands had been part of Great Britain's holdings in Central America, but after pressure from the United States they were returned to Honduras in 1859. The English settlers protested and when they received no help from the home government they turned to the famous filibuster.

British warships were on Walker's trail from the time his schooners entered Honduran waters, so he continued on to Trujillo. His men clambered over the walls of the old fort at night, putting to flight the small Honduran garrison. In his old style Walker issued a proclamation to the Hondurans declaring that he came to free them from bad government. When he seized the customs the British warship *Icarus* sailed into the harbor to threaten him with naval guns, for this money was applied on the Honduran debt to Great Britain. The filibusters retreated into the jungles, hoping to make their way to Nicaragua. Honduran soldiers were on their trail and cornered them in a small camp near the shore. There they held out until the commander of the *Icarus* landed a boatload of sailors, demanding that Walker surrender to His Britannic Majesty. Walker lost his chance of protection as an American citizen by insisting that he was the President of Nicaragua.

Shut up in the fort at Trujillo, he was turned over to the Honduran government by the British commander. The troublemaker met his end before a firing squad of brown, barefoot soldiers in the old fort on September 12, 1860, to the relief of the United States, England and Central America.

After the downfall of William Walker, Nicaragua passed into a remarkably orderly period known as the "thirty years," under the Conservative party. Men of moderation passed the presidency from one to another, entrenching themselves so firmly that the Liberals were unable to organize successful revolts. Managua, a village on Lake Managua between the warring cities of León and Granada, was chosen as a compromise capital. It was little more than a village for many years. During this peaceful period Nicaragua acquired some roads and schools and little rail lines were built from the new Pacific port of Corinto to León, and from Managua to Granada.

Soldiers of fortune had found their way to Central America, however, and Honduras became their favorite hunting ground. This state, because of its central position, had been involved in most of the wars of other states, in addition to suffering from revolutions within the country. There was little chance to build up a strong state when people of different sections were kept apart by lack of roads in the mountainous terrain. The highland towns were also quite separated from the tropical north coast on the Caribbean Sea, inhabited mostly by indolent mixed-bloods and Negroes.

Countrymen of the highlands, eking out a poor living on tiny farms, found guerrilla fighting for one general or another an exciting change from monotonous labor. There was unlimited opportunity for foreign adventurers—footloose, restless men of various nationalities—to carve out gainful careers for themselves by aiding or instigating revolutions.

The tropical region of Mosquitia in Nicaragua was also a paradise for soldiers of fortune. Rum-soaked, black King Robert Charles Frederick gaily handed over millions of acres for gallons of rum. Samuel Shepherd of Jamaica thus acquired a huge territory, from the Bluefields River to the San Juan, part of which he sold to an American, Kinney, during Walker's time in Nicaragua. Kinney intended to colonize the region with American adventurers, but the United States blocked his enterprise and Walker refused to cooperate.

Greytown was typical of the forlorn, lazy little ports in this coastal region of Nicaragua and Honduras. Clusters of thatched huts under leaning palm trees lined the shore, backed by a wall of forest. A few stark wooden buildings housed British and American consuls or other foreigners who lorded it over a mixed population of Indians, zambos, Negroes. Monkeys and parrots screamed in the trees—children, pigs and chickens mingled companionably in and out of the huts. Occasionally the arrival of a schooner or **a foreign warship** broke the listless monotony of the days.

When North **Americans** learned to eat bananas, and **foreign** promoters discovered that the tropical coast lands, particularly in Honduras, were ideal for banana cultivation, life changed in this neglected region of Central America. Foreigners made money in territory Central Americans had been unable to use profitably, and foreign corporations became concerned with the political stability of the republics.

CHAPTER 19

BANANAS AND RAILROADS

FOR CENTURIES the Caribbean coast lands of Central America were of little use, either to the colonial people or the Spanish Americans of the republics. Swampy plains, lagoons, and meandering rivers, jungle forests dense and choked with vegetation; heat, fevers, heavy rainfall—all these factors made much of the territory unfavorable for white men. There were some sugar and cacao plantations which required overseers; in the small coast towns there were a few Englishmen and Americans engaged in trade with Central Americans who handled native products. Brown or black skins were the rule in the scattered population of primitive native Indians, Negroes, zambos and other mixed breeds.

Large areas were not only isolated from the highlands but not even under the control of the republics. Great Britain owned the colony of Belize in coastal Guatemala and kept her old protectorate over the Nicaraguan Kingdom of Mosquitia until about 1894. Diplomatic pressure from the United States was a factor in Great Britain's withdrawal and the black "kings" were persuaded to surrender their territory to be incorporated into Nicaragua. The United States wanted Nica-

323

ragua to have control of her coast lands, but American and English traders, operating in Bluefields and Greytown, preferred orderly British management to the uncertainties of life under unstable Nicaraguan rule.

Yankee shipmasters, sailing their schooners on individual trading ventures, knew every stagnant little harbor town of Nicaragua and Honduras as well as island ports of the West Indies. They dropped anchor in the harbors to barter whiskey, rum, beads, ready-made clothes, kerosene, flour, pork, for such tropical products as coconuts, rubber, sarsaparilla. Sometimes they took on board as an experiment a few bunches of a curious tropical fruit, the banana; red ones from Cuba and yellow ones from Jamaica. In the clipper ship era bananas were sometimes part of the cargo from the West Indies. Often the fruit spoiled before the home port was reached, due to delays from calms or storms. At the best it had only a small local sale so the fame of the banana did not spread far.

It was, nevertheless, the promotion of the banana as a rare tropical fruit, delicious and nourishing, that brought life and progress to the Caribbean lowlands. The banana trade built docks and dredged harbors, built railway lines, established telegraph lines, efficient shipping service, and eventually radio communication.

This fruit of humble origin grows with exotic appearance on a plant that looks like a tree but is not one. Its sturdy stem is composed of many tightly rolled leaf sheaths that break out at the top in the crown of immense, drooping, green leaves. Under the protecting umbrella of leaves the queer fruit and flower stalk curves downward, tipped by a large purple bud below the upward-tilted clusters of bananas. Each plant bears only one bunch, or stem, of bananas, but shoots grow up beside the mother tree to take its place when cut down.

The banana was not native to tropical America. Of Asiatic origin, it made a long journey around the world. Migrating peoples took dried roots along with them from India to Arabia, Africa, the Pacific islands. When finally the banana reached the West Indies and Central America it had practically circled the globe.

Negro tribes of the Guinea coast of Africa cultivated the fruit and banana is their African name for it. Portuguese explorers, slave-hunting on the Guinea coast, transplanted bananas to the Canary Islands. From there root stocks went to Hispaniola in the hands of a Spanish missionary, Fray Tomás de Berlanga, soon after the first Spanish settlements were made. Later, as Bishop of Panama, he introduced bananas for mission gardens, and very rapidly the useful fruit passed from the islands and Panama to all tropical sections of Spanish America.

Grown from root stocks called rhizomes, the banana plant throve in any hot, moist climate and provided farmers with a steady crop of fruit. Two varieties of the banana family became in Central America one of the staple foods of poor folk—and of pigs; the small, honey-sweet banana edible raw when golden ripe, and the large meaty plantain, always boiled or roasted. Every small native farm or cluster of huts had the great green fronds of banana plants near by.

It was not until after the middle of the nineteenth century that bananas attracted enough attention to warrant shipmasters' risking much of the perishable cargo. Owners of a schooner line plying between the Bay Islands and New Orleans developed a market for the yellow bananas grown in the islands, and Carl B. Franc, a steward on the line, saw a future in bananas. He started some plantations on the Isthmus near Colón and sold his fruit so successfully in New Orleans that he became the Banana King of Panama.

Boston, home port of schooner and clipper-ship captains, received its first shipment of bananas in 1870 when Captain Alonzo D. Baker, a Cape Cod skipper, brought a few bunches from Jamaica on his return trip from the West Indies. The fruit arrived intact and sold so well that fruit jobbers welcomed further shipments. Andrew D. Preston, canny Yankee salesman in one of these firms, decided to go seriously into the banana trade. With Captain Alonzo Baker and other shippers and business men, the Boston Fruit Company was organized in 1885. Sailing ships were replaced by steamers in order that speedier voyages and better packing facilities would cut down the risk of loss.

There were hard times, disasters and failures, for they were dealing with a perishable product. Shipments were irregular, sometimes when the fruit arrived there was no market, or it spoiled in transit. Native planters in Jamaica and Cuba, and men of the Boston Fruit Company who started plantations, raised their fruit more by luck than skill in those days, more by the grace of nature than agricultural science. And nature could ruin the hopes of planters and shippers by floods, by hurricanes that flattened a whole plantation, or banana disease that killed the plants.

Various companies tried to make a success of the banana trade, but the Boston Fruit Company was one of the few that survived. The yellow luscious fruit was gradually making its way with the American public, yet at the Philadelphia Centennial in 1876 bananas were an exotic sensation. Individual bananas wrapped in tinfoil sold for ten cents apiece as a tropical luxury.

Railroads came into the banana picture through Minor C. Keith, one of the vigorous, daring promoters of an age of big enterprises. His uncle was the famous railroad builder in Chile and Peru, Henry Meiggs; the man who, faced with the towering Andes, said, "Anywhere a llama can go I can take a train." His nephew was a man of like caliber. In 1871 Minor C. Keith went to Costa Rica to join his uncle and three brothers in the project of building a railroad for Costa Rica from the tropical Caribbean coast to the highland capital. The President of Costa Rica asked the Keiths to undertake the work. It was the second railroad in the tropics, even more difficult to carry through than the Panama Railroad.

The work camp was at Limón on the bay of that name, on a shore lined with coconut-palm groves behind which lay miles of deep, swampy pestilential jungle, an impenetrable tangle swarming with mosquitoes. The steaming black swamps were breeding places of fevers. In this region of year-round rainfall the storms of the rainy season are merely heavier deluges. Northers, hurricanes, torrential downpours, frequently had the crude little settlement under water.

Costa Ricans refused to work there and the Keiths imported hundreds of laborers from the United States, most of whom died soon of fever. More were recruited and many Negroes were brought from Jamaica. During the first year of work only four miles of track were laid, and in the second year twenty more. Those first twenty-four miles cost four thousand lives. Henry Meiggs and Minor Keith's three brothers died of fever but he survived several attacks of illness to carry on the work alone.

Then the Costa Rican government ran out of funds to continue the road, which had not advanced far enough to reach the coffee-growing districts of the highlands. Minor Keith found more funds and set about creating freight for his trains to haul. From Carl B. Franc's banana plantations in Panama he imported root stocks and suckers to start plantations in the

Costa Rican lowlands. He went into partnership with Franc to export bananas and other products to the United States.

The gleaming lines of steel pushed on into the highlands through cuts in the jungle and along the course of the wild Reventazón River, which boils down from the mountains through highland valleys and deep precipitous gorges. Every inch of progress was won against engineering difficulties and the terrible fevers. The workers continued to succumb and the funeral train was a daily service.

The enterprises of Keith and Franc were expanding. Costa Rican banana plantations did so well that plantings were extended into Nicaragua. Keith established a series of general stores at the little coast towns from Limón and Bluefields to Belize. Two coastwise steamers were used to supply them with goods and collect vanilla beans, rubber and tortoise shell for export. Keith cleaned up Limón, built a sea wall to prevent floods, installed a water plant and sewerage system, filled in some of the swamps which bred mosquitoes.

It took nineteen years to build that railroad. By the time it was completed, in 1890, Minor C. Keith had become a famous, highly respected character in Costa Rica. Traveling on the railroad today one wonders at the courage, persistence and skill that carried it through; in teeming swamps and thick jungles of the lowlands, crawling under the beetling walls of cliffs, winding up and down mountainsides, spanning the deep rocky clefts of gorges on spidery trestles. It is a fascinating day's ride in which one passes through the whole gamut of Costa Rican landscape and climate and ways of living.

The successful partners, Keith and Franc, importing bananas from Panama and Central America, joined forces in 1898 with the keen New Englanders of the Boston Fruit Company, importing from the West Indies, and the United Fruit Company was born. With their great capital and resources business expanded enormously. Large tracts of jungle land were bought or leased from Costa Rica, Nicaragua, Guatemala and Honduras. Fruit companies of New Orleans—Cuyamel, Standard Fruit—entered into competition in Honduras and for sixty to seventy miles back from the north coast the land, ideal for bananas, was covered with the thick green mat of plantations.

Small spurs of railroad track were built to connect plantations and transport the fruit to the shipping ports, Tela, Ceiba, Puerto Cortés. The companies bought the fruit of native farmers and employed hundreds of poor villagers as well as the Jamaican Negroes imported for labor. The United Fruit Company, operating great plantations in Colombia, Panama and the West Indies as well as Central America, became the giant among fruit companies, owner of a banana empire.

Company towns grew up at the ports and headquarters of plantations, with neat rows of screened wooden houses for the American employees and officers, with small schools and churches. Sanitation was introduced and treatment of malaria for the employees. In some places the hospitals of the United Fruit Company were the best medical institutions.

The barracks in which the plantation laborers lived were nothing to boast of in the early years but they have changed for the better. They now have screened doors and windows for protection from malaria-carrying mosquitoes and are set upon posts above the ground to avoid the mud of the rainy season.

In Honduras the native workers first came from their inland villages to work on a seasonal basis on the plantations, but now most of them prefer to live all the year round in the plantation barracks. Sons of employees grow up, marry and go to work for the Company. At its best the relationship of the Company to its workers seems to be a paternalistic one.

Banana culture by the great fruit companies became an advanced agricultural science. The plantations were orderly forests, aisles of tall fronded treelike plants from eighteen to twenty-five feet in height, producing huge bunches of perfect fruit. From being a tropical product that took its chances with weather and disease, the banana became the most pampered of fruits; nurtured, shielded, disinfected and sprayed from the sprouting of the young plant to the time when the bunch of fruit hung heavy under the screening leaves.

The cutting of the bunches, or stems, is done by the most exact system at the present time. The bananas must be fully grown but green. Even natives who eat bananas from their own trees cut them green and hang them in the shade to ripen, for if allowed to ripen on the plant they lose savor and texture. Three men and a mule compose each cutting team, proceeding through the aisles to the designated trees. The cutter, with a razor-sharp knife on a long pole, partly severs the bunch and, as it bends over, the backer receives it on his shoulder and lowers it to the ground. Then the whole plant is slashed down.

The bunches, packed in leather slings, are hung over the mule's back, one on each side, to be driven to the nearest railroad spur and transported on hand cars to the main loading station. There the bunches are dipped many times in acid solution and pure water to cleanse them from copper-sulphate spray, are wrapped in paper and packed carefully in freight cars on beds of dry banana leaves. Off goes the train to the port where the ship is waiting.

In the early days of the banana trade there was difficulty in getting the fruit cut and transported to the seaport at just the right time to meet the incoming ship. Now, with modern telegraph, telephone and radio service, the time of the ship's arrival is flashed to the plantation from which bananas are to be shipped, instructions are telephoned to the section where fruit is to be cut, and the whole process of cutting, transporting and loading on shipboard is done in one day. No more loss of fruit from too much heat or cold on the voyage, for the bananas are packed in refrigerated holds of swift steamships, the temperature and ventilation watched as carefully as though the bananas were delicate human patients instead of pampered fruit.

The United Fruit Company's operations are one vast, complex, exceedingly efficient organism, the last word in modern equipment and scientific skill. The tremendous holdings, financial resources, and the big market in the United States and Europe, enabled the Company to make a science of the raising and shipping of one fruit. At the present time raising bananas is only one of the agricultural projects for which the United Fruit Company employs the talents of trained tropical agriculturists.

The banana lands of Central America were developed in the period when promoters with money and technical experience exploited the resources of the so-called colonial countries. These nations, particularly the small Central American republics, could not build their own railroads or develop their mineral and agricultural resources. They needed the aid of outside capital, but with the industrial and mechanical advancements brought to the countries by promoters came foreign domination.

British and American capital built and owned Central American railroads and other public utilities; the old Spanish gold and silver mines of Honduras were revived and brought to rich production by American mining companies; the fecund lowlands became huge banana plantations through the enterprise of American fruit companies.

Ruthless exploitation was the big business pattern of that period. Foreign concessionaires obtained complete control of plantations and mines and depended on abundant cheap native labor to help them build up large profits from their holdings. The banana companies were no exception to the rule.

At the time the banana empire was growing in the Caribbean countries Porfirio Díaz of Mexico was handing over mines, haciendas and petroleum deposits to foreign concessionaires. Foreign corporations reaped profits from the natural riches of Mexico and Central America and exerted influence over governments.

The banana companies, like other promoters, were interested in building up successful enterprises, not in what they could contribute to the countries—that was incidental. The United Fruit Company became a great monopoly, controlling the marketing of bananas. The material improvements brought into the countries by the banana industry were offset in people's minds by the fact that they were foreign-owned.

Native planters did not have the financial backing to stand up under losses or disasters, but they resented the prosperity of the huge plantations, while they received only a small price for the bananas they sold to the United Fruit Company. Central Americans saw large tracts of land, where banana diseases or other disasters had ruined plantations, abandoned by the companies to become useless and overgrown with jungle once more. Politicians made use of the money obtained for the land and from export taxes, hundreds of poor natives had jobs, yet the profits from the banana industry went out of the countries.

The small republics were provided with railroads, telegraph lines, radio, swift steamer communication with the United States, by foreign capital—but they did not like foreign ownership of these utilities. The corporations operating in the countries were accused, probably with reason, of bringing about the overthrow of governments which did not favor their interests, or of aiding friendly dictators to remain in power.

Costa Rica owed its first railroad to the genius of the promoter, Minor C. Keith, and this man of many interests continued his railroad-building when he joined with British and American capitalists in the construction of the International Railways of Central America. The road was built from the new banana port of Guatemala, Puerto Barrios, to the capital; from there to the Pacific coast and along the Pacific lowlands to the border of Mexico. A branch line carried the railroad to El Salvador so that little country had an outlet for shipping its coffee and other products at Puerto Barrios.

Educated Central Americans scorned such practical occupations as surveying, engineering or the business of railroading, so it was energetic Yankees who built the railroads, overseeing gangs of native laborers. Footloose wanderers who had been aimless soldiers of fortune became railroad men in the tropics, and eventually taught Central Americans to run trains and keep rolling stock in repair.

Transport by rail released the highland people of Guatemala and El Salvador from their economic isolation and opened to usefulness large agricultural areas. The rail line from Puerto Barrios to the capital replaced the old, slow, laborious transport by mule trail. The track was built from the low hot country up through the plateaus, barrancas and broken mountains of that exceedingly rumpled country. Construction was difficult in Guatemala, but not so overwhelming as it had been in Costa Rica.

The railroad hauled the bananas of native planters and the fruit company plantations; it hauled the coffee of the growing coffee fincas on the Pacific slopes of Guatemala and El Salvador, and the productive Cobán district of Guatemala, colonized by industrious Germans. With an outlet to markets, coffee became the leading crop and chief economic dependence of El Salvador and Guatemala as it was of Costa Rica. The products of highlands and lowlands could be exchanged by train, and there was an outlet to travel by sea for the people of the highlands.

At the present time, if one is a sturdy traveler, there is great charm in journeys on that railroad of tropical Central America. The trains are small and very leisurely, stopping to rest at an infinitesimal number of tiny stations. First class, or *primera,* passengers sit on leather or wicker seats, while countryfolk and Indians, with their babies and children, their baskets of produce and fruit, crowd into the wooden-seated *segunda* coaches. Every station stop is an entertainment, for Central Americans, like Mexicans, fortify themselves with food and drink along the way.

Women and children trot back and forth below the train windows holding up baskets of fruit, plates of tortillas and fried stuff, clay jugs of coffee, crying their wares in a chorus of soft country speech. Fruits of the region are offered— bananas, plantains, oranges, zapotes, melons, *granadinas.* Zapotes are the fruit of the tree producing chicle for chewing gum and granadinas are pomegranates. In the Pacific hot country women chop off the tops of great green coconuts with a machete and hand them in the train windows. Central Americans have a technique for tossing off the mild, sweetish coconut liquid directly from the shell.

If one were to follow the entire route of the International Railways in Guatemala one would pass through a panorama of hot lowlands and central plateau country. On the Pacific slopes one would pass small tropical towns, stretches of pale-green sugar cane, cacao and banana plantations, coffee fincas with their delicate trees shaded by bananas and tall tropical trees. There would be glimpses of finca mansions down avenues of palms, and of adobe workers' huts.

As the train puffed up the steeps to Guatemala City the landscape would change to deep wooded barrancas, rolling fields, rims of irregular mountains and the smooth cones of volcanoes. Winding down toward Puerto Barrios one would have glimpses of peasant farmers' thatched huts clinging to steep hillsides; each with its banana trees and corn patch, pigs and shy brown children in the dooryard, placid brown women with braids down their backs, and lean, grave-faced farmers.

Eventually the train would wander down to the lush exuberance of hillsides velvety with vegetation and to acres of banana plantations. And if the season were right the hillsides on the way down would be a glory with flowering trees; the spectacular scarlet "flame of the forest," trees of golden, white, pale-mauve bloom, or the violet bouquets of the jacaranda tree.

The people of Guatemala and El Salvador have an advantage over their neighbors in Nicaragua and Honduras because of the extent of territory served by the International Railways. They undoubtedly wish that the railroad was owned by Central Americans rather than foreigners, but they certainly could not do without it, for the movement of people, the linking of small towns, or the shipping of produce.

CHAPTER 20

PASSAGE FROM SEA TO SEA

THE AGE-OLD dream of a water passage from ocean to ocean became a matter for practical planning in the last quarter of the nineteenth century. The United States had become a nation spanning the continent, with need for effective ship communication, as well as railroads for commerce. The nations bordering on the Pacific were important to the trade of various powers, particularly Great Britain, and the world had been drawn closer together by steam navigation.

A canal across the narrow waist of the Americas was of paramount importance. The question was, which country had the more feasible route—Nicaragua or the Isthmus of Panama?

People in the United States favored a Nicaraguan canal. The Transit route to California and the exploits of William Walker had made the public conscious of this Central American country. It was there that the political and commercial rivalry was strongest between the brash young United States and powerful Great Britain. The Manifest Destiny spirit extended itself to this part of Central America as a region where American influence should prevail.

Both nations, in the Clayton-Bulwer Treaty of 1850, had

pledged themselves to the principle of international control of any canal, but before many years sentiment in the United States began to veer toward exclusive American control. Trade with the West Indies and Central America had increased, particularly as the banana companies built up their big industry. Merchants and shippers wanted protection for their interests and the route to the West Coast must also be protected. As early as 1880 President Hayes in a message to Congress, declared: "The policy of this country is a canal under American control and the United States cannot consent to surrender this control to any European power."

In its young days the United States had warned off European nations, by the Monroe Doctrine, from attempting to obtain any further territory in the Western Hemisphere. That principle came into play more intensively as the republic grew up into a nation with expanding commercial interests in the Caribbean.

While the United States was engaged in the War between the States, Napoleon III tried the experiment of setting up a French empire in Mexico with the aid of reactionary Mexicans. But as soon as the war was over, the United States informed the French ruler that French troops must leave Mexico. Napoleon found it politic to heed the warning and abandoned the unfortunate Emperor Maximilian to his fate.

When Great Britain became involved in a controversy with Venezuela over the boundary of British Guiana in 1895, Secretary of State Olney, bringing pressure to bear for arbitration of the dispute, further defined the American position. "The United States is practically sovereign on this continent and its fiat is law," he declared; a statement which gave a bad jolt to all Latin Americans. The Monroe Doctrine, first regarded as a protection to them, began to look like an instrument for North American domination.

With the United States speaking up so strongly for American control in the Caribbean region, Europeans considered the building of a canal by private enterprise, to be internationally controlled for the benefit of all nations. Their choice of a route was the Isthmus of Panama, belonging to New Granada. That state, after a series of political upheavals and changes of name, had become the Republic of Colombia.

As we know, the government of New Granada had tried in the past to interest Great Britain or France in undertaking the building of a canal, or other means of transit across Panama. At various times New Granada had granted concessions to individual promoters who made plans and surveys for a canal, but nothing came of the projects. Nonetheless engineers continued to study the route, hoping to find financiers to support the work. In 1879 a congress of scientists, engineers and promoters, with delegates from various nations, met in Paris to discuss plans for a canal.

Many engineers presented their schemes, but the Frenchman, Ferdinand de Lesseps, was the shining light of the Congress. He was a man of note in France, immensely popular because of his success in building the Suez Canal against tremendous obstacles. De Lesseps was a promoter with sweeping ideas and confidence in himself, but not a practical engineer. His plan, for a sea-level canal across the Isthmus, was adopted by the Congress, and the Panama Canal Company was incorporated under French law, with De Lesseps as president. To the French engineers and the public it was a project undertaken for the glory of France.

De Lesseps bought the concession which Colombia had granted to a company of promoters, among them Lieutenant Wyse of the French Navy, and Baron Jacques de Reinach. They had done nothing to develop their concession. De Lesseps threw himself into the canal project with vigor, although he was an old man of seventy-four. Stock in the company sold successfully among the French people who believed that anything De Lesseps undertook was sound.

Work was begun in 1881 after it had been inaugurated with celebrations and a visit from De Lesseps himself. From that year to 1888 excavation and construction progressed slowly, meeting many disasters from landslides and floods. The plan to build a sea-level canal proved to be impracticable, while brazen extravagance and corruption in financial management further wrecked the project.

Tropical fevers caused terrible loss of life, for although the French had good doctors and hospitals they had not learned that mosquitoes carried yellow fever and malaria. Men worked in swampy jungles, the native towns of Colón and Panama were filthy and unsanitary. The French made the mistake of building lily pools in their gardens and putting flower pots on hospital window sills, fine breeding places for the dangerous anopheles mosquito.

The Company went bankrupt in 1888, and two years later the Panama scandal burst in France. Finances had become hopelessly involved in speculation and politics, hundreds of small investors were ruined. De Lesseps and other officials of the Company were called swindlers, they were brought to trial, accused of misuse of funds and of bribing legislators. De Lesseps and his son were finally proved honest themselves, though involved in shady deals they did not entirely understand.

Philippe Bunau-Varilla, chief engineer of the French Company, was determined to continue the work, to retrieve the reputation of the engineers and give France the prestige of having built the canal. A new company was organized and financed, machinery, dredges and engines of the old company were used when possible. Bunau-Varilla started to build a lock but the work could not be finished for lack of funds. The French people were disillusioned with Panama and would not support the project. In 1898 the company was faced with abandoning everything they had put into it, or of selling the concession. Bunau-Varilla set out to sell it to the United States.

The Isthmus was second in favor in the United States because reports of engineers who had made surveys indicated that it would be more difficult and costly to build there. Nicaragua, with a river and lake and only thirteen miles through which to dig a ditch on the Pacific side, seemed more feasible. The French failure in Panama was also discouraging.

Events of 1895–98 had stepped up American interest in a canal, for it was then that the United States, in an altruistic spirit so far as public sentiment was concerned, went to war with Spain to aid the Cubans in their struggle for independence. There were less disinterested motives under the surface, of course.

When the warship *Oregon* had to make the tremendous voyage from the Pacific around Cape Horn to join the fleet in Cuban waters, people realized how important it was for defense of the coasts to have a speedy route between the oceans.

The United States emerged from that war a nation with colonial possessions—the Philippines and Guam in the Pacific, Puerto Rico and a protectorate over Cuba in the Caribbean. It was at that time, also, that the Hawaiian Islands were annexed. American capital moved into Cuba to organize great sugar and tobacco plantations.

The new status of the nation with interests and territory outside its borders, and the effect of the war which, for a lot of young men, had been high adventure, created a blustering spirit of expansionism. The people were all for a canal to strengthen the nation's political and commercial position, to aid in developing Pacific coast states. Although the canal would be for the use of all nations it must be owned and operated by the United States.

After the Spanish American War, Teddy Roosevelt of the Rough Riders was the man of the hour, the hero of vigorous young men who had taken part in the war. When Roosevelt became president the determination of the United States to become arbiter in the Caribbean region shaped up under his aggressive leadership. Roosevelt was set upon building the canal —world trade needed it, the United States must control it.

With the prospect of France controlling a waterway across the Isthmus, American plans for building in Nicaragua had gone ahead, but no work had been done. It remained for the Frenchman, Bunau-Varilla, to turn sentiment in the country, Congress and State Department from Nicaragua to Panama. He and a New York lawyer, Nelson Cromwell, used every propaganda method; in the press, by lobbying in Washington, by interviewing the President and Secretary of State. The Frenchman even played up the fact that Nicaragua was a land subject to earthquakes and volcanic eruptions while Panama was not. The volcano Momotombo on an island in Lake Managua obligingly staged an eruption to point up his argument. Bunau-Varilla found a Nicaraguan postage stamp picturing Momotombo in eruption and when he had bought up the issue he sent the stamps to Congressmen.

At this time Great Britain decided to play on the side of the United States, and a new treaty was drawn up between the governments releasing the United States from the pledge of international control over a canal.

Congress and President Roosevelt finally decided on the Panama route. There followed long controversies, proposals and counterproposals, with the Colombian government. Aloft in their Andean eyrie, Bogotá, the politicians quarreled over the canal question. They could not bring themselves to grant the United States the concession, or control over a strip of their territory. They were jealous of Nicaragua, but believed that Roosevelt's declaration that if they did not sign a treaty he would make one with Nicaragua was Yankee bluff. Colombians wanted the canal, but they allowed the issue to be clouded by political quarrels and the desire to get all the money possible out of the deal. The Congress seemed to take pleasure in haggling with the Colossus of the North for a higher price than the United States was willing to pay.

Roosevelt finally negotiated a treaty with the Colombian minister in Washington which was ratified by the American Congress. The United States proposed to buy the French concession for forty million dollars and asked for perpetual control over a strip of territory not more than six miles wide. The Colombian Congress held up ratification while the Senators indulged in fiery oratory over their rights, their sovereignty, the danger of granting so much to the Colossus of the North.

Colombians were foolishly proud, unrealistic in not coming to terms for the sake of the great advantage of the canal. but they might have been won by patience, tact, and an attempt to understand Colombian problems. These were not the methods of aggressive Roosevelt. He took it upon himself personally to bring Colombia into line, and his harsh intolerance, impatience and obvious scorn for Colombian nationalism further antagonized the hypersensitive Latin Americans.

Meanwhile Panamanians were in a great state of mind. The canal was the dream of generations, they well knew that their only hope for prosperity lay in the waterway. They were sick of the political upheavals of Colombia; neglect of their interests, the distance from the seat of government, made them anxious for independence. Panamanian delegates threatened the quarreling Congress with secession if the treaty was not signed, but even that did not bring the proud *políticos* to their senses.

Leaders in Panama planned revolt and Bunau-Varilla encouraged them to believe that the United States would support them. American officials of the railroad were hand in glove with the plotters. Busily lobbying in Washington, Bunau-Varilla dropped hints that the Panamanians were in revolutionary mood and satisfied himself that President Roosevelt would favor a movement of secession.

When the shortsighted políticos of Colombia rejected the treaty in October 1903, the spark was struck for revolution in Panama. On November 3, the Revolutionary Junta hastened to declare independence before Colombian troops could reach the country.

How much Roosevelt had to do with the revolution remains a mystery. Certainly he was aware of what was going on and quick to take advantage of circumstances. Warships were sent to hover in the neighborhood of Limón Bay and the cruiser *Nashville* was conveniently at hand to steam into the Bay and prevent a Colombian gunboat, coming from Cartagena, from landing troops. American Marines went ashore to protect the railroad and keep the transit open according to the treaty of 1846.

Marines and railroad managers refused to transport Colombian soldiers already on shore to Panama City, on the ground that fighting would disrupt railroad service. Thus they aided the revolutionists. As the garrison of Panama City had been bought over by the revolutionists, it was easy to take possession of the capital. The Panama revolution went through without casualties except for a harmless Chinese shopkeeper, hit by a shell from a Colombian gunboat.

The Colombian troops went home, Panamanians organized their government and proclaimed Panama an independent state. Three days later President Roosevelt recognized the new republic and European nations were not far behind. Crafty Bunau-Varilla, appointed minister to the United States, hurried to Washington to negotiate a canal treaty for Panama.

There were enraged outcries from Colombia, accusations of direct intervention, of having violated the treaty of 1846 which guaranteed Colombian sovereignty over the Isthmus. The intervention of warships and Marines, the speed with which Roosevelt made sure of his canal treaty, shocked Latin Americans and much of the North American public as well. Later, Roosevelt boasted, "I took the canal zone," and to all intents and purposes he did. The highhanded, aggressive spirit of the President and government in the whole affair laid the foundation for years of fear and resentment in Latin America. All her sister nations sympathized with injured Colombia.

The Colossus of the North was astride Latin America and Theodore Roosevelt was the manifestation of its spirit. Roosevelt of the Big Stick was the man who initiated the theory that it was the moral responsibility and duty of the United States to keep the Latin American countries in order, particularly Mexico and Central America, the nearest neighbors. This new interpretation of the Monroe Doctrine made that document hated in Latin America. What price safety from European powers if they were to be dominated and perhaps absorbed by the Colossus of the North? Rubén Darío, famous Latin American poet, expressed their feeling when he chanted, "Roosevelt, thou foe of Free America!"

Relations with Colombia did not improve until President

Wilson, in 1914, negotiated a treaty to pay that nation twenty-five million dollars indemnity for the loss of Panama, with an expression of "sincere regret." The treaty was not ratified for some time, but since Colombia then wanted American promoters to develop her new petroleum fields, she was in a receptive mood and agreed to recognize Panama in return for the indemnity. Before the treaty was finally ratified by the American Congress however, the apology disappeared from the document. Colombia became a stable republic, the canal brought advantages to the country, and the two nations have lived in amity ever since.

The building of the Panama Canal, begun in 1904, was a colossal undertaking, a saga of science, engineering skill and labor, solving the difficult problems of locks and dams, working against the tropical enemies that had helped to defeat the French. There were delays, incompetence, bungling and red tape; heart-rending struggles with washouts, landslides and tropical swamps.

The Canal Commission was finally turned over to the army in 1907 under the chairmanship of Colonel George W. Goethals. It took all the technical knowledge and indomitable energy of United States' army engineers to build the marvelous locks, dig through the Continental Divide in Culebra Cut, and make the cut safe from the landslides that caused so much trouble; to build the great Gatun Dam and others, to create Gatun Lake from the Chagres River and its valley. Until Lake Mead was made at Boulder Dam, Gatun was the largest artificial lake in the world.

The tropical diseases which had been so disastrous for the French were conquered. Heroic scientists, working in Havana, discovered the mosquito carriers of yellow fever and malaria, and that unhealthy tropical city was cleaned up. The knowledge gained in Havana was applied with complete success to the Zone by Colonel Gorgas and his staff of doctors and inspectors. From being one of the most pestilential regions of the tropics the Isthmus became one of the healthiest. Malarial swamps were treated with oil, inspectors studied every inch of the Canal Zone and the dirty native towns near by. Panama City and Colón had street paving, safe water, medical control. The terminal American towns—Cristóbal on the Atlantic side and Balboa on the Pacific—were models of order and cleanliness. American employees and officers, called the "gold payroll" people, because they were paid in gold, had houses surrounded with screened verandas for circulation of air and vegetation was kept at a safe distance from the houses. Natives and West Indian laborers, paid in silver and called the "silver payroll" people, had their screened barracks. To this day in the Zone the whites are called "gold payroll" and the dark-skinned "silver payroll" people.

The tremendous works of excavation and construction going on in the Canal Zone—the monstrous steam shovels, dredges, cranes, trucks, the mighty cement locks—were a startling sight in that hazy, luxuriant tropical setting. When the work was completed the neat, spick-and-span, well-regulated Canal Zone was an amusing contrast to the disorderly exuberance of the landscape and the colorful, easygoing native life outside.

For ten years the gigantic project moved slowly toward completion under the administration of three presidents—Theodore Roosevelt, William Howard Taft and Woodrow Wilson. During that time, in America, the Mexican Revolution had taken place and the United States had moved from the Big Stick policy of Roosevelt to the period of Dollar Diplomacy in the

Caribbean area. The little republic of Panama had managed to maintain its existence under the giant shadow of the Canal Zone government and the United States. The relations between American and Panamanian officials were delicate, requiring skillful diplomacy. The United States got what it wanted from Panama, but the republic did remain a Latin American state with a life of its own outside the Zone.

As the Canal neared completion in the spring of 1914, the attention of Americans, Anglo and Latin, was turned from their own affairs to the menacing clouds hanging over Europe. Those clouds broke in the storm of World War I before the date set for the ceremonies to celebrate the opening of the Panama Canal. With the attention of all nations focused on Europe the gala celebration was given up.

On August 15, 1914, the Panama Railroad liner *Ancon* sailed through the channel in Limón Bay, mounted the triple flight of locks to Gatun Lake, sailed through the lake and Culebra Cut and descended by the other series of locks to the Bay of Panama. It was a quiet, efficient passage of nine hours and forty minutes. On board were the Secretary of War, the President of Panama and his cabinet, the diplomatic corps, officers of the Canal Commission and army, and guests.

Thus uneventfully, without fanfare and rejoicing, was celebrated the realization of a centuries-old dream, the waterway through the continent. The will-o'-the-wisp which had lured all the ancient navigators, the strait to lead to the fabled Orient —here it was, a marvel of twentieth-century scientific efficiency. Across this narrow strip of land between the oceans had passed the Spanish gold trains with the wealth of Peru, and the commerce of the colonies with Spain; across it had labored the Argonauts of Forty-nine in search of gold. Henceforth the argosies of world commerce would pass in stately procession, in two-way traffic, through the locks and lakes from ocean to ocean.

"The Land Divided; the World United," was the motto of the Canal, but it was opened to traffic just as the twentieth-century world passed into the era of disunity and chaos from which it has not yet emerged.

Simón Bolívar, the Liberator, had realized the strategic importance of Panama. It was here that he called the first Pan American Congress, at which the United States was not represented, to consider a continental alliance of American states for mutual protection and assistance. The American nations of both continents moved toward that when their Foreign Ministers met at Panama in the anxious year 1939, to consider measures for preserving the neutrality of the Americas.

Since 1914 the Isthmus has become a crossroads of the world, with people and ships of every nation passing through the Canal, and a mixture of many races inhabiting the terminal native towns, Colón and Panama. Hundreds of thousands of persons have watched, fascinated, from the decks of ships that smooth passage of the vessels; the raising and lowering in the locks, the clocklike precision of the operation, the uncanny skill of the "electric mules" that haul the ships through the locks. The Canal has been of inestimable benefit to all the nations of the Americas as well as the rest of the world. In fact, one could not conceive of the world today without the Panama Canal.

The control of this waterway has meant that the United States has to be concerned with what happens in all the nations near it. And, in World War II the defense of the Panama Canal was vital to all the Americas.

CHAPTER 21

DICTATORSHIP AND REVOLUTION IN MEXICO

UNDER Benito Juárez was begun the Mexicans' plan for making their country a liberal republic free from the supremacy of the privileged classes—army, clergy and landowners. Church and state were separated, monastic orders were broken up, church institutions lost many of their great estates. The reformers did their best to improve social conditions, but at the end of the Juárez period Mexico was still a backward, semi-feudal country of illiterate, poverty-stricken people contrasted to wealthy old families and great landowners. Each section of the country was isolated from others by lack of good roads or railways.

Porfirio Díaz made himself President by a successful revolution in 1877. From the beginning of his long dictatorship to the present time Mexico has been so completely revolutionized that only a full-length book could cope adequately with the story.

This dictator was different from those who had gone before. In addition to his drive for personal power, he was determined to bring Mexico up to the standard of advanced nations in material prosperity. He pushed the country ahead into the

349

modern world and won international prestige, but at the expense of all but the upper class of the population.

The world acclaimed Porfirio Díaz as a great statesman, the benefactor of his country—and of foreign business. Heads of governments sent telegrams of congratulation each year when he celebrated his birthday in conjunction with the national commemoration of Padre Hidalgo's *Grito de Dolores*.

Mexico, under Porfirio Díaz, presented to the world a fair picture of peace, order, prosperity. Finances were stabilized, the nation's credit was good, investments were safe, foreign concessionaires received every favor. Travel was safe on roads, and railroads were built with foreign capital. There were telegraph and telephone lines, banks, a good post-office system. The capital had public utilities, foreign-owned, and when automobiles came in Don Porfirio and the most wealthy of his official family had theirs.

Mexico City became a cosmopolitan capital with its foreign colonies of diplomats, businessmen and their families—German, French, British and American—who found Mexico under Don Porfirio's rule a delightful country. Society in the capital was gracious and elegant in the European manner. The aristocracy had French mansions furnished in the ornate, ugly style of late nineteenth-century Europe. Wealthy families spent some of their time in European capitals and sent their sons abroad for education. Art and literature were based on Parisian models.

When Porfirio Díaz, the successful dictator, was fifty-one he married the young daughter of a high-born Spanish family, Carmen Rubio. Carmencita, as friends called her, was convent-bred, a devout Catholic and a delicate aristocrat. In her expert hands the mestizo soldier of strong body and gruff manners became a gentleman, and a white man in his whole outlook.

Don Porfirio's clothes were made by the best tailors, and his upright figure was impressive in top hat and frock coat, or in uniforms blazing with decorations. There was dignity in the bronzed countenance, with imposing waxed moustaches twirled upward like those of Kaiser Wilhelm. Indeed, the German Emperor and the Strong Man of Mexico appreciated one another and a martial portrait of the Kaiser hung in the National Palace.

Porfirio Díaz, the mestizo, repudiated his youth of courageous fighting for liberal principles, and the Indian companions with whom he had shared the hardships of guerrilla mountain camps.

He was surrounded by a close group of advisers called the Científicos, who believed that Mexico's destiny was to become a white nation of European culture, maintaining the most friendly relations with foreign governments and capitalists. The Científicos were upper-class gentlemen, lawyers, economists, bankers and such. Their guiding principle was scientific efficiency in the administration of business and finance. Progress in wealth and prestige must be achieved by suppression of political action and development of the nation's resources through concessions to foreign capital.

Don Porfirio agreed with them entirely. He left it to them and to Carmencita's social tact to keep all powerful groups happy—the Catholic hierarchy, the foreign diplomats, most especially the foreign corporations. Meanwhile he kept the generals and big políticos in line by favors and the dictator's method of divide and rule.

When Díaz became President he brought the warring elements under his iron hand by the clever scheme of *Pan y Palo* —Bread and the Club. Favors and soft jobs were offered to recalcitrant men, who throve if they played along with the dictator and became subservient followers. Ruin, jail, or sometimes death were the alternatives.

Bandits and guerrillas who had terrorized the countryside and made travel unsafe were transformed into the *rurales,* the mounted police, adored by hacendados and the administrators of towns. They fared well by the exchange of lawless banditry for official status, for they were all-powerful in their districts and were permitted to become the most spectacular armed force in the country. Mounted on beautiful horses and armed to the teeth, they wore a handsome charro costume of gray suede, liberally ornamented with silver buttons and braid, their sombreros were weighted down with silver and a scarlet blanket was slung over one shoulder.

The rurales were quick on the draw, and the hardihood gained in their lawless days served them in good stead when they were sent to hunt fugitives in mountains or jungles. They were useful to hacendados in hunting runaway peons and bringing them back to be whipped into submission. They rounded up rebellious mountain Indians, particularly the Yaquis of the north, to be sent in gangs to slave labor in the tropics. Factory owners found them useful in putting down revolts of oppressed workers.

The principle of *Pan y Palo* worked well all along the line in bringing about the dictator's rigid control over political activity. Governors of states were regional chieftains, free to re-elect themselves and rule a dynasty so long as they played the game and did not try to encroach on the absolute power of Don Porfirio. Too ambitious governors were checked by other officials sent to their districts to be rivals.

All the way down, from governors and generals, through *jefes políticos* who administered towns, to the lowliest government employee, the cynical habit was ingrained of thievery and extortion. Every official in the complex political bureaucracy lined his pockets by graft from funds of the office and with money extorted by threats from those below.

Foreign capital built not only railroads and public utilities but textile and paper mills, breweries, smelters, iron works, meat packing plants. Concessionaires were attracted by favors from the government and the opportunity to make great profits from their properties with cheap, submissive labor.

There was an old Spanish law, incorporated in the Constitution of 1857, by which the subsoil resources were declared the property of the state. They could not be sold, only leased for use. The dictator's lawyers corrected that with a new law. Porfirio Díaz sold outright to foreigners the fundamental resources of his country, the wealth of minerals in its earth.

British and American corporations bought the fabulously rich petroleum lands around Tampico for less than a dollar and a half per acre and were not even required to pay taxes on the oil they produced for their own profit. Gold, silver and iron mines were developed with great efficiency and profit for their British and American owners.

Both Mexican and foreign hacendados and land companies had their grip on all the best lands, their enormous estates sometimes comprising millions of acres. Great tracts of the public domain were handed over to loyal políticos as reward for services. The land companies had control over waters necessary for irrigation, so that if Indian villagers were rebellious the water for their fields was cut off. When they left the barren tracts in despair, the land was taken over by hacendados and brought back into production.

Indian communal village lands, the ejidos, were almost wiped out of existence, seized by various pretexts. By one pernicious law village tracts were "denounced" as being illegally held. The Indians, having no paper titles to ancestral tracts, lost the land, which was put up for sale and bought by land companies. Indian families, driven from the ejidos, were forced to grow their miserable patches of corn and beans on tiny plots of poor soil or on rocky hillsides.

North Americans became great landowners in Mexico as well as proprietors of rich mines and oil fields. Their huge cattle ranches and haciendas prospered greatly. At the end of the Díaz period Mexico's agricultural lands were concentrated in the hands of less than three thousand families—and foreigners owned more of the country than Mexicans themselves. Among foreign landowners North Americans came first and the British second.

In civil suits judges and juries learned the lesson that the foreigner was always right unless an order to the contrary came from Don Porfirio himself. Those Mexicans who were outside the charmed circle of the Científicos, aristocrats and profiteers coined the saying that Mexico was the mother of foreigners and the stepmother of Mexicans.

The proud old landowning families of Spanish blood lived luxuriously in their stately mansions in the capital when they were not in Europe. These families had been the "notables" of the Maximilian period and were the social elite of the Díaz régime. It was left to the administrators of their numerous estates to produce wealth from cattle, sugar cane, cotton, coffee and maguey from which pulque was made. The families visited the haciendas for gay house parties in their manor houses where they were served by innumerable brown, barefooted retainers.

It was a patriarchal system in which the house servants and field laborers were as subservient to their masters as slaves on the plantations of the Old South. There may have been hacendados who felt some responsibility for the welfare of their peons; there was sometimes affection between the women of the family and their favorite maid servants, but on the whole there was none of the kindly patriarchal relationship true of the best plantation families in the Old South. The Americans lived on their estates, while the Mexicans left affairs in the hands of overseers.

Outside the great walls of the hacienda domain clustered the huts of the Indian peons' village—dark, windowless, mud-floored huts. The families lived in the utmost squalor and poverty, the men laboring in the fields from dawn to dusk. They were required to buy their simple necessities from the hacienda store at any price the storekeeper chose to ask, and their purchases were charged against their pitiful wages. Heads of families never caught up and so they were chained to the hacienda by debt passed on from father to son.

The craving for pulque to deaden misery, the purchase of little things to help celebrate a baptism or burial added to their debt. Peon families, devoutly religious, found momentary joy in saints' day fiestas at their church. When the master's family staged a fiesta the peons, crowded in the great courtyard, took vicarious pleasure in the gay doings.

For the exclusive inner circle at the top, the landowners, the most favored politicians, lawyers and generals, the reign of Díaz was a golden era. But under the fine surface of the Paz Porfiriana Mexico was a nation in two parts. The prosperity at the top did not trickle down to the mestizo middle-class professionals, small tradesmen and rancheros. As for the mass of Indian peons and villagers, they lived in poverty and servitude worse than that of their ancestors under Spanish rule.

Porfirio Díaz and his counselors ignored the fact that the

majority of the people lived from the soil; that Mexico had always been a nation of villages, poverty-stricken, isolated from town centers in mountains, plateaus and tropics. Nothing was done to improve irrigation or farming methods, or to help small farmers. Even the large haciendas were not run efficiently. An agricultural nation, except in the most productive years, imported the staple foods, corn, rice, wheat and beans.

Wages of peons on the haciendas and village day laborers remained stationary while the prices of staples rose steadily. Villagers were lured into factories by slightly higher wages, but the cost of living and bad working conditions made their lives no better.

To the Científicos and aristocrats the Indians were an ignorant stupid mass who could never take part in national life. It would be a mistake to try to educate them, they were fit only to provide cheap labor for their betters.

Education was for the well-born, those who were destined by social position and white blood to rule the nation. Middle-class families of towns sometimes managed by scrimping and saving to send their sons to the National University, but few careers were open to them. They might be professors, small-town lawyers or doctors, or hold minor bureaucratic jobs in government. Mexicans could not find employment with foreign owners of mines, mills or factories except as semi-skilled labor. The proud sons of old families considered it beneath a gentleman to enter a profession or do any work except to check the administration of their estates.

The great statesman, Porfirio Díaz, allotted eight million pesos annually for education, while he spent on his last regal birthday party twenty million pesos. At the end of his long rule seventy-five per cent of the people were still illiterate.

Many another dictator has been praised by the world because

he made trains run on time, built roads, stabilized business and finance. Many another dictator has modernized his country in a showy way at the expense of the spirit and progress of his people. The population, in the golden age of Díaz, was apathetic under the deadening weight of fear, oppression and corruption.

Porfirio Díaz began his rule by declaring adherence to the principle of no re-election, incorporated in the Constitution. He allowed a loyal general to be elected after his first term, but then his lawyers fixed amendments giving a show of legality to his successive stands for the presidency. The dictator saw to it that other candidates were nonentities without popular appeal.

The people had no political guidance from newspapers. Any editor who expressed liberal ideas or criticism of the régime was sent to cool his ardor in jail. Only a minority bothered to vote in presidential elections, knowing that the ballot urns would be stuffed with prepared ballots by election officials. Eight times the Strong Man was re-elected by the "will of the people."

In their own groups, however, men of brains and patriotism discussed the situation in their country, the problems of land, poverty, constitutional government. Some wrote studies of problems and plans for reform which were eagerly read.

Bitter resentment smoldered among all the forgotten people of town and country. Migratory workers, returning from the United States, brought to laborers in mines and mills the idea that labor had a right to win better wages and living conditions. There were a few strikes, mercilessly put down by troops.

Leadership in breaking the iron rule of the dictator came from a most unexpected quarter, from a member of one of the immensely wealthy landowning families of the north, the

Maderos. The family had vast holdings in lumber, cattle, cotton, as well as interest in banks, and the Madero men had friends in high places.

The younger brother, Francisco I. Madero, was a black sheep in that wealthy, conservative family. He was a slender little man with a compassionate heart and idealistic spirit. His family smiled at his crotchets, his vegetarianism, his belief in spiritualistic séances.

Francisco spent his share of the family fortune in trying to improve the lives of Indians on his land; starting cooperatives, feeding the children, while he became deeply concerned over the misery of the Mexican people. His brothers thought "Panchito" a harmless idealist until he published his book, *The Presidential Succession,* arguing for old ideas such as genuine suffrage, no re-election, constitutional government.

In the presidential campaign of 1910 Francisco I. Madero announced his candidacy. His ideas were mild enough and political rather than social, but they roused a wave of enthusiasm in the country.

Don Porfirio was not greatly perturbed by the appearance of this innocuous idealist, but his political henchmen became alarmed by the rise of *maderistas* in towns and cities, campaigning with flaming speeches. The dictator thought he had the country well in hand by the usual methods, but just to be on the safe side he put an embargo on all the Madero estates and sent Francisco to jail. Let out on bail, he escaped to the United States. His brothers Gustavo and Ernesto were so alarmed for the family fortunes that they decided to finance Francisco's revolution.

In Mexico all was quiet for the celebration of the Centennial of Independence and the Strong Man's birthday on September 16, 1910. His admirers at home and abroad rejoiced that the old man was still vigorous and hoped he would fill the presidency for many more years. Representatives of important countries came to honor the statesman who had made Mexico respected among nations.

Once more the old man, a distinguished figure with white hair and moustaches, appeared on the balcony of the National Palace to give the *Grito de Dolores*. The call to liberty was an ironic echo of the past in that celebration of thirty years of absolute dictatorship. There were flamboyant processions on the avenues, balls and banquets for distinguished society.

In October Díaz was elected as smoothly as in former years, but within a few months federal troops were fighting bands of guerrillas in the north, led by rancheros and a cattle rustler called Pancho Villa. In the southern sugar state of Morelos a mestizo leader, Emiliano Zapata, was leading his followers in raids on haciendas.

All over the country there were sporadic revolts, a stir and upheaval, a boiling anger rising from the roots of the nation against age-old exploitation, age-old oppression. It was like the rumblings and earth-shakings preceding eruptions of the great volcanoes.

Pancho Villa and his riders captured Ciudad Juárez on the border and United States troops were lined up along the Rio Grande. Francisco I. Madero crossed the border to join Villa, to lead the revolution. He came with an apostolic mission to bring the Mexican people land and liberty.

The government was in a panic over the revolts, fearful of American intervention. There were conferences with the maderistas and a deal for peace was made with Madero's counselors rather than with the dreamy idealist himself. Díaz and the Científicos must go. A provisional president would be appointed until elections could be held.

When the news reached the capital irrepressible crowds milled and shouted in the Zócalo. Soldiers fired on the demonstrators from the National Palace, leaving dead and wounded on the ground. Throngs surged about the heavily-guarded house of the dictator roaring, "Down with Díaz! *Viva la revolución!*"

While tumult went on outside, the old man within was writhing with pain from an infected jaw, angrily refusing the pleas of his wife and friends that he sign his resignation. All night they pleaded with him and at last he put his signature to the document. The household was hurried in closed cars to the station for the train to Vera Cruz, and the ship which bore the Strong Man of Mexico to spend his last years in France.

The train from the north, bringing Francisco I. Madero to the capital, was surrounded at every station by throngs of ragged Indians, rancheros and townsfolk, eager to see and hear the man who had given them hope. They did not understand politics, but they pinned their faith on Madero. He had promised them land, bread and liberty.

Francisco I. Madero entered Mexico City to the accompaniment of an earthquake that cracked walls and toppled buildings, fitting symbol of the storm about to break over Mexico. It did not prevent the people from giving him a joyous welcome. And when, in October 1911, he was elected President by an overwhelming majority in a free election, it seemed that the revolution had been won. To the people the apostle of liberty was a saint. They expected the promised good things of life to materialize immediately.

President Madero was too compassionate to deal ruthlessly with his enemies, too trusting to cope with the intrigues of generals and Díaz politicians. General Reyes and Felix Díaz, nephew of the dictator, revolted at Vera Cruz and when they were defeated Madero refused to execute the leaders. From their prison cells in Mexico City they continued their plotting. The President had to contend with the scorn and bitter opposition of the foreign interests, bombarding him with demands for indemnity and protection. He was a tragic figure in the vast salons of the National Palace, harassed and tormented on every side.

There were men of good brains in Madero's government with constructive plans for agrarian reform, but in the political turmoil there was little opportunity to advance their work. In the north some land was taken from large estates for Indian villagers, but they did not know how to manage it and many sold the plots back to the hacendados for paltry sums. Emiliano Zapata refused to disarm his men, declaring that they would fight until the ejidos, taken under Díaz, were returned to the villagers. Gentle Madero, who hated bloodshed, was forced by pressure to send troops against Zapata.

Henry Lane Wilson, American Ambassador, called Madero a madman. He took the lead in harassing the President continually with demands for disarming the revolutionists, protection for foreign holdings, payment for damages to property.

Fifteen months after Madero was inaugurated, in February 1913, the generals staged their revolt from the Ciudadela in Mexico City. General Reyes and Felix Díaz were released from prison to take command and troops marched to the National Palace to capture Madero.

Loyal General Villar and Gustavo Madero persuaded the garrison to defend the Palace, but General Villar was so badly wounded that he could not continue in command. Fatefully, Madero gave the defense of the government to General Victoriano Huerta, an old Indian fighter, a drunkard and scoundrel of the worst kind.

There followed ten days of horror, known as the Ten Tragic Days, when the capital was a battlefield. Rebels in the Ciudadela and defenders in the National Palace bombarded each other over the rooftops, wrecking houses and killing civilians. Machine gunners and snipers swept the streets with gunfire, making it almost sure death to go out. When women crept out to find food they carried sheets tied to broomsticks as flags of truce.

Ambassador Wilson bustled about among politicians and diplomats, definitely taking a hand to make a government for Mexico that would please the foreign colonies and American businessmen. Working hand in glove with Felix Díaz and the generals, he chose unscrupulous, treacherous General Huerta for leader.

Huerta invited Gustavo Madero to dine, with a great show of friendliness, and from that dinner table the President's brother was carried to the Ciudadela and brutally murdered. Francisco Madero, the Vice President, Piño Suarez, and the loyal General Angeles, were imprisoned in the National Palace.

The diplomatic corps was called together by Ambassador Wilson, who presented the list of officials chosen for the new government, Victoriano Huerta to be provisional President. One of the diplomats inquired, "And what do you intend to do with Madero?" Cynically, the Ambassador shrugged, with the remark that after all that was not his affair; it would not do for him to interfere in the internal affairs of Mexico!

Victoriano Huerta swore by all that was holy that Madero would be allowed to leave the country in safety. The President's friends pleaded for protection for him at the American Embassy without success. Hired thugs broke into the room where the prisoners were held, bundling Madero and his two companions into a carriage on the pretext of taking them to a safer place. Next day it was announced that the three had been shot "while attempting to escape" and their bodies were found dumped by a wall in a deserted street.

Madero was murdered on February 22, and all the best people, including the foreign colonies, rallied around Huerta. Ambassador Wilson brazenly asked President Taft to recognize the government of the man who was responsible for the deaths of the President and his brother. The governments of Great Britain, France and Germany hastened to recognize Huerta, but President Taft's administration was nearly over and the ticklish question of recognition was left to the incoming Democrats.

Woodrow Wilson wanted friendship and fair dealing with Latin America and was ashamed of some acts of American imperialism. He recalled the Ambassador, repudiated his intervention and told him that Huerta must go.

Supported by powerful groups in the capital, the old reprobate, Huerta, enjoyed himself. He did business over bottles of cognac in his favorite bars where diplomats and politicians had to seek him out for interviews. Nonetheless, the people had been awakened and they worshipped the memory of gentle, martyred Madero. While politicians schemed in the capital The Revolution, as Mexicans call it, with a capital R, continued.

There was no concerted plan, no definite program, no one leader. The Revolution was an elemental surge of people released from bondage. Mountain peasants had their chieftains and their hideouts in the sierras. Other groups had headquarters on ranches or in small towns. At first their common goal was the fierce urge of the dispossessed to seize what they wanted, but as time went on the Revolution took form in the demands for land and liberty, labor's rights, freedom from foreigners.

Until 1920, when Alvaro Obregón became president, Mexico was to know no peace. There were few periods when government functioned in the capital or when there was an occupant for the presidential chair. Gradually the mighty sweep of the Revolution crystallized around a few dramatic chieftains, each differing in character and aims. The land was prostrate under the armies of the chiefs, stripping the country like a swarm of locusts. Hacendados made fortresses of their mansions against raiders, peasants moved in on land they wanted, townsfolk lived in terror and individuals fended for themselves as best they might.

In Morelos and Guerrero, there was Emiliano Zapata with his burning, single-minded drive to win land for the dispossessed campesinos. He was close to the Indians in blood, a countryman himself, and no Mexican leader has been more completely devoted to the people than he. Out of his deep union with the people of the soil he coined the slogan which was the battle cry of the Revolution, and will never die in the hearts of the Mexican masses—"the land belongs to him who works it."

Zapata was a slim, quiet man with an Asiatic face, intense black eyes and drooping black mustaches. Dressed in a tight ranchero costume of dead black and a huge white sombrero, he was a dramatic figure, a hero to his followers, a menace to landowners. The *zapatistas* knew every trail and byway of the country. From the hills they swooped down on the great estates, raided the houses, seized and burned land documents. Then Zapata invited the villagers to come in and cultivate the land. When they were not on the march the zapatistas melted back to their villages and huts to tend their crops, so that it was difficult for the federal troops to catch them.

In northern Sonora and Chihuahua, Pancho Villa, daring ex-bandit and cattle rustler, was adored by the rough men on horseback who flocked to his leadership. He was a primitive creature of violent impulses, whose boyhood as an abused hacienda peon had made him the defender of the poor, ruthless to their exploiters. Villa's spectacular Dorado cavalry galloped over the desert plains in furious raids on haciendas and railroad stations; hid in the mountains and dashed out again to terrorize, loot and celebrate.

Venustiano Carranza, Governor of the northwest state of Coahuila, was a decided contrast to the wild Villa. He was a ranch owner with political ambitions, a middle-class conservative who had been one of Madero's ministers. Carranza called himself First Chief of the Revolution. He was convinced that he alone could save Mexico.

He had a conservative program for constitutional government, church reform, the creation of a middle class of professionals, small businessmen and farmers. His long white beard and spectacles gave the old man a false air of benevolence, for under the Santa Claus appearance Carranza was a cold, stubborn, ambitious man, a patriot, but far from a revolutionist.

Then there was a man of Sonora, Alvaro Obregón, a ranchero and mechanic, a man of genial personality. More than Carranza or Villa he understood what the Revolution should accomplish, for he was in close touch with labor unions and had constructive social ideas. His influence gave the Revolution direction and a plan. When he gave his support to Carranza his military ability brought the First Chief to power.

As the people's armies swarmed over Mexico songs were born out of the excitement and surge of revolt; impudent songs like *La Cucaracha,* sung by the *carrancistas;* or *Adelita* and *Valentina,* songs of love and war and the valiant *soldaderas* who fought beside their men. These were sung in melting strains by *zapatistas* and *villistas.* Corridos, people's ballads, were born and sung in village market places, extolling the deeds of guerrilla chieftains.

In the north the main battles were along the railroad to capture telegraph stations, towns and payrolls. The armies were a mass movement of brown men in cotton suits and sombreros or khaki suits and boots, accompanied by the family swarm of women and children.

Stuffed into freight cars and camped on top, the armies crawled by train over the vast barren country. The soldaderas in long full skirts, babies slung in rebozos on their backs, squatted among the singing men on the car tops. Cheerfully they fed the crowd, patting tortillas, cooking coffee and beans over tins of charcoal.

On foot marches the soldaderas were the commissary department, raiding the countryside for food, or dropping their work to snatch guns and fight with the men. Children had their part in carrying messages, searching for food, even fighting at times. Brown Indian Mexico, from mountain and village and peasant hut, was on the march.

The chiefs, known as Constitutionalists, made their separate campaigns against the Federals supporting counter-revolutionist Huerta, and they soon had the Federals on the run. By April 1914, Huerta held only the capital and the oil coast from Vera Cruz to Tampico.

President Wilson was determined to get Huerta out, but his well-meaning moves to aid the revolutionists were misunderstood and resented. Mexicans appreciated sympathy and arms slipped across the northern border, but intervention they would not have, however friendly the intention. When a German ship bringing arms for Huerta approached Vera Cruz, Wilson made the mistake of sending the fleet to take the port, to prevent the arms from being landed. There was some bloodshed and the presence of bluejackets, even though temporary, sent the cry of gringo invasion ringing through the land. American flags were trampled in the streets, consulates were stoned and American residents hastened to get out of the country.

As the armies closed in on the capital General Huerta fled the country in a German ship and the Constitutionalists marched in. Carranza announced that the Revolution was over. He, the First Chief, would organize government. Meanwhile the people must obey, campesinos must get off the land they had seized, strikers must stop striking, everyone must preserve discipline.

This was not what the people had been fighting for or what Villa and Zapata wanted. They refused to accept Carranza as president. Generals took sides while the war went on. Villa's Army of the North moved toward the capital while Zapata's Agrarian Army came from the south. Carranza removed his government to Vera Cruz for safety.

The inhabitants of the capital trembled as the zapatistas of terrible reputation marched into the city. However, the dreaded fighters in their cotton suits and sombreros acted like the naïve countrymen they were. Horses were the only loot taken, and when the Indians needed food they knocked on householders' doors, politely asking for a little bread. In the imposing salons of the National Palace they wandered about, staring wonderingly at mirrors, paintings and rich furnishings.

When Villa's army arrived the two chiefs made an impression riding down the Paseo de la Reforma between cheering crowds of common folk. The villistas treated the city to the looting people had feared. To amuse himself the burly Villa had his picture taken lolling in the presidential chair under the golden eagle, with slim Zapata in his huge sombrero beside him.

Obregón's skillful generalship brought success to Carranza's cause and in 1915 the First Chief was once more installed in Mexico City. President Wilson recognized Carranza's government but that did not bring peace to the land.

Irrepressible Villa, out of revenge, tried to force American intervention by making daring raids on settlements north of the border. General Pershing, with cavalry and infantry, was sent to capture the bandit. Until 1917, when General Pershing was needed in Europe, Villa and his wild horsemen played hide and seek with American troops in the deserts and mountains. The presence of United States soldiers on their soil was resented by all Mexicans and anti-gringo sentiment increased.

General Obregón went after Villa, crushed the famous Dorado cavalry by meeting their charges with barbed-wire entanglements and trench warfare, and destroyed Villa's romantic reputation. With his army melting away the picturesque chieftain accepted the gift of a fine estate, where he settled down to enjoy farming until an assassin's bullet ended his life.

In 1917 World War I was in its third year, ships were streaming through the Panama Canal, the Russian Revolution had begun. Woodrow Wilson had been re-elected "because he kept us out of war" only to lead the nation into the conflict.

It was in that year that the Mexican Revolution reached its first important milestone, the framing of the Constitution of 1917. Left-wing and labor delegates, supported by Obregón, overrode the conservatives. Delegates were guided by two brilliant men, the writer Enriques Molina and Francisco Mújica, a revolutionary general with clear-cut ideas.

The document born of that convention was a great charter of social betterment and independent nationalism for the Mexican people—on paper. Despite failures in execution, or betrayal of its principles at times, the Constitution of 1917 remains the basis on which the modern Mexican nation lives and grows. The most significant articles had to do with land, labor and conditions under which foreigners might use the resources of Mexico.

The distribution of land, the most fundamental problem, was provided for. Ejidos were declared to be the woods, waters and lands needed by the villagers, the title to be vested in the village as a whole. Ejidos, seized during the Díaz régime, were to be restored to the villages. Lands were to be taken from huge haciendas to satisfy the needs of peasant farmers, the owners to be compensated with government bonds.

Laws regarding foreign concessionaires were worked out. The nation's ownership of subsoil resources was restated. Oil and mineral concessions were to be limited and expropriation of properties for public welfare could be demanded. National resources could be leased for use, but not sold. These laws were to cause endless controversies with foreign corporations.

The charter for labor in the Constitution was no more radical than the rights labor had won in the most industrialized countries, but for Mexico it was a tremendous leap ahead. Workers of all classes were assured of the right to form unions, strike and bargain collectively, to have the eight-hour day and double pay for overtime. There was to be compensation for illness or accidents, no child labor, protection for women workers and pregnant mothers. Large industries must provide schools for the workers' children.

In education a move was made to lessen the control of the Church by decreeing that public education was a government function. Secular teaching, instead of that by priests and nuns, was decreed for all primary schools.

Conservative Carranza did not like the Constitution, but the pressure of left-wing sentiment was such that he accepted it. Nonetheless, he did little to make the provisions for land distribution effective.

Carranza's government was characterized by such brazen thievery among officials that it was a byword even in Mexico. The stubborn domineering First Chief, who would not take advice, lost the support of revolutionary groups. People indulged their flare for political satire in bitter jokes. The only thing they liked about "Old Whiskers" was his stiff attitude toward the United States and the foreign interests who were raising howls of protest over the new Constitution.

Emiliano Zapata refused to give up the fight for land. Bitterly he accused Carranza of having failed to fulfill the Revolution. Ejidos had not been returned, land had not been distributed, greed and speculation were cheating the people of what they had fought for. "The hopes of the people have been mocked," cried Zapata.

To make an end of the agrarian revolt Carranza sent a brutal general to Morelos who went through the country burning villages and hanging campesinos. The fiery leader himself was finally captured through treachery. An officer, pretending that he wanted to join the agrarians, persuaded Zapata to meet him at a certain hacienda. As Zapata rode into the courtyard a file of soldiers fired a volley and he fell, riddled with bullets. His body, slung over a mule, was exhibited in Cuautla, the capital of Morelos, to prove to the campesinos that their leader was dead.

To the grieving men who passed by the murdered body Zapata was not really dead. He had been a worshipped hero in life and when he was gone he became a legend. The people still believe that in mountain storms Zapata of the true heart rides his white horse.

The people's chieftains, Zapata and Villa, were out of the picture. Neither one of them would have been capable of governing the nation. Carranza was soon to follow. When election time came around he did not dare campaign for himself, but tried to put up a harmless conservative candidate. The country would have none of this man or of "Old Whiskers"—everybody wanted popular Alvaro Obregón.

When a new revolutionary army swept down from the north Carranza and his grafting officials packed everything they could collect into trains, to make for Vera Cruz. The trains were ambushed and wrecked, and Carranza escaped into the mountains with a peasant guide whom he trusted. As the tired old man slept in a hut this man killed him.

So, by violent death, the three war chiefs passed from the scene. The capital gave Carranza a stately funeral, then turned to the ways of peace under the new president, Alvaro Obregón.

During a decade of struggle, bloodshed and confusion the Revolution had found direction, the principles on which a reborn Mexico could be built. Out of that fiery crucible came ideals for a national life and culture intrinsically Mexican. The Revolution is a continuing process with the end not yet in sight. Through failures, betrayals, backslidings, Mexicans periodically return to its basic principles; land for the people who need it, education for all classes, labor's rightful place in industrial life, a nation standing on its own feet, dealing on a basis of equality with other nations.

The 1920's were, in many ways, wonderful years in Mexico. They were years when the people were inspired with joyous hope and enthusiasm for their brave new world.

Guerrillas hid their guns in the thatch of house roofs and returned to their plows, soldiers became farmers, hundreds of ejidos were returned to the villages. Solemn campesinos gathered around government land officials to receive paper titles to plots taken from the great haciendas. A modern agricultural school was founded at Chapingo on the former estate of a rich general and other agricultural schools began to function in various parts of the country.

José Vasconcelos, the Minister of Education, was a brilliant man, at that time devoted to the principles of the Revolution. He has changed his position completely in recent years. Some of his educational plans were visionary, others practical. Education was divided into three sections—libraries, art, schools.

It was at this period that missionary teachers, men and women, went out on horseback to remote villages of plains and mountains. With selfless devotion they gave themselves to improving the lives of the villagers, teaching old and young better farming, elementary sanitation, as well as reading and writing. The whitewashed adobe schoolhouse, built by their own hands, was the symbol of a new life to the villagers. The teacher, the school, the mystery of books, were regarded with reverence.

Mexican intellectuals and artists discovered their Indian heritage and made much of it. The folk songs and arts of the people were appreciated, the intrinsic artistic ability of the Indians was extolled. One painter and poet who took the Aztec name Dr. Atl, wrote and illustrated *Los Artes Populares de Mexico,* a fine study of Indian folk arts. Dr. Atl, during the revolution, had edited posters and propaganda sheets illustrated by José Clemente Orozco, which were printed on a press set up in a box car.

Indian children were given paints, brushes and paper. Joyously they went to work, reproducing their village life in vivid naïve pictures that amazed the art world. At Xochimilco and elsewhere children covered the walls of their schools with enchanting frescoes, and talented young Indians were aided to become painters. Archeologists began to excavate and study the site of ancient Toltec culture at Teotihuacán, even while sociologists studied the needs of Indian people living in the region.

Mexico, particularly in the capital, throbbed with creative activity. Writers, artists and educators came from the United States to study what was going on, some to give their help in educational problems. The genius of the nation flowered in a powerful original art unlike anything that had been known in the Americas.

Painters demanded walls on which to tell the story of the Revolution. Working for masons' and plasterers' wages, they donned overalls and mounted scaffolds in public buildings, while Indian students ground colors and mixed plaster for them.

Walls were covered with monumental, earthy figures composed with powerful design and rich color, telling the story of the Mexican people in villages, mines and fields, and their hopes for the future. The sweep and anger of the Revolution, its profound feeling, were best expressed in the passionate compositions of José Clemente Orozco. This painter, and Diego Rivera, David Siquieros, and many another, made names for themselves and gave Mexico international prestige in art. Conservative Mexicans shuddered at this proletarian art and some university students tried to deface the murals in the National Preparatory School of the capital.

On the walls of many public buildings in Mexico City and

other centers the magnificent frescoes remain an eternal tribute to the Revolution, and an eternal reminder to those who fail to work for the welfare of the Mexican people.

Out of the surge of the Revolution writers produced the beginnings of a Mexican literature. Mariano Azuela, a military doctor, wrote, out of his experiences with the fighting campesinos, *Los de Abajo,* a classic of the underdogs. Martín Luis Guzmán wrote many books, of which the best known is *El Aguila y El Serpiente.* Others expressed in their writings the fury, confusion and excitement of the revolutionary period.

The rebuilding of Mexico did not progress smoothly even in this period when people believed that their sufferings were to be vindicated and their hopes fulfilled. Alvaro Obregón was popular because of his kindliness, humor and simplicity. The people trusted him and expected him to expropriate lands of great estates at once. Obregón believed in the land program but his cautious common sense feared drastic moves, and he followed the path of expediency in dealing with national problems and with the United States. Neither Obregón nor his ministers were willing to take over lands on a large scale.

Although eight hundred and fourteen villages received ejidos in his administration, there was discontent among peons who did not receive land, or those who did not know what to do with large plots. Agricultural training did not go hand in hand with land distribution.

Obregón allowed labor to organize but he was exceedingly impatient with strikes. He did permit the opposition to express itself in Congress and the press, which was an advance.

Under his successor, Plutarco Elías Calles, the agrarian program moved ahead faster. Huge tracts of national land, handed over to land companies by Díaz, were recovered. Thousands of small farmers were settled on plots, irrigation projects and agricultural schools increased, fifteen hundred and seventy-six villages received ejidos.

Both Obregón and Calles had a constant battle with Mexican and foreign landowners over the expropriation of tracts, as well as with the owners of mines and oil fields. Their governments yielded to the insistence of British and American corporations that the law forbidding ownership of subsoil resources should not be retroactive. To Presidents Harding and Coolidge, to the oil and mining magnates, the Mexicans were nothing more nor less than Bolsheviks. Conflicting economic interests were reflected in strained political relations between the United States and Mexico.

Revolutions are not noted for proceeding consistently toward their goal and that of Mexico was no exception to the rule. Progress was hindered by lack of courage and no clear-cut program for sweeping away old abuses. Human greed and love of power lured many leaders from their first sincerity.

Some leaders of the underdogs became the upperdogs, taking unto themselves all they could grab of the good things of life while the people waited for the promised land, bread, security. The story of Plutarco Elías Calles, who halted the Revolution, and of Lázaro Cárdenas, who brought it back to life, belongs in another chapter. Mexico had next to go through the period of the Millionaire Socialists.

CHAPTER 22

CENTRAL AMERICANS AND THEIR BIG NEIGHBORS

THE SMALL NATIONS, strategically situated between two oceans, had to live within the orbit of the big North American neighbor whether they liked it or not. The opening of the Panama Canal and the Spanish American War had made the United States the big boss in the Caribbean region. It meant protection for the small nations from European aggression, but their fear of being swallowed up in North American expansion won for the United States the unflattering title, Colossus of the North.

Fortunately that time is past. Central America and the United States are linked by mutual political and economic interests, by the exchange of natural products and manufactured goods. An era of cooperation has begun, and the small nations look forward to the time when they may become economically independent, free to deal with the United States or any other nation on a basis of equality. An unpleasant chapter of the past, however, cannot be passed over.

Central Americans have another important neighbor, Mexico, even closer to them than the United States. Probably North Americans do not realize how much influence the large state next door to them has had on Central America.

376

Under Spanish rule Mexico was the headquarters of the great Viceroyalty of New Spain and the Central American provinces were subject to remote control from the Viceroy in Mexico City. Colonial traders frequently complained of interference from richer and more favored Mexicans. When the provinces became independent many patriotic groups resisted the attempt of Augustín de Iturbide to add Central America to his empire.

Guatemala, having a long border with Mexico in sparsely inhabited country, has been especially alert to aggression from the larger state. Wilderness territories were vaguely defined in colonial times. The province of Chiapas, joined to Mexico at the time of independence, was a subject of border controversies which have now been amicably settled.

Political stability in Central America had become extremely important to the United States as the twentieth century opened. To a lesser degree it was important to Porfirio Díaz of Mexico to have peaceful states south of the border. When there seemed no solution for the constant turmoil among Central American states, this powerful Latin American President, and President Theodore Roosevelt, made friendly offers of arbitration. It was under their leadership that the first constructive plans were worked out for cooperation among the Central American republics.

Peaceful living together was something these states seemed unable to achieve. For seventy years, after the Provincias Unidas del Centro de America was dissolved in 1839, they had been engaged in futile wars. Sixteen attempts had been made between 1839 and 1906 to revive the federation. They had united temporarily to rid themselves of William Walker and after that Nicaragua had known thirty years of peace, until the young leader of the Liberal party, José Santos Zelaya, captured the presidency in 1893.

Among the lesser fantastic caudillos who rose to power in their states, there were two strong men who dominated Central American affairs during the troublous years of the nineteenth century. They were José Santos Zelaya of Nicaragua and Justo Rufino Barrios of Guatemala.

In Guatemala, under the long rule of the mestizo dictator, Rafael Carrera, the wealthy old families and church institutions had been secure by keeping on good terms with him. The Guatemala that counted for anything, politically or socially, was centered around the capital, Guatemala City. Never had the mountain region Los Altos, or its chief city, Quezaltenango, submitted willingly to rule from the capital. Quezaltenango was the place where resentment smoldered against the haughty dominating whites, for Los Altos was almost wholly Indian and *ladino,* as men of mixed blood are called in Guatemala.

Justo Rufino Barrios, young man of a poor provincial family, studied in Quezaltenango and absorbed its spirit. When he made the acquaintance of García Granados, an exile living in Chiapas, he became a reformer. García Granados had been banished for seditious speeches in Congress. In Mexico he had met and talked with Benito Juárez and doubtless was influenced by the ideas of the Mexican reformers.

Across the border in Chiapas, Granados was assembling arms and followers to stage a revolution in Guatemala and Barrios became his chief aide. In 1871 they made their entry, the Liberals flocked to them, and after a campaign of ninety days they had the capital. García Granados became president of a reform government with a program for crushing the political power of the Church, for state education and public improvements. Ladinos were to be given opportunities in government posts.

It was not long before strong-minded, dynamic Barrios

pushed aside the gentle President who wanted to reform abuses slowly and peaceably. Granados retired, leaving the presidency to Justo Rufino Barrios. This strong man intended to reform the backward country by drastic methods.

He began by suppressing the religious orders, expelling their members and confiscating their properties. Religious liberty was decreed, almost unheard of in the Latin America of that time. It is one of the reform acts in which Guatemalans take pride, for to this day freedom of worship is theirs, although Catholicism is the prevailing creed.

Justo Rufino Barrios reformed by decree, ruling either without a legislature or with one subservient to his will. Guatemalans honor him as a great reformer and it is understandable that it should be so. He did modernize the country in many needed ways, by building roads, by fostering the International Railway, by establishing telegraph lines, a postal system, municipal light and power. Something was done for education and some middle-class men gained posts in government.

No opponent dared raise his head, however, or express criticism of the dictator's acts. Barrios instituted the vicious spy system, used so brutally by future dictators, a most effective means of nipping opposition in the bud.

His reforms did not extend to the Indians, almost two thirds of the population. He appointed loyal generals and politicians, *jefes políticos,* to administer the provinces, who had a free hand to make their fortunes so long as they kept the provinces quiet. Indian labor was a source of profit. Indians were rounded up in gangs and practically sold to the plantation owners for seasonal work and to the state for labor on roads.

Nothing was done to improve the peonage, similar to that of Mexico, in which Indian families lived in virtual slavery on the haciendas. These methods of exploiting the Indians prevailed in Guatemala unchanged until recent times and are only partially reformed now.

The great ambition of Justo Rufino Barrios was to revive the federation of Central American states with himself as dictator. To this end he courted the United States and Mexico, hoping to have their backing. Union by peaceful means would have pleased the United States, but not union forced on the states by war. Mexico was placated by a favorable boundary settlement, but Porfirio Díaz did not look kindly on a rival dictator ruling a strong state to the south.

Liberals in the various states hoped for federation, but not under the domination of Guatemala. Nicaragua and Costa Rica were opposed to Barrios, but it was the President of El Salvador who prepared to defy him by force of arms. Barrios led his army against the presumptuous small state and in a battle on the frontier he was killed in 1885.

Perhaps Justo Rufino Barrios has retained his place of honor in Central America because he was removed from the scene before he had become dictator over all the states. In his own country he is remembered as a symbol of progress, the first president to advance Guatemala toward becoming a modern state.

Little can be said in favor of the strong man of Nicaragua, José Santos Zelaya, who became president in 1893. He was the leader of the Liberal party, but there was not much difference in principle between that party and the Conservatives.

Zelaya did, at the beginning of his rule, do some constructive things for his country. The little town of Managua was improved so that it was more like the seat of government. Something was done to improve transportation and to provide schools for public education. The local strife between Liberal

León and Conservative Granada hampered him, as it did all Nicaraguan presidents.

By distributing concessions to friends with a lavish hand and encouraging monopolies, Zelaya won support from those who profited with him in robbing the country. The nation was burdened with intolerable debt to British and American bankers, but the money went to politicians instead of public works.

Imprisonment was the mildest punishment for opposition; confiscation of property, torture and murder were the dictator's favorite methods against his enemies. In the sixteen years of his tyranny Zelaya's name became a symbol of brutal despotism in a country all too accustomed to oppression.

Zelaya used his country in a large way as his personal domain. He kept the other states in turmoil by meddling in their politics, working to make himself dictator of all Central America. In his vanity he hoped to win attention from large nations by playing one off against another. When he embroiled himself with North American interests he prepared the way for intervention in his unhappy country, but that was yet to come.

Soon after the turn of the century, when successive peace treaties between the states had been broken by one or another, the United States and Mexico offered their services as mediators.

In 1907 the five Central American states agreed to a peace conference in Washington, to be presided over by President Díaz and President Theodore Roosevelt.

Five weeks of discussion produced documents which laid the foundation for a new era in Central American life. The most progressive spirit of Central Americans, their hopes for peace and union, went into the agreements. The governments signed a treaty of peace and amity for ten years. The principle was laid down that any attempt to change a constitutional government by violence was a threat to the peace of all. The governments agreed to submit all differences not settled by diplomacy to a court which was also to judge cases of alleged violation of treaties or other injustices.

The judicial body for settling disputes was to be the Central American Court of Justice to be situated at Cartago, Costa Rica. The founding of this court and the plans for fostering interests common to all the republics were the great achievements of the Washington Conference. There was to be an international bureau to consider means for fusing Central American people into one nationality through a uniform educational system, a press association and other cultural activities.

With glowing enthusiasm and hope the Central American Court of Justice was formally inaugurated in the first capital of Costa Rica, the old town of Cartago. Delegations from the United States and Mexico were honored participants, for the two big neighbors were looked upon as the godparents of the Court. While Latin rhetoric pointed up the solemnity of the occasion in the formalities, throngs of eager people watched outside the building. It was the most inspiring thing that had happened to Central Americans in many years.

The Central American Court of Justice was, in a way, a league of small nations founded with hopes for peace and justice within their group not unlike the hopes of the world League of Nations at Geneva. It had similar weaknesses, in that the member states refused to abide by its decisions when their interests were affected, and the Court had no power to enforce its decisions.

The United States, which helped to bring it into being also helped to destroy its effectiveness, as we shall see. Despite failures, the Washington Conference and the Central American

Court of Justice constitute a bright landmark in Central America's stormy history.

The first to upset the applecart of the new order was Nicaragua, where revolt against Zelaya began in 1909, led by a Conservative, Emiliano Chamorro of Granada. With this revolt began the direct intervention of the United States in Nicaraguan affairs and the era of Dollar Diplomacy.

The United States had declared itself the arbiter in the Caribbean region, and Theodore Roosevelt had assumed the responsibility of keeping the states in order with his Big Stick. Very well, said the British, if the Monroe Doctrine is to prevent European nations from intervening to collect debts or protect investors, the United States must take on the job. So it was that United States' officials took over the customs in Haiti, Santo Domingo and Nicaragua. Debts of the erring countries were paid by loans from New York bankers, and American officers, administering the customs, applied the money to repaying the loans. The bankers, in Nicaragua, got holdings through their loans which were very profitable to them. Companies of Marines were stationed in these countries to protect foreign interests, maintain order and back up the American administration of finances. The governments were thus controlled by American political and financial power supported by armed forces. That was Dollar Diplomacy.

It must be admitted that diplomatic officials and foreign investors had their difficulties in dealing with the unstable governments and unscrupulous políticos of Central American states. Many of them, like Zelaya, used their country's resources for personal profit. Some Nicaraguan políticos invited protection from the United States, and sold their country into bondage to what Latin Americans call "Yankee imperialism."

In Nicaragua and elsewhere caudillos handed out concessions

to foreign capitalists in order to win backing for their régimes. At that time it was understood that the flag followed American business into semi-colonial countries. Behind the mining corporations, the banana companies, the bankers and businessmen, there was the shadow of the United States' fleet and the Marines.

When General Chamorro began his revolt in Bluefields on the east coast he had the backing of many Nicaraguans and of the foreign residents of the town, because everyone wanted to get rid of Zelaya. Juan Estrada, governor of the town, and Adolfo Díaz, employed by an American mining company, joined the revolt.

The dictator had set the United States against him by high-handed acts. There were controversies over commercial claims and alleged violation of the Washington conventions. American concessionaires objected to new grants made by Zelaya.

Two American soldiers of fortune were caught laying mines for the rebels in the San Juan River and were shot. They were adventurers with no right to protection, yet Secretary of State Knox sent a sharp note of reprimand and severed relations with Zelaya's government.

With the weight of the United States against him, Zelaya resigned on the advice of Porfirio Díaz, and went to Mexico where he was received with honor.

Zelaya's successor, Madriz, was a distinguished Liberal of León, but the United States refused to recognize his government. The American government supported the Conservative party and definitely intervened to aid its revolt, even though Zelaya was out of the picture. Madriz' attempt to blockade Bluefields where the rebel troops were cooped up was prevented by the commander of an American warship, who declared the town a neutral port for the protection of foreign residents. The Liberal forces were thus forced back into the highlands and defeated, and the Conservative revolt was successful.

With an American diplomat guiding affairs, an election was held, resulting in Juan Estrada for president and Adolfo Díaz for vice president. From that time on the United States government and American investors in Nicaragua supported the Conservative leaders who, in succeeding years, kept themselves in power through the political and armed intervention of the United States.

In order to understand the wars and counter wars one needs to have some picture of the character of the country which kept various sections isolated from each other. Nicaragua is about the size of New York State, but the greater part of it is mountainous interior and jungle east coast, hampered in development by lack of roads. The settled part of the country was, and is, in the lake region near the Pacific—a very small section of the whole. From this Pacific region across to Bluefields, where foreigners put their fingers in the Nicaraguan pie, communication was blocked by unsettled country and impassable jungles. It could only be crossed by mule trail and river canoe. The mountainous section, Las Segovias, north of the lake country, was the scene of the rebel Sandino's battles with Nicaraguan and American troops.

During the conflicts which resulted in complete control of Nicaragua by the United States, the Central American Court of Justice offered its mediation to the opposing parties, but was refused. Nicaraguan writers, later in this humiliating period, accused the United States of having gone back on its former policy of humanity and justice toward Central America. The United States had fostered the Washington Conference and its treaties, yet it intervened to keep one party in power. While most Nicaraguans directed their resentment toward the Colossus of the North. some denounced even more severely the unworthy politicians who invited armed intervention to keep themselves in power.

Estrada's government was recognized by the United States in 1911, but before the year was out dissensions among the Conservatives and clashes with Liberals caused him to resign and Adolfo Díaz became President. Among the politicians who went in and out of office during the period of intervention he was President for the longest period, the man who worked hand and glove with the State Department and relied on the protection of the Marines to keep his place.

Nicaraguans were not the only ones who accused Díaz of being the creature of the American bankers. Those in the United States who opposed the policy of Dollar Diplomacy also called him the yes-man of the bankers, the puppet of the State Department.

The period of intervention in Nicaragua was also the time when American oil magnates, who owned a large part of Mexico's petroleum lands, were resisting the attempt of the Mexican government to curb their power, and were urging intervention in behalf of their interests.

"Yankee imperialism" was the cry of all Latin Americans. The United States, to be sure, was not trying to acquire territory as in the days of Manifest Destiny, but economic imperialism was certainly the spirit of American financiers and corporations. They had no respect for the people of the countries where they operated, no regard for their rights, and they expected the American government to back and protect their enterprises.

When Adolfo Díaz became President the country was in wild disorder. Another Liberal revolt began in 1912 under

General Mena. Foreign properties were being seized and protests were made to the State Department by European diplomats. Díaz appealed to the United States for help, declaring he could not protect the lives or properties of foreigners.

One hundred Marines were landed at Corinto August 4, 1912, to protect the Legation at Managua and keep the railroad open. They took an active part in the war and soon other companies were sent from the Canal Zone to support the government. Disheartened by such a force and beaten in battle, the Liberals gave up and General Mena surrendered to the American commander. Military intervention had cost more in lives and property than Nicaraguan revolts and caused outspoken protest from the other Central American republics.

Thereafter, for twenty years, Nicaragua was occupied almost continually by the Marines, either as a Legation guard or in large companies when wars were going on. Most of the time American warships were stationed in the harbors of Corinto and Bluefields, ready to land bluejackets to keep order. Sometimes British warships hovered near by prepared to protect their nationals if the United States did not do so.

It was a dreary assignment for the Legation guard in Managua. There was nothing for them to do in the dull little town. As bored, lonely men do, they got drunk and became involved in brawls with the inhabitants. The Marines were tough, but some of them made friends with the people. They taught Nicaraguans to play baseball and a few married Nicaraguan girls and settled down in the country.

After Dollar Diplomacy had been at work in Nicaragua the chaotic finances were straightened out, debts paid by loans from New York bankers, the customs money efficiently collected by an American official to repay the bankers. A National Bank was founded and the railway rebuilt with money obtained from the bankers who, through their investments, owned both bank and railroad for some years. Eventually the Nicaraguan government was able to buy them back. Marines guarded the railway to keep communications open between the port of Corinto and the capital.

The best that can be said for United States control of Nicaragua is that efficient management did stabilize finances and reduce the country's debts. To patriotic Nicaraguans and all other Central Americans it was done at the sacrifice of Nicaragua's independence. The country was in the hands of American financiers and the government, dependent on the United States, was in their opinion under orders from the State Department.

The Liberal party had the backing of the people in its attempts to throw out the men who were subservient to the Colossus of the North. The bondage of Nicaraguans was a shame to them and to their sister republics, who feared for their own independence.

The United States government declared that its policy in Nicaragua was undertaken for the benefit of the people, to assure the establishment of orderly constitutional government and the election of presidents by honest voting; to teach Nicaraguans how to manage their finances and pay their debts.

If statesmen had good intentions the muddled policy they pursued was unfortunate to say the least. They blundered through insufficient study of Nicaraguan conditions and the mistaken policy of supporting only one party. The American pattern of constitutional government could not be imposed upon an undeveloped country by threats from warships and intervention by Marines.

Every nation has to follow its own road to government by and for the people. In a country of feudal background and illiterate population it was a long road indeed. Nicaragua could have been aided by friendly counsel as all Central America was aided in the Washington Conference. It could have been helped to improved agriculture and education and therefore prepared, by raising the standard of living, for representative government. American intervention did none of that. Nor could the people look on the United States as a friend while it was the real master of their country.

Adolfo Díaz used the canal route as bait to make a close alliance with the United States for the benefit of himself and his party. If a canal was built he offered to give the United States the right to intervene to keep order, as had been the case in the old treaty between New Granada and the United States regarding the Isthmus of Panama, before the Panama revolution. The plan caused widespread apprehension in Central America. This clause was rejected by the United States Senate, but a canal treaty was negotiated with President Wilson and Secretary of State Bryan—the Bryan-Chamorro Treaty —signed in 1916.

It gave the United States a ninety-nine-year option on building a canal and sovereignty over the route. Naval bases on islands in the Caribbean and on the Gulf of Fonseca were granted. For this the Nicaraguan government received three million dollars.

The other Central American states protested vigorously against the treaty. Nicaragua had negotiated it without consulting the others whose territorial rights were involved. Costa Rica's territory bordered on the San Juan River and she had rights in the harbor of San Juan del Norte or Greytown. El Salvador and Honduras as well as Nicaragua bordered on the Gulf of Fonseca and the three nations were supposed to have equal jurisdiction over its waters. None of the protesting states, at that time, liked the idea of granting naval bases to the United States.

Costa Rica and El Salvador brought suit against Nicaragua before the Central American Court of Justice, over the violation of treaties and disregard of their rights. The Court agreed that Nicaragua had no right to negotiate the treaty without consultation with the other states, but it could not declare the treaty void because it had no jurisdiction over one of the parties, the United States. Neither Nicaragua nor the United States would abide by the Court's decision or revoke the treaty. This was the last blow for the Court which had tried in vain to fulfill its function of settling quarrels between states.

The attitude of the United States in the treaty controversy lost for the nation the last of the prestige it had gained as a friendly big neighbor in the Washington Conference. The United States had sponsored the Court of Justice and now helped to destroy it. Woodrow Wilson, despite his good intentions, did little better in Central America than Taft, the friend of American capital.

Possession of the canal route has always made Nicaraguans the prey of international ambitions and of adventurers. Sometime, it is to be hoped, this new waterway between the oceans will bring to Nicaragua and all Central America the advantages they should have from it.

The Marine guard remained at the Legation until 1925. Elections went through in the usual way with the party in power controlling the votes. Martial law and repressive measures prevented open rebellion, but the constitutional government the United States was supposed to insure did not exist. There was pressure of public opinion in the United States against indefinite policing of a foreign country and the government removed the Marines in August 1925.

Politicians immediately began a scramble for power. Emiliano Chamorro seized the government by such barefaced manipulation that he was not recognized by any foreign power. The deposed President and Vice President left the country, declaring that their lives were in danger. Chamorro was soon ousted and the Congress, in 1926, took up the task of designating a man to occupy the presidency. There was much controversy and difference of opinion, but the legislators finally chose Adolfo Díaz, the man the State Department wanted because he worked well with American officials.

Juan Sacasa, the Vice President, living in exile, proclaimed himself the legal successor to the presidency. In Mexico he found support and arms for the revolt he started on the east coast.

It is difficult to understand why political strife should have turned all Nicaragua into a disordered place where armed bands fought each other, where pistols bulged from the pockets of townsmen and farmers followed their cows and pack mules with rifles slung over their shoulders.

The inherited strife between the parties had become a bitter, personal matter. Every Liberal was the enemy of every Conservative. Men of one party found it difficult to make a living in towns controlled by the other. One or another of the old families of Granada ruled when the Conservatives were in power. The Liberal party traditionally had the support of the less-privileged and darker-skinned population and their stronghold was León, the center of the country's intellectual life. The professional men were on the Liberal side, and the resentment of the people against American intervention led them to support Sacasa's revolt.

The revolution, under the skillful leadership of General Moncada, spread rapidly from the east coast. Guerrilla chiefs of the interior, among them Sandino, joined the revolt. President Díaz appealed once more to the United States. He declared that Mexico was acting with open hostility, that with the revolt making such progress he could not protect foreign lives and property.

Having intervened so far the United States was committed to further control over a country flaming with revolution, for the protection of all foreign interests. In 1927 a Marine guard was sent once more to Managua. Naval forces guarded the railroad from Corinto to the capital, and troops, at Díaz's request, occupied the fort protecting the city. Neutral zones were established on the east coast under the guard of warships and bluejackets.

The country was weary of war and of the depredations of deserting conscript soldiers who ran away from the armies to live off the country as bandits. The rainy season was approaching, the planting time, when farmers and peasants needed to get back to their fields to insure the next year's crops. Leaders of both parties came to the conclusion that the only way out of the deadlock was a new election under American supervision to prevent fraud.

Then President Coolidge sent General Henry L. Stimson to Nicaragua as his personal representative, to study the situation and make a report. He arrived in April 1927, and proved to be the successful mediator between the warring parties.

After conferences with both parties a meeting was arranged between President Díaz and General Moncada. Díaz agreed to a general amnesty and promised to give Liberals provincial posts at once. Both leaders consented to American supervision of the election, and to insure its peacefulness they agreed to order their armies to surrender arms to the Marines.

General Stimson promised that the plan would have his

government's support if President Díaz asked for supervision of the election and issued the decrees for amnesty and surrendering of arms. Every Nicaraguan soldier was to receive ten Nicaraguan dollars for each rifle and machine gun turned in. Only the guerrilla chief, Sandino, refused to obey General Moncada's order to surrender arms. He would have no truck with the Yankees and called Moncada a traitor for coming to terms with them and Díaz. With his followers he retreated into the interior toward the Honduran border.

Dusty little Managua was a sight when General Moncada's wild soldiers rode in to give up their arms in a ceremony presided over by President Díaz and General Stimson. The town swarmed with Díaz' enemies shouting, *"Viva la revolución! Viva Moncada!"* Díaz was a man rejected by his countrymen, branded by Latin Americans in general as a traitor, nominal President in a capital controlled by American troops. All Latin America resented the spectacle of a North American remaking Nicaragua.

Nonetheless, the sincere efforts of General Stimson to bring about harmony had good results. The registration of voters was supervised by Marines aided by Nicaraguans of both parties. The election itself went through without disturbances, bringing triumph to the Liberals.

General Moncada was elected President and Juan Sacasa was appointed Minister to Washington. By the votes of the people the Liberals were returned to power in the first free election ever held in Nicaragua. Even Nicaraguan journalists and politicians agreed that the process had been fair and orderly.

Some years before, it had been proposed that American officers train a native constabulary to act as a national police force to replace the Marines. The presidents had done nothing about it because they wanted the Legation guard to remain. In President Moncada's administration the constabulary, called the Guardia Nacional, was organized and trained.

If American military activity had been confined to training and the Marines had been promptly withdrawn, the United States would have been saved the stigma of taking part in the Sandino war.

Moncada's first use of the Guardia Nacional, with American troops, was to go after the rebel Sandino in the interior. It was an indefensible use of foreign troops in an internal quarrel and cost many more lives than if Nicaraguans had settled it themselves. Whatever the people thought of the guerrilla chieftain —and there were those who considered him a heroic patriot— the killing of their countrymen by American guns and bombing planes was a worse wound to national spirit than the presence of Marines in the capital.

Augusto C. Sandino was a man of Las Segovias, growing up in that mountainous region of mines and small farms. Moncada told General Stimson that he was a mercenary who returned after years outside the country to profit from banditry, but Sandino's friends denied it.

Sandino had worked a few years in Guatemala, Honduras and Mexico. In Mexico he absorbed the spirit of men fighting for land, liberty and decent wages. When he returned to Nicaragua in 1926 he worked in a mine of Las Segovias, teaching his fellow workers what he had learned in Mexico. As an independent leader he fought with guerrilla followers in the Liberal revolution. Sandino was a firebrand, bitter against Yankee domination. He was determined to bring dignity and a better life to humble Nicaraguans who had no spokesman.

The war dragged on for several years, a forgotten war about which the outside world heard little. Sandino's men met the

Marines and the Guardia Nacional with guerrilla tactics in the wild country they knew by heart. There were fierce and bloody battles, ruthless and cruel on each side. American planes tried to bomb Sandino out of his mountain strongholds.

When the Marines were finally withdrawn in 1933 the *sandinistas* boasted that they had driven the Yankees from the country. At any rate, the rebel was still uncaptured. Moncada's successor, Juan Sacasa, made a peace pact with Sandino for the surrender of arms in return for amnesty and land. But in 1934 the rebel of Las Segovias was killed in cold blood by members of the Guardia Nacional. Just what was back of his death remains something of a mystery. Some, at least, of his fellow countrymen remember Augusto C. Sandino as a patriot in a humiliating time.

With the departure of the Marines in 1933 the period of armed intervention came to an end. Those years of Yankee imperialism left a spirit of distrust and fear that is hard to live down. Intervention is a sore subject in Central America and elsewhere in Latin America.

The United States inevitably retains a powerful influence in Central America, but there is more give and take in the relationship. The people have had faith in the Good Neighbor policy because they believed in the sincerity and real friendship of Franklin D. Roosevelt. The big neighbor is now giving the friendly, constructive aid that might have been given all along. Advisory commissions and technical experts sponsored by the United States government are helping to build up malaria control, sanitation, public health services. Other commissions work with the local governments for the improvement of agriculture and education. Public health services and the sanitation projects are long-range enterprises from which the

United States expects to withdraw when they are well established. They have been financed on a fifty-fifty basis by the United States and the government concerned.

The interdependence of the United States and Central America was proved when the Japanese attack on Pearl Harbor threatened the security of all. The republics promptly stood by the United States with declarations of war, and did their part faithfully. They provided naval and air bases, furnished raw materials and food, as well as harboring on their soil large camps of the United States Air Corps and other military groups.

The republics also maintain close relations with their next-door neighbor, Mexico. Liberal-minded journalists, politicians, educators, spend periods in Mexico, sometimes as exiles. They discuss with their colleagues the problems common to them all in building democracy. Ever since the Revolution, Mexico has been working out its destiny on a new basis and, having advanced farther in labor organization and social legislation than the smaller states, she has a strong influence on progressive Central Americans. Reactionary groups, to be sure, are convinced that "communism" is fostered in Central America by Mexican influence.

Mexico's growing industries find a market in Central America, while in the field of entertainment Mexican music and movies are popular. As the big planes of international aviation companies fly back and forth between Panama and Mexico the peoples of Middle America are entering an era of close acquaintance.

CHAPTER 23

THE MEXICAN PENDULUM

SOCIAL and political changes in Mexico did not proceed consistently toward a clear-cut goal. The men who led the nation sometimes did not know where they were going, or did not carry through the reforms they started. There were swings forward and backward; from revolutionary idealism to Millionaire Socialism, from the "heroic madness" of Lázaro Cárdenas to the middle-of-the-road policies of Avila Camacho.

Plutarco Elías Calles was apparently sincere at first in his somewhat confused socialistic thinking, and in his intention to bring the people the lands, schools and wages they needed.

A man of Sonora, like Obregón, he came of a poor family and knew hardship in his youth. He worked as a bartender and teacher before joining the Revolution to fight under General Obregón. General Calles was one of President Obregón's cabinet ministers, the two men were loyal friends, and Calles was the man groomed by Obregón to succeed him.

Calles was a man of dynamic energy and powerful personality, with a hard face that matched his iron character. He was an excellent administrator, demanding efficiency in government departments. He became the Supreme Chief of the

Revolution, the power behind the throne while other men occupied the presidency, until after Lázaro Cárdenas was elected in 1934.

During Calles' term as president rural education progressed in thousands of little schools because men of brains and sincerity worked in the Ministry of Education, and devoted teachers lived on starvation salaries while they helped poor communities. Ejidos were returned to villagers, thousands of small farmers were settled on public lands or tracts taken from large haciendas, dams and irrigation canals were built.

"Mexico for the Mexicans" was a slogan coined by President Calles. It crystallized the long-felt resentment of the people over foreign political domination and control over national resources. While he was President, Calles fought the determination of British and American corporations to retain their great power, and their attempts to evade the labor laws of the nation. Although he went back on the principle, Lázaro Cárdenas revived it, and it remains a guide in Mexico's dealings with other nations.

After Calles' term in office Obregón was reelected, but unfortunately he was assassinated within a month by a religious fanatic. Emilio Portes Gil filled out his term to be followed by Ortiz Rubio. He resigned after two years, when Abelardo Rodriguez became president. These men were civilians, not generals, who took a businesslike view of Mexican affairs. Calles retired to his mansion in Cuernavaca but did not leave politics. He was the Supreme Chief, dictating policies while others occupied the presidency.

During the early part of Calles' term as president industrial workers and countrymen were pleased with progress toward better living conditions. Before long, however, there was growing dissatisfaction as the powerful políticos and labor leaders became richer and richer. They flashed over the new paved highways in handsome cars; their ornate villas, swimming pools and flamboyant parties became notorious.

Men grown rich by dubious methods built villas that outdid Hollywood in the fashionable suburb, Lomas de Chapultepec. Calles and the top-ranking politicians chose lovely, semi-tropical Cuernavaca for their florid pink and white mansions of rococo decoration. Some laughed at the Millionaire Socialists, but the people used the term wryly, in bitter disillusion. The famous street of candy-box mansions was called the Street of the Forty Thieves, as well as the Street of the Millionaire Socialists.

Luis Morones, an electrician and man of little education, rose to be head of the national organization of labor unions—Confederación Obrera Mexicana, or CROM. A fat, self-indulgent, expansive person, Morones managed to be persuasive to the workers as he built up the unions, and in many cases won higher wages from the industrialists.

He was a labor racketeer of a kind familiar in the United States, but with fancy Mexican frills. Morones had a passion for wearing diamonds and for owning high-powered cars. When, in union meetings, the men began to look glum at the appearance of their flashy leader, Morones told them he was just proving that "we proletarians can ride in cars too." None of the workers had automobiles, however, and few had good food or more money to care for their families.

Other labor organizers, following Morones' example, used their position to enrich themselves. Strikes were cynically bought and sold as the leadership in CROM became corrupt.

There were bitter conflicts with the Church over the enforcement of the severe anti-clerical laws. The attempt of the Ministry of Education to impose non-religious teaching and more modern methods in the schools caused intense opposition from church schools and Catholic people. There were strikes of parents and children, attacks on rural schools, even the murder of teachers.

There was fanaticism on both sides in the struggle between anti-clerical government officials and educators, and the church authorities backed by their parishioners. Bands of ignorant superstitious men, called the Cristeros, went marauding and were responsible for the worst attacks on country schools and teachers. Radicals retaliated with insults to priests and religion. Some fanatical officers rode their horses up church aisles and scoffed at the images of saints.

Anti-clerical laws of the Constitution required the registration of priests, limited their number and put a ban on those of foreign birth. The Church refused to accept these laws and priests went on strike, refusing to hold services in the churches. They ministered to the faithful privately in their homes. Some churches remained open, cared for by citizens so that people might go in to pray and leave offerings of flowers before the saints who meant so much to poor people. A compromise was finally arranged between church and state and the enforcement of the most severe laws was relaxed.

While President Calles was still pursuing his program of reform and fighting the oil companies, President Coolidge sent Dwight W. Morrow to be Ambassador to Mexico. Since he was a partner in the House of Morgan, left-wing Mexicans suspected his intentions. He proved to be the first American Ambassador who wanted to understand Mexico. He loved the country and appreciated its culture, but his job was to improve relations between the Mexican government and American corporations, and in this he succeeded. Morrow's tact and personal charm won him popularity and the friendship of strong man Calles.

Over ham-and-egg breakfasts in Morrow's lovely old house in Cuernavaca or in Calles' mansion, the two discussed informally the needs of Mexico. Radicals said that the Ambassador was beguiling the Supreme Chief away from the revolutionary program. It was noticeable, indeed, that after Morrow's three years in Mexico the foreign corporations were no longer harassed.

The big políticos, as well as Mexican business, profited from the reassured foreign capital that flowed into the country. The rule that foreign business must be encouraged, not molested, replaced the slogan "Mexico for the Mexicans."

In these prosperous years Mexico acquired paved highways radiating from the capital to important regions. American plumbing and gadgets, even moderate skyscrapers in the capital, were adopted. Mexico came definitely into the modern world of radio and airplanes.

During the presidency of Emilio Portes Gil the political groups of the country were organized in the Partido Nacional Revolucionario—PNR. At that time all the top men in government posts had a background of some share in the Revolution. The same is largely true today. The government called itself "the revolutionary family" and even when its members gave only rhetorical lip service to the cherished principles, they were still "the revolutionary family." By its machinery PNR had absolute control over presidential elections; the official candidate was sure to win.

In 1933 the PNR began to look around for a candidate to be elected the next year. They must find a safe man who would obey dictator Calles, yet they must throw a sop to discontented left-wing politicians, the agrarian leaders, and all who were disgusted with the excesses of the dictatorship.

Already Calles had called a halt to the agrarian reform program. He declared it had been a failure and that after a certain date the distribution of land would be stopped. Everyone was dissatisfied with the progress of this fundamental reform. Although many ejido communities were functioning well others had been failures.

Greed and graft among local politicians and ejido directors wrought harm to many helpless agricultural workers. Some agrarian leaders got hold of estates allotted to villagers and became new hacendados. The Banks of Ejidal Credit, established to help small farmers, sometimes fell into the hands of profiteering politicians. The people were then under the thumb of bankers instead of hacendados.

Mexico was still a land of great haciendas with peon laborers living and working on them under the old system. Large tracts of formerly productive haciendas went to waste under the management of Indian cultivators because they did not know how to farm on a large scale. Agricultural training lagged, the Indians were not educated out of their ancient habit of growing just enough corn, beans and chili for their families. The responsibility of growing enough food for the community or nation was not brought home to them.

Public admission of failure in the land program was bad enough, but the dictator's announcement that land distribution was to be stopped came as a shock to agrarian leaders and peasant leagues.

In Mexico the Russian Revolution had had its effect on the ideology of left-wing groups, and of the independent unions that had been gaining strength under the leadership of the dynamic young intellectual, Vicente Lombardo Toledano. These left-wing groups were enthusiastic over Russian experiments.

Calles despised all the tenets of communism, but if the Russians could have a Five Year Plan he would go them one better and devise a Six Year Plan for Mexico, for the next presidential term of six years. The Plan was announced at the PNR convention in 1933. Couched in vague, roundabout phrases, it promised to reform Mexico in a socialistic direction. Nobody took it seriously but the official candidate, Lázaro Cárdenas.

He had been chosen for several reasons. The radical politicians liked him, he had a record of honest, efficient work in important posts. He had always been a loyal friend of Calles, so that the dictator and the PNR expected to manage this quiet, unassuming man.

Lázaro Cárdenas came of a small-town mestizo family of the state of Michoacán and his Indian blood was that of the Tarascans, one of the most upstanding and talented of the Indian races. Like many another Mexican boy, he left his home town, Jiquílpan, as an adolescent to join the Revolution, and had been close to General Calles during the war.

As governor of his native state young General Cárdenas had worked hard for rural schools, land distribution and collective farming. Politicians thought him slightly mad to be so earnest for reform, but that very fact made him a candidate with popular appeal. Cárdenas had been president of the PNR and had held two cabinet posts before he became candidate for president.

In his campaign this man of whom people expected nothing startling began breaking precedents. Instead of confining his speeches to important cities he traveled thousands of miles over the country, by car and train, on horseback or on foot if necessary, to visit small towns and villages of mountains, plateaus and hot lands.

He sat down with townsfolk or villagers to learn what they needed—schools, medical care, water or land. Cárdenas was determined to know at first hand the reality of Mexican life and the people's needs. He knew it as no other leader ever had. No amount of pressure could turn him from his deep purpose of redeeming the common folk of Mexico from misery, poverty and ignorance.

The new President was a tall, well-built man with a body hardened by years in the open and on horseback. Hazel-green, searching eyes were a startling note in his bronzed face. Visitors were met with a grave manner and simple speech that was sincere and convincing.

Society in the capital soon learned that they were not to have in this President the luxurious living and flamboyant behavior of the usual general become president. Cárdenas refused to live in Chapultepec Castle which had been the residence of the presidents. That historic building with its furnishings of Maximilian and Carlota, of Porfirio Díaz and Carmencita, was made a museum where the people might come freely. The beautiful woodlands of Chapultepec Park, surrounding the castle, had been a people's playground since the Revolution.

The President, with his wife and little son, lived in a simple suburban home. Cárdenas did not drink or smoke, he disapproved of bullfights and gambling houses, and discouraged social extravagance.

Immediately after the inauguration it was announced that citizens might send messages free over the national telegraph system every day between twelve and one, to tell the President of their needs. Cárdenas paid attention to the flood of requests that came in. Delegations of campesinos generally had precedence over more imposing visitors in getting interviews with him. Frequently during his six years in the presidency Cárdenas escaped from the intrigues of the capital to make long journeys to country regions.

He liked to arrive unannounced in villages, to sit down on a bench in the plaza with the people around him, to discuss what they needed. The common folk had rarely seen a president of their country in the flesh—he had been a mythical figure in the distant capital. This man was one of them, with the tinge of Indian color in his face and his simple earthy speech which they understood. To thousands of humble people he became Lázaro, the man they trusted and turned to for help. He talked to them man to man and did his best to provide the things they asked for—building materials, a school, a well, a corn-grinding machine.

Cárdenas' administration coincided with Franklin D. Roosevelt's New Deal and Good Neighbor policy. Both countries started a régime of social change for the benefit of the people, of social experiments that brought outcries from the privileged and big business on both sides of the border.

The powerful nation to the north initiated a new policy toward its Latin American neighbors. Henceforth relations were to be conducted in a spirit of fairness, justice and friendly cooperation. That was good news to all Latin Americans, particularly to the Mexican government, as its experiments brought it into conflict with North American corporations.

The new President of Mexico moved slowly at first toward his objectives. He was learning, studying conditions, and when the time came for drastic action he moved swiftly and firmly.

Labor troubles, expropriations of land and other acts brought violent opposition from landowners, industrialists and businessmen whose interests were damaged. Cárdenas had only six years in which to make the changes he deemed necessary for the welfare of the people. It was not strange that those years were a period of confusion and labor strife. Some people were disappointed that the millennium did not arrive overnight, others used failures and mistakes to bolster their contention that Cárdenas was the destroyer of Mexico.

A wave of strikes against foreign-owned industries and public utilities brought about the first break with the master, Calles, who had expected his old friend to be a loyal follower. When Calles denounced the workers for upsetting business and prosperity, the President retorted with the announcement that the rights of workers as well as employers would be protected. He received enthusiastic support from all sorts of organizations while Calles, defending capitalism in that time of unrest, lost the last of his prestige.

The unions, or *sindicatos,* filled with enthusiasm and socialistic ideas, did not confine their strikes to foreign-owned businesses. There were disturbances in the whole labor field in which the government had to be the mediator. Cárdenas and his ministers tried to adjust the demands of the workers for drastic changes and participation in management to the operation of industries and public utilities.

The callistas accused the government of communistic policies; there were disturbances caused by them and by the Gold Shirts, a suspiciously fascistic organization. Cárdenas decided that the country would be better off without the presence of the Supreme Chief. He was roused from bed by an officer accompanied by soldiers and bundled off to the airport. When the old man, broken and angry, arrived in California, he told reporters that he had been exiled because he tried to save Mexico from the dictatorship of the proletariat.

In the big swing to the left, reaction from the Calles period, the ideology of world socialism and communism was adopted enthusiastically by radical politicians, industrial workers and peasant farmers. Theories and demagogic phrases were freely used without real understanding of what they meant.

Marxist theorists in the Ministry of Education tried to impose socialistic, anti-religious teaching in the schools, with the result that there was more violence in the country and more rural school teachers were murdered. Professors, and the always politically active university students, went on strike against the socialist school program and interference with the established curriculum.

Industrial workers of the sindicatos wanted not only the collective bargaining, wages, working conditions, schools, due them under Mexican law, but fought for control of the industries. Their lack of technical skill and ignorance of practical management did not bother them.

Filled with their vision of power for the working class the sindicatos went farther in their socialistic ideas than old established unions of more industrialized countries. Naturally, there was chaos when the sindicatos tried to manage such important public utilities as the railroads. In the present postwar period of widespread labor strife and paralyzing strikes Mexico's chaotic labor upheavals in Cárdenas' administration do not seem so startling as they did at the time.

After the Revolution, Mexican workers began their organization and action anew. They were far behind industrialized countries, and entered late the world-wide struggle of the industrial age. The people went about it in their own way, and in the socialistic enthusiasm of the 1930's tried to accomplish everything at once.

Vicente Lombardo Toledano became the powerful left-wing

labor leader. Although he belonged to an upper-class family and started his career as a scholar and philosopher, he devoted his brilliant intellect and dynamic personality to the cause of labor. From leadership in Mexico he has gone on to a position of great influence in Latin American labor organizations and has represented them in international labor conferences. At the present time he is an outstanding personality in Mexico.

When Toledano lost his post at the National University because of his radical teaching, he founded the Workers University in Mexico City. For a small registration fee anyone may study there, taking classes in languages, history, literature and political theory from the Marxist point of view.

Industrial and peasant workers were organized in 1936 under Toledano's leadership in a new national body, the Confederación Trabajadores Mexicanos—CTM. The old organization, CROM, and its leader, Luis Morones, were discredited. Within a few years CTM became a powerful body, winning labor victories, improving social conditions for workers, throwing its political influence to candidates who would help labor.

After 1936 the tremendous strikes organized by CTM led to the most sweeping expropriations of property and land.

Land for the people who needed it was the reform closest to the President's heart. During his first two years in office Cárdenas distributed more land than all his predecessors put together, but he did more than that. He tried to make it possible for village communities and small farmers to make a living from their plots.

Cárdenas was not a communist, although often accused of being one. He never recognized the Soviet government and gave Stalin's arch enemy, Trotsky, asylum in the country. He may have been influenced by the Russian collective farm plan, but he was also interested in the Swedish cooperatives.

The revolutionists' ideal of thousands of small peasant proprietors, Cárdenas believed, could not succeed in the modern world. Agriculture must be organized on a large scale with modern farm machinery. Therefore, when he expropriated tracts of land for the benefit of the workers, he organized large ejido communities. Heads of families, the ejiditarios, who were allotted sections, worked the land on a cooperative basis. The Banks of Ejidal Credit advanced money for seeds, implements, weekly wages; they sold the crops in the national or international market, and after the loans had been repaid the profits, if any, were distributed among the ejiditarios.

Some ejidos succeeded, others were failures for a variety of reasons. The large ejidos had to start with the expropriation of properties, which naturally brought against them the active opposition of the former wealthy owners. It took more than a few years to transform untrained landless workers into cooperative farmers of ejido communities. Efficiency, honesty and funds were needed for every project, all difficult to attain. It is not yet certain that the ejido community is Mexico's solution for the land problem.

In the most successful projects as, for example, the Laguna cotton district, workers were able in a few years to buy tractors, irrigation pumps and other machines, to improve the cultivation of the fields, and to add crops such as wheat and alfalfa.

Many ejido communities organized cooperative stores, chicken runs, a mill for grinding corn, and other enterprises to make life easier for all. They had schoolhouses and improved homes. Group medicine plans, in some places, worked to combat the diseases of the Mexican poor—amoebic dysentery, typhoid, tuberculosis.

When land was taken from great haciendas, the owner was allotted a certain number of acres, sometimes the *ingenio* or sugar mill on sugar-cane haciendas, or the mill for processing hemp fiber from henequen in Yucatán. The owners, of course, were indignant over the loss of their lands and had little faith in the government bonds with which they were indemnified. There was bitter opposition to the land program. Every mistake or failure, every instance of graft, was played up as proof that Cárdenas was ruining agriculture.

It was the expropriation of petroleum lands and properties that caused the greatest sensation outside the country and brought down on Mexico the full might of outraged capitalists.

The British and American oil companies had fought every government since the Revolution to hold their ownership of the petroleum lands sold to them by Porfirio Díaz. The dictator had circumvented the old Spanish law incorporated in the Constitution of 1857, declaring the subsoil resources the property of the state, which could not be sold, only leased for use. That law had been reaffirmed in the Constitution of 1917. The oil companies had persuaded the presidents before Cárdenas to agree that the law should not be retroactive, and had therefore held on to their lands.

In November 1936, a law had been added to the Constitution giving the government the right to expropriate any property when necessary for the public welfare, the owners to receive indemnity within ten years.

Cárdenas had been within the law in his expropriation of agricultural lands such as the Laguna district, and was within the law in the expropriation of the oil companies' properties.

The oil companies had always been more arrogant toward government and labor than other foreign corporations and Mexican resentment was directed especially toward them. Their properties were efficiently managed and brought great profits to the owners. They were well able to give their workers the wages, medical care, social benefits and schools due them under Mexican law, but they had always evaded these responsibilities.

Lázaro Cárdenas knew at first hand the misery of the oil workers, for he had been at one time the officer in charge of military operations in the oil zone.

Tampico was a flamboyant boom town, a place of incredible existence. It was the scene of extravagant spending by foreign officials and employees, and of a mad scramble for oil and fierce competition between British and American companies. It was a place of gaudy night clubs, luxurious hotels and shops selling American luxuries.

Officials had their fine mansions with gardens and swimming pools on the hills above the miasmic swamp lands, and all foreign employees had comfortable screened houses in good situations. The settlements of Mexican workers' shacks along the edge of stagnant malarial swamps or the Pánuco River were in tragic contrast to the other Tampico. Whole families lived in dark one-room shacks with no sanitation. They were listless from malnutrition and malaria, having little medical care and poor food.

In the oil region the attitude of foreign employers toward Mexicans was at its worst. Mexican children had little or no schooling, although that was required under Mexican law. They had no playgrounds and were excluded from the swimming pools where the children of foreign employees amused themselves. Mexicans were excluded from technical positions, although they often did, as underlings, the skilled work for which American bosses received high salaries. The discrimination against his countrymen filled Cárdenas with burning indignation.

In 1937 the CTM called a general strike against seventeen

companies, subsidiaries of Standard Oil and Royal Dutch Shell. The hard-fought conflict went on until the petroleum industry was nearly paralyzed and motor transport was threatened with a complete tie-up.

The case was submitted to the Federal Board of Arbitration and Conciliation, and an exhaustive study was made by government economists of the oil companies' management and assets. They reported that the companies were able to pay the raises demanded, with provision for overtime, vacations, better housing, health and schools. All these things were legally due the workers but the companies had neglected to provide them.

The unions went the limit in their demands, perhaps, but Mexicans felt that company ownership was illegal, and the directors had been callously indifferent to the welfare of their workers.

The oil companies took the case to the Supreme Court which handed down a verdict in favor of the unions and gave the companies seventy-two hours to comply. Then the companies defied the Court and refused to accept the decision. It was not a question of money, for at the last moment they had agreed to all but forty million pesos of the amount demanded. It was a question of maintaining their position as it had been heretofore. They refused to agree to the unions' demand for closed shop and workers' representation in management. The directors never imagined that the government would stand out against them.

Then Lázaro Cárdenas made one of his swift, dramatic moves. On March 18, 1938, his quiet voice over the radio informed the nation that the strike had created a national emergency and that the properties of the oil companies had been expropriated for the public welfare. That date is always celebrated in the capital. It is Mexico's declaration of economic independence, its assertion of the nation's ownership of its natural resources.

The response from the nation was tremendous. Cárdenas had raised the people from their sense of inferiority among nations, given them a new pride and self-respect. On March 22 there was a huge demonstration of solidarity in the Zócalo. Under a sea of banners, placards and showers of confetti the people marched—unions, professional groups, teachers and school children, the army. They marched to the stirring strains of the National Anthem and the International played by numerous bands. Food and fruit stands did a big business as Mexicans ate, sang and shouted, making fiesta in their characteristic way.

When the President spoke from the National Palace, explaining his decree and what it meant for the nation, the people shouted themselves hoarse with enthusiasm. Cárdenas called on the nation to raise money toward paying the indemnity to the oil companies, and people responded according to their ability with large and small sums of money. Children collected centavos, women gave their jewelry, country people brought corn and chickens to be sold for the fund.

Castillo Nájera, Mexican Ambassador to Washington, called the expropriation "heroic madness." It was all of that. Mexico was faced with the terrific power of British and American capital, determined to prevent her from making a success of the oil industry. President Cárdenas realized what the nation was up against, but he believed expropriation was necessary. He did not intend, as propagandists declared, to expropriate all foreign properties.

Mexico was not prepared with money or skill to run the petroleum industry. Everything had to be learned and the oil had to be marketed. The fuel oil and gasoline of the American companies had been mostly consumed in the country, while the British products were exported. The great rivals, British and American, joined hands to create a boycott of Mexican petroleum products.

They threatened to have no further dealings with concerns that handled Mexican oil, and small nations with tankers were afraid to carry Mexican products for fear of reprisals. United States' concerns which sold oil machinery and supplies to Standard Oil refused to sell to Mexico.

Before they left the fields, foreign employees did what they could to hamper production by sabotage—flooding wells, breaking pumps and other equipment. At first the pride of ownership and responsibility for proving that they could get along without the foreigners brought unity in hard work and ingenuity from all the workers. That did not last of course. The national industry, Petroleo Mejicano, or Pemex, went through hard years financially, and with technical and labor troubles, but it is succeeding.

When the nation had oil to export there was the great problem of selling it, for the expropriated companies had succeeded in creating a boycott in the American and British markets. Mexico had to acquire tankers and build up a market in Latin America. Germany, Italy and Japan were only too glad to increase their influence in the country by buying petroleum products. The industry was obliged to sell to them since the British and American markets were cut off, and the oil had to be sold for the nation's economy. Fascist propaganda was increasing in Mexico and the oil boycott helped it along. Also, British and American concerns thus aided their countries' enemies to obtain petroleum products for war.

Cordell Hull reassured the Mexican government when he stated publicly that the nation was within its rights in expropriating lands and properties. Increasing pressure was brought by the State Department, however, for full payment of the indemnities to the companies. Arguments with the British led to the severing of relations between Mexico and Great Britain.

President Cárdenas would have liked to settle promptly if the money had been available, and if a just settlement could have been agreed upon. The companies put an extravagant value on their properties and government economists replied by assessing the value on the basis of the companies' own tax declarations. Neither side would yield and the deadlock continued throughout President Cárdenas' administration.

Through turmoil and experiment, opposed by the powerful and trusted by the people, his reforms sometimes sabotaged by graft, Cárdenas forged ahead with his plans for Mexico. He remained as honest and determined at the end of his administration as he was at the beginning. Of course many mistakes were made, some social experiments failed, the country could not be prosperous while such drastic changes went on. Cárdenas was stubborn in putting his theories into practice.

He grew in his conception of what Mexican democracy should be and how to attain a good life for the people. Such improvements as dams, highways, hospitals, group medicine plans, are credited to him. Perhaps more important for the spirit of the nation, he brought pride and self-respect to thousands of poor Mexicans who learned how to help themselves in cooperative enterprises. Some people consider Lázaro Cárdenas the greatest Mexican since Benito Juárez.

When a journalist asked Cárdenas if the Revolution was over he replied, "As long as there are villages without water, as long as thousands of villagers are asking for land, as long as forty per cent of the people still work for starvation wages, the Revolution must go on."

As election time approached, Cárdenas announced that this time there would be no imposition of an official candidate, no interference with the will of the people expressed at the polls. He refused to give his influence to either candidate—Avila Camacho, chosen by the government party, or Juan Andreu Almazán, the choice of the opposition.

The government party—PNR—had been reorganized and named Partido de la Revolución Mexicana—PRM. It was composed of the great labor organizations, peasant leagues and middle-class associations, and declared itself "without any reservation in favor of the democratic form of government."

The PRM had mass support and so did its candidate, Avila Camacho. On the other hand Juan Andreu Almazán had the power of money behind him, the support of wealthy Conservatives, Catholics, big businessmen, people who were tired of social experiments. He was a wealthy Conservative himself, with an expansive manner that won popularity. The reactionary fascist groups in the country also worked for him.

Both candidates were middle-of-the-road men, and the country was in a state of mind to call a halt to experimenting; on the one side to consolidate social gains and move more slowly; on the other to swing back toward safe conservatism. Some people, weary of confusion sighed for "the good old days of Díaz."

The campaign was hot and exciting, the temper of the country so explosive that many feared the election would be followed by civil war. That did not happen, although the election was not the orderly, democratic process Cárdenas had hoped for. There was violence by both parties at the polls, shooting, interference with voters, accusations of cheating and illegal vote counting.

Disorder was wild in Mexico City where women joined in

the fights around the polls, resulting in killed and injured.
When Lázaro Cárdenas visited the scene he said sadly, "Mex·
ico is not yet a democracy."

Avila Comacho, the bland, quiet, solid man, the tranquilizer,
whose words were sober and good, led Mexico forward into its
next phase.

SISTER NATIONS

ISOLATION, due to difficulties of transportation, has kept Central Americans apart from their fellows in South America and their neighbors in North America. The old Latin American way of life is less changed by outside influences than in Mexico and South America.

Except for those who have lived in the countries for diplomatic or business reasons, few people of the United States are acquainted with their near neighbors in Central America. Tourists, now that they have air transportation, are just beginning to discover the beauty and interest of the small republics.

North Americans know little or nothing about Central American history, and they are inclined to think that the people are all alike. As a matter of fact, each country is distinctive in landscape and in the character of its people, although the general manner of life is similar.

Starting with the understanding that Latin Americans are fundamentally different from Anglo Americans in background and culture as well as race, it is an adventure in friendship to learn to know Central Americans in their own countries.

The beauty of the highlands is entrancing to visitors; the lakes and forested ranges, the volcanoes, the rich vegetation of lands where winter never comes, the tropical blossoms and vivid flowering trees. Visitors who make rapid trips from country to country by plane enjoy the landscape but learn litttle about the people.

It is much more rewarding to explore slowly on the ground, traveling with the population on the small railroads or on the busses, rough as that road travel is for the most part. The simplicity and kindliness of people met on such trips and on visits in small towns, their courtesy to strangers, give a broader understanding of Central Americans than that obtained in the capitals.

Racially all the republics have a mixture of Indians and Spaniards but in different proportions. In Honduras, Nicaragua and El Salvador the two have blended so thoroughly that the majority of the population is mestizo. Indians have mingled with the rest of the population, dressing and living like their fellows. Costa Rica, having few Indians and a minority of mestizo people, is predominantly white. In Guatemala the white upper class is small, there are more Indians than mestizos; in fact, nearly two thirds of the population is of unmixed Indian blood.

Due to their feudal inheritance and the slow progress of democratic ideas, class lines are sharply drawn. The gulf between the masses of the population, poor and uneducated, and the small privileged class at the top is extreme.

Every capital has its group of aristocratic old families of pure Spanish descent; very charming people in their social life, people who are acquainted with Europe and the United States through travel, and through education in foreign schools.

Every state has its university in the capital, its writers, teach-

YUMA
ARIZONA
NEW MEXICO
TEXAS
CIUDAD JUAREZ
SONORA
RIO GRANDE
BAJA CALIFORNIA
CHIHUAHUA
SIERRA MADRE OCCIDENTAL
MEXICO
MONTERREY
SIERRA MADRE ORIENTAL
BUENA VISTA
PACIFIC
ZACATECAS
SAN LUIS POTOSI
TAMPICO
DOLORES
GUADALAJARA
QUERETARO
JALISCO
MEXICO CITY
VERA CRUZ
MORELIA
PUEBLA
CUERNAVACA
POPOCATEPETL
ORIZABA
GUERRERO
ACAPULCO
OAXACA
GULF OF TEHUANTEPEC
OCEAN
MEXICO
CENTRAL AMERICA
AND PANAMA

0 100 MILES 500
GULF OF MEXICO
HAVANA
CUBA
JAMAICA
CARIBBEAN SEA
MERIDA
UXMAL
CHICHEN ITZA
CHAMPOTON
YUCATAN
TABASCO
TICAL
BELIZE
BT. HONDURAS
CHIAPAS
PTO. CORTES
QUIRIGUA
CEIBA
TRUJILLO
GUATEMALA
HONDURAS
GUATEMALA
TEGUCIGALPA
EL SALVADOR
SAN SALVADOR
NICARAGUA
BLUEFIELDS
MOSQUITO COAST
LEON
CORINTO
LAKE NICARAGUA
MANAGUA
GRANADA
GREYTOWN
PANAMA CANAL
COLON
CRISTOBAL
PORTO BELLO
PANAMA
GULF OF DARIEN
COSTA RICA
LIMON
SAN JOSE
PEARL IS.
COLO
BALBOA
EAN

ers and journalists. Culture ranks high among Central Americans, and people of the professional fields are honored for their attainments. Each country has small presses publishing some of the works of native authors.

University education is on a different plan from that of the United States, as it is in all Latin American countries. Emphasis is on the humanities, philosophy, law; the aim is toward general culture rather than specialization. Central American students often go to Mexico, Chile or Argentina for university work. Formerly Europe was the goal for special training. More and more, however, young men are coming to the United States for training in engineering, medicine, agricultural science. For many young men ambitions are changing, horizons widening, as they turn from a few traditional careers to engineering projects and modern agriculture, for the advancement of themselves and their countries. Girls, also, are coming to the United States for various kinds of study.

Latin American students always take an active interest in politics, the great game into which they throw themselves with enthusiasm. Central American university students have been in the forefront of recent struggles to get rid of dictators and democratize governments. They have staged demonstrations, suffered in street fights, gone to prison or into exile with older men.

In the arts it is more difficult to make a living in Central America than in the United States. Painters and musicians must make art an avocation while they support themselves by some other means. Guatemala has an Academy of Fine Arts in the capital, and Honduras, in Tegucigalpa, has the most interesting school of arts and crafts in Central America. There poor boys and girls are supported by the government while they study painting, sculpture, wood carving, and attain skill in crafts which may be a means of livelihood for them.

Education for the people at large has lagged, except in Costa Rica, because governments, controlled by the privileged classes, have not seen fit to devote sufficient funds to education or to improve schools and their standards. It is in teaching that warmhearted, intelligent women have found the most satisfying work, so far, outside their homes. They have been the guides of youth except in the universities. Outstanding among them is Doña Josefa de Aguirre of Nicaragua, an old woman now. She has become almost a legend in her country for her years of work in the education of girls, against all obstacles and all political pressure.

In each country there are progressive, educated women who are breaking away from the Latin American tradition that their place is strictly in the home. They are insisting on their right to study and work in professions and are taking the lead in bringing their more conservative sisters into civic activities, to make their influence felt for social betterment and democracy.

The patriarchal Latin American family life and close relations with friends have charm and graciousness. People are extremely social within their own group and home has been the center of entertainment until recently. Young people of towns now want the freedoms of other modern youth. They have more unchaperoned activities outside their homes in sports and parties. In the two most progressive capitals, Guatemala City and San José, middle-class girls need no longer be mere social ornaments until they marry. They go out to work in shops and offices as a matter of course.

The conservatism which has kept family life in the old pattern has also preserved many charming Spanish customs and fiestas, and in some countries great Catholic festivals are celebrated with processions, carrying gorgeous images of saints through the streets. Regional songs and dances are not lost, although they are not so easily heard or seen as in Mexico. Radio and phonograph records are replacing the old-time singing to guitar or piano, but the people keep their love for the thin, tinkling music of the marimba. This large, xylophonelike instrument is carried on Indian backs to Guatemalan village fiestas and marimba bands have become a tourist delight. When raised to high estate as the basis for dance bands, marimbas give an exciting quality to dance music in social clubs.

Only in a few cities are modern houses or apartments replacing the old Spanish type of house—one-storied, with rooms ranged around a garden patio. Streets of these houses present a blank face to the world with their solid walls broken by iron-barred windows and large wooden doors, emphasizing the seclusion of family life within. The roofed corridors around the patio, with pavement of polished tiles, are delightful in the hot regions, or anywhere in the dry season. Sunlight filters down over flowers and shrubs, family meals are served there and friends entertained.

Fortunately for them the mistresses of households have Indian or mestizo servants to mop the expanses of tiled floor, to wash clothes beside the great stone water tank, called a *pila*, in the kitchen courtyard, and to perform all the other chores which such rambling houses entail.

The tempo of life is leisurely in Central America, particularly in the country. These are lands of slow hand labor and poor transportation. Farmhouses and homes in villages and small towns have no conveniences to lighten the burden of housework. People must work hard to support their families and there is little amusement when work is done, except for village fiestas and movies in towns.

Manufactured goods are coming in from foreign countries, but the deliberate work of peasant craftsmen produces many essential things for country people. Craftsmen are the makers of household pottery, they are leatherworkers and sandal-makers, weavers of pita and cabuey fibers into mats, hats, bags, and the hammocks in which many poor people sleep.

Countrymen have always been accustomed to journeying on foot or on horseback. Honduran and Nicaraguan men and boys ride their animals with the ease of those born to the saddle. In Guatemala, where most of the working population is Indian, the packing of loads is generally done on human backs and heads. Some few market people bring their produce to Guatemala City on the train, but the Indian has always trotted over the roads and trails between highlands and lowlands with burdens on his back and he continues to do so.

In the other countries the oxcart is the farmer's mainstay for transporting produce and supplies over rough dirt roads. It is the vehicle for most heavy carting as well. The cart and its slow-moving beasts may be inefficient, but it made transportation of goods possible in countries where roads were rough trails not so long ago, and it is an interesting note in the Central American landscape.

The carts have two solid disks of wood for wheels, with a flat body; in some places with stakes to hold the load, on others with a frame made of a mat of banana leaves interwoven between stakes. Most attractive are the famous painted carts of the Costa Rican farmers, decorated with flowery patterns and drawn by a fine matched team of oxen.

Although busses and trucks rattle over improved roads in El Salvador, Costa Rica and Guatemala, to transport goods, the oxcart with its leisurely driver has not lost its place.

Country roads, outside towns, are alive in the early morning with men and women, carts and laden animals coming in to market. More important than super-markets to North American housewives are the dim, cavernous market buildings of Central American towns to the urban and country population. For the mestizo and Indian families, who sell their produce and buy supplies with the proceeds, there is, in addition to business, the sociability of mingling with crowds. Sometimes town housewives shop in person, accompanied by a servant maid to carry home on her head the huge flat basket of fruit, meat, vegetables, crowned by a bunch of flowers. In some places the pleasant business of bargaining for supplies is left to the cooks.

Markets are endlessly interesting and a good place to study the produce of a country and its folkways. The fruits, vegetables, grains and lovely flowers are to be found there, as well as the handicrafts; the clay pottery, the hats, baskets and hammocks, the saddles engraved in curlicue patterns, the bridles decorated with tufts of colored wool, the leather sandals for countrymen.

Women shop for lengths of cheap cotton fabrics, store shoes, combs, gewgaw trinkets and tinware. Most of the manufactured goods are sold by merchants who import them from the United States.

It is in the capitals, naturally, that upper class and professional life, as well as government, are concentrated. Each one of them has a character of its own.

Guatemala City is the most modern, with smaller San José of Costa Rica a close second. Earthquakes destroyed much of the eighteenth-century capital built after Santiago de los Caballeros was ruined, so that Guatemala City is largely modern. It is modern in Latin American style, however, with its rectangular streets of low, pastel-colored houses with tiled roofs.

The business center, with office buildings, shops, hotels, cafés and movie theaters, is completely up-to-date. American goods are displayed in the shops and some drugstores and food shops outdo the United States in white-tiled immaculateness. The recent dictator, Jorge Ubico, is said to have cleaned up the city by police methods so rigidly that people were afraid to throw a cigarette butt on the washed streets. Present-day democratic Guatemala keeps its city clean without dictatorial methods. The well-kept verdant parks, the limpid skies and surrounding frame of mountains, make Guatemala City a most attractive place.

Progressive Guatemalans, now taking the lead in their country, are alert, intelligent, with a reserve of manner that belies their inner intensity. They retained their independence of thought and fought for their ideas even while living under tyrannical dictatorship. Now that they have freed themselves, they are proving their ability to carry through greatly needed reforms in every phase of life.

Guatemala was the capital of the colonial kingdom. There the wealth of Spanish aristocrats and the Church was concentrated, leaving an inheritance to the modern nation of rare treasures of Spanish colonial arts, furnishings and architecture.

Large churches loom over Indian mountain towns. Within the dark interiors carved and gilded saints and beaten silver altars form a background for the half-pagan worship of Indians crouched on the stone floors. Antigua, the old capital ruined by earthquake, is a dreamy place where simple people of today carry on their crafts and cultivate their fields in the shadow of massive architectural fragments of churches, monasteries and convents. Dignified Spanish mansions are a living reminder of colonial elegance. In one of the old houses Bernal Diaz del Castillo spent his last years and wrote his absorbing chronicle of the Conquest. His original manuscript, in crabbed Spanish calligraphy, is preserved in the archives of Guatemala City.

In Indian life as well as colonial treasures Guatemala differs from the other republics. Mountainous Los Altos with its Indian villages, half-Indian towns, and the patchwork of Indian cornfields on hillsides and mountain slopes, is a world apart. Lake Atitlán, scene of Alvarado's conquest of the Tzutuhils, is breath-taking in the beauty of blue-green waters set in a frame of somber volcanoes.

Books have been written about the culture of these Indians of Mayan stock, their village customs and textile art. They have clung so stubbornly to the ways of their ancestors that they are an absorbing study for ethnologists. Scholars find them a fruitful source of study, artists and visitors enjoy their vivid costumes of handwoven cotton and wool, the colorful markets and interesting villages.

For progressive Guatemalans, however, who are trying to improve health and labor conditions, to educate the children and teach the men to be citizens, this mass of indigenous people presents problems. Indians have always been burden-bearers, servants, laborers on roads, peons on haciendas and coffee fincas. Those who live in remote mountain villages have no wish to change their ancestral ways and are antagonistic to white men. Reform of the peonage system on plantations is one of the big problems of the present government.

Guatemala is a land of great geographical variety, from cold mountain heights to pleasant plateau regions and tropical coasts. It is a land of poor, backward masses, large landowners of coffee, sugar-cane and banana plantations, with a small intellectual class and aristocracy.

The produce of the country is shipped from a few small ports on the Pacific and from Puerto Barrios, the Atlantic port which grew after the railroad was built as the shipping point for bananas.

Bordering on this state are Honduras, the most isolated of the republics until a few years ago, and El Salvador, the smallest and most thickly populated of the states.

El Salvador is the only one of the states with no outlet to the Atlantic except by rail through Guatemala. It has a few small ports on the Pacific for the shipping of products by coastwise steamer.

The small, pleasant capital, San Salvador, is the home of the wealthy aristocracy, the journalists and educators who have an important place in national life, and the center of all progressive activities.

Salvadoreans, in modern times, have been noted for their upstanding spirit, their concern for education and labor organization, their brave struggle for democracy against the opposition of the army officers and privileged class.

Although the coffee business on which the country lives is in the hands of large owners who manage it very efficiently, small farmers also have their coffee trees. They sell their crop to the large fincas. The whole population thinks and talks coffee at the harvesting period. Country people, with clerks, shopkeepers, mechanics, turn to coffee picking and stream to the fincas to harvest the scarlet berries on which national prosperity depends.

In this country of agriculturists the people are fed from the farms. Every inch of good soil is cultivated in the warm highland valleys. Fields are worked by hand labor on mountain slopes and even in the craters of dead volcanoes there are gardens. Small farmers, industrious and ambitious, have won better opportunities for themselves than those of some neighboring countries.

El Salvador does not have the transportation problems of Nicaragua and Honduras. The country is small and compact, there has been sufficient prosperity, and sufficient desire for progress on the part of governments, so that most towns have been linked by good roads or railways.

El Salvador has territory bordering on the Gulf of Fonseca, as do Honduras and Nicaragua. It is a wonderful great bay, with shores of tropical verdure. Near the Honduran coast lies the peaked green island, Isla del Tigre, once the haunt of pirates. Honduras' tiny Pacific port, Amapala, nestles on its shore and connection is made with the mainland by launch.

Before air transport released Honduras from its age-old isolation, Amapala was the best port of entry. Passengers and goods were transported up over the mountains on the only decent highway in the country, to the aloof capital, Tegucigalpa.

The difficulty of making roads in their country of rugged mountainous interior and jungle coast on the Caribbean Sea has plagued Hondurans throughout their history. Lack of communications has kept them apart from their neighbors and hindered national progress. Soldiers of fortune had their heyday in Honduras, internal revolutions and involvement in the wars between states, kept the country in a turmoil. The emotional intensity of the Honduran temperament led upper-class men into armed conflict, while farmers, ekeing out existence in hard, dull lives, were ready to drop their plows for muskets to follow one general or another.

A great change came to Honduras after Lowell Yerex ar-

rived there, in 1929, with one second-hand plane and two companions. Yerex was a New Zealander, an adventurous airman
with a pilot's record in World War I, a soldier of fortune in
the modern manner. His plane transported prospectors, businessmen and goods to remote places with no ground communications. He was so successful that soon more planes and pilots
were added to the enterprise. Out of their air pioneering grew
the Transportes Aereos Centroamericanos—Taca. The whole
country was knit together by air, the mines, the farming and
cattle regions, the coastal towns. Taca has grown into an international company serving all Central America. Its busy local
planes in their regular runs transport every sort of produce,
machines, supplies, as well as people.

Hondurans have become so air-minded that it will be hard
for them to come down to earth, to the construction of good
roads to open up the country.

With an airport in the valley below the town and planes
bringing business and people, Tegucigalpa awoke from its
secluded life. Modern changes have not spoiled the charm of
the old Spanish colonial town or the friendly, easygoing ways
of its inhabitants.

Tegucigalpa is unique among Central American capitals in
its architecture and atmosphere. The steep streets of old houses
with tiled roofs climb in terraces up a mountain slope. From
the upper levels there are sweeping views over the valley and
encircling pine-covered mountains. The colonial character of
the place may be preserved because there is little room for new
building in the compact, mounting streets. Modernism can
have its way in the twin town, Comayagüela, across a little
river spanned by a Spanish bridge and a modern one.

The remote capital has always been a place where men and
women dreamed and grew enthusiastic over ideas. Prose and

poetry have been written and literature is cherished in cultural groups. The inhabitants have been accustomed to having their peaceful occupations interrupted by shots and street disturbances during revolts. There is a quietness in the people now, for they live under repression. They hope to win political freedom and better government without another revolution.

Real Honduran life is in the highlands, in the small quiet towns and farming regions. Sober, brown-faced working people and farmers, of mixed Spanish and Indian blood, have a hard struggle with poverty. They live with little change by the customs of their forebears. New ideas and more goods to improve life will soon come, for roads are being built. It is now possible to travel all the way from the north coast to the capital by a combination of train on the one little railroad and bus on a rough road.

Flying from Tegucigalpa to the north coast on the Caribbean Sea is like entering another country, the heart of the banana empire. A vast green mat of plantations extends inland for seventy-five miles or more. From the air they look like tufted velvet.

The north coast is more foreign than Honduran. It is a place of United Fruit Company port towns, the great efficient network of the banana industry, administration headquarters where American managers and their subordinates live comfortably in a setting of tropical beauty. Native Hondurans work on the plantations and are being employed more and more in higher positions.

Jamaican Negroes are the majority of the working people along the coast and English is the prevailing language. Negroes first came to the coast in the days of lawless adventure and more were brought in by the banana companies.

Part of the coast was the Honduran section of Mosquitia,

so long under British control. It is still a wild region of swamps, rivers and forests inhabited by primitive Indians.

Hondurans have lived for a long time in the shadow of the foreign banana industry, now almost completely monopolized by the United Fruit Company. With its great resources, its control of the railroad, its ownership of a large fleet of steamers, the Company wields great influence in the country.

This republic has wealth in minerals but not the capital to develop mines. Some of the old Spanish gold and silver mines are very productive under American management. Honduras has not yet reached the stage when its own businessmen can finance the development of its fine hardwoods and minerals without the aid of foreign capital.

Next-door Nicaragua, like Honduras, has been hampered in national progress by inaccessible territory, lack of roads and political unrest. The life of the country has always been concentrated in the low hot region around the shores of the two great lakes and between them and the Pacific. Coffee fincas flourish in the hilly section between Lake Nicaragua and the sea. The lake country is a farming region, yet people like to concentrate in towns—particularly the three important ones, Granada, León and Managua.

Outsiders have crossed Nicaragua from sea to sea since Spanish days, many of them lingering and settling down. Englishmen, other Europeans, and North Americans have lived in the country for business and sometimes married into Nicaraguan families. Chinese and other Asiatics have shops and small businesses.

Nicaraguans themselves are often called the gypsies of Central America because of their love of wandering and living in countries other than their own. Their writers and painters pursue their careers in foreign lands instead of at home, to take advantage of better professional opportunities. Rubén Darío, who was the most original and important poet of all Latin America in the late nineteenth century, was a native of León, and his tomb in the Cathedral is a cherished shrine. He spent most of his creative years, however, in Paris.

The long period of United States' intervention has not been forgotten but Nicaraguans are relegating it to the past where it belongs. They feel more confidence in the friendship of the northern big neighbor since American government agencies have given constructive aid on some of the country's problems. The political influence of the United States is strong, and Managua has more of a Yankee veneer than the other capitals.

This town has the advantage of being built on the shore of Lake Managua, so that lake breezes relieve the heat. In 1931 much of the city was destroyed by a devastating earthquake. Rebuilt with modern commercial buildings, banks and paved streets, the business center is quite North American.

The façade of prosperity in the center and in the fine homes of the wealthy on the lake shore or the hilly outskirts, does not conceal the desperate poverty of the population at large. The lavish dress and spending of the wealthy upper class, their handsome social clubs on the lakeside plaza, are in sharp contrast to the misery of the underprivileged.

Nicaraguans, seen in the towns, seem vivacious and sociable. Market people, coming into Managua with their produce on railroad flat cars, laugh and joke as they roll along. People enjoy local trips on the small railroad running between the port of Corinto and Granada. Social clubs provide entertainment for the ordinary folk as well as for the upper class. In Managua, house doors stand open at night and people set their rocking chairs on the sidewalk to rock and chat, while they enjoy the evening breeze from the lake.

Inhabitants of the lake country live in a hot, enervating climate, particularly trying in the dry season, when hot winds raise clouds of dust. They are scourged by malaria and amoebic dysentery and their government has done little to improve sanitation, water supply and general living conditions.

The historic cities, León and Granada, are places of thick-walled old houses and slow-moving life completely Nicaraguan in character. *Coches,* old-fashioned buggies drawn by teams of bony nags, are the means of transportation around the two old cities, and hold their own among the automobiles of Managua. Rocking and bouncing over cobblestones as the horses are urged to a trot, these primitive taxis are hard on passengers.

The two great lakes and the impressive volcanoes give the Nicaraguan landscape its distinctive character. Lake Nicaragua, an inland sea, is the largest body of fresh water between Lake Superior and Lake Titicaca in South America. Few boats are to be seen on its yellow-green waters. A midget steamer has been in service for years, making trips between Granada and San Carlos at the outlet into the San Juan River. Small clumsy sloops, their decks crowded with country people, careen in the wind as they sail slowly among the islands.

This was the land of Chief Nicaragua's semi-civilized people, as well as the home of other Indians of primitive culture about whom little is known. Tall blocks of stone, carved into the semblance of half-animal gods, have been found in several places and many of them have been assembled in the courtyard of the Jesuit College on the shore of Lake Nicaragua. Indian people live on the islands and around Massaya, growing produce and weaving pita fiber into hats, baskets and hammocks for a livelihood.

Nicaragua is the next-door neighbor to small Costa Rica, aloof in its highlands, separated by distance from the other states, without good road connection even with Nicaragua.

As we have seen, Costa Ricans have followed their own path throughout their history, and have built up a thoroughly civilized nation; a country more advanced in education, civic activities and democracy than their neighbors.

That tradition of democracy, of industry and simple living, is reflected in the sturdy self-respecting country people and in the provincial families, who are very conservative in their customs. Class lines are not so sharply drawn as in the other countries, although emphasis is placed on good family and social position.

The Meseta Central means Costa Rica to most of the people, for that region is the nucleus of their civilization. It is the site of their four important cities—Alajuela, Heredia, Cartago and San José. The lovely cultivated valleys, old towns and villages, framed in blue-green mountains, give an impression of peaceful serenity.

This highland region is so compact, its roads and bus services so good, that dwellers in provincial towns go to the capital for amusement, while city people make visits to country friends who have farms or coffee fincas. Landowners have their beautiful homes on the fincas or cattle farms but spend much time in the capital. Travel by automobile is a matter of course for prosperous families. Town dwellers never lose touch with the countryside in Costa Rica.

Costa Ricans boast that they have more middle-class homeowners and more independent farmers than the other republics, as well as a higher living standard. That does not mean that the people in general are prosperous. Wartime conditions have increased poverty among town and country workers. Many small coffee growers, who had mortgaged their farms, have had to lose them and go to work on the large fincas.

There is a large class of peon laborers who make a scanty living working for the big landowners. The wealthy *finqueros* tend to increase the size of their holdings at the expense of the small ones.

Coffee was the crop that brought prosperity to the country in the first place, and it is the economic mainstay of Costa Ricans now, the chief preoccupation of landowners and merchants. Cattle raising is important and many Costa Ricans have banana plantations, selling their fruit to the United Fruit Company. Others have plantations of cacao in the hot lowlands.

In a nation that has consistently spent more on schools than on the army, middle-class young people have good opportunities if their parents can find the money for higher education. Elementary schooling is free and compulsory. Ambitious boys and girls may go on to high school, and the government furnishes scholarships for the training of teachers in the Normal School at Heredia. There are special schools and the university in the capital.

Everything radiates from San José, the charming capital, so small that green country can be seen at the ends of its long straight streets. Earthquakes have done so much damage that in rebuilding, corrugated iron roofing has been used instead of tiles in parts of the city and some small houses have walls of the metal painted to simulate wood.

San José is busy and modern—a sociable town where everyone seems to know everyone else. It is also a place of bookshops and great interest in literary pursuits among its intellectual men. French and English culture influences Costa Ricans very strongly. Although the majority of the pretty Josefinas care more for dress and social life than careers, there is a lively progressive group of women intent on bringing them forward in civic and national affairs. Among the wealthy families the national ideal of simple, conservative living gives way to gay and modern social activities.

Costa Rica now has rail connection from ocean to ocean. Travelers journey from the capital to the Atlantic port, Puerto Limón, over the railroad of spectacular route built by the promoter, Minor C. Keith. From San José to the Pacific port, Puntarenas, a government-owned electric railway makes the trip down from the mountains in four hours, over the route where the slow-moving coffee carts used to spend nine days of travel.

People of San José prefer to take their seaside vacations at Puntarenas, rather than at hot, rainy Puerto Limón. It is a completely Costa Rican resort with a better climate than the Atlantic coast.

The Atlantic port has been the headquarters of the United Fruit Company in Costa Rica, but the shipping of bananas has decreased since disease ruined most of the plantations. New ones have been developed on the Pacific side. Jamaican Negroes were brought in to work on the railroad and later on the banana plantations. They settled down, raised families and became the basic working population of the hot, wet coast, giving a different character to Puerto Limón from that of any other town.

Costa Rica, in the past, had closer relations with Panama than with the other Central American provinces, despite the difficult trails over mountains and through jungles. The Pan American Highway has now been completed to the Costa Rican border and when the Costa Rican section is finished there will be easy communication.

The tiny state of Panama has managed to preserve its independence and its own thoroughly Latin American way of life outside the totally North American Canal Zone. One steps into a different atmosphere just by crossing the street from the American terminal towns to those of Panama.

Many peoples have crossed this narrow strip of land or settled there in both past and present. Indian, Spaniard and Negro mingled in the colonial period. To this day descendants of primitive Indian tribes, who hid in the mountains to escape the Spaniards, live in their forest retreats by the customs of their ancestors. With the opening of the Canal the terminal towns, Colón and Panama City, became a melting pot of races.

Panama is not counted as one of the Central American states but she is their close sister, one of the group of small nations that try to maintain their rights and receive consideration from large nations. Panamanians share with Central Americans similar problems in economic development and relations with foreign nations.

Past relations of the small republics with the United States have been covered in other chapters. How do the people feel now, politically, about the big neighbor? Diplomatic relations have certainly improved since the inauguration of the Good Neighbor policy. Too often, however, the State Department sends men as ambassadors or other diplomatic officials who do not have sufficient knowledge of the countries' historical background or their language, and with too little interest in their problems. There is reason for the occasional complaints of Central Americans about some of the men sent to represent the United States.

The Cultural Department established within the State Department as part of the Good Neighbor policy has done much to win respect and friendship for the United States. Cultural Attachés are stationed in each embassy whose work is to build up cultural interchanges and activities with the people of the country. Some of these Attachés in Central America have been the right men for the job, with sympathetic understanding and intellectual ability.

Cultural Institutes, a collaboration of the United States and Central American governments, are established in some of the republics. Libraries, classes in English and Spanish, concerts and conferences on various subjects, bring North Americans and Central Americans together in work most important for real understanding.

The American Library in Managua, sponsored by the State Department, is a bright spot and a joy to Nicaraguans. The American director has both Americans and Nicaraguans on his staff. Books in Spanish and English serve adults, there are activities for young people, and the Children's Room, with bright-pictured books from Argentina and the United States, is a new pleasure for the children of Managua.

Central Americans are learning through these varied cultural activities that the United States is more than a big country of materialism and power politics.

CHAPTER 25

CENTRAL AMERICA COMES OF AGE

THE REPUBLICS have jumped from the age of the ox-cart and mule to that of the airplane with only partial development of the stages between. They are on the direct line of air travel between the United States and the west coast of South America. Large international planes of Pan American and Taca make daily flights from Mexico to Panama and back again, stopping in the capital of each country. Central Americans fly from capital to capital in an hour or so.

Entering the age of air travel is a boon beyond compare to Central Americans. It is not only easy for them to reach the United States, but they are becoming better acquainted with one another as they skip so quickly from one country to the next.

Central Americans are likely to build more roads rather than railroads for ground communication. Highway construction is going ahead in all the states.

Before long travelers will be rolling in their cars from Laredo, Texas, to Panama City over the Pan American, or Inter-American, Highway; a journey that for variety, human interest and magnificent scenery could not be surpassed anywhere in the world. It will not be a good road for some time to come, but travelers with a spirit of adventure will be exploring Middle America in a way much more interesting than by plane.

The Pan American Highway will be immensely valuable to Central Americans, for busses will run from country to country, serving the people who cannot afford to travel by air. Local roads, radiating from the Highway, will open up inaccessible regions.

Modern transportation brings Central America out of isolation, but in order to become prosperous, stable nations, the republics must develop the agricultural resources of their tropical lands and good soil. They are all agricultural nations, countries of tiny farms and large plantations.

Many of the gifts of kindly nature have always been used by the people for themselves or for export. Fruits whose names sound exotic to northerners are everyday nourishment; papayas, mangos, zapotes, bread fruit, pomegranates and such. Some products are interesting in their history, the way they are gleaned from the wilderness or grown on plantations.

Mahogany has been cut for centuries in the coastal forests of Honduras, Nicaragua, Guatemala. The trees do not grow in groves, but are widely scattered, so that loggers spot them by climbing a high tree to look for the spreading crown of a great mahogany above the lower treetops. Laborers go up the rivers in the dry season. The logs are cut by moonlight for coolness during the rainy season because the sap then gives the wood its best color. Logs are dragged to rivers by oxen and rafted downstream to the mills.

Chicle, the sap of the zapote tree used for chewing gum, has been profitable to Guatemala for a long time. Most of the trees grow in the primitive forests of El Petén, the flat northeastern section of the country. Where once the Mayan hierarchy of priests and rulers lived in cities of temples and palaces, and traders carried on commerce between them in river canoes, the *chicleros* hack their way through jungles to find the trees.

Chicleros are a special breed of men, generally forest Indians or half-breeds, accustomed to the wilderness. They work on contract, promised a minimum price for a stated amount at the delivery points on lake or river.

In the rainy season they set off with their simple equipment on muleback to spend months in the lonely, sopping jungle finding the trees, collecting the sap, boiling it to a gummy syrup in iron kettles. The syrup is poured into wooden molds to harden into solid blocks of chicle. In their wanderings chicleros often come upon sculptured stones or temple ruins, and have guided archeologists to important discoveries.

Formerly the transport of chicle blocks to delivery points by mule, and by boat to the seacoast, was a long, slow business, but aviation has changed all that. Small planes now hum over the mat of forest, descend to miniature clearings where land-ing is rough, rise above the treetops with their load and speed off to the coast. One of the tiny landing fields is at the foot of the ruined temples of Uaxactún.

Until 1935 it took mule train and boat two weeks, with the best of luck, to transport four thousand pounds of chicle from Uaxactún to Puerto Barrios. Now a plane carries that much in one load and makes the trip in one hour and forty minutes. On the return trip the plane brings all necessary supplies and building materials to the forest settlement.

The island town in Lake Petén-Itzá, named Flores by Her-nán Cortés, was the place where he left his horse to become a creature worshipped by the Mayan inhabitants. Flores has be-come the trading center for the chicle industry and other forest products from El Petén. Canoes paddle to the island and planes take off, connecting this remote spot with the outside world.

Fringing the shores of these tropical lands are hundreds of coconut-palm groves. They are exceedingly useful to the people. The long, spiky leaves make hats, mats and thatch for roofs, and the trunks make house posts. Coconut meat is food and the mild milk of the green nut, *agua de coco,* is a refreshing drink. The shells make bowls, dippers and spoons for peasant families.

In their coconut palms Central Americans have potential wealth. Copra, dried coconut meat, is the source of oils used by millions of tons in industrial countries, for the manufacture of soaps, cosmetics, candles, pharmaceutical products and many other things. The outside fibers make brushes and doormats. Central America could be a great center for coconut products if the industry were developed commercially.

Cacao is another of the historic native riches of these lands. Cacao, or cocoa beans, were currency and food to the Indian peoples. Spaniards learned the energy-building value of the gruel the Indians made by grinding cocoa beans with corn, chili and herbs. They changed it to suit European palates by substituting sugar and cinnamon for corn and chili. Many a Spanish colonial landowner profited from his cacao plantations, and Central Americans were chocolate drinkers until coffee became popular. Spaniards introduced chocolate to Europe where it became the fashionable beverage in the eighteenth century.

Under the shelter of tall tropical trees the silvery-barked cacao trees stand in shady aisles on plantations. The large pods, like elongated cantaloupes, sprout from the trunks. As they range from green to gold and dull crimson in ripening, the plantation of delicate trees has a unique beauty. Men and women gather the pods in baskets, chop them open with machetes and remove the large white beans to be fermented and dried in the sun.

Nicaragua, Costa Rica, Guatemala and Panama have large cacao plantations producing cocoa beans for local use and export. Old-fashioned methods by hand labor are being replaced with machines and mechanical processes in preparing the beans.

The United States, largest buyer of cocoa beans in the world, imports a good deal from Central and South America, but obtains the greater part of its needs from Africa. That situation could be changed with modern development of tropical America's cacao plantations.

Coffee and bananas stand at the top of export crops most important to the republics. The humble banana became the king of fruits through the operations of large companies with financial resources and technical skills. Although there are many native planters the growing of bananas on a large scale is really a foreign industry.

Coffee growing, on the other hand, is the business of Central American planters, with the exception of a few British and American owners, and the Germans in Guatemala, whose holdings were confiscated during the war.

In Costa Rica, El Salvador and Guatemala coffee is the mainstay of the people; prosperity rises and falls by the state of the coffee market. The Pacific slopes and part of the highlands have the ideal climate and mineralized volcanic soil to produce coffees of the finest flavor. Coffee growers of any of the three countries boast that their product is the best in the world.

Like cacao plantations, coffee fincas are one of the interesting sights of tropical America. The glossy green trees, sheltered by tall feathery ones, are beautiful when they are loaded with scarlet berries or when, in the blossoming season, they are covered with a sheen of fragrant white bloom.

A coffee finca has the fine home and gardens of the *finquero* and the primitive adobe huts in which live the *colonos,* the peon families who live all the time on the fincas. There are the great cement drying floors on which the beans are dried in the sun, raked and turned every day, and there is the mill with its modern machinery for processing and packing the crop.

The tending of the trees all the year round, the picking, sorting and drying are all done by hand labor in which women and children take part. Extra workers are hired for the picking season, gangs of Indians in Guatemala, country people in the other countries.

Central Americans have depended for prosperity on only a few of the products already growing or capable of development in their lands. World War II suddenly cut off the oriental market with the store of essential tropical products imported by the United States from across the world. It was then realized that these products could be found or raised right here in the Western Hemisphere, on the doorstep of the big buyer, the United States.

Drastic wartime needs for hemp, rubber, quinine, palm oils and waxes, tung oil, kapoc, oil grasses, mahogany and balsa wood, sent experts of the Department of Agriculture to study the resources of the Caribbean countries and South America. The Defense Supplies Corporation, aided by the Department of Agriculture and sometimes by the United Fruit Company, started many projects in Central America to supply wartime needs.

One of the most valuable and successful of the projects was the raising of abacá on United Fruit Company plantations.

The abacá plant looks like the banana plant and belongs to that family. It is native to the Philippines and the islands were the chief producers of the strong hemp for Manila rope processed from the stalks and leaves. When the Philippines were captured by the Japanese the tremendous need for rope for the navy and merchant marine led to a contract between the United Fruit Company and the Defense Supplies Corporation.

Already, as one of their agricultural experiments, the Company had raised some acres of abacá in Panama. They had the plant stock, the land, money and man power; they and the Department of Agriculture had the experts. Thousands of acres of abacá were raised in Panama, Honduras and Costa Rica and the hemp was processed in modern mills built for the purpose. Colonies of workers' barracks grew up around the mills and millions of bales of abacá hemp went out to help win the war.

Abacá is one of the products that should eventually be turned over to native planters to become a permanent source of prosperity. Plant stock, and instruction in the technique of raising abacá are at the service of native planters, but it will be a long time before they can build up successful plantations. It requires a large outlay of money and the planters must be assured of a market.

Wartime projects, if continued, may point out a road to prosperity for native farmers, who are hardworking and intelligent, say those who know them. If they are aided technically and financially, and if favorable trade treaties give them a market in the United States, the agriculturists of Central America may be on the way toward greater economic independence.

It will be a long road, for modern agriculture depends on science and machines, on the study of soils, irrigation, plant diseases, diversified crops and many other factors.

Guatemala and Costa Rica have National Schools of Agriculture for the training of young farmers. In Nicaragua and El Salvador the governments, with the cooperation of the United States Department of Agriculture, have established agricultural experiment stations.

The advancement of agriculture is a problem for all the Latin American countries. They have combined now, with the United States, in founding the Inter-American Institute of Agricultural Sciences at Turrialba, Costa Rica. Turrialba lies in a rich highland valley rimmed with mountains and bordered by the Reventazón River, half way up from Puerto Limón to San José. The site was chosen because both tropical and semitropical plants flourish in the climate and the planting season is all the year round. Experts and students from all the Americas will conduct experimental projects in crops, forestation and livestock. The Institute, opened in 1943, has beautiful buildings in Spanish style and the work is well under way.

For many years trained experts on the staff of the United Fruit Company have studied the problems of soil, diseases and tropical plant life at the Lancetilla Experiment Station near Tela, Honduras, in a beautiful tropical valley. It was founded by Dr. Wilson Popenoe, an agricultural scientist working with the Company.

In the nurseries the plants, shrubs and trees of many semitropical or tropical countries are raised experimentally. Native farmers may obtain plants and seedlings for enterprises of their own, and advice as to how to raise new products.

A modern enterprise of the greatest value for Central Americans is the Escuela Agricola Panamericana in Honduras. The school was founded by the president of the United Fruit Company and is supported by the Company. Lands of a famous old hacienda at Zamorano, near Tegucigalpa, were purchased from the Honduran government. The school is a gift to the young farmers of Middle America, for students come from every country between Mexico and Panama.

Everything is free for the students—food, tuition, books, clothing, implements, medical and dental care. The boys are chosen by a board of regents from a list of eager applicants. Character, intelligence and ambition are the primary requirements. Promising boys are chosen, who often have had no more than the elementary schooling they could obtain in villages or small towns.

It is the aim of the school administration to give this opportunity to boys whose families could not afford to send them away for study, but of course there are some from more prosperous homes. The students are expected to return to their home villages and farms to raise the standard of farming for their neighbors as well as themselves, and to help the communities through the knowledge they have gained of health and sanitation.

Zamorano is in a high fertile valley surrounded by forested hills and fed by a river. Around the efficient, attractive buildings of the school spread the cultivated fields, pastures, orchards and nurseries worked by the students. They raise cattle, poultry, pigs and sheep; slaughter and refrigerate their meat, learn dairying in a modern creamery. The boys spend their mornings in field work and their afternoons in class, studying a variety of subjects as well as those having to do with agricultural science. Some of the instructors are Latin Americans, others from the United States.

The first classes were begun in 1943 and already the school is a growing concern. Besides their technical training these boys from a number of Latin American countries are learning to know one another, to develop comradeship and cooperation.

That is important, for it is breaking down prejudices and narrow nationalism.

Central American states have grown up into nationhood. They would like to be economically independent, to have full control over their mineral and agricultural resources. Foreign operation of mines and plantations could be helpful if the corporations were more cooperative than in the past. If foreign management aids native people toward economic security and higher living standards by good wages and decent working conditions, if some of the money made in the countries is contributed toward technical and educational advancement, a better relationship between foreigners and natives may be established.

It is a policy of intelligent self-interest for foreign business to help raise living standards; people with a little money in their pockets will be able to buy the manufactured products they need, and which foreign business wants to sell. The more prosperity there is among the people of the small countries the better neighbors we shall all be. As Cordell Hull once wisely said, "the road to market is the road to peace."

Central America has its part in the world struggle between the people, striving for democracy and security, and the forces of reaction. They formed their governments on the republican system, but with their background the progress toward democratic procedures has been more difficult than in the United States.

Progressive groups in each country know that they cannot achieve democracy without raising the mass of the people from the illiteracy and poverty that pains the heart of a sympathetic visitor. The people must have economic security, education and health in order to become an integral part of national life.

The most progressive politicians are learning that the basis of democratic government lies in honest elections and in abiding by the result of those elections. The day is past, they hope, when a defeated candidate for president retires to a neighboring country to foment revolution to overthrow his successful opponent.

Leadership toward democracy comes from journalists, university professors and students, progressive men in the professions and business. Industrial workers and employees of public utilities are becoming better organized and more articulate.

Central American reformers have begun to use the modern weapons of mass protest, general strike and a popular front of political groups instead of the historic armed revolt. Progressive women have led their sisters out to walk through the streets in dignified protest against injustices, a new thing indeed for sheltered Latin American women.

In the spring of 1944 Salvadoreans rid themselves of the cruel dictator, Hernández Martínez, whose long rule had been extremely oppressive. A successful nation-wide strike caused him to resign and leave the country. To be sure, the head of the police force, Osmin Aguirre, soon seized power by a military coup d'état, but he was not recognized by the United States or by Costa Rica and Guatemala. The military dictatorship gave way to an elected president. Castanedo Castro was not the people's choice, but he has to respond to the pressure for democratic reform in order to maintain his government.

Guatemala followed suit in June 1944. Mass protests, strikes, and political organization of democratic groups brought about the resignation of General Jorge Ubico after fourteen years of iron rule. Jorge Ubico was one of the dictators admired by outsiders, praised for introducing modern improvements and stabilizing finances. Work and obedience were his rules for the people, and he was supposed to have required honesty in government officers, but that applied only to the little fellows. Ubico's rule became a despotic tyranny. The ubiquitous spies and terroristic methods kept progressive Guatemalans silent, in jail or in exile. The condition of schools, hospitals, health and sanitation, after fourteen years, do not constitute a good record.

General Ponce, appointed provisional president by Ubico when he resigned, tried by the old brutal methods to prevent preparations for a free election. Then Guatemalans resorted to arms, but the revolution was short and snappy.

On one wild night, October 20, 1944, the great plaza before the National Palace, and streets near by, echoed to machine-gun fire and the rumble of tanks, seized from the citadel.

In the morning a Revolutionary Junta of three young men was in control, and continued to manage the country until after the election and reorganization of government. Dr. Juan José Arévalo, candidate of the Democratic Front, was elected president. He is a civilian, a scholarly educator, who spent some years in Argentina after he found he could not carry forward his educational ideas under Jorge Ubico.

With the most hopeful enthusiasm groups of reformers tackled Guatemala's many problems; rural education and civic training, public health service, labor organization, democratization of government. One hesitates to make definite statements about politics in these troubled times, but at present Guatemala appears to be a workshop of democracy in Central America.

Tiburcio Carías Andino of Honduras and Anastasio Somoza of Nicaragua are heads of parties, but they are dictators nonetheless. They have the support of party leaders who profit from belonging to the régime in power. They maintain their rule by suppression of political action and control of the army, equipped with Lend Lease planes and machine guns obtained from the United States.

The argument of Carías' supporters that twelve years without a real revolution have enabled the country to advance has some weight. There have been revolts, however; opposition leaders have been imprisoned, all freedom of opinion is stifled, and many of the most progressive people live in exile because existence is too difficult at home.

Anastasio Somoza of Nicaragua has exploited his people in a most heartless manner and employed spies and terror to suppress opposition. He is the old-time caudillo in modern dress, despite his protestations of democratic sentiments. The miserable poverty of the people, the backward condition of the country, are an indictment of his long rule. The Guardia Nacional, organized by American officers, is an effective instrument for keeping the people in their place.

Both El Salvador and Guatemala have long had good newspapers, edited by courageous, progressive journalists. Their papers have been suppressed, some editors have been imprisoned, a few have been assassinated, others have saved their lives by temporary exile in other countries. Journalism is a favored career with Central American intellectuals. As freedom of speech wins its way the editors will continue to be educators of public opinion.

Costa Ricans are accustomed to a free press. That small country has steadily built up a foundation of orderly political life on a democratic basis. There have been dictators, but of a milder variety than in the other countries. The people have a tradition of free discussion, and expect to choose their presidents in honest elections.

The people are not always satisfied with their politicians

and national government, they sometimes fear for their precious democracy, but they have the means to express their will in traditional political processes.

"Just another revolution," people are inclined to say when they read of disturbances in Central America. The stormy history of the republics has given them that reputation, but there have never failed to be men and women of progressive spirit working for the betterment of their countries. In the present effort to advance democracy the devoted services of the most patriotic citizens are needed.

Democracy will advance in Central America when the governments concern themselves with the health, economic security and education of the basic population; when the people themselves learn to organize and work together to win what they need. Those who are working toward that end look for the sympathy and understanding of their North American friends.

In the National Park of San Josè, Costa Rica, there is an impressive bronze monument symbolizing the five sister republics of Central America. It was erected to commemorate the united action of the states to oust the filibuster, William Walker. The states are sisters; despite their quarrels, any threat from outside draws them together. They have the same problems in trade and agriculture and in their relations with foreign nations.

The dream of union is not dead. In each country there are groups who believe in it and work for it. Just recently the Presidents of Guatemala and El Salvador met to discuss the possibilities of federation. Many thoughtful people think it is a dream impossible of fulfillment because of national jealousies and suspicions. It may be, however, that the future will see one strong federated nation of Central America.

CHAPTER 26

MEXICO THE LEADER

LESS THAN four decades have passed since the storm of the Revolution broke over Mexico, starting the people on a new path. In that short span of years the nation has become a leader among sister Hispanic American nations in political and social thinking and culture.

Other Latin Americans watched, some with horror, some with hope, while Mexico went through successive revolutionary changes, social and agrarian reforms, labor struggles which resulted in strong organizations of the workers.

Often from the outside the progress of post-revolutionary Mexico has seemed to be one step forward for two steps back, but through it all the nation has continued to build a civilization distinctively its own. It is a civilization in which the character and talents of both Indian and mestizo have their place. Mexico has had men of intellect and constructive spirit, whether of pure Spanish descent or of mixed blood, to lead it forward.

The creative genius of the nation, released by the Revolution, has given Mexico an important position in art, music and literature. The great fresco painters are still at work while many new talents in painting and sculpture contribute to the country's reputation.

Mexico has musicians and composers and a famed symphony orchestra in the capital. Musical artists of world-wide reputation come to Mexico City as guest conductors or to give concerts. The Orquesta Típica, delight of the capital and a favorite in the United States, gives in professional form the regional songs and dances and performances of the typical wandering ballad singers, the *mariachis*. The new National Ballet gives opportunity for dancers and choreographers. Stunning décor and costumes for the ballets are designed by such important artists as José Clemente Orozco and Carlos Mérida.

The motion-picture industry vies with that of Argentina; Mexico has its popular movie stars and the actor, Cantinflas, is the Charlie Chaplin of Latin America. In the theater Mexican audiences delight in the *variedades,* a sort of vaudeville, where witty comedians make jibes at political events and characters in skits sandwiched between dances and ranchero singers.

A host of talented writers and scholars have given the country an interesting national literature concerned with the interpretation of Mexican life and history. The capital is a place of book publishing and large comprehensive bookshops. Street stands overflowing with newspapers, magazines and even books indicate a reading public.

The United States has made a friendly gesture with the Benjamin Franklin Library, sponsored by the State Department—a delight to students, children and general readers. The Library is introducing to Mexicans the value of a circulating library where children and adults may borrow books to read at home. The book fair idea has appealed to publishers and writers. In 1944 Mexico City put on a most successful Book Fair, bringing together the publications and authors of Latin America.

Across the border from the mechanistic United States, harried North Americans have found escape from bustle and drive among their leisurely neighbors. There is something in the very atmosphere of Mexico, in its landscape and color, its old colonial towns and deep-rooted ways of life that have cast a spell over generations of visitors.

The mingling of Indian and Spanish talents in colonial times, and the strength of tradition, have given Mexico a wealth of beautiful folk arts, of regional songs, dances and costumes. This rare heritage has been cherished both by Mexicans and their friends from other countries.

Neighbors learn from each other, so that while North Americans revel in Mexican customs and arts the Mexicans themselves adopt all sorts of machine-made articles and Yankee ways from across the border. They build luxurious resorts for tourists and tend to commercialize the lovely things visitors like to buy. All friends of Mexico hope that in becoming a tourist paradise the country will not lose its intrinsic charm and the quality of its handicrafts.

The country of Hispanic blood and background proved its racial brotherhood when it welcomed Spanish Republican refugees, escaping from fascist General Franco's tyranny. When the Spanish Republic was crushed with the aid of Germany and Italy, Mexico opened its doors to refugees of all classes. They found sympathy, help and means of livelihood among their Mexican friends. Spain's finest artists, writers and scholars, pursuing their professions in Mexico, enriched the cultural life of those who welcomed them in a dark time.

Leaders of the parties that composed the Spanish Republican government have organized on Mexican soil, with sympathetic sponsorship, the legal government in exile to replace the one driven from Spain. The Spaniards await only recognition from the powerful nations and the downfall of the fascist Spanish government to bring Spain back into the company of democratic nations.

Rich, reactionary Spaniards reached Mexico earlier, when their privileges were undermined by the Republican government. Falangists, the Spanish fascists, as well as Nazi agents, had a powerful network of underground activity in Mexico. The Axis powers, expecting triumph in Europe, hoped to use Mexico as a base for attack on the United States. General Franco and the Falangists, with their call to blood and history in Hispanidad, hoped to link Latin America to a fascist Spanish state.

Then came the test of developing inter-American solidarity when World War II in Europe threatened the security of the Western Hemisphere. The American republics, Latin and North American, had the machinery for consultation set up, which went into action with conferences of the Foreign Ministers at Panama in 1939 and Havana in 1940.

After the Japanese attack on Pearl Harbor brought the United States into the war, most of the Latin American republics realized that a threat to one was a threat to all, and that their security lay in union. Most of the republics promptly stood beside the United States with a declaration of war, or by breaking relations with the Axis powers.

In 1942 Mexico declared war, creating an astounding situation in the country. Many people, always suspicious of the big next-door nation, opposed the declaration. Simple folk could not understand why their country should fight beside the gringos, their traditional enemies. General Lázaro Cárdenas, recalled to the government as Minister of War and organizer of the army, was able to reassure the people who trusted him.

Mexico defended its coasts and provided raw materials and

food, while the United States provided machinery and materials for industry, military training and weapons of war. A Mexican air squadron, trained in the United States, went into action in the Pacific. When the "Mexican eagles" returned home after victory they were received with delirious joy and triumph.

Mexico's cooperation was the result of groundwork laid by men of tolerance and good will and farsighted vision on both sides of the border. President Franklin D. Roosevelt and Secretary of State Cordell Hull, President Avila Camacho and Foreign Minister Ezequiel Padilla, worked out the closest and most friendly relations on practical grounds that had ever existed between the two nations. The long-standing dispute between the expropriated oil companies and the Mexican government was settled on a fair basis and the indemnity paid.

For the first time in history a president of the United States paid a visit to a president of Mexico in his own country, when Roosevelt journeyed to Monterrey to confer with Avila Camacho. The Mexican president returned the visit with a trip to the United States.

Ever since the Good Neighbor policy instituted a new era in Pan American affairs Mexican statesmen have been a strong influence for inter-American cooperation. That nation's leadership in Latin American politics was established at the third conference of Foreign Ministers held at Rio de Janeiro in January 1942, to draw up a pact of unity and mutual assistance among all the American nations. They met in an atmosphere of doubt and suspicion, the outcome of the war was uncertain, and some states were unwilling to align themselves with the United Nations.

Then it was that Mexico's Foreign Minister Ezequiel Padilla, by his eloquence and ardent belief in inter-American solidarity, swung the conference to united action. The American nations spoke with a collective voice before the world, although all was not well within the family. Argentina was the only state that failed to carry through the resolution recommending that every state sever relations with the Axis powers.

Mexico took the lead again, when the Inter-American Conference of February 1945, was invited to meet in Mexico City. Historic Chapultepec Castle was turned over to the delegations from twenty nations, meeting on a basis of equality to pledge themselves to unity of action in war and peace. They were to plan multilateral principles for protection in which all had a part, instead of the outworn unilateral protection of the Monroe Doctrine with the United States dominating. Argentina, by the fascist policies of her military government, had isolated herself from her sister nations and was not represented.

Committee rooms, press rooms, secretaries, microphones—all the paraphernalia of international conferences—made Chapultepec Castle a scene of intense activity all day. Delegates, in friendly spirit, conferred amid reminders of all Mexico's history. Portraits of conquerors, viceroys, presidents, looked down upon them from the walls; the furnishings of Mexico's great ones surrounded them. The boudoir of Carmencita, wife of Porfirio Díaz, was turned into a lounge and free bar where soft drinks and sandwiches were served.

The Chapultepec Conference was a most important landmark in the history of Pan American relations. "The unity of the Americas is indivisible" was the principle unanimously adopted. Statesmen of all the republics, with the sad exception of Argentina, worked out a regional system of collective security against dangers which may threaten the Americas from within or without. Economic agreements, planned for future prosperity and cooperation among the nations, were as important as security against aggression. The Conference, if the nations abide by its principles, laid the foundation for a peaceful, secure future in the Western Hemisphere.

Advancement to a position of leadership, and the stepping-up of industry for wartime needs, has pushed Mexico on into a phase of industrial expansion. Statesmen and businessmen want the country to reach economic independence and greater self-sufficiency through manufacturing at home many of the goods they now buy from abroad. Mexicans want to process their raw materials in factories near the source, instead of selling them to foreign manufacturers and buying them back in the form of goods at high prices. Textiles, furniture, glass and leather goods are among the best of Mexican-made products.

Mexico produces its own gasoline, fuel oils and kerosene from the fields and refineries of the national petroleum industry, Pemex. Tires are manufactured for home use and export.

The nation has a number of small airlines covering the country, as well as the national company which is a subsidiary of Pan American Airways. The huge airport of Mexico City is a hub of international air traffic, coming and going in all directions. Young Mexicans have gone into aviation enthusiastically and proved themselves expert pilots and mechanics.

There are big projects under way for dams, power plants, factories for which American machinery is needed and the assistance of technicians. Cooperation with foreign business on terms fair to both sides, in enterprises that shall operate under Mexican laws, is encouraged. By law the majority of employees in any foreign concern must be Mexicans. The time is past when foreign capital can monopolize the best resources of the country and export the greater part of the profits.

The present drive for industrial expansion and big business

is understandable in a nation growing in power, and it is perhaps inevitable. It seems to many friendly observers, however, that Mexico is on the wrong track in trying to become an industrialized nation. The country is not suited for large industries except in a few places. Modernized agriculture, producing larger and better crops for home use and export is more important to the welfare of the people. But there again capitalistic enterprise, running agricultural projects, may defraud the people once again of their hopes.

Mexico remains a country of villages where the greatest number of people depend on the soil, and their problems have not been solved.

In the urge for modernization timeless Mexico City goes through another phase in its long story. Old buildings and whole streets of houses come down, to be replaced with the latest models in structures of glass, cement and steel for business buildings and apartment houses. Traffic roars and snarls through the narrow old streets of the center and streams in a glittering flood over the Paseo de la Reforma.

Terrible wartime inflation and the reckless spending of newly rich Mexicans, wealthy Europeans who got out with their money, and escapists from the United States, have made the contrast between luxury and dire poverty in the capital more heartbreaking than ever. Black markets, speculation in the necessities of life, torment Mexicans even more than people of the United States. The result is worse in Mexico, where the masses of poor people have always lived at a bare subsistence level.

The spectacle of an expanding, ambitious, get-rich-quick Mexico has its ugly aspects, but North Americans should not be too critical. It was not so long ago that the United States went through a period of boastful expansion when cynical political corruption and profiteering was on a much larger scale and more ruthless than that which Mexico is experiencing.

The profound vitality and talents of the Mexican people which have made them able to survive one of the most violent histories of any nation will doubtless bring them through this phase. They have gone forward since the Revolution despite every obstacle and failure. Mexico shares with the rest of the world the postwar chaos in which the progressive forces of humanity are pitted against the dark forces of greed and power, in the struggle to create a world of brotherly cooperation.

Modernization may change some of the romantic surface charm of Mexico, but if it brings better health, food and education to the patient masses of the people it will be worth-while. Factory jobs, if the powerful labor organizations insist on good wages and decent working conditions, should raise the standard of living for industrial workers. Improved farming methods and machines begin to replace the old methods of hand labor and the ox-drawn wooden plow. Some ejido communities are learning to get the best results from their land by large-scale farming and cooperative enterprises.

In hundreds of cottage homes the sewing machine for making the family garments is the pride of the mother. Iron beds are replacing sleeping mats on the floor. In towns and villages the Molino de Nixtamal, the corn-grinding machine, releases women from the ancestral labor of stooping for hours over the grinding stone, the metate. Every day children of poor families carry bowls of soaked corn to the Molino and return with the meal for the essential tortillas.

"Machines and schools will be the emblem of our determination," said President Avila Camacho in a speech to Congress in September 1945. Machines to facilitate labor in the fields, to manufacture the nation's raw materials. Schools to teach the management of the machines and the methods of improved agriculture, to redeem the nation from ignorance and teach citizenship.

Community activities create hundreds of thousands of small, self-respecting groups all over the country. Information and amusement come to villages through movies and community radios. Drawn together by voices on the air, isolated communities begin to learn that they belong to a nation, something beyond their own *tierra* or *patria chica*. News of the country, messages from the president, give them a sense of participation.

Lázaro Cárdenas showed the people, by visiting among them and talking over their problems, that the President of Mexico was a human personality instead of a distant figurehead. They do not see so much of President Avila Camacho, but when he visits a region to inaugurate the completion of a dam, a housing project, a school or some other government enterprise, he renews for them their feeling of belonging to the nation. The training in citizenship goes on by radio, by government projects and by education.

Many remote communities heard over the radio the President's impassioned plea for all to join in the nationwide campaign to conquer illiteracy by the unique basic principle of "each one teach one." Every man, woman and child in the country who could read and write was called upon to teach one less-favored neighbor. The bold campaign was dramatized by vivid posters, by articles and cartoons in the newspapers, as well as over the radio.

The outstanding Minister of Education, Dr. Jaime Torres Bodet, who is poet and scholar as well as educator, worked out the plan of organization with his talented assistants. They toured the country, visiting every state to study the situation and advise the state and municipal authorities in their local organization. A year was given to the work of propaganda and organization, then the government order went into effect.

The problem was enormous, for in 1944, after all the efforts of governments to provide elementary schooling, forty-eight per cent of the people could neither read nor write. The problem was further complicated by the existence of Indian tribes in remote regions who spoke a number of Indian dialects and had never learned to speak Spanish. They must be taught that language before literacy training could begin.

When the campaign was announced by President Avila Camacho in great meetings in August 1944, it met with enormous response. It brought hope to poor fathers and mothers who will work and sacrifice to send their children to school. Idealistic Mexicans responded, as always, to a great idea.

Time has proved that temporary enthusiasm could be channeled in the patient labor, complex organization and public-spirited endeavor necessary to make the plan a success. Dr. Jaime Torres Bodet reported in a speech made in Los Angeles in May 1946, that a million illiterates had been taught. He stated his belief that illiteracy could be conquered in six or seven years.

Groups and individuals from every walk of life are taking part in the work. Banking, industrial and commercial circles build *centros* and pay teachers for the unlettered gathered there for study. Individuals give their time to teach people of their neighborhood; hard-worked teachers help in the centros after hours. Factories have installed centros for the workers; state and municipal authorities, industries and small communities give time and funds for the work. All over the country old and young who have the boon of literacy are teaching their fellows.

The educators devised a primer, clever and effective in its simplicity, each short lesson visualized by a line drawing.

The primers are distributed free, by the millions, to towns, villages and centros. As the student learns printed and written syllables and words, he is led on from the family and farm, the village and market town, to the concept of the nation that belongs to them all. Posters are now prepared with simple news of the day printed in large letters, to be set up in Indian villages for the newly educated.

The pride and self-respect engendered in the people as they are released from the blight of ignorance and learn their part in national life is laying a foundation for democracy.

In the present confused period of Mexico it is well to listen to the purpose of the government leaders, summed up in a recent speech by President Avila Camacho. "To interrupt the program of the Revolution would be to assume the effacing not only of thirty-five years of our life and more than a century of our history, but to lose the war which the democracies won, and to lose it in our country. Our union, in order to be Mexican, has to be revolutionary; because among people whose majority still suffer from ignorance and hunger the Revolution does not constitute a party, but a thirst—a thirst for redemption, collective and burning."

Two democracies, Mexico and the United States, have every reason to foresee a future of increasing friendliness and co-operation. Linked by air, railroad and highway, the people pass back and forth freely. There is no difficulty whatever in friendship between the people of the two countries. They know and like one another, through travel and study, through living each in the other's country.

There are those in Mexico who cannot forget the bitter past, who still fear the United States and resist collaboration. Ezequiel Padilla has lost favor politically, and among many people, because he is thought to be too willing to work closely with the American government. Subversive elements have worked up anti-gringo sentiment among the poor by blaming their wartime sufferings on the big nation across the border.

There are those in the United States who are too aggressive in their dealings with Mexican neighbors, too superior and impatient in their attitude. And, in the border states, there are too many people who allow racial discrimination to make life difficult for Mexicans living in their midst.

Undoubtedly Mexico has become a listening post for Latin America. Her statesmen have great influence in preserving or wrecking inter-American solidarity. If Mexico and the United States build up close friendly relations they may be a potent influence in maintaining unity.

The greater burden of responsibility rests on the United States because of its power, wealth and industrial development. If diplomats substitute fair dealing between equals for power politics; if businessmen act on the principle that economic independence and decent living standards in Latin American countries create mutual benefits and stalwart neighbors—then the future may be good.

It rests with the government and people of the United States to prove that their democracy means more than eloquent words that raise hope among oppressed peoples; that it is a principle of life at home and abroad. The United States must prove that it stands for freedom of peoples, rather than for reactionary political elements in the other nations.

Latin Americans must also prove their faith in democracy by more than words; by permitting freedom of speech and action among their peoples and the growth of really representative government.

Fundamentally inter-American democracy rests with the peoples themselves, for if they are determined to go forward on the path of democracy they can swing governments in that direction. More than all, it rests with the youth of the countries who are becoming acquainted through travel and study, for they are the builders of the future. Working together with mutual respect and understanding, they can make the unity of the Americas a reality.

BIBLIOGRAPHY

Andagoya, Pascual de: *Narrative of the Proceedings of Pedrarias Davila in the Provinces of Tierra Firme of Castilla del Oro*. Tr. by Clements Markham. Hakluyt Society.

Alvarado, Pedro de: *An Account of the Conquest of Guatemala in 1524*. Ed. by Sedley J. Mackie. Cortes Society.

Anderson, Dr. C. L. G.: *Old Panama and Castilla del Oro*. Page & Co.

Baker, Nina Brown: *Juárez, Hero of Mexico*. Vanguard Press.

Baldwin, Leland Dewitt: *The Story of the Americas*. Simon & Shuster.

Bancroft, Hubert Howe: *History of Central America*. Vol. I. A. L. Bancroft & Co.

Beals, Carlton: *Porfirio Diaz, Dictator of Mexico*. J. B. Lippincott.

—— *Rio Grande to Cape Horn*. The Macmillan Company.

Biesanz, John & Mavis: *Costa Rican Life*. Columbia University Press.

Blom, Franz Ferdinand: *The Conquest of Yucatán*. Houghton Mifflin Co.

Boyle, Frederick: *A Ride across a Continent; Wanderings in Nicaragua and Costa Rica, 1868*. R. L. Bentley & Co.

Brenner, Anita: *The Wind That Swept Mexico*. Harper & Bros.

Brinton, Daniel C., ed.: *American Hero Myths*. H. G. Watts & Co.

—— *The Maya Chronicles*. Library of Aboriginal American Literature.

—— *The Annals of the Cakchiquels*. Library of Aboriginal American Literature.

Bunau-Varilla, Philippe: *Panama: the creation, destruction and resurrection*. Robert M. McBride & Co.

Calderón de la Barca, Frances. *Life in Mexico*. E. P. Dutton & Co.

Cortés, Hernán. *Letters to Charles V*. Tr. by Francis Augustus MacNutt. G. P. Putnam's Sons.

Cox, Isaac Joslin: *Nicaragua and the United States*. World Peace Foundation Pamphlets 1927, Vol. X, no. 1.

Crowther, Samuel: *The Romance and Rise of the American Tropics.* Doubleday, Doran & Co.

De Sahagun, Fray Bernardino: *A History of Ancient Mexico.* Vol. 1. Fisk University Press.

De Landa, Bishop Diego: *Relación de las Cosas de Yucatán.* Tr. by Alfred Tozzer, Peabody Museum of American Archeology.

Díaz del Castillo, Bernal: *The True History of the Conquest of Mexico.* Tr. by D. Howden Smith. Argonaut Series. Robert M. McBride & Co.

—— *The Discovery and Conquest of Mexico.* Tr. by Alfred D. Maudsley. G. Routledge & Sons.

Dunn, Henry: *Guatimala, or the United Provinces of Central America in 1827-28.* G. C. Carrill Co.

Gage, Thomas: *A New Survey of the West Indies, 1648; or, the English American, his travails on land and sea.* G. Routledge & Sons: The Argonaut Series. Robert M. McBride & Co.

Gann, Thomas, & J. Eric Thompson: *The History of the Maya.* Charles Scribner's Sons.

Green, Lawrence: *The Filibuster; the Career of William Walker.* Bobbs, Merrill & Co.

Gruening, Ernest: *Mexico and Its Heritage.* The Century Co.

Hill, Roscoe: *American Marines in Nicaragua.* Hispanic American Essays, ed. by H. Curtis Wilgus.

Jones, Chester Lloyd: *Guatemala Past and Present.* University of Minnesota Press.

—— *The Caribbean since 1900.* Prentice-Hall, Inc.

Joyce, Thomas A.: *Central American and West Indian Archeology.* Philip Lee Warren.

—— *Mexican Archeology.* G. P. Putnam's Sons.

Keleman, Pal: *Medieval American Art.* The Macmillan Co.

Kelly, John Geoghan: *Pedro de Alvarado, Conquistador.* Princeton University Press.

Kelsey, Vera, & Lilly de Jongh Osborn. *Four Keys to Guatemala.* Funk & Wagnalls Co.

Kirkpatrick, F. A.: *Latin America, a brief history.* The Macmillan Co.

La Farge, Oliver, & Douglas Byers: *The Year Bearers People.* Middle American Research Series, no. 3. Tulane University.

Mack, Gerstle: *The Land Divided; history of Panama Canal and other isthmian canal projects.* Alfred A. Knopf.

Mason, Gregory: *Silver Cities of Yucatan.* G. P. Putnam's Sons.

—— *South of Yesterday.* Henry Holt & Co.

Maudsley, A. P.: *A Glimpse of Guatemala and Some Notes on Ancient Monuments of Central America.* J. Murray Co.

Millan, Verna Carlton: *Mexico Reborn.* Houghton, Mifflin Co.

Munro, Dana G.: *The Five Republics of Central America.* Oxford University Press.

New Pan Americanism, The: Part III. Central American League of Nations vol. III, no. 1.

Niles, Blair: *Passengers to Mexico.* Farrar & Rinehart.

Osborn, Lilly de Jongh: *Guatemala Textiles.* Middle American Research Series. Tulane University.

Padilla, Ezequiel: *Free Men of America.* Ziff-Davis Co.

Popenoe, Dorothy: *Santiago de los Caballeros de Guatemala.* Howard University Press.

Prescott, William H.: *The Conquest of Mexico.* Harper & Bros.

Priestley, Herbert I.: *The Mexican Nation.* The Macmillan Co.

Quintanilla, Luis: *A Latin American Speaks.* The Macmillan Co.

Rippy, J. Ford: *Justo Rufino Barrios.* Hispanic American Essays. Ed. by H. Curtis Wilgus.

Ruhl, Arthur Brown: *The Central Americans.* Charles Scribner's Sons.

Sands, William Franklin, with Joseph M. Lalley. *Our Jungle Diplomacy.* Chapel Hill Press.

Simpson, Eyler N.: *The Ejido, Mexico's Way Out.* Chapel Hill Press.

Spinden, Herbert J.: *Ancient Civilizations of Mexico and Central America.* American Museum of Natural History. Handbook Series no. 3.

Squier, Ephraim George: *Nicaragua; its People, Scenery, Monuments, and the Proposed Interoceanic Canal, 1851.* D. Appleton Co.

Stephens, John L.: *Incidents of Travel in Central America, Chiapas and Yucatán.* 2 vols. Harper & Brothers.

—— *Incidents of Travel in Yucatán.* 2 vols. Harper & Bros.

Stimson, Henry L.: *American Policy in Nicaragua.* Charles Scribner's Sons.

Strode, Hudson: *Timeless Mexico.* Harcourt, Brace & Co.

Tannenbaum, Frank: *Peace by Revolution.* Columbia University Press.

Warren, Thomas R.: *Dust and Foam; or three oceans and two continents, 1859.* Charles Scribner's Sons.

Wheeler, Senator Burton K.: *Dollar Diplomacy at Work in Nicaragua and Mexico.* Speech delivered at Ford Hall, Boston, March 6, 1927. U. S. Government Printing Office.

Willard, T. A.: *The City of the Sacred Well.* The Century Co.

Wilson, Charles Morrow: *Challenge and Opportunity: Central America.* Henry Holt & Co.

Vaillant, George: *Aztecs of Mexico.* Doubleday, Doran & Co.

SPANISH

Aguilar, Arturo: *Hombres de la independencia de Nicaragua y Costa Rica.* León, Nicaragua.

Aleman Bolaños, G.: *Sandinol Estudio completo del heroe de las Segovias.* León, Nicaragua.

—— *El Pueblo de Nicaragua y los Estados Unidos.* Managua, Nicaragua.

Argüelles, Leonardo: *El Caso Nicaragua.* León, Nicaragua.

Barbarena, Santiago I. *Historia de Salvador: Epoca antigua y de la conquista.* San Salvador.

Bolio, Antonio Mediz: *La Tierra del Faisan y del Venado.* Ediciones Botas. Mexico, D. F.

Centro America Libre, Organ Oficial de Union Democratico Centro Americano. Octubre y Noviembre 1944.

Díaz del Castillo, Bernal: *Verdadera y notable Relación del descubrimiento y conquista de la Nueva España y Guatemala.* Edición conforme al manuscrito original que se guarda en el Archivo de la municipalidad de Guatemala.

Durón, Rómulo E.: *Bosquejo historico de Honduras.* San Pedro Sula, Honduras.

Guardia, Ricardo Fernández: *Cronicas Coloniales.* San José, Costa Rica. Trejos Hermanos.

—— *Cartilla historica de Costa Rica.* San José, Costa Rica. Libreria y Imprenta Lehmann.

—— *Cosas y Gentes de Antaño.* San José, Costa Rica. Trejos Hermanos.

Milla, José: *Historia de la America Central.* 2 vols. Guatemala.

Mancisidor, José: *Miguel Hidalgo; constructor de una Patria*. Mexico D. F. Ediciones Xochitl.

Muñoz, Rafael: *Santa Anna*. Mexico, D. F. Ediciones Botas.

Obarrio de Mallet, Mathilde: *Bosquejo de la vida colonial de Panamá*. Panamá. Academia Panameña de la Historia.

Obregón, Luis Gonzales: *Las Calles de Mexico*. Mexico, D. F. Ediciones Botas.

—— *Cuauhtémoc*. Secretaria de Relaciones Exteriores. Mexico, D. F.

Orozco, Luis Chavez: *Historia economica y social de Mexico*. Mexico, D. F. Ediciones Botas.

Panama *Star and Herald*, 1903: "*La Independencia del Isthmo de Panama.*"

Salgado, Felix: *Nuestra independencia de España*. San Salvador, Revista del Archivo Biblioteca Nacional.

Salvatierra, Sonfonías: *Contribución a la Historia de Centro America*. Managua, Nicaragua.

Tiempo. Semanario de la Vida y la Verdad. vols. 1945-1946. Mexico, D. F.

Trejos, José Francisco: *Origen y desarrollo de la democracia en Costa Rica*. San José, Costa Rica. Trejos Hermanos.

Yañez, Agustin: *Fray Bartolomé de Las Casas*. Ediciones Xochitl. Mexico, D. F.

INDEX

MIDDLE AMERICA
GULF of MEXICO
CUBA
Jamaica
CARIBBEAN SEA
PACIFIC OCEAN